MOVING FORWARD

policies, planning, and promoting access of Hispanic college students

Bilingual Press/Editorial Bilingüe

Publisher
  Gary Francisco Keller

Executive Editor
  Karen S. Van Hooft

Address
  Bilingual Press
  Hispanic Research Center
  Arizona State University
  PO Box 875303
  Tempe, Arizona 85287-5303
  (480) 965-3867

MOVING FORWARD

policies, planning,
and promoting access
of Hispanic
college students

EDITED BY

Alfredo G. de los Santos Jr.

Laura I. Rendón

Gary Francisco Keller

Alberto Acereda

Estela Mara Bensimón

Richard J. Tannenbaum

Bilingual Press/Editorial Bilingüe
TEMPE, ARIZONA

© 2018 by Bilingual Press / Editorial Bilingüe

Library of Congress Cataloging in Publication Control Number: 2017043781

ISBN (cloth) 978-1-939743-25-1
ISBN (paper) 978-1-939743-26-8

PRINTED IN THE UNITED STATES OF AMERICA

Cover art: *El Futuro* (1998), silkscreen, by Malaquías Montoya
Cover and interior design: John Wincek

Jorge Chapa

Jorge Chapa, professor of Latino/Latina Studies at the University of Illinois at Urbana-Champaign, died unexpectedly on Monday, October 19, 2015. Jorge, his wife Belinda De La Rosa, and Blanca Rincón were working on an article for *New Directions: Assessment and Preparation of Hispanic College Students*, the companion volume to this one, when he died.

A prolific writer, Jorge was author, editor, coauthor, or coeditor of twelve books; he also published fifteen articles in refereed journals and eighteen book chapters as well as book reviews, documentaries, computer models, and more. His 2004 book *Apple Pie and Enchiladas*, coauthored with Ann V. Millard, has become the standard treatment for the very important demographic, political, and social changes in the Midwest.

His first book, *The Burden of Support: Young Latinos in an Aging Society*, was a groundbreaking treatise on the consequences of Latino population growth and won the 1989 *Choice* Outstanding Academic Book Award.

He was a great scholar, our best demographer, a gentle giant of a man, an activist, a thinker, a great teacher and mentor, *un hombre de compromiso* who sought equal opportunity for all, an expert witness, a loving husband and father, a wonderful friend . . . y mucho más. He will be missed.

We were delighted that Blanca and Belinda continued to work on the article, which is an important contribution to *New Directions*.

Table of Contents

PART I   POLICIES

PART II   PLANNING

PART III | **PROGRESS**

Index

Download the index for this book at https://bilingualpress.clas.asu.edu
/book/moving-forward-policies-planning-and-promoting-access-hispanic
-college-students

Foreword

Timothy P. White, CHANCELLOR, CALIFORNIA STATE UNIVERSITY

E ducation has a unique role as either a gateway or, in its absence, a barrier to social mobility, economic prosperity, and civic engagement and responsibility. Therefore, equitable access to quality education is an important issue in the advancement of Latino/a communities.

The authors explore the forces at play in the academic lives of Latino/a students with tremendous depth and care. Problems and solutions—from restructuring federal and state policy to better speaking about racial and ethnic issues—are addressed.

Indeed, one of my favorite articles challenges us to provide more success stories as examples for students from underrepresented communities. Reading Dr. Fernando Valle's story—from "waterboy" to professor—crystallized in my mind how many success stories I have heard from California State University faculty and staff.

CSU faculty and staff are appropriately student focused and typically defer telling their stories in order to tell the stories of our students and alumni. This is an admirable instinct, but I would encourage those of us who have a responsibility for the teaching and care of students to begin telling our own stories, because doing so will be one more way in which we help inspire students to achieve at higher levels. It is only fair, then, to begin by acknowledging how the forces of prejudice, privilege, opportunity, and empowerment played out in my life.

My parents emigrated from Argentina when I was a young child. They left because of the political unrest that afflicted my birthplace of Buenos Aires. Canada at first and then the United States opened their doors for my family. It is my tremendous privilege to be a naturalized US citizen. Yet, one of the few regrets from my childhood is that I did not grow up

speaking conversant Spanish. The educational practice during my childhood was total immersion. English only at school and also encouraged
at home. It was complete language replacement and assimilation, cutting
many people—including me—from a part of our heritage.

So, my life took shape as an English-speaking, white, heterosexual male
in the United States.

Even from this position of multiple privilege, my opportunities would
have been severely curtailed without public higher education. The California Community Colleges, California State University and University of
California allowed me to become the first in my family to attend college,
the first to earn a bachelor's degree, then a master's degree, and finally a
PhD. In this way, I and so many other first-generation students exceeded
the expectations that others had for our destiny. One could rise from the
working class into the middle class or upper class. Public higher education
was—and still is—a socioeconomic ladder.

Yet, too many are denied the type of educational opportunity I received.
The authors confront that reality, presenting solutions to address both
active and passive forms of exclusion in higher education. They have done
so in a way that builds on the federal construct of Hispanic-Serving Institutions (HSIs)—a distinguished group that grew out of a grant-eligibility
designation, becoming an association of peer institutions able to learn
from each other and share best practices. These institutions form a solid
foundation for study and examination, and the authors have applied their
considerable talents to building from this base.

This work contributes greatly to the ongoing conversation among
HSI peers, with ramifications that will reach all public higher education
institutions. Together, we must acknowledge that ou r economic and social
advancement as a nation depends on the success of Latino/a students. This
is not an opinion, rather a statement of objective fact.

That is why the focus of these articles is critical. We cannot advance
as a society without addressing the realities for those who continue to be
excluded from educational opportunity. As is often the case when talking
about prejudice and privilege, exclusion is both active and passive. Neglect
can be just as deterministic as hostility.

Introduction

Alfredo G. de los Santos Jr. and Gary Francisco Keller

ONE PROJECT IN TWO VOLUMES

The two volumes that we introduce here, *New Directions: Assessment and Preparation of Hispanic College Students* and *Moving Forward: Policies, Planning, and Promoting Access of Hispanic College Students*, are the product of a larger undertaking that includes not only these publications but also an academic conference and an alliance of professors and other specialists in fields related to assessment, academic preparation, and access. The overall project is known as the New Directions project (ND). ND is an academic alliance that covers many dimensions of research, policy, and advocacy about Hispanic student assessment and achievement. Our twenty-six papers were written separately and coterminously with each other. This New Directions project and its resultant two volumes are not intended as publications with separate chapters that each build upon the other, working incrementally toward a cumulative effect and final conclusion. Quite to the contrary, the project has a number of separate and related conclusions reflecting the multiculturalism and language registers of numerous contributors from all over our nation. ND reflects all of the Hispanic cultures that make up the vibrant Hispanic population of the entire United States. They are not intended to blend every strain of our multicultural nation into a single, homogenous, and nicely packaged product. We take seriously the overarching reality of the Hispanic communities of the United States: *juntos pero no revueltos.*

Thus, unified by our common ground that encompasses the entire nation, each contributor has produced a paper that is internally coherent, self-standing, and individually cogent. Each contributor was master of her or his house; the authors produced their work independently of each other, addressing particular broad themes of the ND alliance. No wonder, then, that both the ND project and the two volumes we have produced reflect heterogeneity and inclusiveness within the academic world. The edited collection reflects a variety of papers by a wide spectrum of academics ranging from professors with endowed chairs through full professors, associate professors, and tenure-track assistant professors to advanced graduate students. In addition, research scientists and policy experts at the Educational Testing Service (ETS) and two national organizations based in Washington, DC—Education Trust and *Excelencia* in Education—contributed papers. By design, the papers before you reflect the Hispanic within multiculturalism and the distinctive emphases and registers of the Hispanic communities and interest groups that populate every region of our nation.

The kernel, the acorn from which these multiple oaks grew, as it were, came from the inspiration of Beth M. Bouloukos, PhD, senior acquisitions editor at the State University of New York (SUNY) Press.

In 1991 SUNY Press published a book on which the current volumes have been loosely modeled: *Assessment and Access: Hispanics in Higher Education*, edited by Gary D. Keller, James R. Deneen, and Rafael G. Magallán. This volume was a landmark that was well received and highly influential. The publication had substantive participation from ETS and the College Board in that coeditors James R. Deneen and Rafael G. Magallán were senior administrators of the ETS and the College Board, respectively.

Assessment and Access led to decades of valuable collaboration among Arizona State University (ASU), the College Board, and ETS, which in November 2005 celebrated their twenty-six years of partnership with a seminal conference, "Latino Achievement in the Sciences, Technology, Engineering, and Mathematics." The conference, in turn, led to the publication of a special issue of *ETS Policy Notes: News from the ETS Policy Information Center* devoted entirely to the theme of the conference. The conference papers were published in the July 2006 issue of the *Journal of Hispanic Higher Education*. The guest editors for the issue—Alfredo G. de los Santos Jr., Gary D. Keller, Michael T. Nettles, and Rose Payán—represented the three organizations that organized the conference.

Now, approximately twenty-five years have transpired and much has been achieved that urgently cries for elucidation. In 2014, Beth Bouloukos suggested to Gary Keller that it would be desirable and exciting for a new book to be published that would update developments in the field. Keller was enthusiastic and in turn contacted his colleague, Alfredo G. de los Santos Jr., a research professor in the ASU Hispanic Research Center

(HRC) and emeritus vice-chancellor of the Maricopa County Community College District.

De los Santos, with equal enthusiasm and in addition an extraordinary network of contacts, brought these two volumes to fruition. He was key in identifying the contributors whose scholarship and advocacy grace these pages. He developed a list of some thirty possible authors and assumed the role of lead editor, culling information about the proposed contributors' interests and publications to facilitate development of the proposed contents. His early involvement as founding vice president in the creation of the American Association of Hispanics in Higher Education (AAHHE) and his long working relationship with Loui Olivas, AAHHE founding president and professor emeritus at ASU, provided another invaluable source of possible contributors: the programs for AAHHE's annual conferences.

During the discussion of what we sometimes playfully called "Assessment and Access 2.0," we mutually agreed that, in addition to inviting senior scholars to contribute to the book, we would provide professional development opportunities for junior faculty and emerging scholars. We are proud of the fact that many professors and associate professors involved either assistant professors or graduate students in the preparation of their contributions to the books. In a few instances, a graduate student took the lead, under the guidance and supervision of the professor, and is listed as the lead author. We are also pleased that the authors represent a wide range of institutions and organizations from around the entire nation.

Once the proposed volume was complete, the final articles were submitted to SUNY Press as a single manuscript. Beth Bouloukos viewed the contributions as the extraordinary result of an ambitious analysis of the key elements pertaining to the academic preparation, assessment, and promotion of access and achievement of Hispanic students. Equally extraordinary was the response from the academic community to the editors' invitation to contribute to this project. Beth judged that, as a matter of practicality, the project in its entirety should be published as two separate, closely related volumes, and the editors agreed. The revised proposal for two separate books was enthusiastically accepted by the SUNY Press editorial board. The five original organizing sections for the entire research publication appear in the two volumes as follows: assessment and academic preparation in the *New Directions* volume, and policies, planning, and progress in *Moving Forward*.

And then an unexpected development! Originally anticipating publication by SUNY Press, the six coeditors signed a contract for the two volumes. Unfortunately, issues of timing and control over design suddenly loomed large. The American Association of Hispanics in Higher Education (AAHHE), ably led by Prof. Loui Olivas, decided to make a major investment in the books and to feature them at its annual conference in 2018. The president of ETS, Walter D. MacDonald, committed to write the foreword to *New Directions* and to give the keynote at one of the plenary sessions at the conference, and the chancellor of the California State University System, Timothy P. White, agreed to do the same with respect to *Moving Forward*. Selected authors representing both volumes will present their papers during the conference's concurrent sessions.

As the date of the AAHHE conference is highly time sensitive, the organization's major involvement in the project led to the necessity of having both volumes published relatively quickly by academic standards. A distinctively Hispanic design was called for with respect to the book covers and interior pages. Both a casebound and a softcover book were needed. At our request, SUNY Press graciously agreed to cancel our contract, and the result is that the Bilingual Press, which only publishes Hispanic-related texts—over 250 titles—has undertaken the project. The issue of timing is further facilitated because editors de los Santos and Keller, AAHHE and its leader Loui Olivas, and executive editor Karen Van Hooft and the editorial offices of the Bilingual Press are all housed together in the Hispanic Research Center (HRC) of Arizona State University.

THE EDITORS

Alfredo G. de los Santos Jr., the lead editor of these volumes, is a research professor at the Hispanic Research Center of Arizona State University. He is emeritus vice-chancellor of the Maricopa Community College District and the founding president of El Paso Community College. In addition, he was a founding vice president of AAHHE, which established the Dr. Alfredo G. de los Santos Jr. Distinguished Leadership in Higher Education Award in his honor. He has been a member of the board of trustees of the College Board, the Educational Testing Service, the United States Open University, the Carnegie Foundation for the Advancement of Teaching, the Council for Higher Education Accreditation, the Tomás Rivera Policy Institute at the University of Southern California, the American Association of Community Colleges, the American Association for Higher Education, American College Testing, and the American Council on Education. He is the recipient of the 1998 Harold W. McGraw Jr. Prize in Education, the Lifelong Dedication to Hispanic Education Award from the Hispanic Association of Colleges and Universities, the Profesor Honorario Award from the Universidad Autónoma de Guadalajara, and the 1993 Education Achievement Award from the National Science Foundation.

Laura I. Rendón, University of Texas at San Antonio professor emerita of educational leadership and policy studies, was named in 2013 one of the Most Powerful and Influential Women in Texas by the National Diversity Council. Rendón is also a nationally recognized education theorist, speaker, and advocate for low-income, first-generation students. She developed the theory of validation that faculty and student affairs practitioners have employed as a student success framework. Rendón is also a teaching and learning thought leader. She is the author of the book *Sentipensante (Sensing/Thinking) Pedagogy: Educating for Wholeness, Social Justice and Liberation* (2009). As a leader in the field of college access and achievement, Rendón's research has been featured in the *Chronicle of Higher Education* and the PBS documentary *The College Track*. She is cofounder and past board chair of the National Council for Community and Education Partnerships and past president of the Association for the Study of Higher Education (ASHE), a leading scholarly organization focusing on higher education research.

Gary Francisco Keller is Regents' Professor and director of the Hispanic Research Center at Arizona State University. He is the author of over thirty books and more than one hundred articles on Latino literature, film, art, linguistics, and language policy. In addition, he has received grants from the National Endowment for the Arts, National Science Foundation, US Department of Education, US Department of Energy, and numerous private foundations. Keller was the lead editor of *Assessment and Access: Hispanics in Higher Education* (SUNY Press, 1991), which was an inspiration for the New Directions project. In 1993 he was awarded a $50,000 prize for "Pioneering Achievement in Education" from the Charles A. Dana Foundation for his design and successful administration of Project 1000. He was featured in a 1989 issue of *Hispanic Business* magazine as among the "one hundred of the nation's most influential Hispanics." Keller received the 2006 National Association for Chicana and Chicano Studies (NACCS) Distinguished Scholar Award. In 2017 he was awarded the Dr. Loui Olivas Distinguished Leadership in Higher Education Award by The Victoria Foundation, and in 2018 he received the first AAHHE President's Award of the American Association of Hispanics in Higher Education.

Alberto Acereda is Senior Director, Global Education, at the Educational Testing Service (ETS) in Princeton, New Jersey. He provides overall leadership for business development initiatives and academic outreach in global and higher education. Prior to joining ETS in 2012, he spent two decades at various universities across the United States. Just before joining ETS he was at Arizona State University, where he was professor of Spanish and Latin American literatures and cultures, chair of the Program of Spanish and Portuguese, director of Graduate Studies at the School of International Letters and Cultures, member of the ASU provost's executive committee, and president of the senate of the College of Liberal Arts and Sciences. He is a member of the North American Academy of the Spanish Language (Academia Norteamericana de la Lengua Española), a branch of the Real Academia Española. He is currently a faculty affiliate at Arizona State University's Hispanic Research Center.

Estela Mara Bensimón is professor of higher education and director of the Center for Urban Education (CUE) at the University of Southern California Rossier School of Education. Her current research is on issues of racial equity in higher education from the perspective of organizational learning and sociocultural practice theories. Dr. Bensimón has held the highest leadership positions in the Association for the Study of Higher Education (President, 2005–2006) and the American Education Research Association–Division on Postsecondary Education (Vice President, 1992–1994). In 2011 she was inducted as an AERA Fellow in recognition of excellence in research. In 2013 she was presented with the Association for the Study of Higher Education Research Achievement Award, and in 2015 she received the American Association of Hispanics in Higher Education Outstanding Latino/a Faculty in Higher Education (Research Institutions) Award. In 2017 she was elected to the National Academy of Education; that same year she was presented with the Social Justice in Education Award by the American Education Research Association.

Richard J. Tannenbaum is a principal research director in the Research and Development Division of the Educational Testing Service (ETS). He has strategic oversight for multiple Centers of Research that include more than 100 directors, scientists, and research associates. These centers address foundational and applied research in the areas of academic-to-career readiness, English language learning and assessment (both domestic and international), and K-12 student assessment and teacher credentialing. Prior to this position, Richard was the senior research director for the Center for Validity Research at ETS. He holds a PhD in Industrial/Organizational Psychology from Old Dominion University. He has published numerous articles, book chapters, and technical papers. His areas of expertise include assessment development, licensure and certification, standard setting and alignment, and validation.

ABOUT THE ARTICLES IN *MOVING FORWARD*

Policies

Cristóbal Rodríguez, José Luis Santos, and Patrick L. Valdez, "A History and Advocacy of Federal Policy: Improving Access and Success for Latina/o College Students" is a major historical review of federal policy since the Civil Rights Acts of the 1960s, and especially the Higher Education Act of 1965, as this policy affects Latina/o college students. Special attention is given to Hispanic-Serving Institutions (HSIs). Informed by this historical analysis, the authors provide an important and timely review of the policies that will shape the upcoming reauthorization of the Higher Education Act and that will affect both HSIs and Latina/o access and success.

David R. García, "An Engaged Approach to Public Scholarship: Shaping the Policy Agenda through Research Evidence" is a cogent and agile analysis of the issues that confront academic researchers who stand outside the policy process but who have the potential to shape the policy agenda. García provides a practical guide for researchers of Hispanic higher education to leverage their expertise as researchers in order to shape policies.

Deborah A. Santiago and Emily Calderón Galdeano, "Helping or Hindering? State Policies and Latino College Completion" reviews the state policies that either promoted or impeded Latino student success in higher education. While many of these policies are not specific, the authors' analysis shows that certain policies are critical for Latino college completion. Effective strategies that can increase access and retention to completion are suggested.

Eric R. Felix, Adrián Trinidad, Cheryl D. Ching, and Estela Mara Bensimón, "California's Student Equity Plan Policy: An Unexploited Opportunity among Hispanic-Serving Community Colleges" analyzes the Equity Plans submitted by a subset of HSI community colleges that are the result of policy requiring colleges to identify inequities, develop activities, and create goals for achieving equitable outcomes in higher education. The study seeks to answer the following questions: In what ways do the Equity Plans of HSI community colleges address the success of Latina/o students? Do the Equity Plans reflect on the HSI status of the institution? Do HSI Equity Plans focus on the most serious barriers to Latino/a success?

Rubén O. Martínez, "Neoliberalism and the Context of Public Higher Education for Latinos" is a critique of the societal shift from a social democratic to a neoliberal order as it affects public higher education. The author concludes that by denying the existence of institutional racism, neoliberalism allows the reproduction of and perpetuates exclusionary structures throughout society.

Planning

Tanya J. Gaxiola Serrano and Daniel G. Solórzano, "The Role of Interest Convergence in California's Education: Community Colleges, Latinas/os, and the State's Future" highlights the crucial role of community colleges in educating Latina/o students in California and the need to reduce the educational attainment gap that persists between Whites and Latinas/os. The authors examine the role that interest convergence plays in garnering support from the State of California to improve the retention, degree completion, and transfer outcomes of Latina/o community college students.

Belinda I. Reyes and Umadevi Senguttuvan, "Latino Students in Higher Education: Identifying Critical Issues and New Possibilities at a Multiethnic Teaching Institution" reviews both the successes and continued challenges in not only improving college enrollment and reducing dropout rates among Latino students but in college degree attainment, which for White students is more than twice that of Latino students enrolled at a four-year institution. A host of specific initiatives designed to meet the challenges are described and critiqued.

Fernando Valle and Cristóbal Salinas Jr., "Recognizing Counter-Stories of First-Generation Latina/o Graduate Students: Advancing the Latina/o Graduate College Choice Process" is a qualitative study that focuses on the advancement of first-generation Latina/o graduate students. The study finds counter-stories of first-generation graduate students to be at the heart of the graduate choice process as well as useful models for reframing the master narrative of graduate education.

Juan F. Carrillo, "Schooling Space: Creating Spatial Justice in Carolina del Norte" is a poignant, often personal call for Latin@s to come out of the "demographic shadows" and take advantage of the opportunity to build a spatially conscious vision where Latin@ students are empowered to define their own goals, research concerns, and contributions in order to improve their educational experience.

Progress

Leticia Oseguera and Wil Del Pilar, "Immigrant and Native Hispanic Students and Post-High School Pathways" studies three population groups of Hispanics from the vantage point of Segmented Assimilation Theory: immigrants, children of immigrants, and native students, the latter being operationally defined as second-generation students. The authors uncover a variety of results in addition to the customary one that the immigrant generation does the best among these three cohorts.

Victor B. Sáenz and DeAna Swan, "Latinas/os and U.S. Community Colleges: A Gateway to Opportunity and Success" reviews the striking data related to Latina/o students in community colleges as well as a number of key issues in their education. The fact that almost 1.5 million community college students are Latinas/os—about one of every five credit-seeking students—strongly suggests that the community college experience is key for education of the Latina/o population. Among the issues that the authors focus on are enrollment and degree attainment trends, key matriculation challenges, student success models, and the role of faculty and administrative leadership.

Amaury Nora and Vincent D. Carales, "Latino College Students: A Trajectory in the Right Direction after Years of Despondency" is a highly focused, in-depth study of one Hispanic-Serving Institution that focuses on such variables as the refutation of the deficit viewpoint with respect to Latino students, the establishment of a sense of belonging, the effectiveness of the mentoring experience, and initiatives to address the formidable gender gap between the much higher-achieving women students and their lagging Latino male peers.

Maria Estela Zárate, Chenoa S. Woods, and Kelly M. Ward, "Nineteen Years after Prop 209: Are Latino/a Students Equitably Represented at the University of California?" When Prop 209 went into effect in 1997, reports documented an immediate decline in the representation of Latinos/as at the University of California. However, since 2003, the long-term implications of Prop 209 have not been documented. This valuable study reviews and measures the enrollment status and educational attainment of Latina/o students from implementation of Prop 209 thorough the present.

Nolan L. Cabrera, " 'The Only Racism Left Is That against White People': The Complex Realities of the Campus Racial Climate for Latina/o Students." This essay begins with the election of President Obama, which led to a paradoxical response among some that the United States had entered a "post-racial" period and among others that contemporary anti-White discrimination is more prevalent than anti-Black discrimination. The essay offers suggestions for dealing with the new climate as it affects Latina/o and other students on campus.

PART

policies

A History and Advocacy of Federal Policy

IMPROVING ACCESS AND SUCCESS
FOR LATINA/O COLLEGE STUDENTS

Cristóbal Rodríguez, José Luis Santos, and Patrick L. Valdez

I n the history of federal policy and Latina/o college students, much can be deduced from the development of Hispanic-Serving Institutions (HSIs) and the amendments made to the Higher Education Act of 1965.[1] However, while one may acknowledge the important effect from a pre-college perspective on all diverse students that were informed by the Civil Rights Acts of the 1960s under President Lyndon B. Johnson, the historic place of the Latina/o college student in federal policy parallel that of Black students, and consequently may argue for stronger policy coalitions today. A detailed understanding of the unique advocacy history of the 1970s and 1980s that led to the development of HSIs provides a more in-depth perspective on the context and plight of college access and success for Latina/o students. Therefore, rather than simply presenting the federal policies that inform greater access and success for Latina/o college students, we provide a historical account of federal policy relating to Latina/o college students, aiming to advocate for reinforcement of present federal policy advocacy to improve access and success for Latina/o college students going forward. We also provide an important and timely snapshot of the policy landscape that will shape the upcoming reauthorization of the Higher Education Act that will affect both HSIs and Latina/o student access and success.

FEDERAL POLICIES AND PROGRAMS
AND LATINO COLLEGE ACCESS AND SUCCESS

Under President Lyndon B. Johnson and with the power of the civil rights movements in a post Brown v. Board era,[2] which by then included Latinos

1. *Higher Education Act of 1965,* U.S. Code 20 ch. 28 (1965) § 1001 et seq.
2. *Brown v. Board of Education of Topeka,* 347 U.S. 483 (1954).

13

as a class of their own as a result of Hernandez v. Texas,[3] the 1960s ushered in new efforts to improve the condition of diverse populations. New federal policies indeed further improved both the K-12 education and the college access and success for Latina/o students. President Johnson's "War on Poverty" led to passage of four crucial federal policies: the Civil Rights Act of 1964,[4] the Economic Opportunity Act of 1964,[5] the Elementary and Secondary Education Act of 1965[6] (and later with the addition through the Bilingual Education Act of 1968,[7]) and the Higher Education Act of 1965.[8] Taken together, these vastly improved the conditions that informed the pathway and success to a college education for Latino students. Stemming from these policies, federal efforts addressed school segregation, federal programming for college readiness and outreach, further education funding for children living with poverty and for children whose home language was another language other than English, and overall improvement of access to college.

The most widely known and possibly the federal effort with the greatest direct influence on college access and success are the TRIO programs such as Upward Bound and Talent search[9] that aimed to develop outreach efforts and led to the development of college readiness efforts. TRIO has been historically represented by three federally funded programs: Upward Bound and Talent Search, which targeted college readiness for secondary education students, and Student Support Services that provided college outreach and academic support for college students. Upward Bound began as a result of the Economic Opportunity Act of 1964;[10] its goal would be college readiness for secondary education students identified as economically underserved and as first-generation college students. Today, hosted for the most part by public universities at nearly 1,000 sites, Upward Bound serves more than 65,000 high school students through summer academic enrichment programs and through weekend programming dur-

---

3. *Hernandez v. Texas*, 347 U.S. 475 (1954).

4. *Civil Rights Act of 1964*, Public Law 88-352, *U.S. Statutes at Large* 78 (1964): 241.

5. *Economic Opportunity Act of 1964*, Public Law 88-452, *U.S. Statutes at Large* 78 (1964): 508.

6. *Elementary and Secondary Education Act of 1965*, Public Law 89-10, *U.S. Statutes at Large* 79 (1965): 27.

7. *Bilingual Education Act*, Public Law 90-247, *U.S. Statutes at Large* 81 (1968): 783–820.

8. *Higher Education Act of 1965*, *U.S. Code 20 ch. 28* (1965) § 1001 et seq.

9. Watson S. Swail and Laura W. Perna. "Pre-college Outreach Programs: A National Perspective" in *Increasing Access to College: Extending Possibilities for All Students*, ed. William G. Tierney and Linda S. Hagedorn (Albany: State University of New York Press, 2002), 15–34.

10. *Economic Opportunity Act of 1964*, Public Law 88-452, *U.S. Statutes at Large* 78 (1964): 508.

ing the academic year. The effort has demonstrated that such students were more likely to enroll in higher education, apply for financial assistance, and complete a college degree than eligible Upward Bound students who did not participate in such programing.[11] Full-year college readiness and academic programming that serves each student for several years is demonstrably a model for success, and it has been adapted through other federal and private foundation programs nationally. Although Talent Search, developed by the Higher Education Act of 1965,[12] has no extensive built-in academic preparation component comparable to that of Upward Bound, it serves far more high school students: about 360,000, through almost five hundred public university and high school based partnerships that provide short-term events and activities throughout an academic year. Talent Search has demonstrated college enrollment trends similar to Upward Bound's.[13]

Available reports on participating students in TRIO projects demonstrate that of 840,000 students served by 2,900 TRIO projects (of which 466 are Talent Search projects and 964 are Upward Bound projects), 35 percent are White, 35 percent are Black, 19 percent are Latina/o, 3 percent are Asian, and 4 percent identify as of "Other" race or ethnicity.[14] Despite the benefits of such programs to the students they serve, the programs serve comparatively few of the 10.9 million U.S. school-aged children living in poverty in 2011.[15] Nonetheless, such federal initiatives and policies clearly demonstrate the impact and influence that the federal government can have on improving college access and success for first-generation college students and economically underserved students, a category that reflects the Latino community in the United States. Sadly, given the political turmoil in the U.S. Congress and the continual efforts by conservative politicians to limit nonessential federal programs, often referred to as entitlement programs, such programming is increasingly targeted for defunding. Defending such programs requires an even greater level of advocacy than has been needed in the past.[16]

---

11. "National Studies Find TRIO Programs Effective at Increasing College Enrollment and Graduation," *The Pell Institute,* accessed July 9, 2012.

12. *Higher Education Act of 1965, U.S. Code 20 ch. 28* (1965) § 1001 et seq.

13. "National Studies Find TRIO Programs Effective . . ."

14. "TRIO: History," *Council for Opportunity in Education,* accessed July 19, 2012. www .coenet.us/coe_prod_imis/COE/TRIO/History/COE/NAV_TRIO/TRIO_History.aspx.

15. Ibid.

16. "Self-Inflicted Wounds: Protecting Families and Our Economy from Bad Budget Choices," *Coalition on Human Needs,* accessed April 3, 2012. www.chn.org.

College Readiness and the Reauthorizations of ESEA

On December 10, 2015, the Elementary and Secondary Education Act (ESEA) of 1965[17] was reauthorized as the *Every Student Succeeds Act*,[18] a change from its previous reauthorization as the *No Child Left Behind Act of 2001* (NCLB) in 2002.[19] The ESEA, developed in 1965[20] through President Johnson's "War on Poverty," provided additional funding to states that targeted improved educational opportunity for students living in poverty. The 1965 legislation also provided federal grant programs that improved regulation of elementary and secondary education. While the initial ESEA did provide college scholarships to low-income college students, the 2001 reauthorization (NCLB) maintained a K-12 focus whose accountability measures required measuring and reporting the achievement progress and high school graduation rates for low-income students, racially and linguistically diverse students, and for students with disabilities.[21]

However, between 2002 and 2015 (that is, between NCLB to ESSA), specifically starting in 2009, states had been independently approving an interstate curriculum effort led by the National Governors Association and the Council for Chief State School Officers to align K-12 curriculum with college readiness standards. Called the Common Core State Standards, these have been adopted by forty-two states, the District of Columbia, four territories, and the Department of Defense Education Activity.[22] While the Common Core State Standards is not specifically a federal effort, and short of requiring states to specifically adopt the Common Core State Standards, ESSA does require states to adopt a curriculum aligned with college readiness standards, essentially using language similar to that describing the Common Core State Standards. Regarding Latinos and college access and success related to reauthorizations of ESEA, since ESSA represents the first time federal policy has guided K-12 education to focus on college readiness, and since Common Core State Standards represent a very recent nationwide reform policy, it remains to be seen whether the reauthori-

---

17. *Elementary and Secondary Education Act of 1965*, Public Law 89-10, *U.S. Statutes at Large* 79 (1965): 27.

18. *Every Student Succeeds Act*, Public Law 114-95, *U.S. Statutes at Large* (2015): 1177–391.

19. *No Child Left Behind Act of 2001*, Public Law 107-110, *U.S. Statutes at Large* (2002): 1425.

20. *Elementary and Secondary Education Act of 1965*, Public Law 89-10, *U.S. Statutes at Large* 79 (1965): 27.

21. "Every Student Succeeds Act (ESSA)," *U.S. Department of Education*, accessed January 7, 2016. http://www.ed.gov/essa.

22. "Common Core State Standards Initiative," *National Governors Association Center and Council of Chief State School Officers*, accessed December 15, 2010. www.corestandards.org.

zation will influence Latino college access and success to the same extent as Civil Rights Acts of the 1960s.

THE HISTORY OF ADVOCACY:
TITLE III TO TITLE V AND THE POLICY FORMATION
OF HISPANIC-SERVING INSTITUTIONS

The history of U.S. higher education is well documented in textbooks, but far less documented within such textbooks is the history of Latino higher education. This is especially true of Latino higher education advocacy—advocacy that led to the expansion of Title III in 1986 and to the Hispanic-Serving Institution (HSI) designation in 1992. Since 1992 an increasing amount of literature has focused on the institutional characteristics, best practices, and the role that HSIs play in educating the nation's fastest growing student population. Yet not enough extant literature focuses on the history of the HSI designation, specifically the advocacy of Latino organizations in the 1970s and 1980s that led Congress to recognize institutions of higher education (IHEs) with a 25 percent or more Latino student population as HSIs.[23] This section will provide insight into the formation of HSI policy and the role that early advocates of Latino higher education played in shaping the current higher education landscape.

1975-1976: Early Higher Education Advocacy

A review of congressional records indicates that between 1967 and 1974 Latino advocacy groups, among them the Incorporated Mexican-American Government Employees (IMAGE), National Congress of Hispanic American Citizens, and Service, Employment, Redevelopment (SER), provided testimony before Congress on large-scale social issues facing the Latino community. Testimony during this period focused on the broad social issues affecting the general welfare of the Latino community, from bilingual education to migrant labor to the number of Latinos employed by federal government agencies. Advocacy for increasing Latino access and success in higher education began to occur in 1973, with the establishment of the LULAC National Education Service Centers (LNESC). In 1975, shortly after LNESC's establishment, Richard Salvatierra, LNESC's

23. Patrick L. Valdez. "An Overview of Hispanic-Serving Institutions' Legislation: Legislation Policy Formation between 1979–1992." in *Hispanic-Serving Institutions in American Higher Education: Their Origin, and Present and Future Challenges*, ed. Jesse Perez Mendez, Fred Bonner II, Josephine Méndez-Negrete, and Robert T. Palmer (Virginia: Stylus Publishing, 2015), 5–29.

assistant national director, testified before the Senate Subcommittee on Education; he called for increasing Latino student access to higher education by expanding Titles III, V, and IX.[24]

Salvatierra's testimony indicates LNESC recommended that an equitable amount of Title III funding be awarded to two-year institutions serving Hispanic students as compared to Title III funds that had been awarded to four-year institutions serving Black students. LNESC's recommendation rested on the following, as stated by Salvatierra.

> In 1972, Black institutions were awarded 96 grants totaling $30 million. Grants for support of programs for the Spanish-speaking in the same year totaled 18 in the amounts of over $2 million. This is a difference of over 1,100 percent in grant funds for Blacks as opposed to Spanish-speaking programs. Taking one more step we discover that the average grant for the Black programs was $322,055, while for the Spanish-speaking program it was $156,444. This also happens to be the case for most other years. We in no way wish to suggest that funding for Black programs be reduced. However, we simply want to point out that the Hispanics are not receiving a fair share.[25]

As illustrated by Salvatierra's testimony, Latinos were not looking to reduce the amount of monies awarded to institutions serving Black students, but they believed administration of the program by the Office of Education would benefit from Latino representation. "In addition, we also favor language that seeks to maintain adequate representation of each minority group in the division of OE that executes Title III."[26]

Ten years after the Civil Rights Act of 1965 passed—a period that witnessed racial and civil unrest—Latinos were the second largest minority group in the nation, of which 85 percent were Mexican American. Despite the long history of Latinos in the U.S. at the time, educational attainment rates lagged and Latino leaders, many who had grown up or attended college during the 1960s era, begin to organize at the local and national level. In addition to LNESC, the National Chicano Council for Higher Education (NCCHE), founded and presided over by Dr. Arturo Madrid, begin producing research and data on the state of Latinos in higher education. Research and the use of data, along with the establishment of a few

24. Higher Education Act Amendments of 1976: Hearings before the Subcommittee on Postsecondary Education, Committee on Education and Labor of the House; Committee on Education and Labor, 94th Cong. 1 (1975) (Statement of Richard Salvatierra, League of United Latin American Citizens, Washington, DC).

25. Higher Education Act Amendments of 1976, 477.

26. Higher Education Act Amendments of 1976, 478–479.

small colleges founded to educate Latinos, laid the foundation of advocacy for the expansion of Title III. One of those colleges, Eugenio de Hostos Community College, founded in 1968 in New York City's South Bronx, was led by Dr. Candido de Leon.

While Salvatierra's testimony called for an increase in Titles III, V, and IX, de Leon's testimony during the 1976 HEA hearings focused specifically on "the need to evaluate the use and appropriations of Title III funds."[27] Accompanied by Pepe Baron, executive director of El Congreso Nacional de Asuntos Colegiales, the only Latino-based higher education organization in Washington at the time, de Leon's testimony questioned the grant application process used to award Title III funds for qualifying institutions. De Leon's testimony was supported by two Government Accounting Office (GAO) reports issued in January 1974 and October of 1975 that criticized (1) the difficulty in identifying characteristics that could be used to distinguish a developing institution from a developed one, for purposes of measuring the title's success (1974), and (2) the administration of the program's grant application process (1975).[28] Like Salvatierra, de Leon was sensitive to the plight of traditional Black institutions when recommending that a greater amount of Title III funds be awarded to institutions serving Latino students:

> I would like to preface the comments that I am about to make with one observation. I think that it is unfortunate that in our presentation of the views it may appear that the views of one group are necessarily against the views of another group. I want to clarify that before we start. I support all of the comments that have been made about the need for the Southern Black institutions and the excellent job that they have done. My comments are directed to making sure that the constituents I have, in our community, which are primarily Puerto Rican, are able to receive just as much support as everyone else is receiving. So, if for any reason, anything that I say is misunderstood to be an attack, I would be happy to clarify that later.[29]

The testimony given by Salvatierra and de Leon signified a changing of the guard, from broad-based Latino civic and social organizations advo-

---

27. Higher Education Act Amendments: Hearings before the Subcommittee on Education, Arts, and Humanities of the Committee on Labor and Human Resources, 94th Cong. 1 (1976) (statement of Candido de Leon, President, Eugenio de Hostos Community College, Washington, DC).

28. Patrick L. Valdez. "Anatomy of the Hispanic-Serving Institution (HSI) Designation: An Overview of HSI Policy Formation" (paper presented at the Hispanic-Serving Institutions in the 21st Century: A Convening, El Paso, Texas, April 28–29, 2015).

29. Higher Education Act Amendments of 1976, 208.

cating for higher education access at the student level, to a more directed approach to increasing federal funding to institutions serving Latino students. This change was accompanied by the arrival of a new group of Latino higher education advocates who appeared in Washington during the mid-1970s. According to one advocate at that time, "We (those of us with higher education backgrounds) knew that we had to start carving out a place for ourselves that would articulate our own interest because none of the national Latino organizations had higher education functions."[30] While Latino civic and social organizations had added student access to postsecondary education to their advocacy agendas, they lacked specific knowledge about higher education to make a focused push. The focused push, however, arrived in 1978 when Latino advocacy groups coalesced into the Hispanic Higher Education Coalition (HHEC).

1978: A New Vanguard:
Hispanic Higher Education Coalition (HHEC)[31]

On March 29, 1979, Dr. Alvin Rivera, representing the Hispanic Higher Education Coalition (HHEC), formed in the fall of 1978, appeared before the Subcommittee on Postsecondary Education and provided testimony focused on expanding Title III funding with the following recommendations:

> (1) the title be changed to Strengthening Developing Institutions and College Programs. This change is directed toward providing incentives through effective and innovative college programs. The college programs will be designed to serve substantial numbers of economically disadvantaged students and students who come from environments in which the dominant language is a language other than English;
>
> (2) the Coalition recognizes the contribution that community colleges make to higher education. We know that over 50 percent of Hispanic students start in community colleges. In the past, Title III has received a disproportionately large number of applications from community colleges. However, the set-aside for community colleges presently is limited to 24 percent. The Coalition recommends that the current 24 percent set-aside for community colleges be increased to 40 percent.[32]

---

30. Proponent 4, personal communication, May 25, 2012.

31. Valdez, "An Overview of Hispanic-Serving Institutions' Legislation," 22–23.

32. Hearings on the Reauthorization of the Higher Education Act and Related Measures, Part 1: Hearing before the Subcommittee on Education, Arts, and Humanities of the Committee on Labor and Human Resources, U.S. Senate, 96th Cong. 1 (1979) (statement of Alvin D. Rivera, Hispanic Higher Education Coalition, Washington, DC).

Established in the fall of 1978, the HHEC was comprised of eight Latino advocacy organizations: ASPIRA of America, El Congreso Nacional de Asuntos Colegiales (CONAC), League of United Latin American Citizens (LULAC), Mexican American Legal Defense & Educational Fund (MAL-DEF), National Association for Equal Educational Opportunities, National Council of La Raza (now UnidosUS), Puerto Rican Legal Defense & Education Fund (LatinoJustice PRLDEF), Inc., and U.S. Catholic Conference.[33]

As the first broad-based Latino coalition committed to higher education advocacy, members felt a sense of urgency and obligation to gain political recognition within the higher education legislative community. As stated by one Latino advocate involved in the HHEC, "We knew that we had to start carving out a place for ourselves that would articulate our own interest because none of the national Latino organizations had higher education functions. Almost none of them except maybe MALDEF had any scholarships, and theirs were just small ones and they were just only for law students not undergraduates. So there was a sense that we were way far behind and we had a long way to go."[34]

This sense of urgency was reinforced by the state of Latinos in higher education at the time: educational attainment remained at the ninth-grade level, dropout rates soared over 50 percent, participation in four-year, graduate, and professional schools rested between 1 percent and 2 percent, and unemployment rates of Hispanic youth were upwards of 30 percent.[35] HHEC members shared de Leon's sentiments that Title III program funds were being distributed disproportionately to traditional Black universities since the title's inception in 1965, but HHEC's sentiments were also tied to Rivera's experience working as a fellow in the Department of Health, Education, and Welfare (HEW), which, at the time, housed the Office of Education. As an HEW Fellow, Rivera worked in the Developing Institutions program and testified that his experience in HEW was "insightful, disappointing, and often demoralizing."[36] Moreover, he expressed concern that the lack of Latinos involved in the administration of federal policies and programs would limit their benefit for the Latino community:

> Effectiveness of Federal education programs for Hispanics will be stifled unless sufficient participation of Hispanic staff in policies and progress occurs. For example, it should be noted that there

33. Valdez, "An Overview of Hispanic-Serving Institutions' Legislation," 7.

34. Proponent 4, personal communication, May 25, 2012.

35. Reauthorization of the HEA, Part 1, 326.

36. Reauthorization of the HEA, Part 1, 325.

are only two Hispanic professionals in the entire Bureau of Higher
and Continuing Education. This is continued evidence of the insen-
sitivity of the Federal government to the need of Hispanics.[37]

Rivera's frustrations stemmed not only from the lack of Latino representation in federal government agencies but from the realization that Latinos
had yet to establish themselves within the Title III higher education policy
system. As a result, although Senate and House committees on higher education heard testimony three times in 1979, HHEC recommendations that
would have directly benefited institutions serving Latino students were not
adopted until the HEA of 1980. HHEC advocacy did, however, lead to a
"Senate and House resolution that established a new Title III, divided into
three parts: Part A, Strengthening Institutions; Part B, Aid to Institutions
with Special Needs; and Part C, Challenge Grants (established a separate
matching grant program). A set-aside for schools historically serving Black
students was applied to Part B, and limited Title III funding to these institutions to 50 percent for fiscal year 1979 was added."[38]

1984: Amending the HEA, Expanding Title III, and Narrowly Defining Institutions Serving Latinos

By 1984, HHEC members had testified at Title III, Title IV, and the
Hispanic Access to Higher Education hearings, which was the first-ever
congressional hearing that focused on Hispanic higher education.[39] Yet
despite their increased advocacy between 1979 and 1982, no specific
definition or set-aside for IHEs serving Latinos students had been added
to HEA legislation. Understanding the way to increase funding to IHEs
serving Latino students was through Title III, Dr. Arturo Madrid, former
director of the Fund for the Improvement of Postsecondary Education
(FIPSE), urged Congress to increase federal support to colleges and
universities serving Hispanics during the Hispanic Access hearings in
1982;[40] following the Hispanic Access hearings, Senator Claiborne Pell
(D-RI) introduced H.R. 5240 during the 1984 HEA reauthorization
hearings. Included in H.R. 5240 was "an institutional eligibility amendment for Title III funding predicated on 40 percent Hispanic student

37. Reauthorization of the HEA, Part 1, 329.

38. Patrick L. Valdez, "Anatomy of the Hispanic-Serving Institution (HSI) Designation," 4.

39. Hispanic Access to Higher Education: Hearing before the Subcommittee on Postsecondary Education of the Committee on Education and Labor, House of Representatives, 97th
Cong. 1 (1982).

40. "Hispanic Access to Higher Education," 17.

enrollment that authorized a $10 million set-aside under Title III: Part D: Reservation for Hispanic Institutions."[41]

Subsequently, Rafael Magallan, executive director of the HHEC, provided testimony during the 1984 HEA reauthorization hearings recommending institutional eligibility predicated on a minimum of 30 percent (not 40 percent) Hispanic student enrollment.[42] The recommendation to reduce the percentage threshold from 40 percent to 30 percent was based on HHEC calculations that the majority of IHEs with 40 percent or more Latino student enrollments were located in Puerto Rico. Thus, any institutional eligibility amendment drafted to support "Hispanic Institutions" on the US mainland required a lower percentage threshold. When asked why negotiations related to the percentage threshold were important, and why it was important to gain a $10 million set-aside for these institutions, an HHEC advocate stated, "There was such an extraordinary concentration of Hispanics and just a handful of institutions . . . we had a lot of discussion in terms of how broadly or how narrowly do we want to try to make the case for Latino institutional support."[43] In addition to the 30 percent threshold, the HHEC recommended that eligibility also reflect an institution's (1) geographic location; (2) proximity to elementary and secondary schools with significant Latino enrollments; (3) cooperative agreement with Local LEAs; (4) Title V TRIO programs enrolling more than 50 percent Latino students; (5) significant Latino staffing patterns; (6) special programs to increase Latinos in underrepresented academic and professional areas; and (7) a five-year master plan that illustrates commitment to Latino students. Using these and the 30 percent criteria, the HHEC identified seventy colleges and universities on the U.S. mainland, and all thirty-four in Puerto Rico, that were eligible for the Title III set-aside.[44]

In the final version of the HEA of 1986, Pell's Part D recommendation authorized Part A, Section 312 (f)(3), identifying "any institution of higher education which has an enrollment of which at least 20 percent are Mexican American, Puerto Rican, Cuban, or other Hispanic students on thereof" eligible for Title III funding.[45] The 20 percent (or more) eligibility

---

41. Valdez, "Anatomy of the Hispanic-Serving Institution (HSI) Designation," 5.

42. Hearings on the Reauthorization of the Higher Education Act: Hearings before the Subcommittee on Postsecondary Education of the Committee on Education and Labor, House of Representatives, 98th Cong. 1 (1984) (statement of Rafael Magallan, Executive Director, Hispanic Higher Education Coalition, Washington, DC).

43. Valdez, "Anatomy of the Hispanic-Serving Institution (HSI) Designation," Proponent 2.

44. Reauthorization of the HEA 1984, 808–809.

45. Higher Education Amendments of 1986, Pub. L. 99-498 (1986).

amendment added to HEA in 1986 was the first legislative definition used to identify a developing institution as a Hispanic Institution for purposes of awarding Title III funding.[46]

Testimony provided during the 1985 HEA hearings was the last time that members representing the HHEC presented on behalf of Title III. That same year, a group of Latino college presidents gathered at Our Lady of the Lake University in San Antonio, Texas, and established the Hispanic Association of Colleges and Universities (HACU). The establishment of HACU in 1986 allowed the HHEC, which was comprised of Latino advocacy groups with much broader social agendas, to turn over its efforts to an association whose founding members were executives and presidents representing eighteen colleges and universities.[47] Because HHEC was comprised of members representing several advocacy groups, the transition from a coalition to an association made up of colleges and universities was vital for continued advocacy and sustainability. Much like HHEC members who held specific expertise in higher education, compared to advocates focused on broad social issues, HACU members held expertise in delivering and implementing services to students at the institutional level. To date, little is known about the HHEC and its members who testified before Congress from 1979 to 1985, yet the influence they had on advancing Latino higher education and the role they played in shaping the current HSI designation is unarguable. While continued research is needed to fully understand the efforts of the HHEC, a first step in understanding Latino advocacy at the federal level is recognizing its existence.

1992–1995: HACU and HSI Designation

Since its inception, HACU has led "the effort to convince Congress to formally recognize campuses with high Hispanic enrollment as federally designated HSIs [in 1992] and to begin targeting federal appropriations to those campuses."[48] With the passing of the baton from HHEC, HACU began its advocacy to increase Title III funds to IHEs serving Latino students in 1986. HACU advocacy efforts between 1986 and 1991 culminated with HACU testimony given by Cesar Trimble, vice president of HACU, in May of 1991. During his testimony, Trimble stated, "We are a coali-

46. Valdez, "Anatomy of the Hispanic-Serving Institution (HSI) Designation," Proponent 2.

47. "About HACU/HACU 101," *Hispanic Association of Colleges and Universities*, accessed January 16, 2016. http://www.hacu.net/hacu/HACU_101.asp.

48. "About HACU/HACU 101."

tion of public and private, nonprofit two-year and four-year colleges and universities where at the institution the minimum Hispanic enrollment overall is 25 percent . . . our recommendation [to Title III] is that you strongly consider initiating the Hispanic-Serving Institutions part of Title III."[49] Additionally, HACU recommended that a $30 million set-aside be appropriated in Title III to fund IHEs with a 25 percent or more Latino student enrollment; in 1992, Trimble reported that 112[50] institutions met the recommended 25 percent threshold—institutions that ranged from two-year to four-year, public and private. HACU's testimony and presence as an association made up of college and university leaders moved Congress to act. In 1992 the 102nd Congress amended the 25 percent HSI designation to Title III and approved a $10 million dollar set-side.[51] Although the set-aside remained unfunded until 1995 when Congress appropriated $12 million,[52] HACU's efforts advanced the work of the HHEC by increasing the percentage threshold from 20 percent to 25 percent and adding the term HSI to the higher education lexicon.

The coining of the term HSI in 1992 and codification of appropriations to specifically fund HSIs in 1995 were major legislative victories for HACU and Latino higher education. This success and the rapid growth of HSIs in the mid-1990s led to increased HACU membership, the majority of those institutions in California and Texas, and legislative clout. Through this increased capacity, HACU moved Congress to amend funding for HSIs to title V in 1998. Since 1998 there has been much discourse about the 25 percent designation and what it means to be an HSI, and since 1992 a growing body of literature has emerged to define and identify HSI characteristics.

Thus, the existence of the term HSI as a federal designation not only increased federal funding to HSIs, but it also stimulated new scholarship focused on Latino higher education that has led to new and current advocacy efforts. Such scholarship and advocacy is needed, but equally important is recognizing the efforts of Latino higher education advocates that paved the way for HSI designation. This section introduced the efforts of Latino higher education advocates which begin as part of the Civil

---

49. Access to College and Program Simplification: Hearings before the Subcommittee on Postsecondary Education of the Committee on Education and Labor, House of Representatives, 102nd Cong. 1 (1991) (statement of Cesar Trimble, Hispanic Association of Colleges and Universities, Washington, DC).

50. Reauthorization of the HEA 1991, 161.

51. Higher Education Amendments of 1992, Pub. L. 102-325 (1992).

52. "About HACU/HACU 101."

Rights era and continue into the current decade. Recognizing these efforts and connecting past and present Latino advocacy, "we are reminded that equity for Latinos has never been freely given."[53]

FEDERAL AID POLICY AND COLLEGE ACCESS

Financial Aid Policy

Federal financial aid has been key in helping to transform higher education from an elite system of higher education to one that is more responsive to the masses. Government support started with the Servicemen's Readjustment Act of 1944[54] (the GI Bill) and continued with the National Defense Student Loan Program of 1958,[55] through the Guaranteed Student Loan program in 1965[56] and the Pell Grant in 1972.[57] The earlier policies focused on helping veterans reintegrate into society from wartime or targeted dollars to educational systems to meet the demands posed by national security needs—that is, to compete with the former Soviet Union in the areas of science and technology. Later financial aid policies focused on directing aid in an effort to increase college access, choice, and affordability. These policies have substantially mitigated costs and increased access for low-income students and students of color. Even so, at every level, there are disparities in educational attainment among White, Black, and Latina/o students, and these disparities widen as students' progress through the educational pipeline. Evidently, college attendance is on the rise, but disparities still exist.

Over the past forty years, we have made a lot of progress regarding college access. Between 1975 and 2015, college attendance rates for all students climbed from 50.7 percent to 69.2 percent.[58] During this same period, college attendance rates for Latinas/os increased from 58 percent to 68.9 percent.[59] Moreover, during that period, college attendance rates among low-income young people climbed from 31.2 percent to 69.2

53. Laura I. Rendon. "Introduction" in *Hispanic-Serving Institutions in American Higher Education: Their Origin, and Present and Future Challenges*, ed. Jesse Perez Mendez, Fred Bonner II, Josephine Méndez-Negrete, and Robert T. Palmer (Virginia: Stylus Publishing, 2015), 1–4.

54. Servicemen's Readjustment Act 1944.

55. National Defense Student Loan Program of 1958.

56. Guaranteed Student Loan Program of 1965.

57. Pell Grant 1972.

58. "The Digest of Education Statistics 2016" (Table 302.10), NCES. https://nces.ed.gov/programs/digest/d16/tables/dt16_302.10.asp?current=yes. Accessed on October 24, 2017.

59. "The Digest of Education Statistics 2016" (Table 302.20), NCES. https://nces.ed.gov/programs/digest/d16/tables/dt16_302.20.asp?current=yes. Accessed on October 24, 2017.

percent.[60] However, proportionately fewer low-income students than did wealthy students in the mid-1970s.[61] In addition, gaps between Whites and underrepresented groups still exist. In short, more students overall are going to college and more Latinas/os, and low-income students are enrolling. This is great news, but access isn't the only issue of concern. What about college affordability and college success for low-income students and Latinos?

Attainment Gaps among Poor Youth and Latinas/os

Even though, overall, more students are attending college and more low-income and students of color are attending, large attainment gaps still exist and some students are far more likely than others to attain a college degree. Today, Latinas/os complete college at lower rates than their White counterparts. Six-year graduation rates for White students (63 percent) almost 10 points greater than Latino students (54 percent).[62] In 2016, 19 percent of Latinas/os ages twenty-five to twenty-nine held at least a bachelor's degree, compared with 37 percent of their white peers.[63] In short, Whites attained bachelor's degrees at two times the rate of Latinas/os. In addition, there is a large and growing income gap in degree attainment. In 2012, individuals from the highest-income families were more than three times more likely than individuals from low-income families to obtain a bachelor's degree by age twenty-four.[64] Of the low-income students and students of color who do go to college, many don't graduate with the degree they seek.

60. "The Condition of Education 2010" (Table A-20-1), NCES, accessed on October 24, 2017. http://nces.ed.gov/pubs2010/2010028.pdf and "The Digest of Education Statistics 2016" (Table 302.30), NCES. https://nces.ed.gov/programs/digest/d16/tables/dt16_302.30.asp?current=yes. Accessed on October 24, 2017.

61. "The Condition of Education 2010" (Table A-20-1), NCES, accessed on October 24, 2017. http://nces.ed.gov/pubs2010/2010028.pdf and "The Digest of Education Statistics 2016" (Table 302.30), NCES. https://nces.ed.gov/programs/digest/d16/tables/dt16_302.30.asp?current=yes. Accessed on October 24, 2017.

62. U.S. Census Bureau, Educational Attainment in the United States: 2016. Based on Fall 2009 Cohort. https://nces.ed.gov/programs/digest/d16/tables/dt16_326.10.asp?current=yes. Accessed on October 24, 2017.

63. U.S. Census Bureau, Current Population Survey 2016, Detailed Tables 1 for Non-Hispanic White alone and Hispanic (of any race) and author's calculations, "Educational Attainment in the United States 2016." https://www.census.gov/data/tables/2016/demo/education-attainment/cps-detailed-tables.html. Accessed on October 24, 2017.

64. Brookings, "How Can We Track Trends in Educational Attainment by Parental Income, 2015," (Note 4). https://www.brookings.edu/research/how-can-we-track-trends-in-educational attainment-by-parental-income-hint-not-with-the-current-population-survey/. Accessed on October 24, 2017.

Higher Education Act (1965)

Before 1965, colleges across the country were mostly populated by white males and middle-to upper-income families. Even though the GI Bill provided federal aid and covered college costs for tens of thousands of veterans after World War II, it was disproportionately used by whites. So, a racially segregated society and a limited federal role in higher education allowed for higher education to remain an exclusive and largely self-governing sector in society before the 1960s. Today we have a higher education "system" that is more diverse and not as elite as its beginnings. It is still a stratified system; albeit more students of color and low-income students have been able to access higher education. As mentioned earlier, between 1975 and 2015, college-going rates among low-income young people increased. In addition, during the same time, longstanding gaps between students of color and other young Americans narrowed. However, two significant problems undercut this positive trend. First, because Pell Grant spending has not kept pace with the rapid rise in college costs, more low-income students go to two-year colleges or low-cost institutions where they are less likely to graduate. Many of these low-income students are Latinas/os. Moreover, many historically underrepresented minorities who do go to college don't graduate.

Financial Aid Policy Shifts

Since the 1992 Higher Education Act Reauthorization, there has been remarkable growth in student loans. During this decade, we also observed the initiation of state merit-based grant programs led by the Georgia HOPE Scholarship Program and the creation of the federal higher education tax credits. This shift has been pronounced at the federal and state level and has had enormous implications for college access. In addition, public colleges and universities have also enacted financial aid policies that favor merit-based aid over need-based-aid.

Essentially, these substantial policy shifts at the federal, state, and postsecondary levels have undermined the primary purpose of aid policy. Financial aid programs were designed to increase college access by enabling those who could not afford college to attend. These fairly new aid programs, such as merit-based grants, tax credits, and savings incentives, are popular and very attractive to middle- and upper-middle income families; however, they do not serve the financial needs of low-income students and Latinas/os who overwhelmingly rely on need-based aid grants.[65] Here lies an opportunity to advocate for change in federal financial aid policy that is better targeted for low-income students.

For many, loans have become the primary way to pay for their college education because the Pell grant's purchasing power has substantially diminished over time and does not cover the same amount of the expenses it had originally intended. For Latinos, this is particularly problematic, given that 50 percent of Latinos rely on Pell as a critical source of aid.

HEA Today

The HEA is the main vehicle for institutional support through Title III and for student financial assistance through Title IV. Latina/o students are greatly benefited by these two titles in HEA. Anyone interested in advocating for improving access, affordability, and success for Latinos and the institutions they attend should care about HEA and its upcoming reauthorization, which is likely sometime in 2018. What follows is a brief description of the two titles of interest and some funding levels.

HEA Title III: Strengthening Developing Institutions

Title III was established in the 1965 HEA to support institutions that serve low-income and minority students. Today, it supports Historically Black Colleges and Universities (HBCUs), Predominantly Black Institutions (PBIs), Tribal Colleges, and Hispanic-Serving Institutions (HSIs). In 2010, the Student Aid and Fiscal Responsibility Act, otherwise known as SAFRA provided $100 million to HSIs. These funds can be used to increase the number of Latina/o and other low-income students pursuing STEM fields and to develop transfer agreements among two- and four-year schools. From the $100 million to HBCUs and PBIs. Eighty-five percent of these funds are to be used to prepare students for careers in STEM and languages; 15 percent are for competitive grants for STEM, international affairs, teacher education, or improving outcomes for African American males. Fifty-five million dollars are dedicated to MSIs. Five million of these funds are to be used to support institutional capacity to serve Native Americans. However, this authorization expires in 2019.

---

65. Deborah Santiago and Alisa Cunningham. "How Latino Students Pay for College: Patterns of Financial Aid in 2003–04" (2005), *Excelencia in Education and the Institute for Higher Education Policy*, accessed on January 20, 2016. http://www.edexcelencia.org/research/how-latino-students-pay-college-patterns-financial-aid-2003-04

In 2015, the Department of Education called for applications for the First in the World Grant (FITW).[66] These were competitive grants, and, of the $60 million that was allocated and awarded, $16 million was set aside for Minority Serving Institutions (MSIs). For the 2015 award period, seventeen colleges and universities of three hundred applicants were awarded the funds. Of the seventeen awardees representing fourteen states, only two HSIs received awards: California State University, Los Angeles ($2.8 million) and Miami Dade College ($2.8 million). That is, HSIs were awarded $5.7 million or 9.5 percent of the total FITW award and 17.5 percent of the total MSI set aside.[67] In short, HSIs represented only 11.76 percent of the MSIs that received an award and received a small share of the overall award.

HEA Title IV: Student Assistance

However, the heart of the Higher Education Act that provides funding to students through federal financial aid is in Title IV of the HEA. For Pell grants, this translates to a $32 billion investment annually. For student loans, it translates to a $110 billion investment annually. This also includes a $2 billion campus-based student aid formula. Student eligibility for financial aid (expected family contributions, income thresholds) and the authorization/rules on the Free Application for Federal Student Aid (FAFSA) are defined here as well.

With respect to Pell grants, there are key financial provisions of importance. Half of Latina/o students receive Pell and more than 80 percent of Pell dollars go to students with family incomes below $40,000.[68] The maximum grant award is currently $5,775 and will be adjusted for inflation in 2017. The Pell grant has generally enjoyed bipartisan support in Congress, in fact, in 2017, Congress restored "year-round Pell Grant" and the Pell Grant program surplus. It is unfortunate that the surplus was cut, however, Latinas/os should benefit from "Summer Pell" given that they are most likely to benefit from the availability of Pell during the Summer months. We believe this presents an opportunity to shift the conversation from cutting "students' "

---

66. *US Department of Education*, accessed on January 20, 2016. http://www2.ed.gov/programs/fitw/index.html.

67. "Department Awards $60 Million in First in the World Grants to 18 Colleges, Universities and Organizations," *US Department of Education,* accessed on January 20, 2016. http://www.ed.gov/news/press-releases/department-awards-60-million-first-world-grants-17-colleges-universities-and-organizations.

68. Jose Luis Santos & Kati Haycock "Higher education's critical role in increasing opportunity in America: What boards should know and 10 questions they should ask." *Trusteeship.* Washington, DC. Association of Governing Boards, 2016, accessed on September 27, 2017. https://www.agb.org/trusteeship/2016/januaryfebruary/higher-educations-critical-role-in-increasing-opportunity-in.

benefits to considering other ways to reallocate dollars into this important program—one that Latinos heavily depend on for college access and success. Given the country's changing demographics, led by a fast-growing Latino/a population, failing to put enough students into and through college is bad for Latino/as and bad for our country. We should be advocating for the restoration of Pell's buying power and not allowing for its fast diminishing purchasing power trend. The Pell Grant program used to cover more than three-quarters of the average attendance cost at a public, four-year college; today, unfortunately, it covers less than one-third. Even after receiving state and institutional aid, the average low-income student in a four-year college must contribute roughly 70 percent of her family's entire income—a far greater percentage than any other economic group.

DREAMERS currently cannot apply for the FAFSA. However, when the Senate debated Comprehensive Immigration Reform in 2013, some federal student aid benefits, namely loans, were expanded to DREAMERs. Moreover, from the state policy perspective, twenty states (red and blue) passed legislation that allows undocumented DREAMER students to receive in-state tuition rates. Of those, five states have expanded state financial aid to DREAMERs: California, New Mexico, Minnesota, Texas and Washington.

HEA Reauthorization

The reauthorization of HEA presents many opportunities for Latino students. However, we, like many others in the higher education policy space, believe that HEA will not be reauthorized this year. Instead, 2017 has been a year of protecting the very programs aimed at helping and protecting various student groups—from Pell to the rollback of the previous Administration's consumer protections. This is a vastly different policy climate with regard to higher education. In the previous year and during the presidential election, college costs was a hot topic on the campaign trail. And there were different plans ranging from the promise of free college to income-contingent repayment plans—all have significant implications for Latina/o students. What we are seeing now is that states are leading the way in trying to reduce the cost of college by passing legislation for college promise programs whereby providing "free tuition" through last dollar programs.[69]

---

69. In a last-dollar program, the amount of College Promise funding awarded to an eligible student takes into account any public funding or grants the student is eligible for, like a federal Pell Grant or some other state grant before the College Program kicks in. See New York's College Promise Program called The Excelsior Scholarship, for example. These types of programs have been known to be beneficial to wealthier students since wealthier students do not qualify for Pell and other need-based aid programs.

At present, the higher education policy discourse in Washington centers around institutional accountability that will undoubtedly affect Latina/o students and HSIs. The discourse is driven by the Senate HELP Committee's white papers on accreditation, consumer information, and risk-sharing.[70] We believe that the most detrimental of the three white papers for Latina/o students could be the HELP Committee's framing of its discussions around risk-sharing as it debates the way forward in a possible 2018 reauthorization scenario. So, what is risk-sharing and why should we care about it for Latina/o students and the institutions that enroll large numbers of them?

Risk-sharing/Skin-in-the-game

In March 2015, the Senate Committee on Health, Education, Labor, and Pensions (HELP), through Chairman Lamar Alexander, put forward a white paper on risk-sharing /skin-in-the-game concepts and proposals. This white paper was designed to engage folks and seek comments on the "skin in the game" concepts as a way forward for thinking about institutional accountability. The goal is to "realign and improve federal incentives so that colleges and universities have a stronger vested interest and more responsibility in reducing excessive student borrowing and prioritizing higher levels of student success and completion" (1). Further, the strategy entails "Design[ing] market-based accountability policies that require *all* colleges and universities to share in the risk of lending to student borrowers."[71] Essentially, the HELP committee believes that if colleges and universities have to share in the risk of student lending, they will not only reduce "excessive student borrowing" but have better outcomes. Many assumptions are embedded in the goal and the strategy; however, if this view of institutional accountability and the effect on the students they enroll is in the future, we should take great interest in this policy frame and the potentially adverse impact it could have on Latinas/os and the institutions that enroll large numbers of Latinas/os. We should be concerned about safeguarding the likely "risk-mitigating" behaviors that colleges and universities might engage in and the penalties associated with failing to address excessive student borrowing. HSIs are likely to face serious challenges under this framework, and institutions may be placed in the position to enroll less "financially risky" students. The white paper drew consider-

---

70. "Alexander Seeks Input from Higher Ed Community on Accreditation, Risk Sharing, and Consumer Information," *US Senate Committee on Health, Education, Labor & Pensions*, accessed on January 20, 2016. https://www.help.senate.gov/chair/newsroom/press/alexander-seeks-input-from-higher-ed-community-on-accreditation-risk-sharing-and-consumer-information.

71. See https://www.help.senate.gov/imo/media/Risk_Sharing.pdf.

able attention, and numerous advocacy organizations, think tanks, college membership associations, and others submitted comments. The comments have not been made public by Chairman Lamar Alexander, but in scanning some of the letters to the Chairman that were posted publicly by various advocacy organizations like the American Council on Education, National Association of Student Financial Aid Administrators, The Institute for College Access and Success, and a joint statement by the American Association of Community Colleges and the Association of Community College Trustees, were overwhelmingly negative, expressing many concerns about students and institutions.[72] One such organization, the Education Trust, made four recommendations that were made to strengthen what had been put forward so far:[73]

1. Increase institutional attention to protecting students' debt investment not just through risk- sharing, but also by focusing on steering their students toward credentials that have labor market value.

2. Make certain that any risk-sharing proposals recognize institutional differences and do not create perverse incentives: the federal government's historical role has been to help low-income students afford college, and that role needs to be expanded to include student success, not curbed.

3. Limit the financial burden that students face by strengthening financial aid to cover the cost of attendance.

4. In choosing accountability metrics, develop and use the institutional repayment rate in place of the cohort default rate. (Loan repayment data is now more readily available through the Department of Education's release of the College Scorecard.)

This framework, moving into the HEA reauthorization conversations, exposes the need for advocacy on behalf of Latinos in the higher education

---

72. "Statements on Risk Sharing," accessed on September 28, 2017.

http://www.acenet.edu/news-room/Documents/Comments-Alexander-Risk-Sharing.pdf;

https://www.nasfaa.org/uploads/documents/comments_senate_consumer_info.pdf;

https://ticas.org/sites/default/files/pub_files/ticas_risk_sharing_response_sdri_one_pager_and_cover_letter_0.pdf;

https://www.acct.org/files/Advocacy/Letters to Congress/Risk Sharing AACCACCT CommentsFinal.pdf .

73. Statement from Education Trust authored by José Luis Santos on April 24, 2016 to Chairman Lamar Alexander of the US Senate Committee on Health, Education, Labor & Pensions. These comments were in response to the Chairman's request for public comments, see https://www.help.senate.gov/chair/newsroom/press/alexander-seeks-input-from-higher-ed-community-on-accreditation-risk-sharing-and-consumer-information. Each organization could make their comments public but the Education Trust chose not to do so. A copy of this Statement with these recommendations is in the possession of José Luis Santos.

policy space, not only on behalf of Latina/o students but the institutions that enroll sizeable numbers of them.

As for accreditation as a vehicle for greater institutional accountability, although there are potential benefits in holding institutions accountable regarding Latina/o outcomes, implementation is complex and, because of the "triad" of actors (federal, state, and accreditors) in educational quality assurance, may not be the quickest path to improving outcomes. Also, these roles are not always clear. Federal agencies should assure that taxpayer funds are used only for acceptable educational activities. Considerable variability exists in the responsibilities different states assume, resulting in uneven coverage of those areas of responsibility specifically allocated to states. As for the accreditors, they play an essential role in determining eligibility for Title IV funding. They should assure that all accredited institutions meet reasonable standards of educational performance and that unacceptably weak institutions are ineligible for student aid. This has been a big problem in recent years, especially in the case of proprietary for-profits (e.g., Corinthian Colleges).

Instead of continuing to fight the War on Poverty from the LBJ era, Congress, unfortunately has shifted its attention to middle- and upper-middle-class voters with tax-based "student aid" giveaways, which quadrupled in size since their inception in the '90s.[74] We believe this approach has been poorly targeted and ineffective in closing attendance and achievement gaps. We view this inefficient use of dollars as a policy opportunity to advocate on behalf of Latinas/os by demanding that Congress recalibrate this share of the pie. In addition, besides refocusing the Pell program, we believe Congress and advocates who care about low-income students and students of color should demand more from colleges in return for the $180 billion the federal government doles out each year. Colleges should be held accountable for access, completion, and success. This must be demanded by advocacy and community groups. We must and should demand more from not only non-MSIs but HSIs alike as these types of institutions mature into their roles.

IMPLICATIONS FOR
LATINO FEDERAL POLICY ADVOCACY TODAY

Clearly, much federal policy that has improved access and success for Latina/o college students has been focused on serving students from low-income backgrounds, except specifically for Title V of the Higher Education Act that gave rise to the development of Hispanic-Serving Institutions. The

---

74. José Luis Santos, "Pell Grants Haven't Kept Pace with College Costs," *Education Week*, accessed on November 6, 2014. http://blogs.edweek.org/edweek/op_education/2014/11/Santos_Restore_Pell_Grants.html.

challenge to Hispanic-Serving Institutions is clearly that it targets improving institutional efforts that have a Latina/o student population of 25 percent and above, which does serve 60 percent of all Latina/o students at public college and universities in the United States.[75] However, there remains a push for specific federal policy efforts that target all Latina/o college students, whether they attend a HSI or not. That said, while there are Latina/o advocacy organizations based in Washington, only one advocacy organization applies policy research to enhance policy advocacy efforts that connect to serving Latina/o college students: *Excelencia* in Education, which targets policy advocacy for Hispanic-Serving Institutions. While organizations such as the Hispanic Association of Colleges and Universities (HACU) and the National Council for La Raza (NCLR) provide a degree of advocacy and support for the Latino community, the authors assert that when it comes to research and policy advocacy targeting Latina/o college students, *Excelencia* has uniquely positioned itself to provide such means, although it targets policy only for Hispanic-Serving Institutions. What is evident is the demand for a coalition of policy advocates that specifically targets policy to improve Latina/o college students' access and success, especially if such policy efforts are based on language that serve all students from low-income backgrounds, given the history of the numerous federal policies as a result of Johnson's 'War on Poverty' and the Civil Rights movements of the 1960s.

From the history and current understanding of Latina/o college students and federal policy, we encourage organizations to coalesce around the common desire to push for policies that are in the best interest of Latinas/os and to form advocacy coalitions in the same manner that precollege experiences were informed from the coalition efforts of the Civil Rights movements that gave rise to the numerous Civil Rights Acts of the 1960s. Furthermore, we neither argue nor recommend that such continued policy should be independent from possible advocacy communities and coalitions, because even though the development of Hispanic-Serving Institutions created tensions between Black college student advocacy, the advocacy was in constant respect for the advocacy gains that had been made for Black college students and argued for new moneys instead of a division of the pot.

REFERENCES

Access to College and Program Simplification: Hearings before the Subcommittee on Postsecondary Education of the Committee on Education and Labor, House of Representatives, 102nd Cong. 1991.

---

75. "*Excelencia* in Education," accessed on January 20, 2016. http://www.edexcelencia.org /hsi-cp2/research/hispanic-serving-institutions-2013-14.

Hearings on the Reauthorization of the Higher Education Act and Related Measures: Hearing before the Subcommittee on Education, Arts, and Humanities of the Committee on Labor and Human Resources, U.S. Senate, 96th Cong. 1979.

Hearings on the Reauthorization of the Higher Education Act: Hearings before the Subcommittee on Postsecondary Education of the Committee on Education and Labor, House of Representatives, 98th Cong. 1984.

Higher Education Act Amendments: Hearings before the Subcommittee on Education, Arts, and Humanities of the Committee on Labor and Human Resources, 94th Cong. 1976.

Higher Education Act Amendments of 1976: Hearings before the Subcommittee on Postsecondary Education of the Committee on Education and Labor, House of Representatives, Cong. 1975.

Higher Education Amendments of 1984, H.R. 5240, 98th Cong. (1984).

Higher Education Amendments of 1986, Pub. L. 99-498 (1986).

Higher Education Amendments of 1992, Pub. L. 102-325 (1992).

Hispanic Access to Higher Education: Hearing before the Subcommittee on Postsecondary Education of the Committee on Education and Labor, House of Representatives, 97th Cong. 1 (1982).

Hispanic Association of Colleges and Universities. "About HACU/HACU 101." Accessed January 16, 2016. http://www.hacu.net/hacu/HACU_101.asp.

Rendon, Laura I. "Introduction." In Hispanic-Serving Institutions in American Higher Education: A Guide to Overcoming Obstacles to Student Learning, edited by Jesse Perez Mendez, Fred Bonner II, Josephine Méndez-Negrete, and Robert T. Palmer, 1–4. Virginia: Stylus Publishing, 2015.

Santos, José L., & Haycock, Kati. "Higher Education's Critical Role in Increasing Opportunity in America: What Boards Should Know and 10 Questions They Should Ask." Trusteeship. Washington, DC. Association of Governing Boards, 2016.

Valdez, Patrick L. "An Overview of Hispanic-Serving Institutions' Legislation: Legislation Policy Formation between 1979–1992" In Hispanic-Serving Institutions in American Higher Education: Their Origin, and Present and Future Challenges, edited by Jesse Perez Mendez, Fred Bonner II, Josephine Méndez-Negrete, and Robert T. Palmer, 5–29. Virginia: Stylus Publishing, 2015.

Valdez, Patrick L. "Anatomy of the Hispanic-Serving Institution (HSI) Designation: An Overview of HSI Policy Formation." Hispanic-Serving Institutions in the 21st Century: A Convening, El Paso, Texas. 2015.

An Engaged Approach to Public Scholarship

SHAPING THE POLICY AGENDA THROUGH RESEARCH EVIDENCE

David R. García

Aaron Wildavsky's classic book, *Speaking Truth to Power*, is inspirationally titled and is the rallying cry of academics searching for a higher purpose for their scholarship. Yet if one reviews the state of affairs on research utilization in education policy, it becomes clear that the academics may be "speaking truth to power" but few appear to be listening.

Why? Because Wildavsky's "evaluation man" holds a privileged position in the policy process and one to which few academics have access. He is at the table; close enough so that when he talks there is a chance that someone in power will listen. Wildavsky's counsel is about how to make the most of the opportunity to "speak truth to power"—once you get in the door.[1]

Academics and academic research, however, stand on the outside of the policy process. Yet being on the outside is not the same as being on the margins. Outside the policymaking process is a highly productive space in which to shape the policy agenda. Academics can be extremely influential from the outside, if they shift their perspective and learn how to function from that position.

This article is devoted to an engaged approach to public scholarship to shape a research-based Latino education policy agenda. I seek to help those interested in taking the ideas articulated elsewhere in the book and translating them into actionable policies that improve educational conditions for Latino students. An engaged approach to public scholarship reconsiders the traditional boundaries between academics and politicians while leveraging the strengths of academics to shape policy through research evidence.

---

1. Aaron Wildavsky, *Speaking Truth to Power: The Art and Craft of Policy Analysis* (Toronto: Brown and Company, 1979).

I begin by describing my chosen approach to the policy process that serves as the backdrop of the article. Next, I distinguish two key types of institutional policy actors: 1) elected officials and appointees, and 2) professional staff, because the former are those who set the policy agenda. Last, I detail four concrete strategies for influencing policy through research.

POLICYMAKING IS AN INTERACTIVE PROCESS

The problem-solving model is most commonly used to understand how research is used in the policymaking process. Weiss observes, in describing the problem-solving model, "The expectation is that research provides empirical evidence and conclusions that help to solve a policy problem. . . . A problem exists and a decision has to be made; information or understanding is lacking either to generate a solution to the problem or to select among alternative solutions; research provides the missing knowledge. With the gap filled, a decision is reached."[2]

The problem-solving model implies a rational and orderly relationship between policy questions or problems, research and answers. Research use can be direct, as when a particular study or series of studies are used to make a policy decision (what Henig refers to as killer studies), or the influence can be more indirect, as when research leads to conceptual changes in how policies are framed.[3]

This rational view of policymaking is favored by academics because it shares many characteristics with the research process, such as logic, structure, and thoroughness.[4] The problem-solving model legitimizes the role of research because research is placed at the center of the policymaking process and decisions are made after an evaluation of research evidence. This approach is convenient and advantageous for academics. Policy makers are expected to approach academics for answers and academics are largely left independent, so that they can focus on research. They are not

---

2. Carol H. Weiss, "The Many Meanings of Research Utilization," *Public Administration Review* 39, no. 5 (1979): 427.

3. Jeffrey R. Henig, "Politicization of Evidence: Lessons for an Informed Democracy," *Educational Policy* 23, no. 1 (2009): 137–60; Huw T. O. Davies and Sandra M. Nutley, *Learning More about How Research-Based Knowledge Gets Used: Guidance in the Development of New Empirical Research* (New York, NY: William T. Grant Foundation, 2008), 31.

4. Erik Albaek, "Between Knowledge and Power: Utilization of Social Science in Policy Making," *Policy Sciences* 28, no. 1 (1995): 79–100.

forced to compromise their values or venture into foreign waters by getting sullied in the political process.[5]

For the purpose of engaging in the policymaking process, I subscribe to Weiss's interactive model: "Another way that social science research can enter the decision arena is as part of an interactive search for knowledge. Those engaged in developing policy seek information not only from social scientists but also from a variety of sources including administrators, practitioners, politicians, planners, journalists, clients, interest groups, aides, friends, and social scientists, too. The process is not one of linear order from research to decision but a disorderly set of interconnections and back-and-forthness that defies neat diagrams."[6]

The interactive model is illustrative because it recognizes several important characteristics of the policymaking process:

1. Social scientists are one of many voices in the policymaking process. And their voice is not privileged. There are many others, most of whom, although they may not possess the same level of technical expertise as the researcher, are valued equally in the policy process.

2. If a diverse group of participants is influential in the policymaking process and many of them do not possess experience or knowledge about education policy or research, then many ways of knowing, in addition to research evidence, contribute to the policymaking process. The interactive model recognizes and validates these multiple ways of knowing and their influence in the policymaking process. For example, personal experiences are an influential way of knowing. When academics engage in the policy process, they are often perplexed when a policy maker's singular personal experience outweighs the preponderance of research evidence. But academics should leverage personal experience because it is a more concrete way of knowing than abstract research evidence.

3. Policy formation is a debate toward reaching the best possible action given the present circumstances. Albeak states, "To understand the linkage between research and the politico-administrative decision-making process, it is necessary to be aware that research is transferred to, and becomes part of, a discourse of action in a philosophical as well as a more everyday practical sense. In this discourse, self-reflecting

5. Jeffrey R. Henig, "The Evolving Relationship between Researchers and Public Policy," in *When Research Matters: How Scholarship Influences Education Policy*, ed. Frederick Hess (Cambridge, MA: Harvard Education Press, 2008), 41–62.

6. Weiss, "The Many Meanings of Research Utilization," 428.

participants deliberate on and debate norms and alternatives with a view to concrete action."[7] It is important for academics to understand that concrete action is the best possible plan, not necessarily the "scientifically best" plan, meaning that "good enough" may be the best possible result.

4. The policymaking process is bounded by the individual participants involved with a specific issue at a given time. The many theories of the policy process are useful as general descriptors, but it is difficult to generalize from these models to learn how to engage in a particular policy setting. Why? The policy process is local and personal. Policy outcomes are dependent upon the actors and circumstances at the time. Thus, personal contact is the most important source of information about research and is an underutilized approach to influencing policy.[8]

DISTINGUISHING PROFESSIONAL STAFF FROM POLITICIANS

To distinguish elected officials and appointees from professional staff, I draw on Kingdon's lasting and extremely useful perspective. He distinguishes elected and appointed officials from professional staff because the former group is the one that sets the policy agenda. Elected and appointed officials are politicians who determine "the list of subjects or problems to which governmental officials, and people outside of government closely associated with those officials, are paying some attention at any given time."[9]

At the district level, elected officials include school board members who come from the ranks of professionals and local community members. At the state level, elected officials include state senators and representatives and may include the state school superintendent in those states where the position is an elected office. At the federal level, elected representatives include United States senators and congressmen.

Political appointees come from organizations such as chambers of commerce, foundations, and civic or community groups. In the business case, politicians consult business representatives because they are regarded as key

---

7. Albaek, "Between Knowledge and Power," 94.

8. Sandra M. Nutley, Isabel Walter, and Huw T. O. Davies, *Using Evidence: How Research Can Inform Public Services* (Bristol, UK: The Policy Press, 2007); John A. Hird, "The Study and Use of Policy Research in State Legislatures," *International Regional Science Review* 32, no. 4 (2009): 523–35.

9. John Kingdon, *Agendas, Alternatives and Public Policies,* 2nd ed. (New York, NY: Addison-Wesley Educational Publishers, 2003), 3.

stakeholders in public education.[10] In other cases, foundation representatives are appointed because they are either involved with or fund a key program of interest to politicians. Finally, civic and community organizations are incorporated into policy positions because of their involvement in social service agencies that support the communities in which schools reside.

In education, political appointees have long played an especially important role in shaping the policy agenda. They are primarily laypersons who come from outside the public school system and are placed, sometimes even thrust, into policymaking positions where they become responsible for crafting education policies that affect the professional lives of educators and student educational experiences.

Conversely, Kingdon describes professional staff as a "hidden cluster of specialists in the bureaucracy and in professional communities" that influence the selection of policy alternatives put forth to carry out the policy agenda.[11] This large and influential group includes state administrators, agency officials or heads, and legislative/administrative staff.

My rationale for separating elected officials and appointees from professional staff for the purpose of advancing a research-based policy agenda is based on two important considerations; 1) professional staff cannot get ahead of elected officials and appointees; and 2) academics often share an academic or knowledge base with professional staff.

Professional staff cannot make decisions that deviate considerably from the publicly stated position of elected/appointed officials. Professional staff serve at the discretion of elected officials or at a minimum work in agencies that are charged with carrying out policies set forth by elected and appointed bodies. They are always constrained by the public positions held by elected and appointed officials. As Kingdon notes, "It is important to remember, however, that staffers do all of these things within limits that are set by the senators and representatives who hire and can fire them. Even respondents with the highest estimates of staff importance frequently refer to the staff's need to 'sell their boss' on an idea."[12] At best, professional staff can take advantage of whatever latitude is available to them to influence the selection of policy alternatives after the policy agenda has been set.

Ostensibly, professional staff are hired because of their academic and professional knowledge in education or education policy. Commonly, professional staff have attended universities or graduate schools and hold degrees in

10. Lorraine M. McDonnell, "Can Education Research Speak to State Policy?" *Theory into Practice* 27, no. 2 (1988): 91–97.

11. Kingdon, *Agendas, Alternatives and Public Policies*, 19.

12. Ibid., 41.

education policy or public policy. Academics and professional staff are likely
to share a common knowledge base; they may have read many of the same
articles and attended many of the same conferences. In fact, many university academics in such positions may be acquainted with professional staff
as current or former students.[13]

Professional staff can be regarded as informed professionals, even experts
in their field. When approaching professional staff, academics do not have to
convince professional staff about the importance of social science research.
Academics can start from a common knowledge base to discuss policy matters with little to no need to start from the beginning or simplify concepts.
Additionally, professional staff are likely to share many of the same social
ideals as academics, such as equity and social justice. "An important characteristic of the more frequent users of social science research is a quality
of the mind or what might be called a 'social perspective,' which, put simply, involves a sensitivity to contemporary social events and a desire for
social reform. They act as if what is happening in the larger society was
from what was happening within themselves."[14]

These similarities make professional staff a receptive audience for
academics to approach with their research. But for the purposes of influencing the policy agenda, it is important to understand that the ability
of professional staff to influence the policymaking process remains constrained—they must still work through politicians.

WHO ARE POLITICIANS?

Elected officials and appointees set the policy agenda. But they differ from
professional staff in one important respect—they are not experts. In fact,
they are novices, by design. Most politicians do not have content expertise
in education. This is not to say that they are uneducated, but simply that
their academic knowledge or professional experience is more than likely
not in education and almost certainly not in education policy. Academics
looking to influence policy through research evidence should not approach
politicians the same way as they approach professional staff. Rather, academics must use the novice status of elected officials and appointees as the
starting point for communicating with politicians most effectively.

13. Stephen R. Nelson, James C. Leffler, and Barbara A. Hansen, *Toward a Research Agenda
for Understanding and Improving the Use of Research Evidence* (Portland, OR: Norwest Regional Educational Laboratory, 2009).

14. Nathan Caplan, "Factors Associated with Knowledge Use among Federal Executives."
Policy Studies Journal 4, no. 3 (1976): 230.

This preceding point may read as intuitive. It may even sound like good old-fashioned commonsense. But in the academic literature, it is an overlooked detail that has escaped how we understand research utilization in the policymaking process. In fact, most of the research utilization literature has been conducted with the professional staff who implement the policy agenda, not the politicians who set it. For example, the foundational work in the field of knowledge utilization along with more recent investments in this field has been conducted on samples that include professional staff such as agency officials rather than those who occupy positions that require communication with the general public. [15]

Politicians are most likely trained in political science or business and hold finishing degrees from law or business schools. Some may never have attended college at all. Hird surveyed a nationally representative sample of legislators and found that 48 percent of respondents identified themselves as "legislators," another 21 percent in professional services to include medicine and law and only 8 percent identified their profession as education. Almost a quarter of the politicians surveyed were not college graduates.[16]

Once elected, legislators have many committee appointments and are often asked to make decisions outside their expertise. It is unrealistic to anticipate that legislators will be content experts in all committees on which they serve or in all public policy areas in which they make decisions. With regard to education policy, politicians can be considered as novices seeking knowledge to make decisions in policy areas outside their professional background.

What does expertise among elected and appointed officials look like? Kingdon's work focused on Congress, but the lessons are applicable to other legislative bodies, such as state legislatures. He found that:

> With some notable exceptions, Congress is not the place to find the detailed, technical types of expertise found in the bureaucracy, in the community of academics and consultants, or among the interest groups that are occupied with the detailed impacts of programs and new proposals on the operations of their members. Certainly among senators and representatives themselves, again with some exceptions, 'expertise' in the congressional context is

---

15. Carol H. Weiss and Michael J. Bucuvalas, "The Challenges of Social Science Research to Decision Making," in *Using Social Research in Public Policy Making*, eds. Carol H. Weiss and Bucuvalas Michael J. (Lexington, MA: Lexington Books, 1977), 213–34; Nelson, Leffler, and Hansen, *Toward a Research Agenda*, 62.

16. John A. Hird, *Power, Knowledge, and Politics: Policy Analysis in the States* (Washington, DC: Georgetown University Press, 2005b), 240.

really a system in which generalists learn enough about a given
subject matter to help other generalists, their colleagues.[17]

The fact that politicians are novices leads to two important implications for understanding how to engage with them in the policy process: 1)
politicians will apply their personal experiences to make sense of education issues and 2) politicians seek places to gain expertise.

A common criticism of politicians is that they are close-minded and
resistant to new perspectives.[18] This is a particularly sensitive complaint
among academics because they often find themselves as the ones bringing new evidence or a dissenting voice to the policymaking process. Yet,
because politicians are usually novices, their resistance is better understood as the tension created when attempting to make sense of new ideas
by comparing them against their existing perspectives and experiences.
Here, the manner in which politicians approach and consider research
in policymaking is similar to the way in which the general public uses
research evidence. Like the general public, most politicians do not read
academic journals and are not aware of academic research or methods.
But they are intensely interested in education and hold strong opinions
about education policies. Howell, in a study on how the general public
approaches research evidence, argues that the general public does not have
sufficient expertise in methodology to assess the quality of research studies. Therefore, they often rely on the organization that produced the report
or the media outlet that reported it to determine its credibility. The general
public is more likely to endorse findings from organizations that align with
their political orientation and findings that confirm their worldview.[19]

The novice status of politicians means that they seek out people and
organizations to gain expertise. In fact, legislative bodies employ professional staff within their organizations to serve this important informational
role.[20] Outside the policy process, however, a crowded field of people and
organizations aspires to serve in an informational role for politicians. This
large group includes lobbyists, think tanks, policy centers, and advocacy
organizations. In education policy, the newest players include foundations

17. Kingdon, *Agendas, Alternatives and Public Policies*, 37.

18. Martyn Hammersley, "The Myth of Research-Based Practice: The Critical Case of Educational Inquiry," *International Journal of Social Science Research Methodology* 8, no. 4 (2005): 317–30.

19. William G. Howell, "Education Policy, Academic Research and Public Opinion," in
When Research Matters: How Scholarship Influences Education Policy, ed. Frederick Hess
(Cambridge, MA: Harvard Education Press, 2008), 135–44.

20. John A. Hird, "Policy Analysis for What? The Effectiveness of Nonpartisan Policy
Research Organizations," *Policy Studies Journal* 33, no. 1 (2005a): 83–105.

and networks.[21] Academics are among this group. They stand outside the process and they possess information, in this case research evidence, for which they are seeking an audience with politicians to influence policy outcomes. Like the many other people and organizations in this space, academics need a strategy to gain access to politicians.

Lastly, academics must understand the communication needs of elected officials and appointees, who communicate in ways different from the ways academics do. Elected officials and appointees need general information to communicate a more general message to a more general audience. Elected officials communicate their message through a platform in which education is one of many important public policy issues. Platforms are short, general, and designed to be understood quickly by a broad range of people. Platforms are marked by poll-tested and emotion-ridden buzzwords intended to connect with their audience. In determining the platform, candidates select a few broad-based issues that resonate with the general public. In setting the policy agenda, elected and appointed officials play a highly public role as they communicate to diverse groups and the media to "soften the ground" by raising the public's awareness to a set of potential policy problems. For this purpose, brevity and clarity of communication are paramount.

After the policy agenda has been set, elected officials and appointees turn to professional staff to provide more detail and to generate specific policy alternatives. The process of generating alternatives requires expertise and much attention to detail. It is at this secondary stage that the skill set of most academics is best suited. Academics have the expertise to recommend and weigh the outcomes of competing policy alternatives with sufficient attention to the detail to take into consideration the consequences of implementation. Many academics who work at the policy implementation stage regard themselves as engaging in the policymaking process, and certainly there are several instrumental contributions that occur at this stage.

At this point, I am compelled to note that we have come full circle. Academics engaged at the policy implementation stage of the process are working alongside professional staff to carry out the policy agenda. They are not working with politicians to set the policy agenda.

The focus of this article, however, is to get ahead of the process and work directly with politicians to set the policy agenda. In the next section,

---

21. Janelle Scott, Christopher L. Lubienski, Elizabeth DeBray, and Huriya Jabbar, "The Intermediary Function in Evidence Production, Promotion, and Utilization: The Case of Educational Incentives," in *Using Research Evidence in Education: From the Schoolhouse Door to Capitol Hill*, eds. Kara S. Finnigan and Alan J. Daly (New York, NY: Springer, 2014), 69–89.

I bring the aforementioned perspectives to bear on a set of concrete ideas that academics can employ to advance a research-based Latino agenda to politicians.

AN ENGAGED APPROACH
TO PUBLIC SCHOLARSHIP

Politicians are novices with respect to education policy. They turn to others they trust for knowledge to help them make sense of complex issues. To become a trusted advisor and shape the policy agenda, an academic must establish relationships with future politicians before they become politicians. When communicating with politicians, academics should provide frameworks that politicians can use in many situations and that can be incorporated into public communications. Lastly, research evidence must be translated to politicians' specific context.

Educate as Novices

If politicians are novices and academics are experts, then it is important to understand how novices think in order to gain insight how to best approach politicians. To explicate the transition from novice to expert, I turned to Patricia Benner, who identified an incremental, five-step transformation model to describe how novices become experts. At the beginning of the process, novices build their knowledge by relying on general rules and concepts. In comparison, experts possess an intuitive grasp of concepts to solve problems.[22] The following is a select list of the key characteristics at each stage of the process from novice to expert:

NOVICE
- "The heart of the difficulty that the novice faces is the inability to use discretionary judgment."[23]
- Relies on general rules and concepts

ADVANCED BEGINNER
- Begins to use guidelines to guide actions
- Unable to distinguish those concepts that are most meaningful, so all concepts are treated as if they are important.

---

22. Patricia Benner, "From Novice to Expert," *The American Journal of Nursing* 82, no. 3 (1982), 402–07.

23. Ibid., 403.

- "Need[s] help in setting priorities since they operate on general guidelines and are only beginning to perceive recurrent meaningful patterns."[24]

COMPETENT

- More aware of long-term plans or goals "based on considerable conscious, abstract, analytic contemplation of the problem."[25]

PROFICIENT

- Perceives and understands situations as whole parts based on a holistic view and performance is guided by maxims
- Possesses the experience to recognize whole situations, and can recognize when "the expected normal picture does not present itself that is, when the normal is absent."[26]

EXPERT

- No longer reliant on analytical principles (rules, guidelines, maxims) to connect situations and determine actions
- Has "an intuitive grasp of the situation and can zero in on the problem."[27]

Daley provided more insight into the learning process to find that novices described their learning as a process of concept formation and assimilation. Novices assimilated information by connecting it to past experiences and made decisions based on the "best-fit," even if they knew the fit was not the most appropriate or correct. They begin to learn as they "acquire information and link that information in unique ways."[28] They look for validation from experts to affirm their decisions.

Experts on the other hand, reported acting based on "blueprints" held in their minds. They described an active learning process based on merging concepts with real-world needs and improvising to pick up new concepts. Experts regarded formal learning opportunities, such as academic research, as background material. "Experts also used their experiences in a different way, learning by assimilating new information with their past experiences or by differentiating their experiences from the new information."[29]

---

24. Ibid., 404.

25. Ibid., 404.

26. Ibid., 405.

27. Ibid., 405.

28. Barbara J. Daley, "Novice to Expert: An Exploration of how Professionals Learn," *Adult Education Quarterly* 49, no. 4 (1999): 139.

29. Ibid., 140.

For academics looking to engage in policy, the path from novice to expert provides some concrete lessons. First, the novice stage is the best opportunity to introduce guidelines and general concepts to shape ways of thinking. This means a return to basics; not dumbing down, but foundational knowledge that can be incorporated into public communication. The key is to put forth general concepts to simplify complex phenomena. For this reason, when academics respond to politicians, they should provide frameworks rather than direct answers or strict advocacy positions. Second, the novice will rely upon past experiences to help make sense of education issues. Therefore, academics should not discount politicians' past experiences. Rather, they should build upon them to introduce new perspectives. Those seeking to advance a Latino education agenda should expose politicians to the educational conditions facing Latino students firsthand. Reading about these conditions, with no experiential knowledge, is not concrete enough to persuade politicians though experience. Third, the novice will seek outside experts, particularly those whom they can trust as advisors. Certainly, the "trusted advisor" is a coveted position. but one has to start early to achieve this status.

GET TO POLITICIANS
BEFORE THEY BECOME POLITICIANS

Despite the crowded and ever-changing field of informants positioning themselves to influence the policy process, a consistent finding in the academic literature is that a few outsiders come to occupy a privileged space as a "trusted advisor" or "insider" source for politicians because these informants possess the expertise and ability screen the available research for those products most relevant to the policy issue at hand.

The trusted advisor is a coveted and logical role for academics. But how does one become a trusted advisor? These relationships are built over time as the politician comes to rely upon and gain confidence in the informant. It may sound counterintuitive, but the best strategy to develop trust is not to approach politicians at all. It's too late at that point. Rather, the more productive, long-term strategy is to build relationships with politicians before they become politicians. There is scant academic literature on engaging future politicians, but there is recognition that getting on the front end of policy formation is an important goal.[30] The engaged approach to public scholarship

---

30. Karen Seashore Louis, "Knowledge Producers and Policymakers: Kissing Kin or Squabbling Siblings?" in *International Handbook of Educational Policy*, ed. Nina Bascia, Alister Cumming, Amanda Datnow, Kenneth Leithwood, and David Livingstone (New York, NY: Springer, 2005), 219–38.

is intended to develop policy influence by leveraging academics' professional strengths as content experts along with their position as outsiders.

There are a number of logical reasons for building relationships with politicians before they are elected or appointed. Once elected or appointed, the politician will be deluged with people seeking influence. At that point, the academic must compete with the many others seeking access. In addition, politicians have already communicated their policy agenda through their campaign platform. Once elected, they begin to implement a policy agenda that has already been established.

Building a relationship with politicians before they become politicians has several strategic advantages. Namely, academics can separate themselves from the crowded field of people seeking access to elected and appointed officials. There are far fewer people seeking access to potential politicians. Also, this preliminary stage when potential politicians are developing the contours of their policy agenda is the opportune time to influence their perspectives on key issues. This early stage is the precise point to introduce the policy ideas articulated in this book to influence politicians. Lastly, this engaged approach is consistent with the literature on research utilization that indicates the importance of engaging with politicians on a personal level.[31]

Where do you find future politicians? Community organizations are productive places to meet future politicians. These organizations include local chambers of commerce, service organizations, and leadership groups. The list of organizations in your local area is available online. The members of these very groups, or their associates, are likely to be appointed to a board or commission, serve on a district school board, or run for public office themselves.

Community organizations often hold an education day or event to inform their participants on the major issues facing their local schools. The action is straightforward—volunteer. Academics are a logical fit as experts on education issues. The academic's goal is to present him- or herself as a knowledgeable resource and to treat the presentation as a networking opportunity. You should be certain to invite participants to contact you directly for more information. And you should follow up with every participant. On many occasions, I have employed this strategy to build opportunities to meet with people as they were considering a run for office or prior to an appointment. These early contacts became the foundation of professional relationships that lasted during the person's tenure as elected or appointed officials.

The reader should remember that this is a long-term strategy. It may take years before an active community member is either elected or appointed to a policymaking position. The repeated exposure and communication with people

---

31. Nutley, Walter, and Davies, *Using Evidence*.

outside your academic field, however, is a productive activity for researchers seeking the skill set to bridge the two communities of research and policy.[32]

PROVIDE POLITICIANS WITH FRAMEWORKS

It is a positive sign of engagement when politicians who are developing policies ask questions of researchers. When responding to politicians or potential politicians, academics have three general responses; answers, advocacy, and frameworks. I will review each response and recommend that academics respond with frameworks whenever possible.

If academics respond to questions with a direct answer, they miss an opportunity to shape the inquiry. Often, when politicians ask a question, the premise of the inquiry has already been established. A direct answer does not alter the premise, and an answer is of limited use to politicians to understand and make decisions on similar issues in the future. For example, politicians may ask academics for the best practices for second language learners to acquire English proficiency. A direct answer could include an inventory of programs or state policies that have resulted in students performing well on standardized tests of English proficiency. The premise of the inquiry, however, is that English proficiency is an isolated pedagogical goal for language learners. A direct answer would miss an opportunity to frame academic achievement to include other subjects, such as mathematics and science, along with English proficiency. In addition, a direct answer may not allow the politician to be introduced to different perspectives on language acquisition that promotes proficiency in more than one language.

Many academics engage in the policy process by advocating a particular cause or policy. Advocates are direct and predictable but may have limited utility as a source of knowledge over time. The advocate's predictable approach makes it easy to know where she or he stands, or would stand, on a given issue. Over time, politicians take advantage of advocates' reactions to specific policies and come to anticipate the type of knowledge they bring to the policy process. If advocates provide no new information or differing opinions, then politicians may use advocates for predictable responses, such as supporting a specific policy or for ammunition against it. Advocates may become limited sources of new knowledge if politicians stop relying on them for new information outside their policies of interest.

Frameworks are the most useful when responding to politicians. Frameworks are analogous to the theories and models that academics use to explain complex phenomena. Frameworks are applicable to understanding

---

32. Nathan Caplan, "The Two-Communities Theory and Knowledge Utilization," *American Behavioral Scientist* 22, no. 3 (1979): 459–70.

more than just a single issue at a specific point in time. They are applicable to understanding many similar issues across space and time.

The field of economics provides the most influential example of how academic frameworks can influence education policy. Brandl, writing as an economist and state legislator, concludes that forecasts and predictions are not the economists' most influential contributions to the policy process. Rather, he observes, "Of somewhat more value to the legislator are a number of simple techniques, aids to reasoning, which can be invoked by politicians and by their advisors."[33] These frameworks are valued because they "transform what was bewildering into a solvable problem."[34]

Frameworks are the type of general principles that help novices become experts. Frameworks simplify complex phenomenon. They are the foundation of the blueprints that novices use to discern patterns and identify problems. They are particularly useful for making sense of seemingly divergent information and scenarios to make decisions. Lastly, they are also helpful for public communication because they synthesize the state of affairs in a comprehensible fashion.

TRANSLATE RESEARCH TO
THE POLITICIAN'S CONTEXT

From the policy maker's perspective, context is the most important consideration with regard to utilization of research. Nelson, et al., conducted a national study of policy makers and concluded:

> In fact, our study identified research relevance to the user's context as the strongest issue across all groups and levels. Users judge all research evidence and other sources of information against their local context, pre-existing understandings, local needs, and expectations. They measure the utility and application of the evidence as it relates (or does not relate) to their specific situation. Policy makers and practitioners in our study placed much more weight on what they considered to be 'practical, real-life, or pragmatic' evidence, including local research, local data, their own experience, and the experience of others.[35]

The dilemma, however, is that research is not intended to be directly applicable to any specific context. There is never a one-to-one relationship between the context studied and the contexts for which the results are

---

33. John E. Brandl, "Distilling Frenzy from Academic Scribbling: How Economics Influences Politicians," *Journal of Policy Analysis and Management* 4, no. 3 (1985): 347.

34. Ibid., 348.

35. Nelson, Leffler, and Hansen, *Toward a Research Agenda*, 19.

applicable. The strength of research is that it is conducted in one context and the findings are then generalized to similar contexts. Understandably, the politician whose paramount concern is how the results apply to a specific context would not find research evidence to be particularly useful.

Academics must translate research results to politicians as concretely as possible.[36] It is important to mention here that translation is not a shortened version of a longer research report. Creating a shortened version of a report or article does not render the findings more applicable to the politician's specific context. Rather, translating research involves developing an entirely new product intended specifically for politicians. The translation of research to a policy context should include all of the following elements:

1. Draw specific examples from the politician's context. Include specific cases from the politician's experiences as examples where the phenomenon under study is likely to occur and where the results are applicable.

2. Describe what the results mean for the politician, not just what they are. Describing what the results are involves detailing the direction and strength of relationships between variables or phenomena. Describing what the results mean involves a clear explanation of how the research findings are applicable to real-world conditions that are getting (or would get) better or worse.

3. Accompany every statistic with a narrative. Politicians frequently use narratives to give issues a "face" when communicating with the public. The same tactic should be applied to research results. Each finding or statistic should be accompanied by a story.

4. Downplay, even delete, methods from the main text. Politicians do not have the time or expertise to wade through the methods before getting to the findings. Present the problem, findings, and solutions. The methods should be referenced last.

5. Present the results on one page, with white space. Synthesize the key points on a single page so politicians can understand the issue(s) at a glance.

6. Make a direct request. Link the results to a request for action on a specific policy. Be prepared to tell politicians exactly what they can do to take action.

---

36. Martyn Hammersley, *Educational Research and Policymaking in Practice* (London, UK: Paul Chapman Publishing, 2002).

CONCLUSION

There are both rewards and perils associated with engaging in public scholarship. But as both research evidence and educational issues become increasingly complex, there remains an unmet need for skilled professionals who can broker the academic and policy worlds.[37] The engaged approach to public scholarship serves as an abbreviated "how to" guide for those interested in undertaking this critical work. Strategically, the approach is built upon the recognition that researchers stand outside of the policymaking process and that sound research evidence is not enough to win the day. Academics can leverage their expertise and engage in the policy process strategically to shape the policy agenda.

The contributions in this book will join a chorus of other research-based policy recommendations, too few of which have found their way into the policy discourse. By engaging in public scholarship, the hope is that the ideas in this book will not sit on the shelf. Rather, anyone invested in improving the educational conditions of Latino students will "speak truth to power" by engaging in the policy process to earn a seat at the table.

REFERENCES

Albaek, Erik. "Between Knowledge and Power: Utilization of Social Science in Policy Making." *Policy Sciences* 28, no. 1 (1995): 79–100.

Benner, Patricia. "From Novice to Expert." *The American Journal of Nursing* 82, no. 3 (1982): 402–07.

Brandl, John E. "Distilling Frenzy from Academic Scribbling: How Economics Influences Politicians." *Journal of Policy Analysis and Management* 4, no. 3 (1985): 344–53.

Caplan, Nathan. "Factors Associated with Knowledge Use among Federal Executives." *Policy Studies Journal* 4, no. 3 (1976): 229–34.

———. "The Two-Communities Theory and Knowledge Utilization." *American Behavioral Scientist* 22, no. 3 (1979): 459–70.

Daley, Barbara J. "Novice to Expert: An Exploration of How Professionals Learn." *Adult Education Quarterly* 49, no. 4 (1999): 133–47.

Davies, Huw T. O. and Sandra M. Nutley. *Learning More about How Research-Based Knowledge Gets used: Guidance in the Development of New Empirical Research.* New York, NY: William T. Grant Foundation, 2008.

Hammersley, Martyn. *Educational Research and Policymaking in Practice.* London, UK: Paul Chapman Publishing, 2002.

———. "The Myth of Research-Based Practice: The Critical Case of Educational Inquiry." *International Journal of Social Science Research Methodology* 8, no. 4 (2005): 317–30.

37. Deborah L. Rhode, *In Pursuit of Knowledge: Scholars, Status, and Academic Culture* (Stanford, CA: Stanford University Press, 2006).

Henig, Jeffrey R. "The Evolving Relationship between Researchers and Public Policy." In *When Research Matters: How Scholarship Influences Education Policy*, 41–62. Edited by Frederick Hess. Cambridge, MA: Harvard Education Press, 2008.

———. "Politicization of Evidence: Lessons for an Informed Democracy." *Educational Policy* 23, no. 1 (2009): 137–60.

Hird, John A. "Policy Analysis for What? The Effectiveness of Nonpartisan Policy Research Organizations." *Policy Studies Journal* 33, no. 1 (2005a): 83–105.

———. *Power, Knowledge, and Politics: Policy Analysis in the States.* American Governance and Public Policy. Washington, DC: Georgetown University Press, 2005h.

———. "The Study and Use of Policy Research in State Legislatures." *International Regional Science Review* 32, no. 4 (2009): 523–35.

Howell, William G. "Education Policy, Academic Research and Public Opinion." In *When Research Matters: How Scholarship Influences Education Policy*, 135–44. Edited by Frederick Hess. Cambridge, MA: Harvard Education Press, 2008.

Kingdon, John. *Agendas, Alternatives and Public Policies.* 2nd ed. New York, NY: Addison-Wesley Educational Publishers, 2003.

McDonnell, Lorraine M. "Can Education Research Speak to State Policy?" *Theory into Practice* 27, no. 2 (1988): 91–97.

Nelson, Stephen R., James C. Leffler, and Barbara A. Hansen. *Toward a Research Agenda for Understanding and Improving the Use of Research Evidence.* Portland, OR: Norwest Regional Educational Laboratory, 2009.

Nutley, Sandra M., Isabel Walter, and Huw T. O. Davies. *Using Evidence: How Research Can Inform Public Services.* Bristol, UK: The Policy Press, 2007.

Rhode, Deborah L. *In Pursuit of Knowledge: Scholars, Status, and Academic Culture.* Stanford, CA: Stanford University Press, 2006.

Scott, Janelle, Christopher L. Lubienski, Elizabeth DeBray, and Huriya Jabbar. "The Intermediary Function in Evidence Production, Promotion, and Utilization: The Case of Educational Incentives." In *Using Research Evidence in Education: From the Schoolhouse Door to Capitol Hill*, 69–89. Edited by Kara S. Finnigan and Alan J. Daly. New York, NY: Springer, 2014.

Seashore Louis, Karen. "Knowledge Producers and Policymakers: Kissing Kin or Squabbling Siblings?" In *International Handbook of Educational Policy*, 219–38. Edited by Nina Bascia, Alister Cumming, Amanda Datnow, Keith Leithwood, and David Livingstone. New York, NY: Springer, 2005.

Weiss, Carol H. "The Many Meanings of Research Utilization." *Public Administration Review* 39, no. 5 (1979): 426–31.

Weiss, Carol H. and Michael J. Bucuvalas. "The Challenges of Social Science Research to Decision Making." In *Using Social Research in Public Policy Making*, 213–34. Edited by Carol H. Weiss and Michael J. Bucuvalas. Lexington, MA: Lexington Books, 1977.

Wildavsky, Aaron. *Speaking Truth to Power: The Art and Craft of Policy Analysis.* Toronto: Brown and Company, 1979.

Helping or Hindering?

STATE POLICIES AND LATINO COLLEGE COMPLETION

Deborah A. Santiago and Emily Calderón Galdeano

OVERVIEW

Everyone deserves a shot at the American Dream—the opportunity for upward social mobility and success derived from hard work in a society with few barriers. More than ever, earning a college education is the prerequisite to the American Dream for Latino/as and others participating in the nation's workforce and civic leadership. At a time when the U.S. job market requires education beyond a high school degree, and the Latino/a population is growing, closing equity gaps by increasing educational attainment among Latino/as is imperative.

Latino/as are making progress in college degree attainment. Over the last 10 years, the percentage of Latino adults in the U.S. with an associate's degree or higher increased from 17% to 22%. However, equity gaps in attainment remain when compared to other groups in the U.S. The percentage of White, non-Hispanic adults with an associate's degree or higher increased from 40% to 46% over the last 10 years—resulting in a current degree attainment gap of 24% between Latino/as and white, non-Hispanic adults (U.S. Census Bureau, 2004; U.S. Census Bureau, 2013). State policies play a critical role in closing equity gaps in educational attainment. Public policy can reinforce the status quo or promote progress to improve college opportunity and student success.

Excelencia in Education (*Excelencia*) works with partners in key states with large Latino/a populations, such as California and Texas, to examine what we are doing, and still need to do, in policy and practice to meet our state and national goals as part of our national initiative, *Ensuring America's Future by Increasing Latino College Completion*. These partners, in turn, lead efforts to improve policy and practice in postsecondary education and increase the degree attainment of Latino/as along with others. *Excelencia in Education* has established a baseline for informing, benchmarking, and organizing stakeholder efforts to increase Latino/a college completion at the national and state levels and tracked progress (Santiago & Callan, 2010). Further, *Excelencia* conducted a preliminary audit of public policy in two states—California and Texas—and their potential impact on closing equity gaps between Latino/as and others in these states and nationally. Our partners for this analysis included The Campaign for College Opportunity (CA) and Educate Texas (TX). Their efforts informed the audits and analysis of state policies and their potential to close equity gaps in attainment that warrant further consideration within each state. The review of state policy was framed with three basic considerations: 1) Current education profile of Latino/as in the state; 2) Current context of postsecondary education in the state overall; and 3) Current state policies that might be helping and/or hindering the acceleration of Latino/a student success.

This article expands the consideration of public policy from national to state governance levels, where the majority of efforts and resources exist to support and improve college completion. The following provides a snapshot profile of Latino/as in California and Texas, and a profile of Latino/a and other post-traditional students. The remainder of this article provides a high-level review of state policies in California and Texas that may be helping or hindering Latino college completion that can compel action to ensure the national imperative of Latino student success is prioritized.

PROFILE OF TWO STATES

Combined, California and Texas enroll over half of all Latino/as in K–12 and postsecondary education in the U.S. today. Latino/as also represent over 20% of the population in each state and have an average age of 27, compared to over 40 years of age for white, non-Hispanics in each state. Further, about 16% of Latino/a adults had earned an associate's degree or higher, compared to more than 32% of all adults in each state.

Profile of Latino and Other Post-traditional Students

Some people are uncomfortable talking about race/ethnicity in public policy and practice and would rather emphasize "educating all students," without disaggregating by race/ethnicity. While race/ethnicity is not the sole characteristic to consider for public policy or postsecondary education, data

FIGURE 1. Snapshot of Latino/as in California and Texas

	CALIFORNIA	TEXAS
State ranking	CA had the largest Latino population in the U.S.	TX had the 2nd largest Latino population in the U.S.
Latino population	K-12 Population – 51%	K-12 Population – 48%
	State Population – 38%	Population – 38%
Median age	Latino – 27	Latino – 27
	White – 44	White – 41
Degree attainment	Latino – 16%	Latino – 16%
	Total – 38%	Total – 32%

Source: *Excelencia* in Education. (2014). *Latino College Completion: U.S.*

show persistent educational attainment gaps between racial/ethnic groups. Equity gaps in educational attainment are evidence that while broad goals of educating all students are inclusive in tone, this generic goal has not been implemented in ways that have resulted in equal levels of educational attainment. Considering race/ethnicity among factors can increase awareness of more specific strengths and needs of students, resulting in more intentional and equitable efforts to increase educational attainment. To be clear, intentionally considering the strengths and needs of Latino/a students in public policy does not require a lack of attention to other students; but addressing the strengths and needs of Latino/a students might help other students with similar strengths and needs. Policy makers have an opportunity to ensure their efforts accelerate the educational attainment of the students in our educational pipeline today, and increasingly, these students are Latino/a.

Whereas the term "nontraditional" is used to describe students that do not fit into a traditional profile, *Excelencia* in Education uses the term "post-traditional" to describe a growing majority of students who have evolved beyond the traditional profile. Latino/a and other post-traditional students are the majority of students in postsecondary education today, and have a profile distinct from traditional students. However, too often federal and state policies addressing postsecondary education focus on meeting the needs of traditional students, who represent less than 20% of students today. The post-traditional college-going population is projected to continue growing and public policy that more aptly addresses their strengths and needs can more effectively accelerate their postsecondary degree attainment.

FIGURE 2. Student profiles

TRADITIONAL STUDENT PROFILE	POST-TRADITIONAL STUDENT PROFILE
College-ready	May need academic prep or remediation
Enroll in a college or university full-time	Enroll at a community college and/or work part-time
Enroll the fall after high school graduation	Delay initial college enrollment while entering the workforce
Live on-campus	Live off-campus with their parents or with their own dependents
Complete a bachelor degree in four tears	Take more than four years to complete a degree
Parents have college degrees	First in family to enroll in college
White, non-Hispanic	Latino, African-American, Asian/Pacific Islander
Do not work while enrolled	Work 30 hours or more a week
Make college choices based on financial aid, academic programs offered, and institutional prestige	Make college choices based on cost of attendance, location, and accessibility

Source: *Excelencia* in Education. (2013). *Using a Latino Lens to Reimagine Aid Design and Delivery.*

Focusing on Latino/a students, as representative of post-traditional students more broadly, provides an opportunity to be intentional in including them in a policy context where too often Latinos are either considered as a footnote, or an aside, if considered at all. *Excelencia* believes acknowledging racial and ethnic trends describes our society in constructive ways, and thus helps us to understand it. The use of data and analysis to identify factors affecting the success of specific student populations establishes a base of information from which to develop more effective policies, engage diverse stakeholders, and, enhance tactical responses to better target limited resources to meet the nation's education goals. Given this recognition, it is worth articulating the profile of Latino/as in order to shape the policies and practices that can better serve these and other students.

- While the majority of the U.S. population is still white, non-Hispanic, Latino/as are the youngest and among the fastest growing racial/ethnic groups in the United States.
- The median age for Latino/as in the U.S. is 27 compared to 42 for white, non-Hispanics.

- Latino/as already represent a growing segment of those in secondary and postsecondary institutions across the country. In fact, Hispanics are currently the second largest racial/ethnic group in the U.S. overall (17%) as well as in early childhood, K–12 education, and postsecondary education. Hispanics represented 25% of children under 9 years of age (U.S. Census Bureau, 2013), 22% of students in K–12, and 16% of students in postsecondary education (*Excelencia* in Education, 2015a).

- The Hispanic population is projected to continue growing.

- The majority of Latino/a students were concentrated in a small number of institutions. In 2013–2014, over 60% of Latino/a undergraduates were enrolled in the 12% of institutions of higher education identified as Hispanic-Serving Institutions (HSIs) (*Excelencia* in Education, 2015b).

- Latinos were more likely to enroll in community colleges than all other groups. In 2012, 46% of Latino/as in higher education were enrolled in community colleges, compared to African American (34%), Asian (32%), and White (31%) students in higher education (U.S. Department of Education, 2013).

- Studies have shown between 30% and 47% of Latino/a students need remediation in postsecondary education (Complete College America, 2012).

- While a relatively small number of Latino/a students are undocumented, the majority of undocumented students in the United States are Latino/a (Motel & Patton, 2012).

- The enrollment of Latino/as along the educational pipeline is significant, but, as noted earlier, their educational attainment is lower than adults overall (U.S. Census Bureau, 2013).

There is a clear opportunity for state public policy to improve the educational attainment for Latinos as a critical component of improving educational attainment for all in the state. The following section provides an overview of the Latino/a population in each state along with a primer of some state policies that might be helping, hindering, or warrant reconsideration to improve Latino/a college completion.

CALIFORNIA

Latino/as are the fastest-growing segment of the population, accounting for 65% of the state's population growth, and are projected to become the state's majority ethnic group by 2020. Approximately 40% of California residents are projected to be of Hispanic origin in 2020, up from 25% in 1990 (California Department of Housing and Community Development, 2013). The following sections provide a primer of state policies that may help or hinder to increase Latino student access and completion of post-secondary education in California.

Policies that May Help

California has state policies that span the higher education pipeline to help increase Latinos' higher education access and completion. While all of these policies have the potential to help, the participation, implementation, outreach, or funding of these policies may limit how state policy is helping. The following three public policy strategies may be helping increase Latino college completion: College preparation activities; student support services funds for community colleges; and transfer reform.

College preparation activities. College preparation includes academic support through curriculum as well as knowledge of opportunities and options through counseling.

Curriculum

Policy context. Too few students in California are graduating from high school who are academically prepared for college. In 2011–2012, only 28% of Latino/a students completed a college prep curriculum, compared to 62% of Asian students, 45% of White students, and 29% of Black students (Institution for Higher Education Leadership & Policy, 2014). Successful completion of the college preparatory curriculum is a requirement for admission to the California State University (CSU) and University of California (UC) systems. This low completion means about two-thirds of Latino/a high school graduates in California are not eligible to apply to a university in California.

State policy. The California Education Code (EC) establishes a minimum set of requirements for graduation from California high schools, generally known as the college prep (A-G) curriculum to be eligible for the state's public universities. The intent of the curriculum is to ensure students have a body of general knowledge to prepare for more advanced study in college. This was a critical attempt to create a clear default curriculum for all students to be academically college ready.

Future consideration. High schools should increase the availability of A-G course offerings, support students to succeed in these courses, and close any gaps by race. Until more high schools see their role as graduating students prepared for college, we will not have enough Latino/as able to succeed in higher education.

Counseling

Policy context. School-based college readiness counseling ensures students receive individualized reviews of their education and career goals. The high school counselor ratio in California is 945 to 1, compared to the national average of 477 to 1 (California Department of Education, n.d.). This places California last in the nation in terms of the student/counselor ratio. Given this high ratio, counselors are too often limited to mitigating personal and social issues rather than providing college preparation and selection options. Considering over half of the K–12 population in California is Latino/a, there is a need for increased focus on college advising.

State policy. The Schools Curriculum: Opportunities for Pupils (Chapter 732, Statutes of 2007) reforms middle and high school counseling programs to ensure that students receive individualized reviews of their career goals, and that they are informed about high school graduation requirements and career technical opportunities in their schools. Further, the California Department of Education and California's P-16 Council launched "Achieving Success for All Students," a multiagency initiative focused on closing the achievement gap between recognized subgroups in the state and federal accountability systems by providing school-based college readiness counseling.

Student support services at community colleges. At community colleges, support services to completion include orientation and education planning services and reporting progress in student completion.

Policy context. Community colleges are generally open admission institutions (enroll all who apply). In California, 70% of postsecondary students are enrolled in community colleges. Similarly, 68% of Latino/as enrolled in college in California are at a community college (Campaign for College Opportunity, 2013). However, completion rates for community college students continue to be low. Per 100 overall undergraduate students enrolled, there are only 9 degrees awarded. For Latino/as, the numbers are even lower with only 7 degrees awarded per 100 students enrolled (Institute for Higher Education Leadership & Policy, 2014).

State policy. In recognition of this disconnect between those who enroll and graduate, the California Community Colleges Student Success

Act of 2012 (SB1456) restructured the way student support services were delivered to improve the assistance that students receive at the beginning of their educational experience, specifically student orientation, assessment, and education planning services. It also requires colleges receiving student support service funds to post a student success scorecard to clearly communicate progress in improving completion rates for all students and closing the achievement gap among historically underrepresented students (California Community Colleges Chancellor's Office, 2012).

Future consideration. Remedial classes are where many Latino/as start in higher education and where they are lost. Only 1 out of 5 students in pre college level courses will earn a degree or transfer within six years. By accelerating curriculum and improving placement methods, community colleges can vastly improve the number of students who go on to receive degrees. Community colleges should expand alternative placement programs, which use high school GPA to place students in college level courses and truly enact multiple measures, not just assessment tests that may understate competency, in order to ensure that we place students properly and improve their time and success in remedial courses when they do need them.

Transfer reform. Transfer reform amplifies the transfer pathway between community colleges and colleges/universities.

Policy context. Community colleges are seen as a gateway to higher education for the vast majority (70%) of students in California. While enrollment has increased, the numbers of transfers to four-year colleges and universities has not seen the same growth. Many Latino/as start their college education at a community college (68%); yet, for students who are interested in continuing their education at a four-year institution, the overall transfer rate is low. Currently, California has an overall community college transfer rate of 23% overall (Campaign for College Opportunity, 2012) and just 4 out of 10 Latino/a community college students either completed their associate degree or transferred to a four-year institution after six years, with rates continuing to decline (Campaign for College Opportunity, 2013).

State policy. California passed higher education transfer reform in 2010 (SB 1440) to simplify the transfer pathway between community college and colleges/universities. The policy created a transfer path for all California community college students, regardless of which college they originally attend. According to SB1440, students who successfully complete 60 units of transferable coursework at a community college will receive an associate degree and guaranteed admission with upper-division junior standing to a California State University system institution. However, as of 2012, those tracking the policy have seen implementation throughout the state has been uneven.

Future consideration. While the transfer legislation is helping, there is still no clear pathway into the University of California that guarantees students a spot. Ensuring full implementation of this transfer pathway AND expanding this program to the UC system would be a tremendous boost for Latino/a students.

Policies that May Hinder

Along with policies that might help increase Latino/a college completion in California, there are also public policies that may hinder their access to and success in higher education. The following three public policy strategies may be hindering Latino college completion: Lack of a centralized database; "Master Plan" eligibility/capacity limits; and lack of support for race conscious efforts.

Lack of a centralized postsecondary education database. As Latino/a representation in higher education is increasing, data can inform policy to improve student outcomes. Lack of a centralized postsecondary education database and easy access for institutions and the public limits the data and information that can inform policy to improve student outcomes.

Policy context. Without a central location for student data and benchmarks for college-going completion, monitors towards these benchmarks cannot be tracked. Lack of data on access and completion rates by race/ethnicity will hinder the state's progress in improving student outcomes and meeting workforce needs. These data can also help inform legislative policies and budget strategies to achieve these goals.

State policy. The California Legislature initially created the California Postsecondary Education Commission (CPEC) in 1973 to coordinate and develop plans for public higher education. It was later expanded to include private colleges and universities within the planning process. CPEC was closed in November 2011 due to perceived ineffectiveness and state budget cuts. The data housed at CPEC has now been transferred to the Chancellor's Office of the California Community Colleges (California Postsecondary Education Commission, n.d.). However, much of that data has not been updated since CPEC's closure and is not as easily accessible. In 2013, the California Assembly passed SB195, which created goals for California higher education policy; however, it did not establish metrics to monitor goals.

Future consideration. At a time when Latino/as are the majority in K–12 having access to a centralized location for data is important to inform public policy about what is or is not working, as these data can help inform policy discussions.

"Master Plan" eligibility/capacity limits. The limited growth of college campuses and "seats" has decreased capacity, with eligible students being turned away or unable to enroll in any classes they need, or the raising of admissions standards to constrain eligibility.

Policy context. Due to decreases in state funding for higher education, institutions needed to make large cuts in expenditures, which have impacted institutional capacity and reduced student access to higher education, at a time when student applications are increasing. The UC system has limited the number of students enrolled, resulting in increased numbers of students staying within the CSU system. With 70% of California post-secondary students attending community colleges, the CSU schools are also unable to enroll all eligible community college students due to lack of space and resources. Combined with increased tuition and fees at all three school systems, higher education completion is becoming more difficult for students who have to bear the burden of these costs and strategize how to complete their education. As a result of these budget cuts, enrollment at all three California systems has decreased by more than half a million students (Campaign for College Opportunity, 2014).

Latino/as are going to college at higher rates than ever before, and this trend is likely to continue (Fry & Taylor, 2013). However, the majority of Latino/as (68%) are enrolled at California community colleges, followed by 14% at the CSU institutions (Campaign for College Opportunity, 2013). For high school students who graduated in 2010, 34% went straight to a California community college, 10% to a CSU school and just 4% to a UC school (Malcom-Piqueux, 2013). These "master plan" eligibility limits will negatively impact students' college completion goals, which will also have an impact on both the students' and the state's bottom line. Students will either have to enroll at multiple institutions, transfer to private institutions that have higher tuition costs, or put their education plans on hold until there is space at the institution they want to attend. The state will lose out on the opportunity to have a more educated populace.

State policy. In 1960, California created a "master plan" for post-secondary education to provide access to education. This plan created three public university systems, the UC system, the CSU system and the California Community College (CCC) system, and aligned their missions to different segments. According to the plan, the top 12.5% of California high school students are eligible for admission to UC schools, which are considered the primary research universities; the top 33.3% are eligible for admission to CSU schools; and the community colleges are charged with providing academic and vocational instruction (University of California, Office of the President, n.d.).

Future considerations. California needs a statewide plan for education that increases college-going rates, improves graduation rates, maintains college affordability, and closes the gap amongst underrepresented students.

Lack of support for race-conscious efforts. Limitation of using race/ethnicity has led to the perception that institutions cannot be inclusive and intentional about serving Latino/a students.

Policy context. In recent years, the college-going rate for Latino/as has increased; however, this is also due to an increase in the overall Latino/a population, and less so on proclivity. Almost half (47%) of the college-going age population (18–24 years) is Latino/a (Campaign for College Opportunity, 2013); yet, they continue to be underrepresented at each of the higher education systems in the state. The lack of institutional support for race conscious efforts has led to a less diverse student body that does not have parity. Latino/a students currently make up 20% of the student population in the UC system, 33% within the CSU system, and 39% in the community colleges (Campaign for College Opportunity, 2013).

State policy. In 1996, California voters approved an initiative that abolished the state's public affirmative action program. The California Civil Rights Initiative (also known as Proposition 209) prohibits preferential treatment based on race, sex, color, ethnicity, or national origin by the State in public employment, education, and public contracting. Immediately after the passage of Proposition 209, higher education enrollment rates for Latino/as and African American students dropped, with the admission rates of Latino/as dropping 8% from 1997 to 1998 (University of California, Office of the President, 2014).

Future considerations. Modifying Proposition 209 to permit the use of race/ethnicity as one of many factors in weighing a candidate's qualifications, is a position consistent with federal rulings by the U.S. Supreme Court, and essential to increasing the diversity of our student body in our four year public universities, especially at the University of California (UC).

TEXAS

It is estimated by 2040, Texas' population will grow to 50 million, with 59% of the net increase being Latino/a (Murdock, White, Hoque, Pecotte, You, & Balkan, 2003). The following sections provide a primer of state policies with a Latino/a lens that may help, hinder, or be worth reconsidering to increase access and completion of postsecondary education in Texas.

Policies that May Help

Texas has state policies that span the higher education pipeline to help increase Latino/as' higher education access and completion. While all of these policies have the potential to help, the participation, implementation, outreach, or funding of these policies may limit how state policy is helping. The following two public policy strategies may be seen as helping to increase Latino/a college completion: P-16 curriculum alignment and the TEXAS (Towards Excellence, Access, and Success) Grant.

P-16 curriculum alignment. Programs developed to assist students enrolling and completing a higher education credential via partnerships along P-16 pipeline can help Latino/a students.

Policy context. College readiness is facilitated by a rigorous and aligned curriculum provided to students throughout the educational pipeline. However, in Texas and other states, it has been a challenge to align K–12 curriculum with the college readiness institutions expect of entering students. Given Latino/a youth represent about half of all students in K–12 education in Texas, there are opportunities to prepare them for success in college through curriculum alignment.

State policy. The Texas Higher Education Coordinating Board (THECB) has developed various programs to assist students in enrolling and completing a higher education credential (Texas Higher Education Coordinating Board, n.d.). GenerationTX, AdviseTX, and TransitionTX are geared toward a more traditional student profile, that of a recent high school graduate, of which increasing numbers in Texas are Latino/as. Pilot programs for GenerationTX began in 2010 in San Antonio and Fort Worth, due to their high numbers of Latino/a and Black students, and are now located in 10 areas across the state. Its focus is to work with school districts and provide a social media blitz to encourage students to pursue postsecondary education. The AdviseTX College Advising Corps is currently located in 5 areas across the state. The student advisers live within their service areas, involving themselves in the communities they serve. AdviseTX focuses on best-fit colleges, encouraging students to attend schools that will serve them well both academically and socially. TransitionTX is designed to help first-generation, low-income, Latino/a and Black students navigate their first year at participating public two-year community colleges. The program is intended to better enable students to complete a certificate or degree within three years, or successfully transfer to a four-year institution. AccelerateTX was created in response to the growing demand for adult basic education services to assist these students to transition from earning a GED to college-level degree and certificate programs. Currently 14 community colleges throughout the state are participating in this program. The program provides intensive advising, support skills classes, and selected workforce certificates that move students through education to employment within a few months.

Future considerations. Via partnerships between K–12 and postsecondary institutions, curriculum alignment is improved through data collection, analysis, and student services. Increased awareness and parental outreach can continue to increase college participation and completion rates.

TEXAS (Towards Excellence, Access, and Success) Grant.

Policy context. Financial support and an institution's ability to provide such support are very important to students, especially Latino/as. In fact, Latino/a and Black undergraduates are more likely to apply for financial aid to pay for college than all undergraduates; however, they receive lower amounts of aid than other groups, on average (Santiago, 2010a). An institution that focuses on ensuring financial support for its students has a positive effect on recruitment, retention, and degree completion (Santiago, 2010b). Undocumented students who graduate from a Texas high school and meet the criteria for the grant are also eligible to receive it and help fund their higher education degrees.

State policy. The Texas Legislature created the TEXAS Grant in 1999 to provide financial support for students attending public institutions within the state. This program can be used by recent high school graduates or by recent community college students who are continuing their education. Students entering the program from high school can receive awards for up to 150 semester credit hours, until they receive a bachelor's degree. Students who enter the program after completing their associate's degree can receive awards for up to 90 semester credit hours until they receive a bachelor's degree. Award amounts vary depending on the type of postsecondary institution the student attends.

Future considerations. TEXAS grants are contingent upon the availability of state funds, and can be cancelled or reduced in the event that state funds are no longer available. When institutions offer students the opportunity to attend college with limited financial burden, that is one less thing for the students to worry about. Providing state financial aid and scholarships beyond federal financial aid can help students continue in their programs.

Policies that May Hinder

It is important to also provide information about public policies that serve as a hindrance to Latino/as and their access to and success in higher education. These policies include a less rigorous high school graduation plan and decreased state support of higher education.

Reduced rigor in high school curriculum. Students interested in career and technical fields may receive less rigorous plans and less preparation if they decide to pursue college credentials. This can have a potentially negative impact on students should they change their minds and decide to pursue postsecondary credentials.

Policy context. A recent study found that HB 5 might lead school counselors to set historically disadvantaged students on a less rigorous degree plan designed for students who do not want to go to college (Obaseki, Kessler, & Freeman, 2013). Those opposed to HB 5 argue that students need college-ready skills to be successful in life, even though they may not want to go to college. They also believe the less rigorous plan will have a negative impact on the numbers of Latino/a and Black students should they change their mind and decide to pursue a postsecondary education in the future.

State policy. In 2013, the Texas Legislature passed HB 5, which reduced high school testing and changed graduation requirements. These changes went into effect during the 2014–2015 school year. The new curriculum dropped Algebra 2 from the standard high school curriculum and created a three-tiered high school diploma system, depending on a student's goals after high school. Two of the graduation plans allow students to earn the credits they need to get into most state colleges and universities, while one plan does not. The less rigorous plan was crafted to give students who want to go into career and technical fields more flexibility to take more classes catered to their interests instead of taking college preparation classes.

Future considerations. The curriculum under HB 5 prioritizes high school pathways that emphasize either college or workforce readiness. However, for students to be eligible for automatic admission to Texas public universities under the Top 10% program, they are required to take Algebra 2. School districts should make either of the top 2 more rigorous plans the default, which allows students more postsecondary options.

State funding of higher education. Increased college costs due to tuition deregulation result in low-income students being hit the hardest.

Policy context. Increased costs of higher education, coupled with stagnant financial aid and less state and federal funding, have made college less affordable for many families and hampered the efforts to increase access to higher education, especially among low-income and residents of color. Institutions along the Texas-Mexico border share a history of limited state financial support to help improve the access to and quality of education.

In addition to inequitable funding for higher education, Texas public school finance policies continue to disadvantage those students who have been historically underserved, Latino/as and Blacks. The pipeline from the public-school system (K–12) to college is leaking as a result of funding inequalities in the public education system, making academic access and preparation for college more difficult. It is critical to understand that although the funding to improve higher education in Texas has increased, the public education system producing academically prepared children of color continues to be flawed.

State policy. Higher education has been confronted by a decline of state and federal government funding, resulting in increased tuition costs for the students. In 2003, the Texas Legislature passed HB 3015, allowing the deregulation of tuition at public colleges and universities. As a result, Texas tuition costs have increased, on average, 40% since 2003.

Future considerations. Funding of programs designed to help attract and retain students, especially those who have been historically underserved, can help close the gaps in higher education attainment. The Texas Higher Education Coordinating Board has noted that although Latinos accounted for the most enrollment growth from 2000 to 2007, the target for Latino/a enrollment in higher education was not met. Community colleges in Texas enroll 56% of all students, and more than 60 percent of all Latino and Black students (Texas Higher Education Coordinating Board, 2010). Therefore, community colleges are well-positioned to educate and train the regional workforce.

ADDITIONAL POLICIES THAT HELP
LATINO/A STUDENTS (BOTH CA & TX)

In-State Tuition for Undocumented Students

The majority of Latino/a students in college are U.S.-born or legal residents (*Excelencia* in Education, 2012). Further, many families have been U.S. citizens for generations. However, there is a proportion of college age, undocumented Latino/as in California and Texas who have been educated in public high schools and have graduated college. California has the largest population of undocumented students, with approximately 40% of all undocumented Latino/a students living in the state (Passel, Cohn, & Lopez, 2011). Other states consider these students foreign/international students for college enrollment and federal financial aid purposes resulting in higher tuition costs. Allowing for in-state tuition for undocumented students provides them an opportunity to continue their higher education at a more reasonable cost.

For undocumented youth, the promise of college affordability appears to be a positive factor in high school graduation. California and Texas are 2 of 13 states that currently offer in-state tuition for undocumented students. Texas and California take this one step further by allowing undocumented students the opportunity to participate in state financial aid programs. These state aid programs consist of state-funded grants and loan programs to encourage timely degree completion.

Hispanic-Serving Institutions (HSIs)

In California and Texas, as in other states across the country, the majority of Latino/a students enrolled in postsecondary education are enrolled in Hispanic-Serving Institutions (HSIs). HSIs are defined in federal law (the Higher Education Opportunity Act (HEOA), Title V, 2008) as accredited, degree-granting, public or private nonprofit institutions of higher education with 25% or more total undergraduate Hispanic full-time equivalent (FTE) student enrollment. To ensure an educated workforce that is prepared to meet the demands of the 21st Century, Texas and California must capitalize on the strengths and locations of Hispanic-Serving Institutions.

SUMMARY

The goal of this article was to explore state policies that either helped or hindered Latino student success in higher education. Although many of these policies are not Latino/a-specific, analysis showed certain policies are critical for Latino college completion and effective strategies can increase access and retention to completion. This article builds on findings in previous research on policies and practices to increase student retention to completion by examining them through a Latino/a lens that uses the Latino/a student profile to accelerate retention and completion in higher education for all students.

The link between education and prosperity is undisputed. Preparing students to earn postsecondary credentials and degrees is vital for the nation's economic future. Higher education should once again be considered a public good. Studies have shown that for every $1 invested in higher education, a state can expect to gain $4 in returns (Stiles, Hout, & Brady, 2012).

Why should we be intentional in ensuring Latinos are included? How do state policies address this post-traditional student profile? Do current state policies help or hinder these students' college degree attainment? Going forward, a much more in-depth discussion of public policy is warranted, but this article lays out some obvious policies to initiate this discussion in a much more intentional way. *Excelencia* in Education and our partners in the Ensuring America's Future initiative will continue these discussions in institutional, state, and federal public policy.

Excelencia believes institutions and communities intentionally acting and measuring their postsecondary success are agents of change in expanding opportunities at institutions and public policy. We have witnessed the unintended impact of public policy that ignores the strengths and needs of the evolving student population and the institutions that serve these students. Therefore, developing networks of institutions and communities that actively pursue effective change and link with other effective practices is needed to graduate more students and provide our future workforce.

ACKNOWLEDGMENTS

The authors are grateful for the constructive review and input on early versions of each state policy section by the following partner organizations: The Campaign for College Opportunity and Educate Texas. This analysis was developed with the generous support of the Ford Foundation.

REFERENCES

California Community Colleges Chancellor's Office. (2012). *Student success initiative, 2012*. Retrieved from: http://californiacommunitycolleges.cccco.edu/Student SuccessInitiative.aspx

California Department of Education. (n. d.). *Research on school counseling effectiveness*. Retrieved from: http://www.cde.ca.gov/ls/cg/rh/counseffective.asp

California Department of Housing and Community Development. (2013). *California housing production needs 1997–2020*. Retrieved from: http://www.hcd.ca.gov /hpd/hrc/rtr/chp2r.htm

California Postsecondary Education Commission. (n.d.). *Commission history*. Retrieved from: http://www.cpec.ca.gov/SecondPages/CommissionHistory.asp

Campaign for College Opportunity. (2012). *Meeting compliance, but missing the mark*. Retrieved from: http://collegecampaign.org/wp-content/uploads/2014/06 /Meeting_Compliance_Missing_the_Mark_Full_Report_FINALfinal-1.pdf

Campaign for College Opportunity. (2013). *The state of Latinos in higher education in California*. Retrieved from: http://collegecampaign.org/wp-content/uploads/2014 /06/State_of_Higher_Education_Latino_FINAL-1.pdf

Campaign for College Opportunity. (2014). *Higher education primer*. Retrieved from: http://collegecampaign.org/wp-content/uploads/2014/06/2014_Higher_Ed _Primer_Final.pdf

Complete College America. (2012). *Remediation: Higher education's bridge to nowhere*. Retrieved from: http://www.completecollege.org/docs/CCA-Remediation-final.pdf

Excelencia in Education. (2012). Analysis of data from National Postsecondary Student Aid Survey (NPSAS) 2008. Unpublished analysis.

Excelencia in Education. (2013). *Using a Latino Lens to Reimagine Aid Design and Delivery*. Retrieved from: http://www.edexcelencia.org/research/using -latino-lens-reimagine-aid-design-and-delivery.

Excelencia in Education. (2014). *Latino college completion: U.S.* Retrieved from: http://www.edexcelencia.org/research/college-completion/united-states

Excelencia in Education. (2015a). *The condition of Latinos in education: 2015 factbook*. Retrieved from: http://www.edexcelencia.org/research/2015-factbook

Excelencia in Education. (2015b). *Hispanic-serving institutions (HSIs) fact sheet: 2013–14*. Retrieved from: http://www.edexcelencia.org/hsi-cp2/research/hsis-fact -sheet-2013-14

Fry, R., & Taylor, P. (2013). *Hispanic high school graduates pass whites in rate of college enrollment*. Retrieved from: http://www.pewhispanic.org/files/2013/05 /PHC_college_enrollment_2013-05.pdf

Institute for Higher Education Leadership & Policy. (2014). *Average won't do: Performance trends in California higher education as a foundation for action*. Retrieved from: http://collegecampaign.org/wp-content/uploads/2014/06/IHELP_AverWontDo _Report_Final.pdf

Malcom-Piqueux, L. (2013). *Addressing Latino outcomes at California's Hispanic-serving institutions: Latina and Latino high school graduates are disproportionately enrolled in community colleges.* A joint report from USC's Center for Urban Education and Tomás Rivera Policy Institute. Los Angeles, CA.

Motel, S., & Patton, E. (2013). *Statistical portrait of the foreign-born population in the United States, 2011.* Retrieved from: http://www.pewhispanic.org/2013/01/29/statistical-portrait-of-the-foreign-born-population-in-the-united-states-2011/

Murdock, S. H., White, S., Hoque, M. N., Pecotte, B., You, X., & Balkan, J. (2003). *The new Texas challenge: Population change and the future of Texas.* College Station, TX: Texas A&M University Press.

Obaseki, V., Kessler, S., & Freeman, K. (2013). *Primary and secondary education.* Retrieved from: https://www.documentcloud.org/documents/813863-ut-study-hb-5-and-minority-students.html

Passel, J. S., Cohn, D., & Lopez, M. H. (2011). *Hispanics account for more than half of the nation's growth in past decade.* Retrieved from: http://www.pewhispanic.org/files/reports/140.pdf

Santiago, D. A. (2010a). *Latinos and financial aid: Applying and receiving, 2007–08.* Retrieved from: http://www.edexcelencia.org/research/latinos-and-financial-aid-applying-receiving-2007-2008

Santiago, D. A. (2010b). *Reality check: Hispanic-serving institutions on the Texas border strategizing financial aid.* Retrieved from: http://www.edexcelencia.org/hsi-cp2/research/reality-check-hispanic-serving-institutions-texas-border-strategizing-financial-aid

Santiago, D. A., & Callan, P. (2010). *Ensuring America's future: Benchmarking Latino college completion to meet national goals: 2010 to 2020.* Retrieved from: http://www.edexcelencia.org/research/ensuring-americas-future-benchmarking-latino-college-completion-meet-national-goals-2010

Stiles, J., Hout, M., & Brady, H. (2012). *California's economic payoff: Investing in college access & completion.* Retrieved from: http://collegecampaign.org/wp-content/uploads/2014/06/Californias_Economic_Payoff_Full_Report_FINAL.pdf

Texas Higher Education Coordinating Board. (n. d). *Division of College Readiness and Success.* Retrieved from: http://www.thecb.state.tx.us/index.cfm?objectid=BCA1DEF2-02B0-B3FB-5A72BD7F7FB2448E

Texas Higher Education Coordinating Board. (2010). *Strategic plan for Texas public community colleges, 2011–2015.* Retrieved from: http://www.thecb.state.tx.us/files/dmfile/StrategicPlanforTexasPublicCommunityColleges2.pdf

University of California, Office of the President. (n.d.). *Master plan for higher education in California.* Retrieved from: http://www.ucop.edu/acadinit/mastplan/mp.htm

University of California, Office of the President, Student Affairs, Admissions. (2014). *University of California application, admissions and enrollment of California resident freshmen for Fall 1989 through 2013.* Retrieved from: http://www.ucop.edu/news/factsheets/2013/flow-frosh-ca-13.pdf

U.S. Census Bureau. (2004). *Current population survey, annual social and economic supplement, Table 1: Educational attainment.* Retrieved from: https://www.census .gov/hhes/socdemo/education/data/cps/2004/tables.html

U.S. Census Bureau. (2013). *Current population survey, annual social and economic supplement, Table 1: Educational attainment.* Retrieved from: https://www.census .gov/hhes/socdemo/education/data/cps/2013/tables.html

U.S. Department of Education. (2013). *Digest of Education Statistics, Table 306.20: Total fall enrollment in degree-granting postsecondary institutions, by level and control of institution and race/ethnicity of student: Selected years, 1976 through 2012.* Retrieved from: https://nces.ed.gov/programs/digest/d13/tables /dt13_306.20.asp

California's Student Equity Plan Policy

AN UNEXPLOITED OPPORTUNITY AMONG HISPANIC-SERVING COMMUNITY COLLEGES

Eric R. Felix, Adrián Trinidad, Cheryl D. Ching, and Estela Mara Bensimón

ABSTRACT

This article examines California's Student Equity Plan policy, which requires community colleges to identify inequities, develop activities, and create goals for achieving equitable outcomes in higher education. We provide an analysis of the Equity Plans submitted by a subset of HSI (Hispanic-serving institution) community colleges and focus on these questions:

- In what ways do the Equity Plans of HSI community colleges address the success of Latina/o students?
- Do the Equity Plans reflect the HSI status of the institution?
- Do HSI's Equity Plans focus on the most serious barriers to Latino/a success (e.g., developmental education and transfer)?

Because HSI community colleges provide a majority of credentials and degrees and they represent a pathway to transfer, we see the potential for HSIs to reduce educational inequality through the Student Equity Plan process and funding ($530 million since 2014). Specifically, do HSIs take advantage of the Student Equity Plan process and funding as an opportunity to build their capacity to produce better and more equitable outcomes for Latinos/as? Or do they approach equity more broadly and generically? Our analysis sheds light on the ways in which HSIs address policy mandates strategically to build their capacity and strengthen their identity.

INTRODUCTION

Latino/a student enrollment in higher education has steadily increased over the last 30 years. In 1976, Latino/a students comprised 4% of total fall under-graduate enrollment; in 2014, that number rose to 16%, representing over 3 million students across postsecondary education. Despite greater participation in higher education, their attendance is stratified by institutional type and sector; in general, Latino/a students are overrepresented in open-access institutions and severely underrepresented in selective institutions (Bastedo & Jacquette, 2011). Furthermore, Latino/a students face major challenges with respect to persistence and graduation (Chapa, 2005; Tierney & Hagedorn, 2002; Villalpando, 2004). Notably, they are placed in remedial courses at a higher rate than their counterparts, which delays their degree completion and overall persistence rates (Contreras & Contreras, 2015).

Many of the open-access institutions that Latino/a students attend are Hispanic-Serving Institutions (HSIs) (Excelencia in Education, 2014). The "Hispanic-serving" designation is given to institutions that have a Latino/a enrollment that is at least 25% of their student population. Unlike historically Black colleges and universities that were designed and established for the benefit of African Americans (Contreras, Malcom, & Bensimon, 2008; Malcom-Piqueux & Bensimon, 2015), with few exceptions (e.g., Hostos Community College in New York and National Hispanic University in California), HSIs were not founded specifically to serve Latino/a students. Moreover, the HSI designation is contingent on the shifting variable of enrollment: if Latino/a students fall below 25% of the campus population, the institution is no longer an HSI. And even if an institution maintains its HSI designation, questions remain about the embeddedness of this identity. As Contreras, Malcom, and Bensimon (2008) found, being an HSI does not necessarily mean that the institution sees "Hispanic-serving" as part of its broader educational mission.

In this article, we examine whether and how community colleges in California with the HSI designation are leveraging the Student Equity Policy (SEP) to improve Latino/a student outcomes. The SEP asks community colleges to eliminate inequities for a wide range of historically underrepresented groups, including students of color, low-income students, foster youth, veterans, and students with disabilities, in the areas of access, basic skills (developmental education) completion, course completion, degree completion, and transfer. By developing and implementing "student equity plans," community colleges are expected to identify where and for whom inequities exist based on an analysis of disaggregated student outcomes data, set goals to close these gaps, propose interventions to meet these goals, and evaluate progress towards achieving equity. In short, the SEP aims to establish at each community college a process of continuous improvement for mitigating inequitable outcomes. To support these efforts, the state has invested 530 million dollars in the policy since 2014.

Given what is required, we see the SEP as an opportunity to investigate whether Hispanic-serving community colleges in California—which comprise over 75% of the sector—take advantage of the Student Equity funds to support Latino/a students in ways that advance their educational outcomes. In our analysis, we focus specifically on Latino/a student outcomes in developmental education and transfer to four-year institutions as these two areas pose the greatest equity barriers for Latino/as (Contreras & Contreras, 2015; Gonzalez, 2015). In our view, developmental education is *the* access issue for Latino/a students in community colleges given their disproportionate placement and limited success in remedial courses, while transfer to a baccalaureate institution is *the* success issue given their low transfer rates despite their intentions to earn a four-year degree.

Our analysis of the Equity Plans is guided by the principles and methods of Critical Policy Analysis and Critical Race Theory. We investigate a subset of Hispanic-serving community colleges' Equity Plans (n=15), as well as relevant policy documents to address the following questions:

1. Do the student equity plans of HSI community colleges reflect their HSI designation?
   a. How do they articulate their status/identity as an HSI?
   b. How do they acknowledge their HSI identity?
   c. Do they focus on the success of Latino/a students?
2. How do the plans address disproportionate impact in basic skills for Latino/a students?
   a. How do they frame inequities in basic skills outcomes?
   b. How do they address the needs of Latino/a students in the goals and activities?
3. How do the plans address disproportionate impact in transfer for Latino/a students?
   a. How do they frame inequities in transfer?
   b. How do they include Latino/a students in the goals and activities?

In addition, we consider whether HSIs take advantage of the planning process and funding to build their capacity to produce better and more equitable outcomes for Latino/a students, or whether they approach equity more broadly and generically. We anticipate that our findings can shed light on the saliency of HSIs' identity in the distribution of resources that aim to close equity gaps in community college.

LATINO/AS IN THE CALIFORNIA COMMUNITY COLLEGES

In 2013, 65% of the first-time freshmen Latino/a students in California enrolled in one of the 113 community colleges in the state. Within these colleges, Latino/a students face significant challenges in developmental education and transfer to four-year institutions (Campaign for College Opportunity, 2015; Gonzalez, 2012). They are overrepresented in the former and underrepresented in the latter (Contreras & Contreras, 2015; Gonzalez, 2015).

Latino/a Students and Developmental Education

Developmental education refers to precollege courses, typically in English and math, that are designed to help students build knowledge, skills, and competencies needed for college-level coursework (Merisotis & Phipps, 2000). Nationally, 68% of community college students enroll in at least one developmental education course (Campaign for College Opportunity, 2015). In California, 74% of all entering students and 85% of incoming Latino/as are assessed and placed in developmental English or math. The number of Latino/a students placed in developmental courses annually could fill the Los Angeles Coliseum (93,000 capacity), more than one and a half times (p. 10). While developmental courses can serve as building blocks toward success, there is a growing consensus that they delay access to degree- and transfer-level courses and contribute to the low rates of degree production and transfer in community colleges, particularly in those that are minority-serving (Attewell, Lavin, Domina, & Levey, 2006; Bailey, 2009; Bailey, Jeong, & Cho, 2010; Ngo & Kwon, 2014). In the California Community Colleges, only 34 of 100 Latino/as who were placed in developmental English, and 14 of 100 who were placed in developmental math, subsequently passed a transfer-level course (Solórzano, Datnow, Park, & Watford, 2013).

Students are typically placed in developmental education courses based on their performance on standardized assessments such as the ACCUPLACER or COMPASS. These assessments attempt to measure college-readiness for English and math, offering an "objective" result that directs colleges to place students in an "appropriate" course for their academic level (Hughes

& Scott-Clayton, 2011; Ngo & Kwon, 2014). Scholars argue that these assessments can be ineffective and weak in their predictive power, creating arbitrary barriers for students' educational goals (Martorell & McFarlin, 2007). For Latino/a students, these assessments magnify the P–12 educational inequalities in academic and college-readiness preparation (Bailey et al., 2010). Once sorted into remedial courses, the progression toward college-level courses can take years, especially for students who attend college on a part-time basis, balancing a course load with work and family responsibilities. This process can lead to Latino/a students feeling educational fatigue, losing academic interest, or even dropping out of college (Contreras & Contreras, 2015). Advocates of reforms in basic skills placement practices and policies recommend the use of multiple measures (Bettinger & Long, 2005; Ngo & Kwon, 2014) and an end to arbitrary cut-scores (Martorell & McFarlin, 2007).

Depending on where a student is placed on the developmental course sequence, a student can be up to seven courses away from a college-level course, and two to four years away from reaching math and English classes that count toward their educational goals. In addition, the rates of "success" are critically low for Latino/a students. Statewide, only 29% of the Latino/a students who first enroll in a developmental math course completed a college level course after six years; for English the "success" rate was 40.2% (CCCCO, 2014). Both of these rates for Latino/a students were below the average completion rate.

Given this reality, developmental education has been described as a "cyclical trap" that sorts and maintains Latino/a students in remediation (Contreras & Contreras, 2015). Access to postsecondary education for Latino/a students must account for the cyclical trap of remediation and the barriers placed on community college students seeking to achieve a bachelor's degree.

Latino/a Students and the Transfer Process

With 159 HSI institutions, California is home to the majority of HSIs across the nation. Most of these institutions are community colleges (n=98) (Contreras & Contreras, 2015), whose multiple identities and missions raise concerns over whether efforts are made to target and serve Latino/a students (Hurtado & Ruiz, 2012). Of particular concern is the transfer function, which has failed to maintain equitable transfer levels for Latino/a students. State policy has attempted to support transfer for Latino/as (e.g., Senate Bills 1456 and 1440, and Assembly Bill 540), but baccalaureate graduation rates remain low (Excelencia in Education, 2014; Contreras

& Contreras, 2015). Given their overrepresentation in the state and community college system (Martinez & Fernández, 2004), Hispanic-serving community colleges are poised to provide transfer pathways to the baccalaureate for Latino/s students in California. Yet, while Latino/as make up 40% of all students in California's community colleges, only 24% successfully transfer to a four-year college or university (CCCCO, 2014). Furthermore, Latino/as' "transfer velocity rate"[1] is 29%, nine percentage points below the average and 24 percentage points below the highest-performing racial/ethnic group. In part, these low transfer rates are affected by community colleges' multiple missions, which also include vocational and workforce development, and continuing education (Brint & Karabel, 1989; Cohen & Brawer, 2008; Martinez & Fernández, 2004). As such, transfer is merely one of several foci, and in some community colleges (i.e., those with a history of technical education), it may sit second to a focus for vocational and workforce training. This is particularly important as research has shown that students of color who enroll in vocational programs are negatively affected by transfer (Crisp & Nuñez, 2014).

In sum, developmental education and transfer are two areas where Latino/as in community college face substantial equity issues. By requiring community colleges to develop equity plans, the SEP creates a space for close examination of basic skills completion and transfer rates, meaningful conversations on why Latino/a students face disparate outcomes, and strategic development of interventions that promise to eliminate the inequities they experience. For community colleges with the Hispanic-serving designation, the SEP provides the opportunity strengthen the conditions that promote Latino/a student success and equitable educational outcomes (Flores & Park, 2014).

STUDENT EQUITY PLANS

The California Community Colleges Board of Governors initiated the SEP in 1993 as a way of addressing equity issues facing underrepresented students in the system, then defined as ethnic minorities, women, and students with disabilities. To ensure equal opportunities for access, success, and transfer for these students, community colleges were asked to develop "student equity plans" that were suited to the needs of "each college's

---

1. The CCCCO (California Community College Chancellor's Office) uses the transfer velocity rate to measure "behavioral intent to transfer." Students who demonstrate intent to transfer must have completed 12 credit units and attempted at least one transfer-level English or math course within six years of initial enrollment in the community colleges.

student population, best fit the particular college's traditions and organizational structure, and have the maximum support from the college's faculty and staff" (Guichard, 1992, p. 3). In the current iteration, student equity plans have to address inequity in five indicators (access, course completion, basic skills, degree attainment, and transfer) for 14 student groups[2], of which Latino/as are one. First, colleges must calculate "disproportionate impact" (DI)—the term used in the policy to describe inequities in outcomes—on each area for each student group. For example, in the area of transfer, the plans are required to demonstrate whether each of the 14 groups are at or below equity. Colleges are obliged to include Latino/as (or any other student group) in the subsequent sections of the plan only if they are found to experience disproportionate impact. Second, the plan must include equity goals based on the DI calculations. The goal should describe the equity gap being addressed, goals to determine progress, and a desired outcome. For example, one goal is as follows: "Increase the number of students completing degree-applicable English courses who began their studies in basic skills English courses." Finally, the plans must outline activities, including strategies and action items that help a college achieve its stated goals. An activity aligned with the goal described above, for example, is: "Scale the proactive counseling model to include at least four counselors and twelve faculty members."

At each college, a committee with representatives from across campus areas (e.g., instruction, counseling, administration, governance, staff, students, community members) oversees plan development and implementation. Drafted plans are approved by local governance bodies (e.g., academic senate), leaders (e.g., president), and the board of trustees. Once approved, the plans are submitted to the California Community College Chancellor's Office for review and accountability purposes.

CONCEPTUAL FRAMEWORK:
CRITICAL POLICY ANALYSIS AND CRITICAL RACE THEORY

Critical policy analysis (CPA) (Alemán, 2007; Ball, 1997; Iverson, 2007) has been used to understand the racialized effects of policies purported to be unbiased, value-free, beneficial for all, or a combination of these. Within education, CPA illuminates the ways policy design and imple-

---

2. These groups are American Indian/Alaskan Natives, Asians, African Americans, Latino/as, Pacific Islanders/Native Hawaiians, Whites, students of some other race, students of more than one race, males, females, students with disabilities, low-income students, current or former foster youth, and veterans.

mentation create negative conditions for students of color. For example, Iverson (2007) shows how university diversity policies meant to convey institutional commitment to creating inclusive campus environments for all students constructs students of color as outsiders, disadvantaged victims, and commodities. Her study used Critical Race Theory (CRT) and CPA to position race as the central issue of interest in understanding the dominant discourse, use of deficit-based beliefs of people of color in plans, and ultimately what is produced in these plans that are intended to improve the experiences of students of color.

Undergirding CPA are critical theories such as CRT, which advance our understanding of issues related to social justice and racial inequality in society. Founded in legal studies, CRT draws from fields like sociology, ethnic studies, women's studies, and education (Ladson-Billings & Tate, 1995). Together, CPA and CRT enable us to better recognize patterns, practice, and policies that perpetuate racial inequality, including those that operate in subtle and covert ways (Villalpando, 2004). They also allow us to examine, deconstruct, and understand racial realities within higher education (Quaye, 2008). These concepts have been adopted by education scholars (Ladson-Billings & Tate, 1995; Smith, Allen, & Danley, 2007; Solórzano et al., 2013; Villalpando, 2004; Yosso, 2006) to discuss the racialized barriers people of color face in accessing, participating, and succeeding in higher education. For instance, Harper, Patton, and Wooden (2009) use CRT to show how policies that broadened educational opportunity for African Americans (e.g., the two Morrill Acts that established numerous historically Black colleges and universities) encouraged segregation and separatism, legitimized the tracking of African Americans into trade and vocational fields, and on the whole benefitted Whites as much or even more than African Americans. Alemán (2007) employed CRT to understand the racialized effects of school finance policy on Mexican American-dominant school districts. He found that the funding policy was drafted as "race-neutral," which failed to account for the historical discrimination in the communities in which the schools were embedded. Focused on equal funding, the policy neglected "property poor, majority-Mexican American schools" and ultimately maintained the inequity the policy attempted to ameliorate (p. 548).

We weave together CPA and CRT as a complementary framework to better understand the ways in which Hispanic-serving community colleges take advantage of the SEP policy. For example, does the process required by the SEP enable practitioners to focus on inequities experienced by Latino/a students? Do institutions use the SEP process as an opportunity to reflect more intentionally on how practices and policies work on behalf of Latino/a student success and take action to remediate them when necessary?

One of the factors contributing to the "closeted identity" of HSIs (Contreras et al., 2008) is the fear of "identity politics" and the potential for divisiveness should campus constituents interpret an emphasis on the HSI identity as preferential treatment to one group. The SEP's design as a policy specifically for the purposes of eliminating inequities in basic indicators of college access, participation, and success provides an unusual opportunity to focus on Latinos/as as a matter of compliance with policy. Thus, in examining the content of these plans, we sought to understand how community colleges utilize the SEP to close outcome gaps for Latino/a students.

METHODS:
DATA COLLECTION AND ANALYSIS

The data presented here is from a larger study examining the Student Equity Policy in California (see Ching, Felix, Fernandez-Castro, & Trinidad, 2017). The plans and related policy documents were obtained from the California Community College Chancellor's Office (CCCCO). For this article, we randomly selected 15 HSIs from the larger sample of plans we initially analyzed (n=28). We identified HSI status based on percentage of Latino/a students enrolled and Title V Grantee status.

We first familiarized ourselves with the policy design of the SEP. Then we reviewed all related documents on the CCCCO website to better understand the implementation guidelines for developing the equity plans at each campus. We also examined the laws and regulations (e.g., California Education Code, CA Senate Bill 860) that created the policy, beginning with its inception in the early 1990s. Once all the documents were collected, we developed an analytical framework based on Iverson's (2007) method of policy discourse analysis to review the plans. Questions in the framework had two levels. In the first level, we examined the policy plan to understand how each college framed issues of equity, how they discussed inequities experienced by students of color, and the ways they articulated potential strategies and interventions. The second level questions focused on whether the community colleges identify as an HSI in the plan (e.g., whether they used specific language when referencing Latino/a students and how proposed goals and activities addressed the unique needs of Latino/a students).

Our data analysis proceeded in three stages. First, we tested our analytical framework on a plan not included in our sample. This allowed us to apply the framework and see how it helped to answer our research questions. An inter-rating meeting was used to revise the framework and standardize our analysis process from the test case. Second, we each reviewed five plans using the protocol. Finally, we met as a team to discuss the emerging insights and themes, and to synthesize our findings.

IDENTIFYING AS AN HSI IN STUDENT EQUITY PLANS

Within our sample of Hispanic-serving community colleges, we had a range of enrollment percentages from 25.7% to 64.3%. Our sample also included eight institutions that received federal Title V grants in 2013–2014. These grants provide funding for HSIs to "expand educational opportunities for, and improve the attainment of, Hispanic students" (US Department of Education, 2015). These funds can be used for faculty development, academic tutoring or counseling programs, and student support services, to list a few. Given our sample, our first question was to determine if and how colleges shared their HSI identity in their student equity plan.

Of the 15 plans in the sample, only 5 mentioned their HSI status, leaving 10 that made no mention of being an HSI throughout the document. It is important to note that the plan guidelines do not specifically require colleges to list or address their HSI status. However, given the common interest of improving educational outcomes for Latino/as, we expected more plans to make note of the colleges' HSI status. Similar to previous researchers (Contreras et al., 2008; Gasman, Baez, & Viernes Turner, 2008; Malcom, Bensimon, & Davila, 2010), we were interested in understanding the salience of the Hispanic-serving identity among the colleges that reported their status. We found that the colleges shared their status in different sections of the equity plan. Three plans shared their status in the executive summary, one described it in indicators such as access and transfer, while another shared their identity in the budget and funding source section. For those that shared their HSI status in the executive summary, Hispanic-serving was a moniker of diversity-serving. Colleges shared their status with other descriptors that showcase the diversity of their student populations. For example, one college stated:

> The college is a Hispanic Serving Institution (HSI), is identified as a Service Members Opportunity College, and serves a small number of foster youth. Also prominent in our community are large numbers of refugees from Iraq, Iran and Afghanistan, and we expect to see the numbers of refugees added to our service area by over 30,000 by the year 2016.

Another plan indicated that

> [College] is home to a diverse student population. The college has the distinction of being a Hispanic Serving Institution (HSI) and will be applying for recognition as an Asian American and Native American Pacific Islander Serving Institution (AANAPISI) with a student population of 36% Hispanic, 24% African American and 14% Asian.

In both examples, being an HSI is one of the college's many diversity identities.

Of the eight colleges that have received Title V funds, only three mentioned their HSI status. One of the colleges identified itself as an HSI only by mentioning the Title V grant in the "Sources of Funding" section: "Since student equity requires institutional commitment, funding for student equity is implicit in the use of all institutional funding resources." The mention of the college's HSI status in this plan served a functional purpose, for its inclusion was a way of demonstrating how the college will coordinate Title V grant and equity plan activities.

One college identified its HSI status in the section of the plan devoted to the calculation of DI (disproportionate impact). The college stated, "Overall, transfer can be an ambitious goal for most students. As a Hispanic Serving Institution, we must provide more resources to our Hispanic students to make this goal attainable." Unlike other colleges that used their HSI status to merely signify the diversity of their student population or to show how it will align different initiatives, this college employed its identity as an HSI as a call to action. Once the college identified Latino/as as a group facing inequity in transfer, it described how being an HSI requires it to do more to make transfer equitable for Latino/as.

PLANNING FOR LATINO/A STUDENT SUCCESS AND EQUITY

In this section, we focus on the three aspects of the equity planning process described earlier: calculation of disproportionate impact, setting goals, and proposing activities. Table 1 summarizes the aspects where Latino/as were addressed directly. In exploring whether colleges found and addressed DI with Latino/a students, we generally found that campuses did not target Latino/a in their goals and activities. When Latino/as were targeted, they were frequently grouped with other racial and non-racial groups (i.e., foster youth, veterans), or were included in other indicators (i.e., access or course completion), but not in basic skills and/or transfer.

TABLE 1. Summary of Latino/a Focus in Equity Plans: Basic Skills and Transfer

	% LATINO/A	BASIC SKILLS ENGLISH			BASIC SKILLS MATH			BASIC SKILLS ESL			TRANSFER		
		DI	G	A	DI	G	A	DI	G	A	DI	G	A
1	37*												
2	48												
3	26												
4	55*												
5	51*								NR	NR			
6	29												
7	49												
8	52*												
9	51*												
10	29												
11	33												
12	48												
13	42*												
14	55*												
15	63												

Notes. DI = disproportionate impact; G = goals; A = activities; NR = not reported; *Title V grant recipient.

Basic Skills

Of the plans we analyzed, all but one identified inequities for Latino/a students in basic skills. Within the SEP, the category of basic skills encompasses three areas: English, math, and English as a Second Language (ESL). ESL was the most identified area for Latino/a students, with twelve of the fifteen plans indicating DI. The second most identified area was English (10 plans) and then math (8 plans). Not only were Latino/a students identified as facing inequities in basic skills, many colleges found that they were the most severely impacted. One college stated, "The data indicate that Hispanic students, who have a 19% success rate in ESL, experience the greatest adverse impact compared to a 43% success rate of Asian students, the highest performing group." Another noted, "Students enrolling in ESL and subsequently completing a college-level ESL or English course show there is disproportionate impact for Latino students." These statements on DI mirror the statewide equity issue in regards to Latino/a students and success. Of those who start in an ESL program only 19.5% complete a college-level course—the lowest of all racial/ethnic groups.

Although 14 of the 15 plans identified DI for Latino/as in basic skills, six plans did not refer to Latino/a students explicitly in their goals. Of the nine plans that included Latino/as in their goals, five offered more specific goals, such as "Increase Hispanic student basic skills completion rate in the next four years to the average of 34% for all students" and "Increase Basic Skills English completion among Hispanic students from 45% to 47%. Another subset of the plans included Latino/as, but as one of a series of students groups that were found to be disproportionately impacted. For example,

> To ensure equity among students, [college] aims to increase course completion rates for each of the following basic skills subject areas: English: African-American/Black and Hispanic students; all sub-groups 25 or older; ESL-Reading: Hispanic, White, and Unknown ethnicity students; all student subgroups 25 or older; ESL-Writing: Hispanic and Unknown ethnicity students; all student subgroups 25 or older; Math: African-American/Black and Hispanic students; students 40 or older; and students with disabilities.

A consequence of including so many different target populations in a single goal is the difficulty of developing specific activities to address inequities for those populations. Plans that included many target groups articulated activities that tended to be race-neutral, to lack cultural relevance, and to build on existing programs and services. One college that took this approach shared a laundry list of activities:

> (1) "get ready" for math and English workshops; (2) provide more tutoring and supplemental instruction; (3) look into "three takes" rules; (4) look into test prep and post-assessment boot camp programs; (5) review SSSP [Student Success and Support Program] data; (6) monitor online orientation and advising efforts; (7) develop and offer summer bridge program; (8) look into acceleration.

Others advocated for general professional development, such as "Engage basic skills instructors in professional learning opportunities." Although these activities may be helpful to Latino/a students, they may not address the needs of Latino/a students directly and consequently may fall short of closing equity gaps in basic skills.

Some colleges proposed activities specifically for Latino/a students. One college intends to redesign its curriculum to be more relevant to the students they serve: "develop and expand culturally specific content into transfer and developmental level English courses (e.g., Puente English Model)." Another college aims to develop better programming within the English Department, to include "strategies and workshops to assist African-American and Latino students who complete their last basic skills level." Some activities also centered on giving Latino/a students the chance to voice their concerns and offer potential solutions through focus groups on their "perceptions of risk and resilience as it pertains to success through the basic skills sequence." In contrast to the race-neutral activities listed above, these activities place Latino/a students front and center. It is important to remember that only a few plans included activities that fell into this category. This may stem from the lack of congruence between the identification of DI (14 plans) to their inclusion in the goal statement (9 plans), to the development of Latino/a specific activities and interventions (5 plans).

Transfer

For the primary pathway to a bachelor's degree and for a student group overrepresented in community colleges, the inclusion of transfer goals and activities centered on Latino/as is an important step toward advancing equitable practices in California community colleges. We found, however, few instances where colleges drafted coherent strategies that carefully considered Latino/a students.

Of the 15 equity plans, 10 identified DI gaps in transfer among Latino/a students. Two plans did not include calculations to identify DI and two other plans did not acknowledge DI, despite providing data that showed otherwise. For example, one college did not identify Latino/as as being disproportionately affected, even though only 50% of students transferred. Most of the plans combined Latino/as with other student groups when identifying inequities and none of the plans noted Latino/as as facing the greatest DI, despite the fact that Latino/as were among the lowest performing group across many indicators. Furthermore, none of the plans used language that expressed significant concern over the inequities among Latino/as.

When constructing goals for the transfer indicator, the colleges did not include Latino/as, listed them among other student groups, or created separate goals intended to serve only Latino/a students. Four plans neglected altogether to include Latino/a students in their goals section. These plans either prioritized other racial/ethnic groups or developed goals for non-racial/ethnic groups. Seven plans grouped Latino/as with other student groups. These colleges created general goals and listed all the groups that were disproportionately affected; for example, "Increase transfer rates for all students with an emphasis on the following groups: Hispanic, African Americans, American Indian, Filipino, Pacific Islander, Southeast Asian (e.g., Hmong, Laotian, Cambodian), and first generation, college-going students." The list looks like a "fill in the blank" format into which student groups are slotted and can just as easily be replaced or removed from the goal. Only four colleges created plans with Latino/a-specific transfer goals such as "Increase transfer rates of Hispanic students from 32.6% to 34.6%." However, among two of these four plans, attention to Latino/as was done as a secondary rather than primary focus. In other words, the plans set generic goals and in the end included the phrase, "specifically for Hispanic students."

As with the activities in basic skills, we found few attempts to create Latino/a or race-conscious activities. Over half (n=8) of plans did not include Latino/a-specific activities. These plans generalized activities towards all students and developed strategies that were race-neutral. Two plans, while race-conscious, used indirect and vague activities such as creating "men of color learning communities" and expanding Puente, an intensive English program intended to help students transfer. The remaining plans (n=5) included Latino/a-specific activities to address disproportionate impact, three of which incorporated a generic strategy that would be customized for Latino/a students. For example, one plan proposed transfer application "clinics" for Black, Latino, and Filipino students, among others. One college proposed Latino/a-specific activities but also explained that the disproportionate impact Latino/as face is the result of cultural limitations, that is, coming from immigrant families who are "intimidated by the prospect of attending college" and who lack social capital. Only one college served as a model of Latino/a specific goals and activities. This college planned to increase transfer rates and decrease time to transfer among Latina/o students through transfer pathways, outreach, or expanded student support services tailored for Latina/o students.

Although SEP is not intended to address inequity only among Latino/as, the limited effort placed to achieve equity for these students is noteworthy in view of their magnitude in the California community colleges and their status as the group with the largest number of students disproportionately affected. As highlighted, very few plans among the ones we reviewed developed comprehensive strategies' centered on Latino/a students. For the most part, the plans articulated one-size-fits-all strategies that seek to address inequities for all student groups without careful consideration of the unique needs of the groups experiencing disproportionate impact.

DISCUSSION AND IMPLICATIONS

As Latino/as attend college in greater numbers, institutions of higher education are faced with questions of how to best support them such that they have quality academic experiences, achieve equitable outcomes, and are well-prepared to pursue personal and professional goals. Unfortunately, the great strides that Latino/as have made in accessing higher education are compromised by attendance in less-selective institutions, and more important, by continued inequities in success and completion. Our purpose in this article was to explore how Hispanic-serving community colleges in California, which enroll the greatest number of Latino/as in the state, intend to address the equity issues facing Latino/a students. We grounded our examination in an analysis of student equity plans, which all California community colleges are required to develop and implement as a way of mitigating disproportionate impact for different student groups. We reasoned that these plans are an opportunity for colleges to remedy inequities for Latino/a students, and thus we sought to discover whether they used the plans in this manner. Since developmental education and transfer represent, in our view, the most critical access and success problems for Latino/a students, we focused our attention on these two areas. Indeed, based on the 15 plans we analyzed, only one did not reveal inequities for Latino/as in basic skills English, math, or ESL, and only four did not find disproportionate impact in transfer.

Despite these results, the plans did not include Latino/a-specific goals and activities. In both basic skills and transfer, we found few examples of plans that offered goals that were developed with Latino/a students in mind. Several included Latino/as in their goals, but they were mentioned alongside the other student groups experiencing disproportionate impact. Finally, there were plans with goals that made no mention of Latino/as. Our analysis of the proposed activities produced similar findings, with only a handful of plans presenting Latino/a-specific and more generally race-conscious strategies to addressing inequities. Most, in contrast, shared one-size-fits-all activities, which may maintain outcome gaps even while raising success rates for all students. Although we can only speculate such a result at this point in time, recent evaluations of interventions designed to improve achievement for all students support this possibility. For example, the redesign and implementation of "accelerated" basic skills math courses in the California community colleges increased the completion rates of transfer-level math courses for all students. Racial and ethnic inequities remained, however, and for Latino/as, the gap increased from four to nine percentage points when compared to White students, the highest performing group (California Acceleration Project, 2015). Our point is not to disparage acceleration, which we believe is creating much-needed curricular reforms that reduce the time students spend in developmental education and that provide knowledge and skills more clearly aligned with college-level work. Rather, we want to emphasize that equity for Latino/a students, indeed equity for all students of color, may very well require additional strategies that attend to their unique needs.

While we think it is crucial that all institutions of higher education address Latino/a student equity in such ways, we are also convinced that doing so may be even more important for HSIs, given that they enroll a significant number of Latino/a students. Yet, we found that except for one plan, this status was neither acknowledged nor invoked meaningfully, a finding that raises the question of whether being an HSI is essential facet of these institutions' identity and mission. In our view, it is not sufficient for the HSI designation to serve as a means of securing Title V grant monies or to signal the diversity of a college's student body. Echoing the arguments of other scholars (Contreras et al., 2008), we similarly assert that it is critical for HSIs to seriously consider what it means to be Hispanic-"serving" and to reckon with how they will be "centers of educational equity and excellence for Latinas and Latinos" (Malcom et al., 2010, p. 3).

REFERENCES

Alemán, E. (2007). Situating Texas school finance policy in a CRT framework: How "substantially equal" yields racial inequity. *Educational Administration Quarterly, 43*(5), 525–558. http://doi.org/10.1177/0013161X07303276

Attewell, P., Lavin, D., Domina, T., & Levey, T. (2006). New evidence on college remediation. *Journal of Higher Education, 77*(5), 886–924.

Ball, S. J. (1997). Policy sociology and critical social research: A personal review of recent education policy and policy research. *British Educational Research Journal, 23*(3), 257–274.

Bailey, T. (2009). Challenge and opportunity: Rethinking the role and function of developmental education in community college. *New Directions for Community Colleges, 145*, 11–30.

Bailey, T., Jeong, D. W., & Cho, S-W. (2010). Referral, enrollment, and completion in developmental education sequences in community colleges. *Economics of Education Review, 29*(2), 255–270. doi:10.1016/j.econedurev.2009.09.002

Bastedo, M. N., & Jaquette, O. (2011). Running in place: Low-income students and the dynamics of higher education stratification. *Educational Evaluation and Policy Analysis, 33*(3), 318–339. http://doi.org/10.3102/0162373711406718

Bettinger, E., & Long, B. (2005). *Addressing the needs of under-prepared college students: Does college remediation work?* Cambridge, MA: National Bureau of Economic Research. (NBER Working Paper No.11325).

Brint, S., & Karabel, J. (1989). *The diverted dream: Community colleges and the promise of educational opportunity in America, 1900–1985.* New York: Oxford University Press.

California Acceleration Project. (2015). *Acceleration strategies that produce powerful results: A planning resource for community colleges.* Retrieved from http://cap.3csn.org/files/2015/10/Powerful-Acceleration-Strategies-CAP.pdf

California Community Colleges Chancellor's Office. (2014). *Student success scorecard, California community colleges.* Retrieved from http://scorecard.cccco.edu/scorecard.aspx

Campaign for College Opportunity. (2015). *State of higher education in California: Latinos.* Los Angeles: Campaign for College Opportunity.

Chapa, J. (2005). Affirmative action and percent plans as alternatives for increasing successful participation of minorities in higher education. *Journal of Hispanic Higher Education, 4*(3), 181–196.

Ching, C. D., Felix, E. R., Fernandez Castro, M., & Trinidad, A. (2017). *Achieving Equity from the BottomUp?: The Student Equity Policy in the California Community Colleges.* Los Angeles, CA: Center for Urban Education.

Cohen, A. M., & Brawer, F. B. (2008). *The American community college* (5th ed.). San Francisco, CA: Jossey-Bass.

Contreras, F., & Contreras, G. J. (2015). Raising the bar for Hispanic serving institutions an analysis of college completion and success rates. *Journal of Hispanic Higher Education, 14*(2), 151–170. http://doi.org/10.1177/1538192715572892

Contreras, F. E., Malcom, L. E., & Bensimon, E. M. (2008). Hispanic-serving institutions: Closeted identity and the production of equitable outcomes for Latino/a students. In M. Gasman, B. Baez, & C. S. Viernes Turner (Eds.), *Understanding minority-serving institutions* (pp. 71–90). Albany, NY: SUNY Press.

Crisp, G., & Nuñez, A. M. (2014). Understanding the racial transfer gap: Modeling underrepresented minority and nonminority students' pathways from two- to four-year institutions. *The Review of Higher Education, 37*(3), 291–320. http://doi.org/10.1353/rhe.2014.0017

Cuellar, M. (2014). The impact of Hispanic-serving institutions (HSIs), emerging HSIs, and non-HSIs on Latina/o academic self-concept. *The Review of Higher Education, 37*(4), 499–530. http://doi.org/10.1353/rhe.2014.0032

Excelencia in Education. (2014). *Hispanic-serving institutions.* Retrieved from http://www.edexcelencia.org/research/hsis

Flores, S. M., & Park, T. J. (2014). The effect of enrolling in a minority-serving institution for black and Hispanic students in Texas. *Research in Higher Education, 56*(3), 247–276. http://doi.org/10.1007/s11162-014-9342-y

Gasman, M., Baez, B., & Viernes Turner, C. S. (Eds.). (2008). *Understanding minority-serving institutions.* Albany, NY: SUNY Press.

Gonzalez, K. P. (2012). Increasing Latina/o college completion rates: Mistakes and opportunities. *Journal of Hispanic Higher Education, 11,* 279–290.

Gonzalez, K. P. (2015). Increasing college completion for Latina/as in community colleges: Leadership and strategy. *New Directions for Higher Education, 172,* 71–80.

Guichard, G. (1992). *Student equity policy: A status report.* Retrieved from http://eric.ed.gov

Harper, S. R., Patton, L. D., & Wooden, O. S. (2009). Access and equity for African American students in higher education: A critical race historical analysis of policy efforts. *The Journal of Higher Education, 80*(4), 389-414.

Hughes, K. L., & Scott-Clayton, J. (2011). Assessing developmental assessment in community colleges. *Community College Review, 39*(4), 327–351.

Hurtado, S., & Ruiz, A. (2012). *Realizing the potential of Hispanic-serving institutions: Multiple dimensions of institutional diversity for advancing Hispanic higher education.* Los Angeles: University of California, Higher Education Research Institute.

Iverson, S. V. (2007). Camouflaging power and privilege: A critical race analysis of university diversity policies. *Educational Administration Quarterly, 43*(5), 586–611. doi: 10.1177/0013161X07307794

Ladson-Billings, G. & Tate IV, W. F. (1995). Toward a critical race theory of education. *Teachers College Record, 97*(1), 47-68.

Malcom, L. E., Bensimon, E. M., & Davila, B. (2010). (Re)Constructing Hispanic-serving institutions: Moving beyond numbers towards student success. *Educational Policy and Practice Perspectives, 6*, 2–8.

Malcom-Piqueux, L., & Bensimon, E. M. (2015). Design principles for equity and excellence at Hispanic-serving institutions. *PERSPECTIVAS: Issues in Higher Education Policy and Practice*, 1–16.

Martinez, M., & Fernández, E. (2004). Latinos at community colleges. *New Directions for Student Services, 2004*(105), 51–62. http://doi.org/10.1002/ss.116

Martorell, P., & McFarlin, I. (2007). Help or hindrance? The effects of college remediation on academic and labor market outcomes. Unpublished manuscript retrieved from www.utdallas.edu/wp_mcfarlin_2010_help_or_hindrance_college_remediation.pdf

Merisotis, J. P., & Phipps, R. A. (2000). Remedial education in colleges and universities: What's really going on? *The Review of Higher Education, 24*(1), 67–85. http://doi.org/10.1353/rhe.2000.0023

Ngo, F., & Kwon, W. W. (2014). Using multiple measures to make math placement decisions: Implications for access and success in community colleges. *Research in Higher Education, 56*, 442–470.

Quaye, S. (2008). *Pedagogy and racialized ways of knowing: Students and faculty engage racial realities in postsecondary classrooms.* Ph.D. dissertation, Department of Education, The Pennsylvania State University, University Park, Pennsylvania.

Smith, W. A., Allen, W. R., & Danley, L. L. (2007). "Assume the position . . . You fit the description": Campus racial climate and the psychosocial experiences of African American male college students. *American Behavioral Scientist, 51*(4), 551-578

Solórzano, D. G., Datnow, A., Park, V., & Watford, T. (2013). *Pathways to postsecondary success: Maximizing opportunities for youth in poverty.* Los Angeles,

CA: UC/ACCORD. Retrieved from http://pathways.gseis.ucla.edu/publications/PathwaysReport.pdf

Stanton-Salazar, R. D. (2011). A social capital framework for the study of institutional agents and their role in the empowerment of low-status students and youth. *Youth & Society, 43,* 1066–1109. doi:10.1177/0044118x10382877

Tierney, W. G., & Hagedorn, L. S. (Eds.). (2002). *Increasing access to college: Extending possibilities for all students.* Albany, NY: State University of New York Press.

U.S. Department of Education. (2015). *Definition of Hispanic-serving institutions.* Retrieved from http://www2.ed.gov/programs/idueshsi/definition.html

Villalpando, O. (2004). Practical considerations of critical race theory and Latino critical theory for Latino college students. In A. M. Ortiz. (Ed.), *Addressing the unique needs of Latino American students: New directions for student services, 105* (pp. 41–50). San Francisco, CA: Jossey-Bass.

Yosso, T. J. (2006). *Critical race counterstories along the Chicana/Chicano educational pipeline.* New York, NY: Routledge.

Neoliberalism and the Context of Public Higher Education for Latinos

Rubén O. Martínez

ddressing the condition of Latinos in public higher education requires a clear understanding of the societal shift from a social democratic to a neoliberal order. That is, the context of public higher education has changed dramatically since the doors to public colleges and universities were cracked open for Latinos and other racial minorities by both the Chicano Movement and the Civil Rights Movement. Despite the fact that education is widely hailed as the pathway to upward mobility in American society, the education gap between Latinos and White[1] Americans has persisted over the past several decades even as important gains were made in those years following the Civil Rights Movement (Martinez and Aguirre 2003).

In the 1960s the social order that prevailed in the United States was social democratic in values and structure. Since then, it has been transformed into a neoliberal order, with changes in politics, economics, and culture. Regarded as a bourgeois revolution, neoliberalism has brought changes in values, policies, and economic dynamics. In relation to public higher education, the shift has meant, among other things, a reduction in public funding, disdain for remedial education despite the poor performance of public education, and narrowing of the curriculum, including attacks on ethnic studies programs and faculty tenure, among other changes. To understand and promote the representation and presence of Latinos in public higher education it is important to take into account the shift from social democracy to neoliberalism and its attendant changes in the political climate, public policies, and the structures of opportunity.

---

1. I use "White Americans" as an ethnic label, and therefore "White" is capitalized.

This article presents the status of Latinos in public higher education within an overarching neoliberal political context that has reshaped the nation as a whole. It provides an overview of the principal elements of neoliberalism, also referred to as free market fundamentalism, and highlights their structural influences on Latinos and public higher education within an ideology that denies the reality of racism. Neoliberalism's basic principles are radical individualism, limited government, and flexible labor. Implementation of policies based on these principles has affected all societal institutions, including public higher education.

All of these features of neoliberalism undermine the public university's mission of serving the public good and seek to put its resources at the service of corporations and private industry, with these entities creeping more and more into positions to shape teaching, curriculum, and research in higher education. In tandem with the neoliberal movement in the U.S. has been a related conservative movement, that of neoconservatism, a reactionary cultural movement that pursues an ideal right-wing view of America.[2] Neoconservatism infuses neoliberalism with political stances that promote attacks on, among other things, affirmative action policies and ethnic studies programs, both of which have given Latinos footholds in public higher education.

Although both Democrats and Republicans promote neoliberal policies, Republicans are much more aligned with views that fuse neoliberal and neoconservative perspectives. Neoliberals align with conservatives on several socially divisive issues because they keep the electorate divided and divert attention from the stealth imposition of neoliberal policies. Neoconservatism aligns with neoliberalism on antitaxation and antigovernment stances, with the two movements comprising core elements of today's conservative movement. Both neoliberalism and neoconservatism deny the structural nature of American racism and promote colorblind approaches in the various life areas, such as education, employment, and so on, with individuals treated, it is claimed, only on the basis of their individual performance and accomplishments. Differences in the material conditions and life platforms upon which individuals pursue their lives are ignored.

---

2. I recognize that from some perspectives neoconservatism is understood as part of the liberalization of markets at the global level. However, it has also been part of the cultural wars of the past four decades. Because neoliberalism is more clearly the economic and political movement that has promoted free market fundamentalism on a global scale, it makes more sense to reserve the term neoconservatism to refer to the cultural reactionary movements that oppose the civil rights policies that benefit women and racial and ethnic minorities.

FROM SOCIAL DEMOCRACY TO NEOLIBERALISM

Rising socialism and the Great Depression, which threatened to bring about the collapse of capitalism, gave rise to reformist policies that brought capital and labor into a compromise based on pursuit of greater equality of income and wealth through redistributive tax and social welfare policies and pursuit of full employment through economic growth. The social democratic compromise did not, of course, mean that class struggle had ended. Class struggle was framed philosophically by conservatives in the early part of the twentieth century as a conflict between individualism and collectivism, with the latter presented as the great threat to freedom (Johnson 1991a; Libertarian Press 1974). The compromise did not resolve the conflict between these two perspectives. Indeed, throughout the period of social democracy (1930s to 1980s), conservative economists, historians, philosophers, business and public affairs leaders were meeting at a Swiss resort to develop perspectives and frameworks to counter the principles and influence of socialism and social democracy (Hartwell 1995).

Formed formally in 1947, the Mont Pèlerin Society held that civilization was in danger due to the decline of absolute moral standards and belief in private property and the competitive market. It was the view of the members of the Society that they were engaged in a battle for ideas, one that had to be won if the rise of *dirigisme*, or state-regulated economies, was to be reversed. Their view held that individual freedom was diminished by state regulation of the economy. From their perspective, collectivism equaled totalitarianism. During the final quarter of the twentieth century, neoliberal ideas ascended to the ruling ideas of the day through the leadership of Ronald Reagan, Margaret Thatcher, and others. These political leaders, however, were simply following the general ideas of the members of the Mont Pèlerin Society.

American Neoliberalism

The roots of neoliberalism in the United States are found among the early participants of the Mont Pèlerin Society and the international network of scholars and businessmen who convened annually and planned to end economic planning as called for by socialism. More broadly, it was right-wing libertarians, anticommunists, and conservative traditionalists who gave rise to the New Right in this country in the 1950s. Barry Goldwater, Jr., the senator from Arizona, rose as the first national leader of the New Right. Known as Mr. Conservative, Goldwater is credited, among others, with the revival of the American conservative political movement that today consists of neoliberalism and neoconservatism; the former using the state to impose radical *laissez faire* principles on society and the latter a cultural reactionary movement that seeks to impose its values on society as it divides the American electorate along myriad social and political issues.

In the 1960s the New Right took on populist tones, became linked to the Religious Right, and, among other things, focused on opposing the progress made by the Civil Rights Movement on social issues. In 1971, Lewis F. Powell, Jr., a corporate lawyer from Virginia and representative of the tobacco industry who would be appointed justice of the U.S. Supreme Court the following year by President Richard Nixon, submitted a confidential memorandum to the U.S. Chamber of Commerce in which he expressed the view that socialist, communist, and fascist forces were destroying America's free enterprise system (1971).

Although Powell was a moderate on the Supreme Court, in his memorandum he presented a perspective declaring college students, liberal professors, and the mass media as responsible for the criticisms of capitalism of the period. His perspective was already evident among libertarians in the 1950s (Libertarian Press 1974). In his memo Powell presented a course of action for the Chamber of Commerce that included the following activities and resources to counter the critiques of the free enterprise system:

> 1) [A] staff of respected social science faculty, 2) a staff of speakers who translate the works of the faculty for the public, 3) a speaker's bureau, 4) scholars to evaluate social science textbooks for balanced and fair treatment of free enterprise, 5) equal time for defenders of the free enterprise system on campuses, 6) balanced faculties on the nation's campuses, 7) surveillance and monitoring of national television and radio networks, 8) scholarly journals for independent scholars to promote the free enterprise system, 9) a mix of publications for the public, 10) paid advertisements promoting the virtues of free enterprise, 11) direct engagement in the political arena, 12) a staff of lawyers to influence the judiciary by acting as counsel amicus at the Supreme Court, 13) mobilization of stockholders through educational and political action programs, and 14) a more aggressive attitude by business to participate in the political arena to promote the free enterprise system and punish those who would oppose it (Martinez 2016, 12-13).

All these activities and resources, he argued, had to meet standards of accuracy and professional excellence. Like other neoliberal thinkers, Powell held that threats to free enterprise were threats to individual freedom and that the nation had moved too far in the direction of collectivism and state socialism. In hindsight, efforts promoting neoliberalism in this country have paralleled and reflected the approach and tactics set forth by Powell.

In 1973, the American Legislative Exchange Council (ALEC), a non-profit organization that has been a powerful behind-the-scenes actor in coordinating the neoliberal policy movement over the past several decades, was founded by a group of conservative legislators. Supported by major corporations and conservative nonprofit organizations, ALEC hosts state and national summits for conservative lawmakers and their supporters to present them with hundreds of model legislative proposals drafted by corporate and ALEC staffers. ALEC legislator participants then return to their respective state legislatures to introduce model conservative bills picked up at the summits (Center for Media and Democracy 2013; Natural Resources Defense Council 2002). For example, during the 1999 and 2000 legislative sessions more than 450 "model bills" were enacted into law (NRDC 2002), and 466 were identified in the 2013 legislative agenda targeting the following areas: 1) Voter ID, 2) Stand Your Ground, 3) wages and worker rights, 4) public education, 5) the environment, and 6) citizen access to the courts (Center for Media and Democracy 2013).

The influence and the products of the Powell Memo and the work of ALEC, along with numerous conservative think tanks, have given and continue to give concrete direction to the neoliberal movement in this country. As with all social and political movements, there are intellectuals whose works influence movement leaders. Both the Powell Memo and the work of ALEC reflect a broader political philosophy and perspective that emphasizes individual freedom, free enterprise and limited government. As a movement, neoliberalism consists of a mix of economic theories and political beliefs and ideologies that motivate, mobilize, and guide a policy movement on behalf of the American capitalist class and its corporate segment that has shaped social and economic policies for more than four decades (Birch and Tickell 2010; Miller 2010).

Based on the ideas of Ludwig von Mises (1951), Friedrich Hayek (1944), Frank Knight (1946), Milton Friedman (1962), James M. Buchanan and Gordon Tullock (1962), and many other free market economists (Ronald Coase, Gary Becker, etc.), the economic theories of neoliberalism emphasize monetarism in the shaping of economic policies (Palley 2004). Monetarists seek to control inflation by controlling the supply of money primarily through the tactical setting of interest rates. Monetarism arose as a response to socialism and to Keynesian economics, which had difficulties addressing the problem of stagflation that occurred in the early 1970s, when the national economy experienced simultaneously the problems of economic stagnation and inflation. Stagflation provided neoliberals with the crisis needed to begin dismantling the social democratic order. The work of Allan Greenspan best exemplifies the monetarist approach in this country at the policy level. A disciple of the radical conservative novelist Ayn Rand, Greenspan headed the Federal Reserve for several years prior to the Great Recession of 2007–2009, and his approach demonstrates efforts to "manage" the economy by controlling the supply of money.

THE PRINCIPLES OF NEOLIBERALISM
AND LATINOS IN PUBLIC HIGHER EDUCATION

The overarching political beliefs and ideology of neoliberalism emphasize free market fundamentalism. To this are added the mutually reinforcing principles of radical individualism, limited government, and flexible labor (see Martinez 2016). Free market fundamentalism, the *sine qua non* for neoliberalism, emphasizes a radical version of laissez-faire ideas in which the economy is minimally regulated by government. According to Friedman (1994), he, Hayek and other monetarists believed in a "free society" in terms of nineteenth-century liberalism. What they mean by the term "freedom," however, is "economic freedom." That is, they held that individuals should be free to pursue profits and wealth in an open market without being hindered by government regulations. According to Friedman (1987), a basic tenet of neoliberal ideology is that individuals should be free to enter voluntarily into relations with others but should not negatively impact or harm others. Moreover, economic freedom is held as the necessary basis of all other freedoms (Knight 1946; Libertarian Press 1974; v and von Mises 1998), a view that, if not purely ideological, is surely open to critique and debate (see Wootton 1945).

Radical individualism emphasizes individual responsibility for economic and social well-being. It privileges individual freedom of choice in the market over notions of the public good, which is viewed as collectivist. Individuals are to pursue their interests within the boundaries of law and order without becoming dependent on government for their well-being. Over the past several decades this has been articulated in terms of an anti-entitlement view, which portrays the beneficiaries of social programs as "welfare cheats" living on government handouts (Reese 2005; Wacquant 2009a). Consequently, the antitax movement has imposed reductions in social programs, including public education, and presented funding cuts as mandatory for balancing national, state and local budgets. Indeed, Margaret Thatcher, Britain's prime minister from 1979 to 1991, was known for her slogan "There is no alternative" to neoliberalism. Framing the cuts in terms of "no alternative" leaves little opportunity for open and serious public discussions about the public good. Instead, reductions are presented to the public as overdetermined. Thatcher's approach exemplifies the way that the public discourse has been structured and, consequently, given the ideology of neoliberalism's hegemonic status in today's society, public policy options are oriented to making market forces dominant over all other institutions.

The principle of limited government calls for the involvement of the state in the maintenance of conditions for the accumulation of capital, including a strong military, while limiting social programs and government services to the citizenry. In this model, the state maintains the order necessary for competitive markets to function with minimum restraints. State involvement in the market beyond this point is viewed both as unfair (Johnson 1991b) and as ultimately leading to socialism (von Mises 1998) or some form of collectivism. Limited government has been promoted through deregulation of the economy and through the privatization of government services. Liberalization of markets, it is argued, allows individuals to be free from the restraints of market regulations and, as such, is a critical cornerstone of neoliberalism.

Deregulation was set in motion with the presidency of Jimmy Carter, gained momentum under Ronald Reagan, and has continued to this day (Cooper 2009; Meeropol 1998). Indeed, with the election of Donald Trump to the presidency, we now have neoliberalism gone wild; with programmatic efforts underway to dismantle the federal government even as globalism (neoliberalism) and nationalism (neoconservatism) collide through the rise of neoliberal nationalism. It is not uncommon to hear elected officials call for the elimination of the Department of Education, the Environmental Protection Agency, and other regulatory units of government. Privatization is evident today in charter schools, prisons and detention centers, private armies, border surveillance firms, and many other entities that carry out functions previously performed by different units of government. According to Martinez (2016, 16), "A legitimating notion underlying privatization is the view that the market is more efficient and effective than government, a view that is not borne out in education, corrections, public infrastructure and other areas in which privatization has occurred" (see Project on Government Oversight 2011).

Finally, the principle of flexible labor holds that, due to economic downturns, employers should have maximum flexibility in determining the terms and conditions of employment, with full power to employ and dismiss workers without the burden of employment protection measures (Solow 1998). The underlying rationale is that this would permit firms to meet the demands of market dynamics and the business cycle. In accord with this principle, the pursuit of collective interests is virulently opposed through aggressive punitive measures intended to break up labor unions and other organizations that support workers and other group interests, except, of course, those aligned with neoliberal principles, which includes all corporations that benefit from deregulation and privatization. The principle of flexible labor is also implemented through the suppression of wages and benefits, accomplished by promoting part-time and temporary employment and low-wage jobs (Abelda and Carr 2012). Economic dependency with limited rights leaves workers with no material platform for organizing themselves. It is this principle of neoliberalism, for example, that underlies the attack on tenure in public higher education and that has given rise to the large number of adjunct faculty members across the nation's public colleges and universities.

Simply put, then, the pursuit of group interests perceived to be aligned with collectivism is seen as wrongheaded, with the freedom of individuals maximized when the conditions detailed above prevail. It is held that those who succeed in amassing wealth under neoliberal capitalism do so by creating and operating firms that provide job opportunities for others to also do well—in this way, wealth is supposed to trickle down to those willing to work hard, with the majority of the population ultimately benefitting.

The Denial of Racism

With regard to racial domination and oppression, the neoliberal perspective holds that racism no longer exists and a color-blind perspective will eliminate all vestiges of it. Individuals, regardless of race, are seen as free to pursue their own material well-being. There is even talk that the nation entered a post-racial period when Barack Obama was elected President of the United States, a perspective that now must address the fact that the White House is filled with white nationalists. From the neoliberal perspective, groups do not exist in reality; that is, they do not have an objective existence, only individuals exist. Thus, structural inequalities also do not exist. Consequently, the U.S. is portrayed as an open society in which structural barriers such as institutional racism do not exist and therefore cannot limit the material well-being of individuals and their families.

The denial of institutional racism, according to Robbins, removes racism from "the realm of history, cultural practices, and social relations of power" (2004, 3). This denial has the effect of removing issues of race and racism from public discourses. Indeed, a few years ago it was common-place to hear White Americans exclaim that they were "sick and tired of hearing about racism." Within the orbit of neoliberalism, then, structural inequalities are hidden by attributing the causes of social problems to the personal sphere. By separating inequalities from the structural features of society and assigning them to the personal sphere, the issue of racism itself is removed from the public sphere (Davis 2007). This diminishes the spaces of public discourses in which racial dynamics and their effects can be framed, discussed and addressed. The result is a political economic climate that intensifies racial oppression by making it invisible, muting resistance by the oppressed, and by indirectly legitimating racist attitudes and behaviors.

Added to these neoliberal and neoconservative pressures on Latino communities is a powerful assimilationist movement that attacks the cultural pluralism that was partially institutionalized as a result of the Civil Rights Movement. This includes attacks on bilingualism in all societal sectors that are promoted by nativist and xenophobic forces within "neo-conservatives." These culturally reactionary forces oppose immigration and the full incorporation of racial and ethnic minorities into the nation's institutions. Instead, they promote exclusionary political efforts based on absolutist values that oppose cultural pluralism and multiculturalism and negatively affect Latinos and other historically oppressed groups across the country. The next section examines the ways by which neoliberalism and neoconservatism diminish opportunities for Latinos to access and succeed in public higher education by defunding and politicizing public educa-tion, attacking ethnic studies, framing students as consumers, and creating university/industry partnerships that narrow the range of studies seen as having value for society.

The Impact of Neoliberalism on Latinos in Public Higher Education

Each of the principles of neoliberalism discussed above threatens Latinos in higher education. Under neoliberalism the general aim is to impose market logic on public higher education and other societal institutions. Public universities are expected to operate as businesses, as the traditions of academic freedom, tenure, and shared governance are undermined on the basis that they lead to inefficiencies. Each of these traditions is targeted because each constitutes a barrier to the imposition of free-market fundamentalist principles and to the continued corporatization of the university. Parallel processes are also occurring in public education, where the imposition of market logic has been ongoing for several decades.

The politicization of education at the K-12 levels, which are critical sections of the education pipeline, constrains Latino student achievement in several ways, but primarily through funding cuts, the imposition of standardized tests, and attacks on ethnic studies programs. Funding cuts have led to school closures and reduced the resources available to provide many students with courses in physical education, the humanities, and the arts. Instead, the emphasis is on using standardized tests to improve student achievement, while the real aim has been to determine the conditions of employment of teachers by identifying "failing schools" and imposing punitive measures on them, including closing schools on the basis of poor performance. Further, the closure of schools removes their assets from Latino neighborhoods and reduces neighborhood capacity for improvement. Narrowing of the curriculum constricts the physical development of children as well as their team-building skills and their aesthetic potential and sensibilities. At the same time, standardized tests diminish the overall quality of education by shifting the emphasis from critical thinking and intellectual development to test-taking, especially under high stake rules. Finally, the threat of reduced funding for low test performance by students diminishes the resources available for education while providing a mechanism by which ideologically driven changes are imposed on this and other institutional sectors in society.

Providing choice in public schools has been a popular approach to reforming public education. More than anything else, charter schools embody the principle of privatization, with public funds transferred to private corporations that are exempt from several legal obligations in exchange for promising improved educational outcomes (Parker 2001). However, charter schools have not delivered the results promised, as evaluation studies show that they produce no better student performance results than do public schools (Gleason, Clark, Tuttle, and Dwoyer 2010), and in some states, such as Indiana, companies received and kept public funds without establishing schools (Center for Media and Democracy 2015).

Also of concern is the fact that charter schools have increased school segregation and provided a new avenue for white flight (Frankenberg, Siegel-Hawley, and Wang 2010; Parker 2001; Renzulli and Evans 2005). Although Latinos are underrepresented in charter schools in the West and over-represented in areas outside the West, the result has been the increased isolation of Latino and other minority students (Frankenberg, Siegel-Hawley, and Wang 2010). Consequently, over the course of neoliberalism the education of Latinos has suffered through increased isolation and segregation in charter schools and the defunding of public education generally.

Continued defunding of public education at K-12 levels ensures that plural approaches to meeting the needs of diverse students are eliminated and the "one size fits all" model is resurrected under the guise that insufficient funds are available for programs that conservatives claim "pamper" students. Thus, bilingual education programs continue to be cut as neoliberals join neoconservatives in attacking multicultural education under the guise that it is divisive to national unity. Arizona has been leading these attacks, first with Proposition 203 in 2000, which eliminated bilingual education programs and made public schooling "English Only." More recently, HB 2281 eliminated Mexican American Studies in the Tucson Independent School District and prohibited similar programs across the state, spurring related efforts in other states. This is occurring at a time when the number of households in which Spanish is spoken is greater than it has ever been in the history of this nation, both in absolute and relative terms.

Elimination of Mexican American Studies in the Tucson United School District deprives Latino students of an epistemological position that promotes intellectual growth among self-conscious racial minorities. Further, it imposes a "Johnny Appleseed" curriculum that fails to resonate with the lives of Latino students. Similar efforts are evident in efforts to "cleanse" high school history courses of an accurate presentation of intergroup relations. HB 2281 in Arizona, for example, declares that students in public schools "should be taught to treat and value each other as individuals and not based on ethnic background" (Arizona HB 2281 2010). It amends Arizona statutes relating to school curriculum and was used to dismantle the Mexican American Studies program at the Tucson Independent School District. HB 2281 prohibits classes designed primarily for members of a particular ethnic group and which promote ethnic solidarity. Yet, the result is a curriculum that promotes white nationalism. More recently, California Governor Jerry Brown, a Democrat, vetoed a bipartisan bill that provided for the development of an ethnic studies curriculum that could be used voluntarily by school districts throughout the state.

Furthermore, neoliberal views are now codified as law in public education in Arizona, where, according to Tom Horne, former Arizona Attorney General and former Superintendent of Arizona's Department of Education, one's race is not important in this society; what is important are the skills and personal characteristics of the individual (*Horne v. Martinez* 2011). Horne's ally, John Huppenthal, former Superintendent of Arizona's Department of Education, who opposes teacher unions and supports charter schools, argues that "we" are engaged in the ". . . eternal battle of all time; the forces of collectivism against the forces of individual liberty . . . right now in our country we're way out of balance. The forces of collectivism are suffocating us, it's a tidal wave that is threatening our individual liberties, and so we need, at the national level, to rebalance this and we need to make sure that what's going on in our schools rebalances this" (Western Free Press 2012).

In higher education today, students are viewed as consumers and expected to pay their way through college with minimum financial aid from the government, causing student debt to exceed more than a trillion dollars (Martinez and Leon 2013). The shift is predicated on the view that a college education is a private good, one that benefits the individual and as such individuals are responsible for its costs. The result is that socio-economic status becomes more intensely correlated with opportunities for a college education than it was in the social democratic order. This change in the opportunity structure leads to increased social inequality and reproduces stratification in society (Kochar, Fry, and Taylor 2011; see also Aguirre Jr. and Martinez 2014; Martinez 2016).

Treating students as consumers replaces the view of students as co-creators of knowledge, which is one of the founding views of Chicano/a Studies and a traditional view of liberal education. The neoliberal view focuses students on the pursuit of occupational careers instead of on becoming educated persons who can engage in the production of knowl-edge that aims to ameliorate the human condition by shedding light on the structural possibilities for improving the lives of peoples, in this case Latinos. And while the pursuit of careers is generally a key goal in the pursuit of a higher education, a college education is much more than career-seeking activity; it is about developing the whole student to appre-ciate all the dimensions of the social and the natural worlds. Students are thereby best positioned not only to pursue careers but to make substantial contributions to the betterment of society across a range of life areas.

Additionally, access to higher education is limited by anti-affirmative action policies that prohibit so-called "preferential treatment" on the basis of race, ethnicity, sex, and so on. Laws that eliminate affirmative action policies at public universities, such those passed and implemented in California, Washington, and Michigan reduce the probabilities for Latinos and other racial minorities of getting admitted to major public colleges and universities. While these laws also tend to prohibit discrimination, this component usually goes unnoticed and unenforced. Interestingly, political views that legitimate anti-affirmative action policies hold that such policies harm minorities themselves and hold them back in society by subjecting them to the stigma of having failed to properly earn positions on the basis of merit. Instead, it is argued, positions were obtained through affirmative action procedures or "preferential treatment" processes. In other words, it is for the good of minorities themselves that affirmative action policies have been and should continue to be eliminated. Ironically, there is no stigma attached to obtaining a position through white privilege, which often leads to mediocrity.

Related to the representation of Latinos in higher education is the fact that they continue to drop out of the educational system in significant numbers before completing the requirements for a high school diploma (Center for Labor Market Studies 2009; Martinez 2011), and that pattern is replicated at the level of higher education institutions. In the fall of 2013, Latinos comprised 14.4% of the total number of students enrolled in higher education institutions (*Chronicle of Higher Education* 2015). Of these, 35.0% were in four-year public colleges and universities, 46.5% were in two-year public colleges, 7.3% were in for-profit colleges and universities, and the remainder in other institutions. Although the number of Latinos obtaining college degrees has increased over time, it has not kept pace with the growth of this population group relative to the country's total population. For example, between 1990 and 2014, the gap in the attainment of a bachelor's degree or higher between White Americans and Hispanics increased from 18 to 26 percentage points (Kena et al. 2015). Moreover, Latino males have lost ground in higher education both in terms of the relative number enrolled and the number of degrees received. Sometime between 1980 and 1990, the tipping point occurred in the decline in the number of Latino males relative to Latinas attending college, and the proportion of men dropped below 50% of the total Latino/a student population in institutions of higher education. At the same time their numbers in prisons across the country increased substantially (The Sentencing Project 2003).

Radical individualism, limited government, and reduced state funding to public colleges and universities have resulted in dramatic increases in tuition and fees (Martinez and León, 2013). Given their socioeconomic status (see Martinez, 2016), increased tuition rates make it much more difficult for Latinos to attend colleges and universities. At the same time that there have been state funding cuts to higher education, there have also been substantial cuts to financial aid programs serving the poor and disadvantaged, and shifts from need-based to merit-based financial aid and from student grants to loans (Heller 2006; 2008).

Merit-based financial aid places Latinos in poor-performing schools in competition with students from better performing schools, a structural disadvantage that perpetuates the educational gap. Further, the shift from financial aid grants to student loans is part of the neoliberal strategy to reduce government support and make individuals responsible for paying their way through college. Although Heller (2008) does not refer to neo-liberalism, he does capture the fit of this shift to loans with neoliberalism:

> Loans fit very nicely with the conception that the economic and nonpecuniary returns to college are predominantly private, rather than social. As policymakers believe that it is the individual who more and more benefits from attending college—spurred, no doubt, by media reports and studies that document the increased lifetime earnings enjoyed by college graduates as compared to those individuals with only a high school diploma—they are likely to grow more comfortable with the notion that loans are an appropriate vehicle for assisting students with meeting the ever-increasing cost of college. (63)

Readers should note that the benefits to society and the public good are lost when the emphasis is on the individual.

Although there have been slight increases in grant aid and tax benefits in recent years, net costs to full- time students have continued to increase (College Board 2014). The result of these policies is that, nationally, the total student loan debt ranks second to mortgage debt and the delinquent rate for student loans is higher than for all other types of loans (Cauchon 2011). Both student loans and defaults on student loans have significant consequences for students, even those who obtain their degrees, as it may take them several decades to pay off the loan, and there are serious con-sequences for defaulting on them. Additionally, there have been constant threats to remediation programs for underprepared students. In effect, the neoliberal message is that individual achievement determines one's lot in life. With the impending departure of Baby Boomers as active participants in the economy and the misalignment between the skilled labor demands of the economy and the available labor force (Sahin et al. 2011), the fail-ure to adequately educate Latinos will be negatively felt in the economy for generations to come. Additionally, the shift from higher education as a public good to a private good also will have negative effects for years to come, even if a policy paradigm shift in the opposite direction were to occur soon.

At the level of faculty, neoliberalism will also continue to have nega-tive effects. With increasing reliance on adjunct faculty, the competition for tenure-track positions intensifies, and with Latino faculty having limited influence in higher education, the likelihood is that they will increase among the ranks of the former and decrease in the ranks of the latter. This has the effect of removing the research interests of Latinos from organized research in higher education. Moreover, with the push for funded research occurring at most four-year, public institutions of higher education as a means for generating revenues through facilities and administrative funds paid on grant awards, especially by federal agencies, the range of studies on Latinos is narrowed to align with the funding priorities of agencies and foundations, and the mission of Chicano and Latino Studies, and thus Chicano and Latino scholars, is diminished and replaced by the perspectives and priorities of funding agencies and foundations. This problem is compounded by the rise of university-industry partnerships and university-industry research complexes which narrow the range of research areas to those of corporate interests, even as they are presented as valuable to society (e.g., STEM). At the same time, the tightening of standards for promotion and tenure serves as a mechanism by which the value of faculty publications are more narrowly centered on the standards of the dominant group.

For example, as part of the accountability emphasis of neoliberalism, departments are pressured to develop lists of professional journals with high impact factors in which faculty members should be publishing their research and creative works. As these lists are developed there is a tendency to use simple impact metrics of journals in deciding which publications are to be valued. This approach re-introduces to the academy the cultural biases of the dominant group as well as its current demographic dominance. That is, Latino scholars are more likely than their White American counterparts to conduct critical studies focusing on the mechanisms of continued domination of Latino populations in American society. Additionally, they are likely to use research methods that are less likely to be valued by the high-impact journals in their respective fields. The result is that those journals that are important outlets for the research conducted by Latino scholars may not be viewed as having scholarly value within the academy. Moreover, the impact values of journals are greatly influenced by the greater numbers of White American scholars relative to those of Latinos. In other words, the production of knowledge is not color-blind. In this context then, research by Latinos is likely to become less valued than what it already is in promotion and tenure processes, leaving them to decide if they should join the ranks of the adjunct faculty, align their research projects with the funding priorities of government agencies, foundations or corporations, or leave the academy altogether.

CONCLUSION

Neoliberalism represents the revolt of the ruling class in capitalist society against social democracy. It combines with neoconservatism to form a contemporary version of the New Right intended to restore the unilateral power of the capitalist ruling class in society and impose policies that promote its interests while the "welfare state" and social democracy are dismantled and Latinos and other minorities are pushed down the socioeconomic structure. In the process, issues of racism are muted through a radical view of individualism and the denial of structural inequality. The result is a high degree of ideological hegemony supported by contradictory but much needed neoconservative (nationalistic) emphases on white privilege, the Alt-right being today's articulation of neoliberal nationalism. That is, without the neoconservative emphasis on divisive social and racial issues, neoliberalism could not have achieved the political (electoral) power required to promote its radical antiwelfare and anticollectivist policies. In this context, Latinos and other minority populations face greater obstacles to full incorporation into the nation's institutions, including public higher education.

Because neoliberalism is a broad political economic movement, its influence is felt throughout society, including the structures of opportunity for Latinos in higher education. The imposition of market logic and market relations throughout all societal sectors has increased social inequality, diminished the quality of public education systems, reduced the influence of policies intended to increase opportunities for racial and ethnic minorities, and put public higher education on a path that reduces it to developing a workforce for the economy and to producing knowledge for industry.

By denying the existence of institutional racism, neoliberalism allows the reproduction of and perpetuates exclusionary structures throughout society. These structures limit opportunities for Latinos and other racial and ethnic minority groups, including poor White Americans, to obtain educational experiences that promote personal growth, expand their stock of knowledge, and increase their technological skills.

REFERENCES

Abelda, Randy, and Michael Carr. 2012. "Low-Wage and Low-Income Workers in the U.S., 1979–2009." *Center for Social Policy Publications.* http://scholarworks .umb.edu/csp_pubs/60.

Aguirre Jr., Adalberto, and Rubén O. Martinez. 2014. "The Foreclosure Crisis, the American Dream, and Minority Households in the United States: A Descriptive Profile." *Social Justice* 40(3): 6–15.

Arizona HB 2281. 2010. https://www.azleg.gov/legtext/49leg/2r/bills/hb2281s.pdf.

Birch, Kean, and Adam Tickell. 2010. "Making Neoliberal Order in the United States." In *The Rise and Fall of Neoliberalism: The Collapse of an Economic Order?*, edited by Kean Birch and Vlad Mykhnenko, 42–59. New York: Zed Books, Ltd.

Buchanan, James M., and Gordon Tullock. 1962. *The Calculus of Consent: Logical Foundations of Constitutional Democracy*. Ann Arbor: University of Michigan Press.

Cauchon, Dennis. "Student Loans Outstanding Will Exceed $1 Trillion this Year." *USA Today*. October 25, 2011. http://usatoday30.usatoday.com/money/perfi/college/story/2011-10-19/student-loan-debt/50818676/1.

Center for Labor Market Studies. 2009. *Left Behind in America: The Nation's Dropout Crisis*. Boston, MA: Northeastern University.

Center for Media and Democracy. 2013. *ALEC at 40: Turning Back the Clock on Prosperity and Progress*. Madison, WI: CMD. http://www.sourcewatch.org/images/8/88/ALEC_report_2013.pdf.

Center for Media and Democracy. 2015. *Charter School Black Hole*. Madison, WI: CMD. http://www.prwatch.org/charter-school-black-hole.

Chronicle of Higher Education. 2015. *Almanac 2015–16*. 61, no. 43. Washington, DC: The Chronicle of Higher Education.

College Board. 2014. *Trends in College Pricing 2014*. New York: The College Board. http://trends.collegeboard.org/sites/default/files/2014-trends-college-pricing-final-web.pdf.

Cooper, Phillip J. 2009. *The War Against Regulation from Jimmy Carter to George W. Bush*. Lawrence, KS: University of Kansas.

Davis, Dana-Ain. 2007. "Narrating the Mute: Racializing and Racism in a Neoliberal Moment." *Souls* 9(4): 346–360.

Frankenberg, Erica, Geneveve Siegel-Hawley, and Jia Wang. 2010. *Choice without Equity: Charter School Segregation and the Need for Civil Rights Standards*. Los Angeles: The Civil Rights Project/*Proyecto Derechos Civiles*, UCLA Graduate School of Education and Information Studies.

Friedman, Milton. 1962. *Capitalism and Freedom*. Chicago: University of Chicago.

———. 1987. "The Future of Freedom." YouTube video, 1:21:06, November 14, 2012. http://www.youtube.com/watch?v=Ub_3x4XDbiE.

———. 1994. "Book Discussion on the 50th Anniversary Edition of F. A. Hayek's *Road to Serfdom*." *Booknotes*. http://www.booknotes.org/Watch/61272-1/Milton+Friedman.aspx.

Gleason, Philip, Melissa Clark, Christina Clark Tuttle, and Emily Dwoyer. 2010. *The Evaluation of Charter School Impacts, Final Report*. NCEE 2010–4029. Washington, DC: National Center for Education Evaluation and Regional Assistance, U.S. Department of Education.

Hartwell, Ronald Max. 1995. *A History of the Mont Pelerin Society*. Indianapolis: Liberty Fund, Inc.

Hayek, Friedrich A. 1944. *The Road to Serfdom*. Chicago: University of Chicago.

Heller, Donald E. 2006. "Merit Aid and College Access." Paper presentation at the Symposium on the Consequences of Merit-Based Student Aid, Madison, WI.

Heller, Donald E. 2008. "The Impact of Student Loans on College Access." In *The Effectiveness of Student Aid Policies: What the Research Tells Us*, edited by Sandy Baum, Michael McPherson, and Patricia Steele, 39–67. New York: The College Board.

Horne v. Martinez. 2011. YouTube video, 1:09:02, March 22. http://www.youtube .com/watch?v=7-1joLIuXvIandfeature=player_embedded.

Johnson, R. 1991a. "A New Road to Serfdom? A Critical History of the 1988 Act." In *Education Limited: Schooling, Training and the New Right in England Since 1979*, edited by Education Group II, 31–86. London: Unwin Hyman.

———. 1991b. "My New Right Education." In *Education Limited: Schooling, Training and the New Right in England Since 1979*, edited by Education Group II, 87–113. London: Unwin Hyman.

Kena, Grace, Lauren Musu-Gillette, Jennifer Robinson, Xiaolei Wang, Amy Rathbun, Jijun Zhang, Sidney Wilkinson-Flicker, Amy Barmer, and Erin Dunlop Velez. 2015. *The Condition of Education 2015* (NCES 2015-144). Washington, DC: U.S. Department of Education, National Center for Education Statistics. http://nces .ed.gov/pubs2015/2015144.pdf.

Knight, Frank H. 1946. "Freedom Under Planning." *Journal of Political Economy* 54(5): 451–454.

Kochhar, Rakesh, Richard Fry, and Paul Taylor. 2011. *Twenty to One: Wealth Gaps Rise to Record Highs Between Whites, Blacks and Hispanics*. Washington DC: Pew Hispanic Research Center. http://www.pewsocialtrends.org/2011/07/26 /wealth-gaps-rise-to-record-highs-between-whites-blacks-hispanics/.

Libertarian Press. 1974. "Original Preface." In *Planning for Freedom and Twelve Other Essays and Addresses by Ludwig von Mises*, edited by Libertarian Press, iii–v. South Holland, IL: Libertarian Press.

Martinez, Rubén O. 2016. "Neoliberalism and Latinos." *Latino Studies* 14(1): 11–32.

Martinez, Rubén O., and Adalberto Aguirre Jr. 2003. "Resource Shares and Educational Attainment: The U.S. Latino Population in the Twenty-first Century." In *Latinos in Higher Education*, edited by David J. León, 37–55. Greenwich, CT: JAI.

Martinez, Rubén O., and David. J. León. 2013. "Conclusion: Future Climbers: Lessons Learned and Final Thoughts." In *Latino College Presidents: In Their Own Words*, edited by David J. León and Rubén O. Martinez, 265–277. Bingley, UK: Emerald Group Publishing Limited.

Meeropol, Michael. 1998. *Surrender: How the Clinton Administration Completed the Reagan Revolution*. Ann Arbor, MI: The University of Michigan Press.

Miller, David. 2010. "How Neoliberalism Got Where It Is: Elite Planning, Corporate Lobbying and the Release of the Free Market." In *The Rise and Fall of*

Neoliberalism: The Collapse of an Economic Order?, edited by Kean Birch and V. Mykhnenko, 23–41. New York: Zed Books, Ltd.

Natural Resources Defense Council. 2002. *Corporate America's Trojan Horse in the States*. New York: NRDC. http://www.alecwatch.org/11223344.pdf.

Palley, Thomas I. 2004. "From Keynesianism to Neoliberalism: Shifting Paradigms in Economics." In *Neoliberalism: A Critical Reader*, edited by Alfredo Saad-Filho and Deborah Johnston, 20–29. London: Pluto Press.

Parker, Wendy. 2001. "The Color of Choice: Race and Charter Schools." *Tulane Law Review* 75(3): 563–630.

Powell Jr., Lewis. F. 1971. *Confidential Memorandum: Attack on American Free Enterprise System.* http://brianholmes.files.wordpress.com/2012/06/5b-powell_memorandum.pdf.

Project on Government Oversight. 2011. *Bad Business: Billions of Taxpayer Dollars Wasted on Hiring Contractors*. Washington, DC: POGO.

Reese, Ellen. 2005. *Backlash against Welfare Mothers: Past and Present*. Berkeley: University of California Press.

Renzulli, Linda A., and Lorraine Evans. 2005. "School Choice, Charter Schools, and White Flight." *Social Problems* 52(3): 398–418.

Robbins, Christopher G. 2004. "Racism and the Authority of Neoliberalism: A Review of Three New Books on the Persistence of Racial Inequality in a Color-blind Era." *Journal for Critical Education Policy Studies* 2(2). http://www.jceps.com/wp-content/uploads/PDFs/02-2-09.pdf.

Sahin, Aysegul, Joseph Song, Giorgio Topa, and Giovanni L. Violante. 2011. *Measuring Mismatch in the U.S. Labor Market*. 2011. http://www.economicdynamics.org/meetpapers/2012/paper_973.pdf.

The Sentencing Project. 2010. *Hispanic Prisoners in the United States*. http://www.sentencingproject.org/doc/publications/inc_hispanicprisoners.pdf.

Solow, R. M. 1998. "What is Labor-Market Flexibility? What is it Good for?" *Proceedings of the British Academy* 97: 189–211.

von Mises, Ludwig. 1951. *Socialism: An Economic and Sociological Analysis*. Translated by J. Nahane. New Haven, CT: Yale University Press.

———. 1998. *Interventionism: An Economic Analysis.* Irvington on Hudson, NY: The Foundation for Economic Education, Inc., 1998.

Wacquant, Loic. 2009a. *Punishing the Poor: The Neoliberal Government of Social Insecurity*. Durham: Duke University Press.

———. *Prisons of Poverty*. 2009b. Minneapolis: University of Minnesota Press.

Weiss, Elaine, and Don Long. *Market-oriented Education Reforms' Rhetoric Trumps Reality: The Impacts of Test-based Teacher Evaluations, School Closures, and Increased Charter School Access on Student Outcomes in Chicago, New York City, and Washington, DC*. Washington, DC: Broader, Bolder Approach to Education. 2013. http://www.epi.org/files/2013/bba-rhetoric-trumps-reality.pdf

Western Free Press. 2012. "WFP Interviews John Huppenthal, AZ Superintendent of Public Instruction." YouTube video, 38:00, December 11. http://www.youtube .com/watch?v=IOqG1niwPx8.

Wootton, Barbara. *Freedom Under Planning*. Chapel Hill, NC: University of North Carolina Press, 1945.

PART

II

planning

The Role of Interest Convergence in California's Education

COMMUNITY COLLEGES, LATINAS/OS, AND THE STATE'S FUTURE

Tanya J. Gaxiola Serrano and Daniel G. Solórzano

INTRODUCTION

Latinas/os are one of the fastest growing demographic groups and the largest Population of Color[1] in the United States with 56.6 million people (U.S. Census Bureau, 2017). The rise in the Latina/o population is transforming the student demographics found in P-12 and higher education institutions (Fry & Lopez, 2012). Although there has been an increase in the enrollment of Latinas/os in institutions of higher education, particularly community colleges, the educational attainment gap still persists, with only 15% of Latinas/os earning a baccalaureate degree compared to 34% of Whites in the U.S. as of 2015 (U.S. Census Bureau, 2017b). Because of the disproportionately high enrollment of Latinas/os in community colleges, it is important to focus on this institutional sector and address its low retention, degree completion and transfer rates as a means of reducing the educational disparities between Whites and Latinas/os (Chapa & Schink, 2006; Moore & Shulock, 2010; Ornelas & Solórzano, 2004).

While the educational disparity gap begins not in higher education but along the educational pipeline of Latina/o students (Yosso & Solórzano, 2006), we focus on highlighting the crucial role of community colleges in educating Latina/o students in California (Ornelas & Solórzano, 2004; Rivas, Pérez, Alvarez, & Solórzano, 2007). Therefore, we heed Richard Delgado's (2004) call for the application of interest convergence by expanding our

---

1. "Population of Color" is intentionally capitalized to reject standard usage. Capitalization here represents a move toward social and racial justice. This rule will also apply to "People of Color," "Students of Color," "Communities of Color," and when naming specific ethno-racial categories, including those referring to specific Persons of Color (e.g., Black).

understanding of this theoretical tool and applying it to California's State Legislature to examine Latina/o community college students. The concept of interest convergence, a principle rooted in Critical Race Theory (CRT), is defined by Derrick Bell (1980) as the moment when the interests of Whites and People of Color converge, albeit momentarily. One of the principal arguments of CRT today is that "racism is normal, not aberrant, in American society" (Delgado, 2009, p. 4) and as a consequence has become normalized over time, making it difficult to address. With this theoretical lens in mind, we focus on the educational injustices and racist systemic practices Latina/o students experience. Incorporating interest convergence will also help highlight how U.S. political and educational institutions work to protect and reinforce Whiteness at the expense of People of Color (Bell, 1992). We seek to answer the following question: What role does interest convergence play in garnering support from the State of California in advancing the degree attainment and transfer outcomes of Latina/o community college students? To better answer this query, we first introduce California Community Colleges, followed by the theoretical groundings of interest convergence. A brief review of the literature concerning the intersection of interest convergence and higher education is provided highlighting the lack of scholarship in this area. Next, we discuss the role of White interests in relation to the success of Latina/o students followed by a section on methodology. More specifically, this article will engage the reader in a counterstory highlighting the relationship between interest convergence and California's state legislative leaders in serving the needs of Latina/o community college students. To do this, we incorporate current educational and economic issues the State of California is facing. A discussion on the future of California, the role of interest convergence as a political strategy, and the Latina/o student population concludes the article.

CALIFORNIA COMMUNITY COLLEGES

California has the largest community college system in the nation with 113 campuses and over 2.3 million students (California Community Colleges Chancellor's Office, 2017). In California, around 80% of the Latinas/os in higher education are enrolled in a community college (Moore & Shulock, 2010; Solórzano, Acevedo-Gil, & Santos, 2013).[2] The disproportionate

2. According to the PEW Research Center, 46% of all Latinas/os in higher education nation-wide are enrolled in community colleges (Krogstad & Fry, 2015).

enrollment of Latinas/os in community colleges can be troubling given the low degree attainment and transfer rates of community colleges. In 2015–16, the California Community College (CCC) system enrolled 1,005,761 Latina/o students, accounting for 43% of their student body— a plurality (California Community Colleges Chancellor's Office, 2017). Unfortunately, only 14% of the Latinas/os in the CCC system persist to transfer to a four-year university, making this one of the largest points of departure in the Latina/o educational pipeline (Solórzano et al., 2013).

WHAT IS INTEREST CONVERGENCE?

Interest convergence was first introduced by Derrick Bell in 1980 when he argued that Whites will tolerate small advances for Blacks only when it is in their (Whites) interest to do so, and not because it is the moral or right thing to do (Bell, 1980). In other words, "the interests of Blacks in achieving racial equality will be accommodated only when it converges with the interests of Whites" (Bell 1980, p. 523; see Figure 1).

To support his argument, Bell (1980) described how the National Association for the Advancement of Colored People (NAACP) had for years argued before state and federal courts for the desegregation of schools for Blacks given the schools' substandard education practices. Yet in 1954 the Supreme Court Case of *Brown v. Board* (1954) ordered the end of *de jure* (by law) segregation in public schools. Bell questioned the nation's sudden interest in the desegregation of schools in *Brown*. This led him to reason that the U.S. finally supported school desegregation, not because of beliefs of social and racial equity, but because it was in its political and economic interest to present itself as a moral nation and mend global and domestic relations. This is especially true given the post-World War II and Cold War context in which the U.S. was competing for global power against

FIGURE 1. A visual representation of Bell's interest convergence

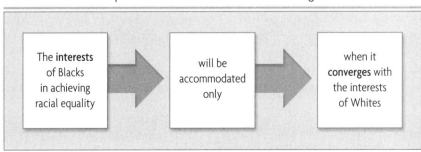

communist countries such as Soviet Union. To gain allies, the U.S. needed to demonstrate to the world its credibility as a moral nation. Bell argued that one way of demonstrating this commitment was to address the racial segregation in U.S. schools (i.e., *Brown v. Board*). Thus, for that moment in 1954 the interests of Whites and Blacks converged (Bell, 1980, 1992). Bell continued to explore and expand on the concept of interest convergence by observing, "regardless of how great the need is he [Whites] only gives *you* [the racially oppressed] when it will do *him* [Whites] the most good!" (Bell 1992, p. 19; clarification added). Here, Bell reminds us that interest convergence is sustained through White supremacy, which upholds and protects the interests of Whites.

Brown shows how the racial equality interests of Blacks, and we would argue People of Color, have been tolerated only when they align with the political and economic interests of Whites. This case was only made possible when the interests of Whites in preserving the credibility of the U.S., nationally and internationally, converged with the school desegregation interests of Blacks. It is important to stress that while *Brown* had a "favorable outcome," full racial equality has remained inaccessible. For instance, in 2014, a report published by the Civil Rights Project found that Latinas/os are the most segregated in the state of California, followed by Blacks, emphasizing the lack of attention to *Brown's* 60-year-old call for racial integration in schools (Orfield & Ee, 2014).

Interest Convergence and Education

The analytical and theoretical contributions of the interest convergence principle have seldom been integrated in higher education research, in contrast to other disciplines such as the law.[3] While legal theorists have shown the usefulness of interest convergence in examining xenophobic legislature such as Arizona's anti-Latina/o and anti-immigrant Senate Bill 1070 (Martinez, 2012), higher education scholars have used interest convergence to investigate the cost-benefit analysis of diversity and affirmative action for People of Color in academia (Aguirre, 2010). Interest convergence as an analytical tool allowed Aguirre (2010) to study how White faculty and administrators benefit from the introduction of diversity requirements, as it provides them the opportunity to gain increased access to valuable resources (i.e., teaching assistants, faculty hires, instruc-

---

3. A search using the key terms *interest convergence* and *community colleges* resulted in 30 source matches from HEINONLINE, a primary law database, compared to only 3 source matches in ERIC, an important education database.

tional funds) while reinforcing the dominant deficit discourse on People of Color. Aguirre (2010) states that "from the interest convergence perspective, academia will develop and implement institutional practices focused on diversity only when it benefits the dominant group" (p. 765) and not Communities of Color. The findings provided by Aguirre (2010) serve as a pillar to the foundation of higher education in which the interests of People of Color will only be addressed when they also benefit the interests of Whites.

Castagno and Lee (2007) demonstrate how policies and practices affecting Students of Color will be supported only for as long as they do not interfere with the interests of Whites. In their study, Castagno and Lee (2007) showed how Indian mascot policies challenging the wrongful appropriation of communities and cultures served as an example of interest convergence. In espousing such policies, institutions of higher education can appease the concerns from the American Indian student body and supporters and develop a caring image as an institution that responds to the needs of marginalized communities. Yet such policies are cautiously crafted in ways that become less proactive and more symbolic. Castagno and Lee (2007) state, "The institution is willing to make concessions toward greater social justice but only to the point at which it stands to lose something" (p. 7), in this case, alumni donations and profits from campus mascot fan gear. It is important to remember that institutions of higher education function to the advancement of White interests, and interest convergence serves as a tool to expose the details found within.

Although interest convergence is gradually being incorporated in higher education, scholars have noted the lack of integration of interest convergence in the field of teacher education. Milner, Pearman, and McGee (2013) argue that interest convergence, a tool not sufficiently used in education, can help disrupt normative practices and policies in teacher preparation programs. Hence, the authors together with the assistance of interest convergence as an analytical tool, "recognize that educational advancements will occur for marginalized students in conjunction with the interests of Whites" even when they might not have a "vested interest in the educational, social, and economic equality of these marginalized students of color" (p. 343). Milner et al. (2013) call for the deliberate incorporation of theoretical and analytical tools that can challenge the White supremacy present throughout educational institutions as a step in understanding the complexities of race and racism in academia.

Similarly, it is our goal to extend the call for interest convergence in other areas of higher education, including community colleges and

Latina/o students. A search of three of the most prominent education research databases (ERIC, Education Source, and PsycInfo) using the terms *interest convergence* and *community colleges* in all text fields resulted in a total of only three journal articles. From these, only an article by Shaun Harper (2009) explicitly centered the applicability of interest convergence in studying the efficacy of race and racism in the transfer outcomes of Black male community college athletes. The alarmingly low transfer rates of Black male athletes encouraged Harper (2009) to "consider the mutual benefits that could accrue for these students and the colleges" (p. 30) when there is an institutional commitment to their success. To do this, Harper (2009) delineates how the interests of community colleges can converge with the interests of Black male athletes. He specifically outlines how community colleges, as institutions in positions of power, can gain in the following four areas when invested in transferring Black athletes: (1) increased institutional transfer rate, (2) an improved reputation, (3) coaches supporting the academic success of students, and (4) student athlete alumni donations. Here, Harper (2009) makes a case for the alignment of the interests of those in the dominant group with the educational equality interests of Black male athletes. While Harper's (2009) scholarship has opened the conversation on interest convergence and community colleges, we focus on the application of the interest convergence principle to the study of Latina/o students in community colleges. Next, we provide a foundation focusing on the role of White interests before engaging in a counterstory centering California's Capitol Hill.

THE ROLE OF WHITE INTERESTS

Race and racism work to benefit Whites under the premise of a "justified ideology of racial superiority and White privilege" (Yosso & Solórzano, 2005, p. 117). It is this same ideology of racial superiority that extends to institutions such as educational systems and leads to prioritization of Whites and marginalization of Students of Color. Whiteness is defined by Gillborn (2009) as "a regime of beliefs and attitudes that embodies the interests and assumptions of White people" (p. 535), which allows for the continued relegation of People of Color. In other words, Whiteness "is a structured advantage that channels unfair gains and unjust enrichments to Whites while imposing unearned and unjust obstacles in the way of Blacks [People of Color]" (Lipsitz, 2011, p. 3). The interests of Whites as the group benefitting the most from the U.S. racial hierarchy have been protected since the inception of the nation. History has continuously demonstrated efforts to reproduce and maintain White supremacy from the expansionist goals of Manifest Destiny to the Jim Crow era of lawful racial segregation and the always-present debate on birthright citizenship—all protective of White interests (Gómez, 2007). Contemporary examples of the preservation of White interests include the high market value and desirability of residential neighborhoods predominantly populated by Whites in comparison to the low economic value of communities largely occupied by People of Color (Delgado & Stefancic, 2012). Correspondingly, it is these same White neighborhoods that enjoy the benefits of well-equipped hospitals, schools, and other institutions that contribute to their social, economic, and health prosperity (Unnatural Causes, 2008). These examples depict how the U.S. has continued to protect and invest in White interests at the expense of the interests of People of Color.

METHODS

To tell the story of interest convergence in California's economic and education future and Latinas/os in the community college system, we will share a counterstory. We define counterstory as a method of telling the stories of those people whose experiences are not often told (i.e., those on the margins of society).[4] The counterstory is also a tool for exposing, analyzing, and challenging the majoritarian stories of racial [White] privilege. Counterstories can shatter complacency, challenge the dominant discourse on race and racism, and further the struggle for racial reform. Indeed, within the histories and lives of People of Color, there are numerous unheard counterstories. By using storytelling and counterstory-telling these experiences can help strengthen traditions of social, political, and cultural survival and resistance.

For this article we use a variation of the composite story method to help understand the concept of interest convergence and how it plays out for Latinas/os in the California Community College System. Composite counter-narratives draw on various forms of data to recount the raced, gendered, classed experiences of People of Color. Using Delgado Bernal's (1998) concept of cultural intuition, we create the counterstory from (1) data gathered from the California Department of Education, the California Community College, the U.S. Census, and the U.S. Social Security Administration, (2) the existing literature on the intersection of California's postsecondary system of higher education (community colleges), California's education and eco-

---

4. This method section draws heavily from Solórzano and Yosso, 2002; Yosso and Solórzano, 2005.

nomic future, and the role of interest convergence in that future, (3) our own professional experiences, (4) our own personal experiences, and (5) our collective experiences and community memory.

Once these various sources of data had been compiled, examined, and analyzed, we created composite characters from the lives of real-life persons to help tell the counterstory. We then got the characters to engage in a real and critical dialogue addressing Bell's (1980) interest convergence tool and how it plays out for Latinas/os in the California Community College System. The first character is the speaker of the California State Assembly, Adrian Reyes. The second individual is the president pro tempore of the California State Senate, Diego Del Rio. These two office-bearers are the two most powerful politicians in the two branches of the California State Legislature. Indeed, their election represents the first time in California history that Latinos/as have held these two powerful positions at the same time. The third character is Lila Bustos, a Latina graduate student doing an education and economic policy internship at the California State Capitol. Emilia Bates, the fourth character, is the former California assembly speaker and the first African American woman to serve as any state assembly's highest-ranking leader. The final character is Malaquías Tamez, a Chicano university professor and Critical Race Theorist.

We ask you to suspend judgment, listen for the story's point, test them against your own version of reality, and use the counterstory as a theoretical, conceptual, methodological, and pedagogical case study.

THE DILEMMA OF INTEREST CONVERGENCE AS A POLITICAL STRATEGY IN LATINA/O EDUCATION

It is a January morning in Sacramento's Capitol Hill and California State Speaker of the Assembly, Adrian Reyes, is running a few minutes late to his meeting with California State Senate president pro tempore, Diego Del Rio. His earlier meeting ran longer than expected, since he is still getting acquainted with his new appointment as California's Assembly Speaker. Upon arriving to his office, Reyes sees Del Rio; they embrace each other and share some laughter as they walk into the office together.

"Reyes, it's really good to see you. How is it being the Assembly Speaker for the largest state in the United States?" Del Rio asks as they both take a seat.

"It's great to see you too, Del Rio. Transitioning to Speaker of the Assembly has been exciting and nerve-wracking at the same time. I know we had previously discussed collaborating on the education of Latinas/

os as this is an area of great concern for the State of California and our economy. In your role as the president pro tempore for the California State Senate, you, like me, are the highest-ranking leader."

Del Rio interrupts Reyes and adds, "And let's not forget I'm also the first Latino in over 130 years to hold this position."

"I believe this is the first time in the history of California that both houses of the state legislature are led by Latinos or even two People of Color (Berestein Rojas, 2015), leaving us with an enormous amount of responsibility to honor our collective experiences and ethical commitments," replies Reyes.

Del Rio nods his head in agreement before remarking, "The last time we had this conversation we left off on a discussion on the changing demographics of our schools here in California. Today, I brought a report my staffers put together that can guide us through our meeting."

California Latina/o Demography

Del Rio hands Reyes a report, which Reyes begins to peruse. Del Rio continues, "In California, we have the largest Latina/o population at 15 million, making us the second state in the nation (after New Mexico) to have a Latina/o plurality as of 2014 (Lopez, 2014; U.S. Census Bureau, 2015)."

Reyes stares intently at a California graph highlighting the fact that, as of 2014, Whites are no longer the majority; Latinas/os are now the largest group at 39% (U.S. Census Bureau, 2015). Del Rio notices and takes the opportunity to share some longitudinal data. "If you turn the page, you will notice a shift in demographic trends showing that in 1970 California was a majority White state at 16 million and a smaller Latina/o populace at 2 million (State of California, 2007). In other words, in the last 45 years Whites declined in population size from 77% to 38% while Latinas/os increased from 12% to 39% in California (State of California, 2007). This is another milestone—Latinas/os are now a plurality of the population in California."

"Let me think out loud for a minute," comments Reyes. "What you're telling me then is that Whites have been on a steady decline while the Latina/o population continues to grow. How did this dramatic shift occur?"

Del Rio responds as he flips through the pages for the section on U.S. birth rates. "You see, nationwide, the median age of Latinas/os is 28 compared to the older age of 43 for Whites, and the numbers are similar for California (Krogstad & Lopez, 2015). What this means is that demographically these are two different populations with very different policy interests. The Latina/o population is younger and of childbearing age, leading to higher birth rates among this group, while the White population is older and no longer at peak reproduction age (20–29 years old). This, in combination with the continuous influx of immigrants from Latin America, contributes to the rapid growth of Latinas/os in the U.S. and even more so in California (Cohn, 2014)."

Latinas/os and Education

Del Rio continues, "This information is important because it has a direct effect on our student population and because we need to know who we are teaching in order to better serve them."

"Good point, we need to understand what the strengths and needs of our student populations are to develop appropriate curriculum, teaching, and policy strategies at every segment of the pipeline," Reyes comments.

"Yes, strategies such as culturally relevant pedagogy (Howard, 2003), community cultural wealth (Yosso, 2005), and pedagogies of the home (Delgado Bernal, 2001) all embody an asset-based framework that allows educators to focus on the experiential knowledge (Delgado Bernal, 2002) of students from historically marginalized backgrounds. But before we get sidetracked, let me share some demographics of our schools here in California to better contextualize the need for improved teaching practices, educational policies, and school funding." Del Rio continues, "As of 2013–14, the majority of K-12 enrollment in California was comprised of Latina/o students, accounting for 53% of the student body in comparison to 25% for Whites (California Department of Education, 2015). These statistics reflect the changing demographics of California and predict that of the nation."

"Yet this demographic change does not apply to the teaching force. An email I received recently stated that only 19% of our teachers in California are Latina/o when our Latina/o students comprise 53% of the K-12 student body (California Department of Education, 2015). Conversely, White teachers are overrepresented, constituting 65% of the teaching force (California Department of Education, 2015)," Reyes notes before shifting the conversation. "Do you have any statistics on the enrollment of Latinas/os in higher education that we can review in this report? I'm wondering if the growth has been as striking as in the K-12 sector."

"It has. They have also reached new milestones!" Del Rio replies. "A report released by the California Senate Office of Research (2014) found that of the 720,000 Latinas/os enrolled in California's higher education in 2010, 82% were enrolled in community college, 13% at a California

State University and only 5% at the University of California. When you look at the California Community College (CCC) system alone, Latinas/os are the plurality with 43% for the 2015–16 school year. Although the Latina/o enrollment has increased across all sectors, we still experience low degree attainment, particularly because of the disproportionate enrollment of Latinas/os in community colleges, a sector with low A.A. and A.S. degree attainment and transfer rates to four-year colleges and universities. A recent research report by the UCLA Chicana/o Studies Research Center (2014) demonstrates how in the state of California, 'Latinas/os fare much worse in degree attainment than any other major racial/ethnic group' (Pérez Huber, Pulido Villanueva, Guarneros, Velez, & Solórzano, 2014, p. 1). For example, in California, Latinas earn bachelor's degrees at a lower rate of 11% in comparison to their White female peers, who earn bachelor's degree at higher rate of 38%. The same pattern applies to Latinos and their White male counterparts and continues throughout the educational pipeline. Again, even though the Latina/o student body is growing in both P-12 and the CCC, it is critical that we find ways to improve their educational attainment outcomes."

Reyes interrupts. "It is very clear that we are failing Latina/o students. A few years back a staffer attended the UCLA Latina/o Education Summit and provided me a copy of the report you just mentioned on the California Latina/o educational pipeline. If I recall, in 2012, for every 100 Latina/o elementary students, 58 earn a high school diploma, 10 graduate with a bachelor's degree, 2 receive a graduate or professional degree, and only 0.2 will earn a doctoral degree in California (Pérez Huber et al., 2014). I am particularly interested in strengthening California's community colleges to improve the Latina/o pipeline in degree attainment and transfer outcomes. This meeting reminds me of a conversation I had earlier this week with a Latina graduate student, Lila Bustos. She is working as an intern here in the Capitol. During our chat, she mentioned her concern for the economic welfare of our nation and state (Hayes-Bautista, Schink, & Chapa, 1988)."

College Educated Workforce Shortage

"I'm going to stop you for a minute," Del Rio adds. "I think I see a connection here. Let me share some information on the nation's educated workforce shortage. According to the 2014 U.S. Census Bureau report on Educational Attainment, 45.2 million people in the United States have a bachelor's degree, with Whites accounting for 36.4 million or 80% and Latinas/os accounting for only 3.4 million or 7%, further emphasizing the educational disparity (U.S. Census Bureau, Educational Attainment, 2014). The nation's demand for a more educated workforce together with the growth in the number of Latinas/os, who have historically low baccalaureate degree attainment rates, represents an important economic concern for the prosperity of the United States. More important, the Public Policy Institute of California (Johnson & Sengupta, 2009) published some alarming statistics on California's college-educated workforce. According to their data, 'California will have one million fewer college graduates than it needs in 2025—only 35 percent of working-age adults will have a college degree in an economy that would otherwise require 41 percent of workers to have college degrees'" (p. 1).

"So we are less than 7 years away from having a California shortage of one million college graduates?" Reyes responds.

"Yes, meaning that we have to act fast and deliberately. As shown in the report, we have to tap into the growing Latina/o community in order to meet this demand. This is why this meeting is so important," Del Rio comments.

"Actually, I believe I have a copy of the *Closing the Gap* report by the Public Policy Institute of California (Johnson & Sengupta, 2009)," Reyes remarks as he looks through a file cabinet next to his desk. "Found it. I see here that the report establishes that 'California was once a national leader in higher education. Today, it has much room for improvement. The state's direct enrollment rate from high school into four-year colleges is among the lowest in the nation, and although students who transfer from community colleges to the University of California (UC) and California State University (CSU) have high success rates, transfer rates are very low' (p. 2). This clearly demonstrates how California's K-12 and higher education systems are not adequately preparing the college-educated graduates the state needs. The statistics you shared earlier also highlight the significant role of Latinas/os in meeting the one million gap, given that they constitute the majority (53%) of students in California's K-12 and the plurality (43%) of students in the California Community College."

"Yes, they do. To me it is clear that we have an amazing resource in the form of Latina/o educational talent that is not being tapped. I know I stopped you earlier from sharing the details of the conversation you had with Bustos, the Latina graduate student intern, but I thought this was relevant. Please, tell me more about what she shared with you," Del Rio asks.

"I think this conversation could benefit from having her involved. Let me see if she's available," responds Reyes.

The Future of the Social Security Program

A few minutes later Bustos enters the office; Reyes introduces her as he begins to share a little about their meeting. Reyes continues, "Thank you for joining us, Ms. Bustos. We were getting ready to discuss the material you shared with me on the future of the Social Security program. Would you please share some of the information we discussed earlier?" shares Reyes.

Bustos takes the reports she had in her hands and passes them to the California Assembly speaker and Senate president pro tempore. She states, "I would be more than glad to share some of the issues Social Security is facing. To start, it is important that we consider the future of Social Security as this program services close to 42 million retired workers and dependents annually across the nation as of 2014 (Social Security Administration, 2015). More important, the number of retired beneficiaries is predicted to 'double in less than 30 years . . . as the members of the post-World War II baby boom continue to reach early retirement age' (Social Security Research Statistics & Policy Analysis, 2010, p. 35). The estimated rise in beneficiaries has led to projections indicating that by 2037 Social Security (2010) will not have enough funds to cover all program costs."

"That is a very disturbing prediction given the large number of people who rely on Social Security as their main income source," observes Del Rio.

"Some of the information compiled in the report demonstrates that in 1950, the Social Security Administration had a ratio of 16 workers for every Social Security beneficiary (Social Security History, 2015). In 2010, the ratio declined to three 'and in 2034 it is projected to be two to one' (Datnow & Solórzano, 2012, p. 1422). This reminds us that the United States needs to produce employees who can continue to support the Social Security program now and after 2037," notes Bustos.

"Yes, we need more employees," responds Reyes. "Employees who are predominantly going to be People of Color as witnessed in the changing demographics of the state and the nation (Hayes-Bautista, Schink, & Chapa, 1988). Because the ratio between employees and beneficiaries is so low, and predicted to decline in the decades to come, we need to ensure that an increasing number of our California employees are college-educated in order to sustain the Social Security program."

"It seems that in order to continue having a sustainable economy we need to invest in our system of education, and pay special attention to the academic success of our Latina/o students. We also need to start thinking of how the predicted educated labor shortage will affect our nation's Social Security program," Bustos adds.

"To do this, our state and federal governments need to invest in the education of Latinas/os to secure their success and entry into the college-educated workforce. Having access to college qualifications will allow Latinas/os to participate in occupations that earn higher salaries, provide better job security, and further contribute to the support of our aging [mostly White] population through Social Security (Datnow & Solórzano, 2012). That's where we come in: we need to develop state legislation that can further strengthen the Latina/o education pipeline in California as a step to solving the issues ahead of us," Del Rio comments.

A Conversation on White Interests

Reyes starts looking through his briefcase. He takes out his notepad and says, "I think we all see the direction that this state needs to take. We can start by focusing on California and the future of Latina/o education. I have an idea. I think we should reach out to former California Assembly Speaker Emilia Bates. As you recall she was the first African American woman nationwide to ever serve as the Assembly's highest-ranking leader."

"That's a great idea!" Bustos responds.

"Okay, how about we call Bates and see if she's available to chat?"

Reyes calls Bates and they chat for a few minutes before he begins to discuss the purpose of his call. "Bates, I'm here with Del Rio and Bustos, and we are discussing a legislative plan that can improve the educational opportunities for Latina/o students in California with a specific focus on community colleges. We wanted to see if you would be willing to share some of your insight as a former and very successful Assembly Speaker."

"Of course I would. I can provide my input and share what I have learned from working with a predominantly White male state legislature and other state and federal entities," replies Bates. "Besides, I firmly believe that a strong commitment to education is the best investment for a strong economy and our future competitiveness in the global market, making your agenda interesting to me. But before we continue, let me ask you, why is it that you are deciding to focus on Latina/o students?"

Reyes and Del Rio look at each other for a split second, deciding who should answer. Del Rio takes the lead: "Bates, this is Del Rio speaking. You bring up a valid question, one that we should be ready to answer if we want to be successful in the passage of our bill. We have decided to focus on the Latina/o populace because of their large and growing population and P-22 enrollment numbers. While we acknowledge that Asian/Pacific Islander, Black, Latina/o, and Native American students share similar negative experiences in education, we are focusing on Latinas/os because of their large numbers in this state, knowing the bill will also improve the educational experiences of all underserved students."

Bustos, who had always been impressed by the accomplishments of Bates, especially given their shared identities as women of color, comments, "It is a pleasure to meet you, Bates. To add to the discussion, it is my understanding that California does not allow for the consideration of race in education or the legislature since the passage of Proposition 209 in 1996. That is, we cannot draft legislation that focuses on the needs of one particular race or ethnicity. Instead we need to use language in our bill that addresses the needs of underserved populations, which on many occasions parallels the needs of many Communities of Color."

Bates replies, "You're both right. Latinas/os comprise 53% of K-12 students, while the aggregate of Asian/Pacific Islander, Black, and Native American amount to only 19% of K-12 in California (California Department of Education, 2015). Additionally, the comment Bustos shared is an accurate one; we need to incorporate language in the proposed bill that avoids a race-conscious discourse and replace it with a general discourse on underserved populations using the data discussed earlier. I think that for now, we can focus the conversation on Latina/o students keeping in mind that oppression in the U.S. has affected People of Color disproportionately. In simpler terms, what affects the underserved Latina/o population also affects the historically under-resourced Asian/Pacific Islander, Black, and Native American communities, making for shared educational interests."

"Sounds like a great plan, Bates," comments Reyes. "Now, how can we ensure our success?"

"First, I would recommend outlining what your specific focus areas are before moving on to a conversation on White interests," replies Bates.

Reyes jots down some notes and explains, "Through our conversation we have been paying specific attention to the need for a college-educated workforce. In California alone, a shortage of one million college degrees is predicted to occur by 2025 (Johnson & Sengupta, 2009). This plus the over one million Latina/o students currently enrolled in the California Community College have led us to focus on the retention, completion, and transfer outcomes for Latina/o students in the CCC. We are all well aware that while community colleges offer many an opportunity to pursue higher education, the educational aspirations of Latinas/os to earn an associate's degree or transfer to a four-year college are rarely met because of the many barriers faced throughout this critical pathway (Solórzano et al., 2013). Personally, as a Latino who began postsecondary education at a community college, I was able to experience and witness the institutional barriers Students of Color experience at this educational juncture."

"Okay, so the focus is strengthening the California Community College by paying particular attention to the large population of Students of Color (68%), eliminating the barriers, and improving their success in transferring to four-year colleges and/or completing other degrees such as associate's degrees. And you consider this to be one solution to the college-educated shortage California is facing, correct?" says Bates.

"'The [Latina/o] achievement gap is not only an educational issue; it is about the strength of our economy. If these students do not have the opportunity to succeed, California's future will be in peril.' Moreover, the report by the Public Policy Institute of California (Johnson & Sengupta, 2009), cited 'increasing transfer rates from community colleges to four-year institutions' (p. 1) as one method of eliminating the educated workforce shortage gap," replies Del Rio.

"Great, so we know what our focus is. Now tell me how the interests of Whites benefit in this scenario. We must remember the work of Derrick Bell in this case. According to Bell (1980), interest convergence occurs when the interests of People of Color align with the interests of Whites, providing limited opportunity for transformative racial equality. In my more than ten years of political experience, I have found that Whites are more receptive to attending to the interests of People of Color when there is a shared political and economic interest to the White community," Bates replies.

"Let me make sure I'm understanding this correctly. You're suggesting that we use interest convergence as a tool to help us predict some of the challenges we might encounter in proposing a bill that focuses on the education of Latinas/os to a predominantly White legislature?" Reyes asks, with a look of confusion on his face. "I must admit this is the first time I've heard of such a strategy."

"Yes, I have found that my work on improving People of Color's conditions has been more successful when I predict White interests. To expand, when I say White interests, I am pointing to the systematic interests of those in power, and as witnessed throughout history in the U.S., this power has been afforded almost exclusively to Whites," Bates notes.

"This sounds like a great approach. 'It is not a matter of compromising or coming to mutually satisfying agreements, but rather a case of strategically aligning the interests of the powerless with those of the powerful' (Ladson-Billings, 2009, p. 347).

"I may be able to contribute something in this discussion," Bustos says. "From what I have gathered, we have identified the educational need in the Latina/o community in California. This Latina/o interest has been narrowed to the strengthening of the California Community College to ensure the success of the growing body of Latinas/os in this higher education sector. Now, we need to be strategic in aligning our interests, those of the Latina/o community, with the interests of Whites. One method of converging the interests of Whites is by focusing on California's need for more college graduates and the benefit that this would have for them. By focusing on this college-educated shortfall, we are speaking to the broader interests of Whites, the prosperity of state of California, and the economic welfare of the nation. This paired with the predicted underfunding and decreasing employee-to-beneficiary ratio in the Social Security program provides a strong case for the alignment of White interests."

"In other words, if Whites are able to comprehend (1) the fragile future of California's economy and (2) the nation's impoverished Social Security program, together with (3) the growth of Latinas/os in California and the U.S., they will become interested in ensuring the success of this group as their future depends on it. The White interests of having a prosperous economy and a robust Social Security Program will align with the Latina/o interests of having access to a quality education at the California Community College that can help ensure their success in transfer outcomes and later degree completion," remarks Del Rio.

"I sense that we are missing something," Bustos says. "When studying for my master's I took a class with two professors who discussed the risks involved when using interest convergence as a political strategy. If it's okay, I would like to video call Professor Malaquías Tamez and consult with him on this strategy."

Everyone agrees, and a few minutes later Dr. Tamez is up-to-date with the conversation. Tamez explains, "As a Critical Race Theorist, I foreground race and racism in my scholarship and activism. While I have seen and understand how some apply interest convergence as a strategic tool, this political strategy does not garner 'our communities [of color] the type of radical, structural, institutional reform that is needed for real social transformation. We have to realize that our interests—if we are truly going to advocate for Latina/o interests—will not always converge with White interests' (Alemán & Alemán, 2010, p. 13). Especially if we are seeking racial equality."

Bates responds, "As members of the state legislature we face a lot of challenges when centering the racialized experiences of People of Color due to the privileging of White interests. To circumvent this, we engage in race-conscious planning meetings behind closed doors, such as this one, followed with coded bills. The outcome is 'color-blind' legislation that fails to challenge the same systems of oppression that limit us from openly discussing race and racism."

"While I understand the need for diverse strategies, I believe that interest convergence was not seen by Bell (1980) as a political strategy but instead as an analytical tool," Dr. Tamez comments. "By aligning the interests of Latinas/os with the interest of Whites, we continue to uphold Whiteness and repudiate permanent social transformation for Communities of Color (Alemán & Alemán, 2010). Although the proposed legislation has the potential to succeed, we must remember that this can only be sustained for as long as there is an alignment of interests. Hence, according to the interest convergence framework, once White interests no longer benefit from providing a quality community college education to Latinas/os, the convergence and support will end, placing Latinas/os in a marginal position once again."

The calls with Bates and Dr. Tamez end and the room remains quiet. Del Rio breaks the silence, "I must say, I was feeling really positive about the future of our proposed bill on Latina/o students in California Community Colleges before discussing the long-term repercussions of our strategy. Gaining the support of California to invest in the higher education of Latinas/os is not as easy as we had imagined."

Bustos nods in agreement as she says, "I believe that understanding how Whiteness and White interests function is helpful when thinking of the potential successes of legislation. But maybe using an interest convergence strategy is not the right solution to the substandard education of Latinas/os."

"The discussion of interest convergence has definitely made me realize the importance of understanding systems of power and oppression that continue to shape educational and government institutions when attempting to center the needs of Asian/Pacific Islanders, Blacks, Latinas/os and Native Americans. It has made me question and problematize some of my strategies and reminded me of the three types of reforms[5] discussed by Andre Gorz (1967). In my position, I do not want to engage in a reformist reform that maintains structures of domination. Instead, I strive to practice revolutionary reforms that can lead to a radical transformation of society. But if I am being honest, I'm still considering drafting this bill and strengthening the Latina/o educational pipeline even if its success does not bring forth the radical success we hope for. In many ways, this bill might be better understood as a form of non-reformist reform—a bill that is capable of improving the lives and experiences of Latina/o students with the

---

5. For more information on reformist reform, non-reformist reform, and revolutionary reform please see the Andre Gorz' 1967 citation.

hopes of providing access to a better position to gain more improvements in the future (Gorz, 1967). Until someone can show me a more permanent race-conscious strategy, I'm going to give this a try. Besides, what other options do we have? . . ." Reyes asks as his voice trails off. There was a mood of uncertainty in the room as the meeting ended.

A NOTE ON THE FUTURE OF CALIFORNIA

By incorporating contemporary issues and interest convergence, we have provided a glimpse into the future of California's postsecondary education system. The educational disparities experienced by Latinas/os need to be addressed not only for the welfare of Latinas/os but for other People of Color in the state of California and United States (Ladson-Billings, 2009). Embedded in our counterstory are implications for the improvement of California Community College's degree attainment and transfer outcomes for Latina/o students as well as the economic and political interests of those in power. While strategies targeting the role of the California State Legislature are offered as one method of investing in the education of Latinas/os, we have also highlighted some of the nuances in applying interest convergence as a political strategy. Some limitations include the reproduction of racial hierarchies given the institutional nature of race and racism and the prioritization of White interests. Though engaging in an interest convergence political strategy can lead to temporary and incremental gains such as improved outcomes for Latina/o community college students, this method does not challenge systematic racism (Alemán & Alemán, 2010). As long as power differences exist between Whites and People of Color, the alignment of interests will continue to reinforce White supremacy and further oppress marginalized communities seeking transformation. Yet Reyes ends the counterstory with a question that deserves our attention: what strategies do we have when attempting to garner the support of state and government officials for the advancement of the Latina/o community, while simultaneously centering the role of race and racism in our nation? While we cannot provide all the answers, one method of doing this is by continuing to examine the endemic role of race and racism in all facets of society and the impact this has on People of Color. Hence, understanding how White interests are privileged in the California State Legislature and Department of Education can help us further problematize our education system.

Although this article centered the education of Latina/o community college students in California, a lot remains unexamined. All segments of the P-22 pipeline deserve the attention of stakeholders in order to facilitate the academic attainment of Latina/o students throughout the educational segments. In P-12 for example, scholarship examining the role of White interests in the limited college-ready curricula available for Students of Color could further dismantle the racially biased practices found within schools. Similarly, while we discussed in depth the important role of community colleges in serving their large Latina/o student body, the postsecondary education of Latinas/os should not be relegated solely to this sector of higher education. Instead, four-year colleges and universities together with K-12 need to implement strategies that can enhance the high school to four-year colleges and universities pipeline for Latinas/os across the nation.

Paying particular attention to the growing Latina/o demographics, this article focused on the important role of California Community Colleges in enhancing the degree attainment and transfer outcomes of Latina/o community college students. Using the California State Legislature as a platform, the counterstory challenges the educational disparities present for Latina/o students. Incorporating interest convergence allowed for a discussion on White interests and the complexities of using the former as a strategic political tool that, while having the potential for success, does not reject the dominant discourse of Latinas/os and education. With the assistance of Bates, Bustos, Del Rio, Reyes, and Tamez the counterstory was able to demonstrate the nuances of interest convergence when used as a political strategy instead of as an analytical or explanatory tool as first introduced by Bell (1980). In sharing our counterstory, we have attempted to answer Delgado's (2004) call for a more complex discussion on the applicability of interest convergence in diverse areas beyond the Black-White binary of race and racism.

REFERENCES

Adelman, L. (Producer). (2008). *Unnatural causes: Is inequality making us sick?* [documentary]. California Newsreel.

Aguirre, A. (2010). Diversity as interest-convergence in academia: A critical race theory story. *Social Identities, 16*(6): 763–774.

Alemán Jr., E., & Alemán, S. M. (2010). "Do Latin@ interests always have to 'converge' with white interests?": (Re)claiming racial realism and interest convergence in critical race theory praxis. *Race Ethnicity and Education, 13*(1): 1–21.

Bell Jr., D. (1980). Brown v. Board of Education and the interest-convergence dilemma. *Harvard Law Review, 93*, 518–533.

Bell Jr., D. (1992). *Faces at the bottom of the well: The permanence of racism*. New York, NY: Basic Books.

Berestein Rojas, L. (2015). Incoming Speaker Rendon wants to bridge east, west on environment concerns. [Southern California Public Radio]. Retrieved from http://www.scpr .org/news/2015/10/20/55127/incoming-calif-assembly-speaker-anthony-rendon-see /Brown v. Board, 347 U.S. 483 (1954)

California Community Colleges Chancellor's Office. (2017). Annual/term student count report. Retrieved from http://datamart.cccco.edu/Students/Student_Term _Annual_Count.aspx

California Department of Education. (2015). Data reporting office, statewide enrollment by ethnicity 2014. Retrieved from https://www.ed-data.k12.ca.us/App_Resx /EdDataClassic/fsTwoPanel.aspx?#!bottom=/_layouts/EdDataClassic/profile.asp ?Tab=1&level=04&reportNumber=16

California Senate Office of Research. (2014). A statistical picture of Latinos in California: Demographic, income, education, health and other social characteristics. Retrieved from http://latinocaucus.legislature.ca.gov/sites/latinocaucus.legislature .ca.gov/files/LatinosInCA.pdf

Castagno, A. E., & Lee, S. J. (2007). Native mascots and ethnic fraud in higher education: Using tribal critical race theory and the interest convergence principle as an analytic tool. *Equity & Excellence in Education, 40*(1): 3–13.

Chapa, J., & Schink, W. (2006). California community colleges: Help or hindrance to Latinos in the higher education pipeline? *New Directions for Community Colleges, 2006*(133): 41–50.

Cohn, D. (2014). Are minority births the majority yet? Retrieved from http://www .pewresearch.org/fact-tank/2014/06/04/are-minority-births-the-majority-yet/

Datnow, A., & Solórzano. D. G. (2012). Low-income youth, access to education. In J. A. Banks (Ed.), *Encyclopedia of Diversity in Education* (pp. 1420–1423). Thousand Oaks, CA: Sage Publications.

Delgado Bernal, D. (1998). Using a Chicana feminist epistemology in educational research. *Harvard Educational Review, 68*(4): 555–583.

Delgado Bernal, D. (2001). Learning and living pedagogies of the home: The mestiza consciousness of Chicana students. *International Journal of Qualitative Studies in Education, 14*(5): 623–639.

Delgado Bernal, D. (2002). Critical race theory, Latino critical theory, and critical raced-gendered epistemologies: Recognizing students of color as holders and creators of knowledge. *Qualitative Inquiry, 8*(1), 105–126.

Delgado, R., & Stefancic, J. (2012). *Critical race theory: An introduction.* 2nd ed. New York: NYU Press.

Delgado, R. (2004). Locating Latinos in the field of civil rights: Assessing the neoliberal case for radical exclusion. *Texas Law Review, 83*, 489–524.

Delgado, R. (2009). Liberal McCarthyism and the origins of critical race theory. *Iowa Law Review, 94*, 1505–1545.

Fry, R., & Lopez, M. H. (2012). Hispanic student enrollments reach new highs in 2011. *PEW Research Center*. Retrieved from http://www.pewhispanic.org/2012/08/20/hispanic-student-enrollments-reach-new-highs-in-2011/

Gillborn, D. (2009). Risk-free racism: Whiteness and so-called "free speech." *Wake Forest Law Review, 44*, 535–555.

Gómez, L. E. (2007). *Manifest destinies: The making of the Mexican American race.* New York: NYU Press.

Gorz, A. (1967). *Strategies for labor: A radical proposal.* New York: Beacon Press.

Harper, S. R. (2009). Race, interest convergence, and transfer outcomes for black male student athletes. *New Directions for Community Colleges, 147*, 29–37.

Hayes-Bautista, D. E., Schink, W. O., & Chapa, J. (1988). *The burden of support: Young Latinos in an aging society.* Palo Alto, CA: Stanford University Press.

Howard, T. C. (2003). Culturally relevant pedagogy: Ingredients for critical teacher reflection. *Theory into Practice, 42*(3), 195–202.

Johnson, H., & Sengupta, R. (2009). Closing the gap: Meeting California's need for college graduates. *Public Policy Institute of California*. Retrieved from http://www.ppic.org/main/publication.asp?i=835

Krogstad, J. M., & Lopez, M. H. (2015). Hispanic population reaches record 55 million, but growth has cooled. *Pew Research Center*. Retrieved from http://www.pewresearch.org/fact-tank/2015/06/25/u-s-hispanic-population-growth-surge-cools/

Krogstad, J. M., & Fry, R. (2015). Hispanics to benefit from Obama's community college plan. *Pew Research Center*. Retrieved from http://www.pewresearch.org/fact-tank/2015/01/20/hispanics-to-benefit-from-obamas-community-college-plan/

Ladson-Billings, G. (2009). Education for everyday people: Obstacles and opportunities facing the Obama administration. *Harvard Educational Review, 79*(2), 345–359.

Lipsitz, G. (2011). *How racism takes place.* Philadelphia, PA: Temple University Press.

Lopez, M. H. (2014). In 2014, Latinos will surpass whites as largest racial/ethnic group in California. *Pew Research Center*. Retrieved from http://www.pewresearch.org/fact-tank/2014/01/24/in-2014-latinos-will-surpass-whites-as-largest-racialethnic-group-in-california/

Martinez, G. A. (2012). Arizona, immigration, and Latinos: The epistemology of whiteness, the geography of race, interest convergence, and the view from the perspective of critical theory. *Arizona State Law Journal, 44*, 175–211.

Milner IV, H., Alvin Pearman III, R. A., & McGee, E. O. (2013). Critical race theory, interest convergence, and teacher education. In M. Lynn & A. Dixson (Eds.), *Handbook of critical race theory in education* (pp. 339–354). NY: Routledge.

Moore, C., & Shulock, N. (2010). *Divided we fail: Improving completion and closing racial gaps in California's community colleges.* Sacramento, CA: Institute for Higher Education Leadership & Policy.

Orfield, G., & Ee, J. (2014). *Segregating California's future: Inequality and its alternative 60 years after* Brown v. Board of Education. Los Angeles, CA: The Civil Rights Project/Proyecto Derechos Civiles.

Ornelas, A., & Solórzano, D. G. (2004). Transfer conditions of Latina/o community college students: A single institution case study. *Community College Journal of Research and Practice, 28*(3), 233–248.

Pérez Huber, L., Pulido Villanueva, B., Guarneros, N., Velez, V. N., & Solórzano, D. G. (2014). DACAmented in California: The impact of the Deferred Action for Childhood Arrivals Program on Latinas/os. *UCLA Chicano Studies Research Center, 18.* Retrieved from https://chicano.ucla.edu/files/RR18.pdf

Rivas, M. A., Pérez, J., Alvarez, C. R., Solórzano, D. G. (2007). An examination of Latina/o transfer students in California's postsecondary institutions. Latino Policy & Issues Brief. Number 16. *UCLA Chicano Studies Research Center.* Retrieved from https://www.chicano.ucla.edu/files/LPIB_16.pdf

Social Security Administration. (2015). Beneficiary data: Number of Social Security recipients. Retrieved from https://www.ssa.gov/cgi-bin/currentpay.cgi

Social Security History. (2015). Ratio of Social Security covered workers to beneficiaries calendar years 1940–2013. Retrieved from https://www.ssa.gov/history/ratios

Social Security Research Statistics & Policy Analysis. (2010). Fast facts & figures about Social Security, 2010. Retrieved from https://ssa.gov/policy/docs/chartbooks/fast_facts/2010/index.html

Solórzano, D., Acevedo-Gil, N., & Santos, R. (2013). Latina/o community college students: Understanding the barriers of developmental education. *Policy Report, 10,* 1–8.

Solórzano, D. G., & Yosso, T. J. (2002). Critical race methodology: Counter-storytelling as an analytical framework for education research. *Qualitative Inquiry, 8*(1): 23–44.

Solórzano, D., Datnow, A., Park, V., & Watford, T. (2013). *Pathways to postsecondary success: Maximizing opportunities for youth in poverty.* Los Angeles, CA: UC /ACCORD.

State of California. (2007). Race/ethnic population estimates, 1970–90. California Department of Finance. Retrieved from http://www.dof.ca.gov/research/demographic/reports/estimates/race-ethnic_1970-90/

U.S. Census Bureau. (2017). Annual estimates of the resident population by sex, race, and Hispanic origin for the United States, States, and Counties: April 1, 2010 to July 1, 2015. Retrieved from https://factfinder.census.gov/faces/tableservices/jsf/pages/productview.xhtml?src=bkmk

U.S. Census Bureau. (2017b). Sex by educational attainment for the population 25 years and over. Retrieved from https://factfinder.census.gov/faces/tableservices/jsf/pages/productview.xhtml?src=bkmk

U.S. Census Bureau, Educational Attainment. (2014). Educational attainment in the United States: 2014—Detailed tables. Retrieved from http://www.census.gov/hhes/socdemo/education/data/cps/2014/tables.html

Yosso, T. J., & Solórzano, D. G. (2006). Leaks in the Chicana and Chicano educational pipeline. Latino Policy & Issues Brief. Number 13. *UCLA Chicano Studies Research Center (NJ1).*

Yosso, T. J., & Solórzano, D. (2005). Conceptualizing a critical race theory in sociology. In M. Romero & E. Margolis (Eds.), *The Blackwell companion to social inequalities* (pp. 117–146). Oxford, UK: Blackwell Publishing.

Yosso, T. J. (2005). Whose culture has capital? A critical race theory discussion of community cultural wealth. *Race Ethnicity and Education, 8*(1): 69–91.

Latino Students in Higher Education

IDENTIFYING CRITICAL ISSUES AND NEW POSSIBILITIES AT A MULTIETHNIC TEACHING INSTITUTION

Belinda I. Reyes and Umadevi Senguttuvan

The past decades have seen a dramatic improvement in Latinos' educational attainment: college enrollment rates are increasing and high school dropout rates are declining (Lopez & Fry, 2013). Since 2010 Latinos have become the largest group of nonwhite students in the U.S. postsecondary educational system (Fry, 2011) and in 2012 Latino high school graduates were enrolling in college at higher rates than whites (Lopez & Fry, 2013). But they still experience a significant gap in college degree attainment—more than twice as many white students who enrolled at a four-year institution earned a degree compared to Latino students (Swail, Cabrera, & Lee, 2004).

As the Latino population grows in the U.S., more universities are becoming Hispanic-Serving Institutions (HSIs), but this has not necessarily led to significant improvements in college completion. In fact, graduation rates for Latino in four-year HSIs lag behind those of Latinos at four-year non-HSIs (Malcom, 2012). On average HSIs are less selective, less expensive, and have more students in financial aid than non-HSIs. Moreover, HSIs lack a guiding framework for engaging Latino students beyond enrollment, and there is no follow-up mechanism to report how successful campuses were at meeting Latino student needs.

The systems of public higher education in California, where we conducted our analysis, have launched initiatives to improve outcomes and close the opportunity gap, but results have been mixed. For example, the Graduation Initiative of the California State University System (CSU) is on the cusp of completing its sixth and final year. While the CSU is optimistic about achieving the overall six-year graduation rate goal—to raise overall graduation rate to 54%—no progress toward its goal of closing the achievement gap was made.[1] Without institution-wide engagement and evaluation of the barriers to Latino student persistence, it is unlikely that equitable academic outcomes for this critical population will be achieved.

The Cesar E. Chavez Institute (CCI) established the Latino Educational Achievement Partnership (LEAP) to assist institutions in going beyond enrolling Latinos. The goal is to enable institutions to become "equity minded"[2] by providing tools for evaluating institutional barriers to Latino success. We are interested in examining the institutions' role in student success, beyond their structural characteristics (e.g., size, HSI status). LEAP involves postsecondary institutions in research and dialogue to yield institutional change that better serves Latino students. The first phase of the work involves analyses of student experiences on campus. For this we conduct student surveys and focus groups with students, faculty, and staff as well as key informant interviews with university administrators.

The second phase of the project will engage the campus in a structured consultation process supported by rigorous research to expand the campus understanding of Latino students' experiences. Using a Participatory Action Research approach, we will engage in a community-wide consultation process to generate a concrete plan for addressing barriers to Latino students' educational success. In this article we summarize the preliminary analysis from our student survey to illustrate an assessment approach to improve Latino students' outcomes.

THEORY AND EVIDENCE

Early research perceived student persistence as a product of student attributes, skills, and pull factors (Tinto, 2006a). For example, Tinto theorizes that students who socially and academically integrate into the campus increase their commitment to the institution and are more likely to graduate (Tinto, 1975). Studies over the past decade continue to draw from the integration theory as the foundation for a student-centered model in which student outcomes are viewed as a product of student attributes and engagement. The exclusive focus on students is detrimental, as it places the responsibility for academic success entirely on the students and tends to ignore the role of the institutions. Furthermore, it enforces a deficit view

1. Review Access to Excellence Progress Report available at: http://www.calstate.edu/access-toexcellence/documents/A2E-2011-13-Progress-Report-May2014.pdf

2. For an analysis of how to make campuses more equity minded, see Estela Bensimon and Malcom (2012).

of students of color, who may be underprepared for college compared to their white counterparts (Contreras, 2011).

Institutional policies and practices have the power to affect student academic and social engagement (Bensimon, 2005). Research indicates that institutional practices are particularly important for students of color, who often lack the financial, social, and cultural resources that allow them to integrate easily into the campus (Nora & Crisp, 2009; Tierney, 1999). In particular, Latino students who are the first in their families to go to college may lack the "know-how" in navigating an unfamiliar bureaucratic, social, and cultural system (Gonzalez, 2002; Karp, 2011; Yosso, 2006) that is critical for academic success (McDonough, 1997).

Nora (2003) found that student characteristics interact with institutional factors to determine student outcomes. It is important to understand how different types of students (e.g., Latino freshmen vs. seniors) experience their learning environment and face unique challenges, as well as to identify institutional practices that perpetuate unequal or poor outcomes for different students. This understanding is critical to designing interventions for academic success. While programs currently exist to improve student outcomes, often these programs are not integrated into the academic life of the campus, and they may be poorly funded. When it comes to student retention efforts, faculty are largely absent, and most do not see student retention as their job (Tinto, 2006b). Below we examine some critical programs and practices that influence Latino student outcomes.

Student Services, High-Impact Practices, and Developmental Programs

Being successful in postsecondary education requires more than the ability to satisfactorily complete college-level courses. Many students, especially Latino college students who are the first in their families to go to college, they need to learn to navigate a new bureaucratic, social, and cultural system (Karp, 2011). They need academic and nonacademic support to succeed in college (Karp, 2011).

Latinos attend K-12 schools that have fewer resources to promote college enrollment than do other students (Perna & Titus, 2005; Wolniak & Engberg, 2010). They often have insufficient access to college preparatory courses, and many score low on standardized tests and high school exit exams (Contreras, 2011; Gandara & Contreras, 2009; Hernandez & Lopez, 2004; Justiz & Rendong, 1989). Meanwhile, we are requiring of this generation more college preparatory and advanced courses than any previous generation in U.S. history (Zusman, 2005). Students with low levels of college preparation are required to take developmental or remedial courses in college. Developmental courses have been found to have a positive effect on student preparation and some have found a positive impact on student persistence towards graduation (Bettinger & Long, 2009; Boatman & Long, 2010), while others find the opposite effect (Martorell & McFarlin, 2011). For some students, remedial courses become a dead-end in their education (Scott-Clayton & Rodriguez, 2012). Not surprisingly, studies have shown that the more remediation students are required to take, the harder it is for them to complete their college education (Charles A. Dana Center et al., 2012).

A set of programs have been identified as high impact practices because they offer students opportunities to enhance their basic skills, activities to acclimate students to the university, and a space for high levels of peer inter-action and faculty student engagement in and outside the classroom (Schnell & Doekott, 2002; Schrader & Brown, 2008). They provide engaged learning experiences to students—e.g., first-year seminars, learning communities, collaborative assignments, writing intensive courses, conducting research with faculty members, internships, capstone courses, study abroad, and community service learning (Kuh, 2008). While high-impact activities help all students, their positive effect is even more pronounced for underserved students. Kuh's (2008) study analyzing large datasets of the National Survey of Student Engagement (NSSE) found that Latino students who engage in high-impact practices experience greater gains in their first-year GPA and a higher probability of retention than do white students. However, on almost all campuses, the use of high-impact practices is unsystematic, to the detriment of student learning.

Campus Climate

Some scholars challenge the integration model's assumption that success depends on students assimilating to the dominant culture on campus (Bensimon & Malcom, 2012; Hurtado & Carter, 1997; Rendón, Jalomo, & Nora, 2000; Tierney, 1999). Students may find it difficult to integrate academically and socially if they feel like outsiders (Hernandez & Lopez, 2004; Murguia, Padilla, & Pavel, 1991). For many Latino students, their collective, respectful, and relational cultural values are in conflict with the individualistic, homogenizing, and competitive approach in higher education (Gonzalez, 2002; Yosso, 2006). The level of racial discrimination they experience also influences students' experience of the campus. Experiencing overt discrimination or covert microaggressions, which involve "incessant, subtle, yet stunning racial assaults" (Yosso, Smith, Ceja, & Solorzano, 2009, p. 660), from faculty, staff, or other students decrease students' adjustment on campus and their academic outcomes (Hurtado & Ponjuan, 2005).

A hostile campus climate can be psychologically harmful as they often lead students to question whether others perceive the student as having the intellectual and academic capacities to be successful in university and whether she or he belongs in college. These feelings of inadequacy are likely to make students feel isolated from their academic environment, affecting their confidence and sense of belonging (Gurin, Dey, Hurtado, & Gurin, 2002; Hurtado & Ponjuan, 2005; Nuñez, 2009, 2011; Nuñez, et al., 2013; Solorzano & Villalpando, 1998; Yosso et al., 2009). Numerous studies on negative campus environments, such as experiences of discrimination and microaggressions, have shown these circumstances to affect self-image and self-confidence of students of color negatively, which often leads them to drop out (Hurtado & Carter, 1997; Massey, Charles, Lundy, & Fischer, 2003; Nora & Cabrera, 1996; Yosso et al, 2009).

Validation, mentoring, and affirmation. Rendón (1994) argues that before students can engage with and integrate into the campus, they need to feel validated. Rendón and Munoz (2011, p.12) define validation as the "intentional, proactive affirmation of students by in- and out-of-class agents (i.e., faculty, students, and academic affairs staff, family members, and peers) in order to 1) validate students as a generator of knowledge and as a valued member of the college learning community and 2) foster personal development and social adjustment." Students need to develop a strong academic self-concept, but they also need to feel that their experience, culture, and community matter. Quevedo-Garcia (1987) suggested that a major developmental challenge for Latino college students is the conflict resulting from the need to establish their personal identity within the framework of their ethnic heritage as well as within the more dominant American culture. Affirming students as knowledgeable and valued provides students with a sense of self-worth that helps them succeed (Pérez & Ceja, 2010). Nora (1987, 1990) emphasized the importance of support and encouragement, and Nora and colleagues (1996, 2011) demonstrated the critical role of affirmation for Latino students. For example, studies have shown that interventions such as nonacademic support and formal mentoring experiences with role models correlate positively with sense of belonging and persistence for Latino students (Arana, Castañeda-Sound, Blanchard, & Aguilar., 2011; Arellano & Padilla, 1996; Bordes, Sand, Arredondo, Robinson-

Kurpius, & Rayle, 2006; Fisher, 2007). Mentoring has also been found to be critical to validating students' culture and identity (Barnett, 2011; Bragg, 2001; Crisp 2009, 2010; Nora & Crisp, 2009). Moreover, a curriculum that values student experiences, such as ethnic studies courses, fosters a sense of belonging and validation (Jehangir, 2009). Family members, staff, peers, and particularly faculty are important in shaping students' confidence and validation within the campus environment (Bragg, 2001; Oseguera, Locks, & Vega, 2009). There are, however, few quantitative studies of validation, and much of the quantitative research has been conducted at community colleges. There is also a need in the literature to examine the construct of validation by identifying particular indicators to capture the concept (Nora et al., 2011).

Course Availability and Enrollment

Course availability, campus policies about registration, and impactions[3] can make it hard for students to get into classes and complete their degree. A consequence of budget cuts and reductions in hiring, the dwindling availability of courses is a serious problem (Bohn, Reyes, & Johnson, 2013). New student enrollment continues to increase, but faculty hiring has not kept pace (Lambert & Reese, 2015). This has resulted in significant competition for fewer classes offered; increased student-teacher ratios; unpredictable schedules; and increases in the number of efforts by faculty to designate the majors in their departments as impacted so as to restrict the number of students who can enroll in their course offerings.

In this article we examine the experience of Latino students at a diverse four-year public teaching institution in California with high proportions of Latino students (25%). As higher learning institutions become more diverse it is critical to examine the experiences of students of color at diverse institutions. We critically examine student characteristics, institutional factors, and student outcomes to determine barriers to Latino students' success. The following key questions guide our research:

---

3. *Campus impaction* (otherwise known as campus-wide impaction) means that a campus has exhausted existing enrollment capacity in terms of the instructional resources and physical capacity of the campus. Because the campus receives more eligible applicants during the initial admission application filing period than can be accommodated, the campus must therefore restrict enrollment at the campus for a specific enrollment category (e.g., first-time freshmen or transfers). *Major impaction* means that the number of applications from fully eligible students to a designated major during the initial filing period far exceeds the number of spaces available in that major. The majors then impose additional requirements for admission.

1. What is the experience of Latinos on campus?
2. What institutional factors are associated with Latino students' academic performance?

DATA AND METHODOLOGY

Between March and May 2014, undergraduate students older than 18 received an email invitation to participate in the Student Life Survey. A 13% response rate resulted in a sample of 2,921 survey participants. Latinos comprised 29% of the respondents, whites 25%, Asians 27.5%, and other races and ethnicities made up 18%[4]. Fifty-seven percent of the students were first-time freshman and 43% were transfer students. The majority of the students (89%) were full-time students. The survey collected data on students' background characteristics, high school preparation, academic efficacy and attitudes, college affordability, use of campus programs and resources, levels of mentoring and support, struggles confronted accessing courses, perceptions of prejudice and discrimination on campus, and overall perception of bias and equity in the treatment of members of diverse groups on campus. We linked responses from the survey to academic records and obtained information on all courses taken by the participants up until the survey and a year after the survey. We used the data to examine students' course completion patterns, GPAs, and progress towards graduation.

To examine the experience of Latino students on the campus, we examined the frequencies of Latino students' survey responses (e.g., participation in social activities on campus) and academic data (e.g., milestones[5]). We also compared them to white and Asian students using a series of analysis of variance with Tukey follow-up tests for continuous data and chi-square tests for categorical data. Moreover, we examined students' cumulative GPAs at the time of survey using multiple regression analyses to determine how institutional factors are associated with students' academic

---

4. The ethnic makeup of the campus in the year of survey was 27% Latino, 27% white, 33% Asian, and 13% Other. Unfortunately, the sample of African Americans was too small to generate significant results. For that reason we had to include African Americans in the "Other" category. They are, however, the largest group of students in "Other."

5. First-time freshmen students were considered as successfully meeting their first-year milestone if they met all three criteria: (a) completed at least 24 units by the end of their first year, (b) maintained a GPA of 2.0 or above, and (c) satisfied their English and math remediation requirement (either did not need remediation or needed and completed remediation) by the end of their first year. Their second-year milestone included (a) completing at least 48 units by the end of their second year, (b) maintaining a GPA of 2.0 or above, and (c) a successful declaration of major.

performance. We empirically tested the role of academic support, high-impact practices, campus climate, and student validation on students' academic performance, while controlling for pre-college characteristics and pull factors.[6]

EXAMINING LATINO STUDENT EXPERIENCE

In general, Latinos differ from traditional college students. We attempt to understand their characteristics to design programs that meet their needs and build on their assets and skills.

As shown in Table 1, Latino students did not significantly differ from white students in their high school GPAs; however, they had significantly lower high school GPAs than Asian students ($F(2, 1382) = 6.21, p < .01$). Latino students differed from white students in other characteristics, such as parental education and pull factors such as off campus work and helping family. Latino undergraduates on our campus had the highest proportion of mothers without college experience of all racial and ethnic groups on campus—70% of the mothers of Latino undergraduates had no college education and 31% had less than a high school education. Furthermore, over half of Latinos were the first in their families to go to college, as compared to one in four African Americans, one in three Asians, and one in ten white non-Hispanics (χ^2 (3, N = 2384) = 296.09, $p < .001$).

Of the survey respondents, 44% of Latino freshmen were living at home while going to college and fewer than 40% reported living in campus resident halls. In contrast, 12% of White non-Hispanic freshmen reported living at home, and 70% were living on-campus (χ^2 (2, N = 411) = 63.45, $p < 0.001$). In some households, Latino males are expected to work and help support the family (Sáenz & Ponjuan, 2009). The results of our survey found that one in four Latino freshmen help support their families—50% of Latino male freshmen, as compared to 8% of white freshmen (χ^2 (2, N = 93) = 11.39, $p < 0.01$).

More than a third of Latino freshmen were working, and of those who worked 75% worked more than eight hours per week. Latino sophomores worked even more than freshmen. A majority of Latino sophomores worked, and 85% worked more than eight hours per week. To accommodate this work schedule, usually students enroll in college part-time. However, in the campus under analysis, most Latinos were enrolled full-time. Moreover,

---

6. We controlled for gender, whether the student is the first in the family to go to college, whether they applied for financial aid, whether they live on campus, and hours worked outside the campus. We also controlled for the students' high school GPA.

TABLE 1. Background characteristics

	ASIAN	LATINO	WHITE
Mean High School GPA	3.28	3.19	3.23
Mother's education			
BA or more	38%	16%	50%
Less than a high school education	16%	31%	-
First in their family to go to college	35%	51%	10%
Living Arrangements			
% of students who live on campus			
Freshmen	26%	39%	70%
Sophomores	10%	27%	43%
Juniors	7%	9%	17%
% of students living at home with parents			
Freshmen	63%	44%	12%
Sophomores	59%	33%	6%
Juniors	55%	39%	23%
Work and Family Responsibilities			
% of students who help support their family			
Freshmen	20%	24%	8%
Sophomores	21%	18%	12%
Juniors	30%	28%	17%
Work outside the campus			
Freshmen	30%	36%	28%
Sophomores	27%	53%	52%
Working more than 8 hours per week			
Freshmen	60%	75%	82%
Sophomores	67%	85%	88%
Enrolled full-time			
First-time freshmen	93%	96%	92%
Transfers	81%	86%	81%
Commuting Time			
More than 30 minutes	42%	44%	32%
More than an hour	14%	18%	12%

Source: Student Life Survey 2014

44% were commuting more than half an hour to campus, and one of every six was commuting more than an hour. This is a challenging scenario, particularly for freshman and sophomores who are still adapting to the campus life.

Student Services, High-Impact Practices, and Developmental Programs

Table 2 shows students' participation in campus academic support services and activities. In general, participants reported low engagement on campus. Students participated the least at athletic events, while more students participated in seminars, conferences, and workshops every semester (27% of Latino students). Close to one in five Latinos participated in cultural (17%) and social (20%) events on campus. Tukey comparisons showed that Latinos and Asians participated significantly more than white students in cultural events ($F(2, 2285) = 9.66$, $p < 0.001$); while Latinos and whites participated more than Asians in social ($F(2, 2276) = 9.54$, $p < 0.001$) and athletic events ($F(2, 2254) = 9.97$, $p < 0.001$).

Among the students interviewed, few participated in high impact practices—among Latinos, only 4% participated in study abroad programs and 9% worked with faculty members on research at least once per semester. Students also failed to seek advice and tutoring even when they felt dissatisfied with their academic performance. Although better than other groups, only one in four Latino students who were dissatisfied with their academic performance met with an academic advisor and half met with a tutor. Latino students (28%) were more engaged in community service learning ($\chi^2 (2, N = 2167) = 17.63$, $p < 0.001$) and learning communities ($\chi^2 (2, N = 2127) = 132.61$, $p < 0.001$) compared to white students.

There are several examples of learning community at the campus under study. These programs work to build students' learning skills, as well as providing nonacademic support to students. In our sample, one of every four Latino students and one of every three African American students participated in learning communities during their first year. Latinos who participated in a learning community had significantly lower academic progress in their first year compared to other students in learning communities—30% met their first-year milestones. Their progress improved significantly by the second year, but they continued to lag behind other students. In the second year, students in other racial/ethnic groups caught up to their counterparts who did not participate in learning communities, but Latinos did not.

Of the first-year Latino students who responded to the Student Life Survey, an overwhelming majority (66%) needed to enroll in remedial

TABLE 2. Students' participation in campus programs, services, and activities

	ASIAN	LATINO	WHITE
Once per semester participated at . . .			
Social events on campus such as dances or gatherings	11%	20%	13%
Cultural events on campus such as concerts, exhibits, or literary events	12%	17%	12%
Athletic games or events	9%	14%	12%
Participated in high impact activities . . .			
Once per semester participate in seminars, conference, workers, films	22%	27%	20%
Once per semester worked with faculty on research	10%	9%	12%
Study Abroad	6%	4%	4%
Community Service Learning	35%	38%	28%
Learning Communities	19%	28%	5%
Membership in Student Organizations			
Student organizations	37%	37%	39%
Fraternity/sorority	7%	7%	7%
Student who feel at least once per semester dissatisfied with their academic performance			
Meet with an academic advisor at least once per semester	37%	43%	41%
Never met with a tutor	57%	51%	66%

Source: Student Life Survey 2014
Contact authors for mean values of participation for the different groups

courses for English, math, or both, as compared to 58% of Asian and 31% of white students (See Table 3).[7] Almost half of Latino freshmen (46%) needed remediation in English; 57% needed remediation in math.

Most students completed their remediation in one year, but the completion rates decreased with increased need for remediation—94% of Latino freshmen who required only English remediation and 85% of those who required remediation only in math completed their remediation in one year. However, close to half (46%) of Latino students who were required to enroll in both English and math remediation were unable to complete both in one

7. At the campus in our study, students take a placement test to determine whether they are academically prepared for postsecondary education. Depending on their score, they are required to take remedial courses that teach students what the campus determines to be the necessary skills to complete the gateway courses in English and math.

TABLE 3. Need for remediation and completion rates— single subject and multiple subjects

	ASIAN	LATINO	WHITE
Freshman Remediation Rate			
English only	26%	9%	2%
Math only	9%	20%	25%
Both	24%	37%	4%
None	42%	34%	69%
Remediation completion rates – Single Subject			
English remediation	79%	94%	100%
Math remediation	78%	85%	73%
Remediation completion rates – Multiple Subjects			
Both Remediations	60%	54%	67%
Only English	27%	23%	33%
Only Math	3%	14%	
Neither	10%	9%	

Source: Student Life Survey 2014 and Student Records Spring 2013

Note: These figures were calculated using student records for the sample of students who responded to our survey. We had students' placement test results and observed course-taking patterns to determine whether a student completed with a grade of C or better in the required remediation series within the first year.

year. If we combine all students who did not complete remediation within one year after entering college, one in five Latino students (20%) were still required to complete English and one in four (26%) still needed to complete math remediation.

Students who need remediation are progressing more slowly toward a degree than their counterparts who do not need this extra coursework. Table 4 shows the completion of first- and second-year milestones for a cross-section of the students in our sample who needed remediation, as compared to students who did not need remediation. Students who needed remediation, particularly students who needed remediation in more than one subject area, were more likely to fall behind than their counterparts. While 80% of Latinos who did not need remediation completed the first-year milestones, only 10% of students who needed remediation in both English and math completed the first-year milestones. They remained behind in the second year as well—37% completed the second year milestones. Fewer than half (48%) completed 48 units two years after entering the campus. For students who needed remediation in only one subject,

TABLE 4. Milestones for Latino students by remediation status

	COMPLETED 1ST YEAR MILESTONES	COMPLETED 2ND YEAR MILESTONES
Single Subject Remediation		
English	45%	71%
Math	29%	52%
Multiple Subjects	10%	37%
No Remediation Needed	80%	69%

Source: Student Life Survey 2014

either math or English, math remediation had a longer-lasting negative effect on course accumulation than English remediation. About half (52%) of students who needed math remediation completed the second-year milestones, compared to 71% of Latino students who needed English remediation only.

Campus Climate

The campus we examined had a very diverse student population, with no majority groups on campus. In our survey, overall students felt that the campus is strongly committed to diversity (80%), two-thirds agree with the statement that the campus "offers students adequate opportunities to learn about other groups and cultures;" and over half of students expressed that their "experience at this campus has improved their ability to interact comfortably with people of other racial/ethnic and cultural groups" (See Table 5). On the average of these items, white students perceived the campus to be slightly more positive than Latino and Asian students ($F(2, 2138) = 8.85$, $p < 0.001$). These results along with their reports of low campus engagement indicate that students recognize opportunities to learn about diversity but seldom take part in activities that contribute to cross-racial and cross-cultural interactions.

Students also reported about their experiences with discrimination and mistreatment by various constituents on campus (See Table 5). Almost one in five students reported witnessing discrimination on campus at least once per year. Far fewer said they experienced discrimination from faculty or staff, but one in six experienced discrimination from other students. On the average discrimination score, Latinos did not differ from whites and Asians, but Asians reported experiencing slightly more discrimination than white students ($F(2, 1934) = 4.48$, $p < 0.01$).

TABLE 5. Campus climate

	ASIAN	LATINO	WHITE
% of students who "agree/strongly agree"			
"The campus is strongly committed to diversity."	80%	80%	83%
"The campus offers students adequate opportunities to learn about other groups and cultures."	66%	70%	71%
"My experience at this campus has improved my ability to interact comfortably with people of other racial/ethnic and cultural groups."	58%	61%	56%
Experiences with discrimination on campus			
Witnessed at least once per year	23%	18%	20%
Mistreated or placed at a disadvantage by a professor	10%	7%	6%
Experienced discrimination yourself from a faculty member at least once per year	8%	7%	6%
Experienced discrimination yourself from staff/personnel at least once per year	7%	5%	5%
Experienced discrimination yourself from a student at least once per year	16%	15%	15%
Procedures to address harassment and discrimination			
The campus has an established procedure	31%	34%	29%
Reported an incident	8%	4%	3%

Source: Student Life Survey 2014

Validation, Mentoring, and Affirmation

The relationships students develop on campus also contribute to student retention. Figure 1 shows student engagement with staff and faculty on campus. Latino students did not significantly differ from white and Asian students ($F(2, 2121) = 0.22$, ns) on average validation score. Half (51%) of Latino students agreed with the statement that a staff member had taken an interest in their professional, academic, and personal development, and 62% of Latinos agreed with the statement that a faculty member had taken an interest in their development. Moreover, 62% of Latino students think that faculty believed in their potential. However, 23% of Latinos who disagreed with the statement that faculty had taken an interest in their development, 10% do not feel that faculty believe in their potential, and 28% neither agree nor disagree. Thus despite reports of high interest among staff and faculty on student development, more time may need to be spent directly with students, and a greater awareness of what students find helpful may be needed. For example, students may not have access to

FIGURE 1. Survey responses to questions about mentors and support

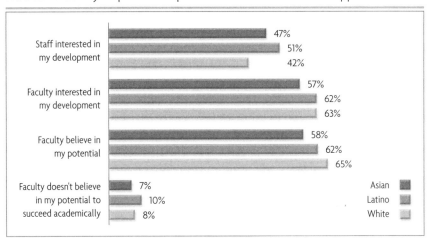

staff and faculty who signal an authentic belief in their potential, because of low numbers of Latinos in these roles on campus.

The growth in the Latino student population has not been matched by a comparable increase in Latino faculty, staff and administrators. Over the five years studied, while the proportion of Latino students grew by 37%, the number of Latino faculty declined on campus. Figure 2 shows the ratio

FIGURE 2. Number of students per tenured/tenure-track faculty of same ethnicity

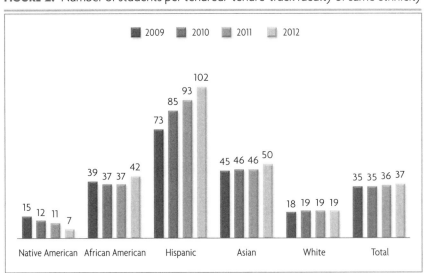

Source: Author calculations from the HR Summary to Dean, 2013

of students to faculty of the same ethnicity. In 2012, there were 102 Latino students for every one Latino tenured or tenure-track faculty member, making Latino faculty the most underrepresented among all ethnic groups in proportion to students of the same ethnicity.

Class availability and enrollment. A significant proportion of students express problems in getting into their selected major on campus because of impaction. All the top six majors preferred by Latino students—criminal justice, sociology, psychology, health education, kinesiology, and biology—are impacted majors. Students are expected to select their major by their sophomore year—36% of Latino sophomores responded that they were unable to get into a major because it was impacted (Table 6). But this is also an issue for freshmen, juniors, and seniors: among Latinos, a third of the freshmen, 28% of the juniors, and 21% of the seniors could not declare their desired major because it was impacted. Latino and Asian students report being impacted more than White students (χ^2 (2, N = 2367) = 32.24, p < 0.001)

In addition to difficulty in gaining access to particular majors, students reported difficulty in gaining access to classes because they were full or canceled. Fifty percent of Latino students reported that at least once per

TABLE 6. Course availability and impaction

	ASIAN	LATINO	WHITE
"Did you want to pursue a particular major, but were not able to because it was impacted?"			
Freshman	31%	33%	22%
Sophomore	46%	36%	36%
Junior	29%	28%	17%
Senior	30%	21%	16%
Percentages of students who reported that at least once per semester . . .			
they had not been able to get into a class in their major/minor because the class was cancelled	34%	32%	28%
Freshmen	46%	35%	35%
Sophomore	63%	64%	62%
Junior	69%	56%	49%
they had not been able to get into a class in their major/minor because the class was full	61%	50%	47%
they were taking classes at a time when campus services were closed	23%	29%	25%

Source: Student Life Survey 2014

semester they could not get into a class in their major or minor because the class was full, and a third could not get into a class because the class was canceled. This becomes even more of an issue for students as they progress in their degree: 35% of Latino freshmen, 64% of Latino sophomores, 56% of Latino juniors, and almost half of Latino seniors reported that at least once per semester they could not enroll in a class because the class was full. Limited class availability and work schedules may be forcing students to take classes at night, when student services are closed; for example, 29% of Latinos take evening classes every semester.

STUDENT OUTCOMES

Student retention and graduation rates have been improving and the gaps in performance between whites and Latinos have been declining over time (Table 7)[8]. For example, in examining one- and two-year continuation rates for first-time freshmen, we observe significant improvements in outcomes, particularly for Latino students. For Chicanas/os and Mexican

TABLE 7. Retention and graduation rates

	ASIAN	CHICANO/ MEXICAN AMERICAN	OTHER LATINO	WHITE
One-year continuation rates				
2007	85%	69%	73%	69%
2012	89%	77%	84%	81%
Two-years continuation rate				
2007	80%	60%	67%	56%
2012	82%	67%	67%	64%
Graduation within 4 years				
2007	10%	10%	10%	16%
2012	16%	15%	16%	23%
Graduation within 6 years				
2007	60%	32%	40%	46%
2012	57%	46%	42%	44%

Source: Author calculations from the Data Book for 2013 and the Graduation Retention Report for FTF 2014.

Note: Continuation rates represent the proportion of a student cohort still enrolled at the same university as undergraduates for a specific year after matriculation.

8. Data was not available for Latinos as a whole, but was disaggregated in two groups. Instead of aggregating the data to match the prior tables, we felt it was important to show the details for the two groups.

Americans, 69% of the 2007 cohort remained for a second year, and this number increased to 77% for the 2012 cohort. For some measures Latinos do better than whites, but gaps are persistent with Asian students.

Even though we see significant improvements, graduation rates are very low at the campus under analysis. Only 15% of Chicano/Mexican Americans and 16% of other Latinos who started on the campus in 2009 graduated in four years. Even the six-year graduation rates are generally low—32% of Chicano/Mexican American and 40% of other Latinos graduated in six years.

Next, multiple linear regression models were estimated to examine students' academic performance. Specifically, we examined the correlation between student performance (i.e., cumulative GPA) and institutional factors (e.g., validation, learning communities) while controlling for student characteristics (e.g., gender, campus engagement). In model 1 we predicted the GPA of the cross-section of first-time freshman students who responded to the survey. In model 2 we examined only students who were in their criti-

TABLE 8. Multiple regression results for first-time freshmen students

	MODEL 1 ALL STUDENTS (n = 1667)	MODEL 2 FIRST YEAR STUDENTS (n = 337)
Intercept	1.76	0.81
Resident Hall	0.07*	0.05
English Remediation Completed	-0.12***	-0.20***
English Remediation Incomplete	-0.24***	-0.88***
Math Remediation Completed	-0.07*	-0.11
Math Remediation Incomplete	-0.22***	-0.41*
Campus Engagement	-0.04*	-0.03
Campus Diversity Policies	-0.04	0.06
Racial Discrimination	-0.09	0.15
Validation/Mentor	0.05**	-0.03
Academic Adviser	0.03**	0.04t
Learning Community	0.02	0.16*
Faculty Research	0.02	0.05t
Ethnic Studies	0.03*	0.06*
R2	0.27	0.34

Note: $^t p < .10.$ $^* p < .05.$ $^{**} p < .01.$ $^{***} p < .001.$
Contact the authors for full model as well as for means and SD of the different variables

cal first year. Results of the multiple regression models predicting GPA are presented in Table 8.

In general, our models revealed remediation to be negatively associated with GPA. Students who were required to complete English and math remediation have a lower GPA compared to students who need no remedial courses. This is true irrespective of whether they completed the remedial courses in their first year or not.

Figure 3 presents the simulations of GPA for the average Latino student on campus.[9] In the first model, we estimated the GPA for a student who did not need remediation at 3.02 at the time of the survey. If she had to complete remediation in math her GPA drops to 2.95, even if she completes it in the first year. If she did not complete it, her GPA drops to 2.8. The same is true for English remediation. But English has an even stronger and persistent effect on GPA than math.

Feeling validated by faculty and staff, having mentors, and meeting with academic advisers were positively associated with GPA in the all-students model (Model 1), whereas participation in a learning community and taking

FIGURE 3. GPA simulation for the average Latino student

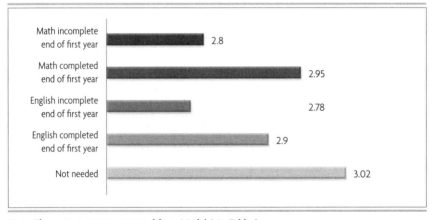

Note: The estimates were generated from Model 1 in Table 8.

---

9. We estimate the cumulative GPA by multiplying the parameter estimates generated from the regression to the average value of that predictor for Latino students. For example, in model 1 the average Latino student on campus had the following characteristics: sophomore, female, a high school GPA of 3.2; registered full-time; first generation college-goer; works more than 8 hours per week off- campus; applied for financial aid; is barely engaged on campus = 2.18 (rarely); perceives positive campus diversity=4.02 (strongly agree); has average contact with mentor=3.42 (neither agree nor disagree) and academic advisors = 3.09 (neither agree nor disagree); did not participate in learning communities; low research with faculty = 1.58 (rarely); and rarely enrolled in ethnic studies courses=2.24.

FIGURE 4. GPA of typical Latino student

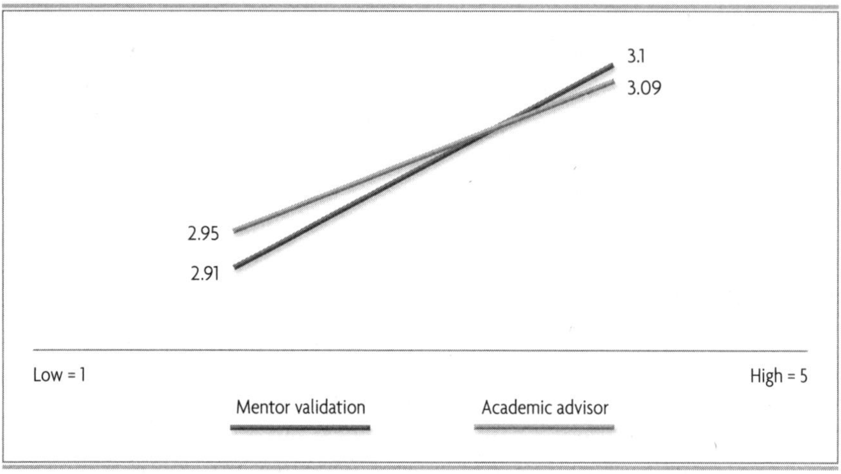

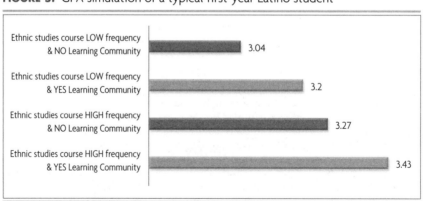

3.1
3.09
2.95
2.91
Low = 1
High = 5
Mentor validation
Academic advisor

Note: The estimates were generated from Model 1 in Table 8.

ethnic studies courses were associated with higher levels of GPA for first-year students (Model 2). Figure 4 represents the change in GPA with change in student's validation (e.g., faculty and/or staff have taken an interest in their development and faculty believe in their potential) and engagement with mentors and academic advisers. It shows a higher GPA as students are engaged in these activities and feel validated on campus. Moreover, Figure 5 shows the positive effect of ethnic studies courses on a student's GPA. For the average Latina in the sample, GPA increases from 3.04 to 3.27 when an ethnic studies course is taken, especially in the first year. For students who

FIGURE 5. GPA simulation of a typical first-year Latino student

Ethnic studies course LOW frequency & NO Learning Community
3.04
Ethnic studies course LOW frequency & YES Learning Community
3.2
Ethnic studies course HIGH frequency & NO Learning Community
3.27
Ethnic studies course HIGH frequency & YES Learning Community
3.43

Note: The estimates were generated from Model 1 in Table 8.

are in a learning community and are exposed to ethnic studies courses, GPA raises to 3.43 at the end of the first year.

SUMMARY AND CONCLUSION

For Latinos, education goes beyond gaining knowledge and individual enrichment. It involves shaping a moral individual engaged with their family and community (Ortiz & Santos, 2009). As such, Latino students differ from other racial/ethnic groups in many ways. The Latino students in our sample face more challenges than other students, among them being first-generation college students, working large numbers of hours off-campus, and helping their families while enrolled in college.

Even though Latino students did not differ from white students in their average high school GPA, more were required to take remedial courses. Our study revealed that remedial courses, at the campus under analysis, are a serious obstacle to academic performance. Remediation was not only associated with low cumulative GPA in our study, but compared to other students, fewer Latino students who took remedial courses completed their first- and second-year milestones. There are some questions about the predictive validity of placement tests and whether students could have passed gateway math and English courses even if they made a low score on the test (Scott-Clayton & Rodriguez, 2012). Although the test is very important for student placement, students are often "unaware of their importance and consequently do not take the time to prepare or apply the necessary focus the exam demands" (Charles A. Dana Center et al., 2012, p. 4). Scholars suggest that campuses use multiple measures to place students in gateway courses and that schools' priority should be to get students into college-level courses. The tests and the courses also focus on a narrow set of skills that may have little relation to the student's preferred area of study. For example, college algebra may not be needed for nursing or photography, while is critical for economics and engineering. Likewise, English writing and reading skills may vary by discipline. Scholars are also testing different approaches to remediation; some promising approaches are integrating remedial instruction within college-level courses, so students are not delayed from starting their area of study (Jenkins & Cho, 2012).

Although the Latino students who responded to this study completed English remediation successfully for the most part, some students may struggle with advanced English courses in the junior or senior year, when courses require a higher level of academic literacy and writing. In a future study we will look at the completion of English requirements to explore the effect of advanced academic literacy on student performance.

Although extant research reveals that engagement on campus improves academic student outcomes (e.g., Tinto 2006a), our study revealed that a very low number of Latinos students (and others) are engaged on campus. More information is necessary to understand the reasons behind this and to improve student engagement in cultural and social activities. Focus group discussions will help with this. Moreover, students are describing serious challenges in accessing courses in their major/minor and are struggling to get into some majors. For Latinos at this campus, the largest Latino majors are affected by these issues. Many students have to take classes at night when student services, advising, and mentoring are generally not available on campus. Thus, reduced class access not only appears to delay time to graduation and adding to students' debt by extending the number of semesters tuition must be paid, but it also limits students' access to campus resources that could improve their academic performance, social support, and financial aid (e.g., tutoring, counseling, and student services).

Our study also showed ethnic studies courses have a positive effect on GPAs, particularly on the critical first year. The effect appears to persist, as seen in our cumulative GPA model of the cross-section of students in our sample. This is an important finding for a multi-ethnic campus, where almost a quarter of students are still witnessing acts of discrimination on campus. Studies show that enrolling in ethnic studies courses can serve as a protective factor enabling students to cope with the college environment and improve their academic outcomes (Harris, 2006; Hernandez, 2000; Laird & Kuh, 2005; McKinney, McKinney, Franiuk, & Schweiter, 2006; Nuñez, 2011).

Our study revealed that having mentors and validating experiences exerts a positive impact on students' academic performance. Individuals who support students, such as role models and mentors, contribute in meaningful ways to Latino students' academic success (Arana et al., 2011; Arellano & Padilla, 1996). Latino students may, however, lack role models of their own ethnicity on campus. Although there is significant diversity in student population on campus, the majority of administrators, staff, and faculty on campus are mostly white. Latinos constitute barely 7% of faculty on campus.

Overall, our results indicate that students exposed to programs that root first-year student experiences using high-impact practices and that encourage mentorship experiences with academic advisers and faculty members do better than students who are not exposed to such programs. To improve Latino student outcomes, campuses should take efforts to understand Latino student experiences on campus; understand and resolve issues related to course accessibility; increase the number of Latino faculty, staff and students on campus, and improve programs that better serve Latino students.

REFERENCES

Arana, R., Castañeda-Sound, C., Blanchard, S., & Aguilar, T. E. (2011). Indicators of persistence for Hispanic undergraduate achievement: Toward an ecological model, *Journal of Hispanic Higher Education, 10*, 237–251.

Arellano, A. R., & Padilla, A. (1996). Academic invulnerability among a select group of Latino university students. *Hispanic Journal of Behavioral Sciences, 18*, 485–507.

Barnett, E. A. (2011). Validation experiences and persistence among community college students. *The Review of Higher Education, 34*, 193–230.

Bensimon, E. M. (2005). *Equality in fact, equality in results: A matter of institutional accountability.* Washington DC: American Council on Education.

Bensimon, E. M., & Malcom, L. (2012). *Confronting equity issues on campus: Implementing the equity scorecard in theory and practices.* Sterling, Virginia: Stylus Printing.

Bettinger, E., & Long, B. T. (2009). Addressing the needs of under-prepared college students: Does college remediation work? *Journal of Human Resources, 44*, 736–771.

Boatman, A., & Long, B. T. (2010). *Does remediation work for all students? How the effects of postsecondary remedial and developmental courses vary by level of academic preparation.* New York: National Center for Postsecondary Research.

Bohn, S., Reyes, B., & Johnson, H. (2013). *The impact of budget cuts on California's community college.* San Francisco: Public Policy Institute of California, March 2013.

Bordes, V., Sand, J. K., Arredondo, P., Robinson-Kurpius, S. E. R., & Rayle, A. D. (2006). Validation of four measures of social support with Latina/o and non-Hispanic White undergraduates. *Hispanic Journal of Behavioral Sciences, 28*, 65–83.

Bragg, D. (2001). Community college access, mission, and outcomes: Considering intriguing intersections and challenges. *Peabody Journal of Education, 76*, 93–116.

Charles A. Dana Center, Complete College American, Inc, Education Commission of the States, and Jobs for the Future (2012). *Core principles for transforming remedial Education: A joint statement.* Retrieved from http://www.completecollege.org/docs/Remediation_Joint_Statement-Embargo.pdf

Contreras, F. (2011). *Achieving equity for Latino students: Expanding the pathway to higher education through public policy.* New York: Teachers College Press.

Crisp, G. (2009). Conceptualization and initial validation of the College Student Mentoring Scale (CSMS). *Journal of College Student Development, 50*, 177–194.

Fisher, M. J. (2007). Settling into campus life: Differences by race/ethnicity in college involvement and outcomes. *Journal of Higher Education, 78*, 125–161.

Fry, R. (2011). *Hispanic enrollment spikes, narrowing gaps with other groups.* Washington, DC: Pew Hispanic Center.

Gándara, P., & Contreras, F. (2009). *The Latino educational crisis.* New York: Teacher College Press.

González, K.P. (2002). Campus culture and the experiences of Chicano students in a predominantly white university. *Journal of College Student Retention: Research, Theory, and Practice, 2*, 69–91.

Gurin, P., Dey, E. L., Hurtado, S., & Gurin, G. (2002). Diversity and higher education: Theory and impact on educational outcomes, *Harvard Educational Review*,
72, 330–366.

Harris, B. A. (2006). The importance of creating a "sense of community." *Journal of
College Student Retention: Research, Theory & Practice, 8,* 83–105.

Hernandez, J. C. (2000). Understanding the retention of Latino college students.
Journal of College Student Development, 41, 575–588.

Hernandez, J., & Lopez, M. (2004). Leaking pipeline: Issues impacting Latino/a college students retention. *Journal of College Student Retention, 6,* 37–60.

Hurtado, S., & Carter, D. F. (1997). Effects of college transition and perceptions of
the campus racial climate on Latino students' sense of belonging. *Sociology of
Education, 70,* 324–345.

Hurtado, S., & Ponjuan, L. (2005). Latino educational outcomes and the campus
climate. *Journal of Hispanic Higher Education, 4,* 235–251.

Jehangir, R. R. (2009). Cultivating voice: First-generation students seek full academic
citizenship in multicultural learning communities. *Innovative Higher Education,
34,* 33–49.

Justiz, M. J., & Rendon, L. I. (1989). Hispanic students. In M. L. Upcraft, J. N. Gard-
ner, & Associates (Eds.), *The freshman year experience: Helping students survive
and succeed in college* (pp. 261–276). San Francisco: Jossey-Bass.

Karp, M. M. (2011). *Toward a new understanding of non-academic student support:
Four mechanisms encouraging positive student outcomes in the community college.*
CCRC Working Paper No. 28. New York: Community College Research Center,
Columbia University.

Kuh, G. (2008). *High-impact educational practices: What they are, who has access to
them and why they matter.* Washington, DC: Association of American Colleges
and Universities.

Laird, T. F., & Kuh, G.D. (2005). Student experiences with information technology
and their relationship to other aspects of student engagement. *Research in Higher
Education, 46,* 211–233.

Lambert, D., & Reese, P. (2015, January 31). CSU using more part-time faculty than
full-time professors. *Sacramento Bee.* Retrieved from http://www.sacbee.com
/news/local/education/article8875895.html

Lopez, M. H., & Fry, R. (2013). Among recent high school grads, Hispanic college
enrollment rate surpasses that of whites. *FACTANK: News in the Numbers.* Retrieved
from   http://www.pewresearch.org/fact-tank/2013/09/04/hispanic-college
-enrollment-rate-surpasses-whites-for-the-first-time/

Malcom-Piqueux, L. E., & Lee, J. M. (2011). *Hispanic serving institutions: Contributions and challenges, college board advocacy & policy center policy brief.* New York:
The College Board.

Martorell, P., & McFarlin, I. (2011). Help or hindrance? The effects of college remediation on academic labor market outcomes. *Review of Economics and Statistics,
2,* 436–454.

Massey, D. S., Charles, C. Z., Lundy, G. F., & Fischer, M. J. (2003). *The source of the river: The social origins of freshman at America's selective colleges and universities.* Princeton, NJ: Princeton University Press.

McDonough, P. M. (1997). *Choosing college: How school and social class structure opportunity.* Albany: State University of New York Press.

McKinney, J. P., McKinney, K. G., Franiuk, R., & Schweiter, J. (2006). The college classroom as a community: Impact on student learning. *College Teaching, 54,* 281–284.

Murguia, E., Padilla, R. V., & Pavel, M. (1991). Ethnicity and the concept of social integration in Tinto's model of institutional departure. *Journal of College Student Development, 32,* 433–439.

Nora, A. (2003). Access to higher education for Hispanic students: Real or illusory? In J. Castellanos & L. Jones (Eds.), *The majority in the minority: Expanding the representation of Latina/o faculty, administrators and students in higher education* (pp. 47–67). Sterling, VA: Stylus Publishing, LLC.

Nora, A. (1990). Campus-based aid programs as determinates of retention among Hispanic community college students. *Journal of Higher Education, 61,* 312–327.

Nora, A. (1987). Determinants of retention among Chicano college students: A structural model. *Research in Higher Education, 26,* 31–59.

Nora, A., & Cabrera, A. F. (1996). The role of perceptions of prejudice and discrimination on the adjustment of minority students to college. *Journal of Higher Education, 67,* 119–148.

Nora, A., & Crisp, G. (2009). Hispanics and higher education: An overview of research, theory and practice. *Higher Education: Handbook of Theory and Research, 24,* 321–324.

Nora, A., Urick, A., & Cerecer, P. D. Q. (2011). Validating students: A conceptualization and overview of its impact on student experiences and outcomes. *Enrollment Management Journal, 5,* 34–52.

Nuñez, A. M. (2011). Counterspaces and connections in college transitions: First-generation Latino students' perspectives on Chicano studies. *Journal of College Student Development, 52,* 639–655.

Nuñez, A. M., Hoover, R. E., Pickett, K., Stuart-Carruthers, A. C., & Vazquez, M. (2013). Latinos in higher education and Hispanic-serving institutions. *ASHE Higher Education Report, 39* (1). Online.

Nuñez, A. M. (2009). Latino students' transitions to college: A social and intercultural capital perspective. *Harvard Educational Review, 79*(1), 22–48.

Ortiz, A.M., & Santos, S. J. (2009). *Ethnicity in college: Advancing theory and improving diversity practices.* Sterling, CA: Stylus.

Oseguera, L., Locks, A. M., & Vega, I. (2009). Increasing Latina/o students' baccalaureate attainment. *Journal of Hispanic Higher Education, 8,* 23–53.

Pérez, P. A., & Ceja, M. (2010). Building a Latina/o student transfer culture: Best practices and outcomes in transfer to universities. *Journal of Hispanic Higher Education, 9,* 6–21.

Perna, L. W., & Titus, M. A. (2005). The relationship between parental involvement as social capital and college enrollment: An examination of racial/ethnic group differences. *Journal of Higher Education, 76*, 486–518.

Pierce, C. (1995). Stress analogs of racism and sexism: Terrorism, torture, and disaster. In Willie, C. Reiker, P., Kramer, B., & Brown, B. (Eds.), *Mental health, racism, and sexism* (pp. 281). Pittsburgh, PA: University of Pittsburgh Press.

Quevedo-García, E. L. (1987). Facilitating the development of Hispanic college students. *New directions for student services, 38*, 49–63.

Rendón, L. I. (1994). Validating culturally diverse students: Toward a new model of learning and student development. *Innovative Higher Education, 19*, 33–51.

Rendón, L. I., Jalomo, R. E., & Nora, A. (2000). Theoretical consideration in the study of minority student retention in higher education. In Braxton, J. M. (Ed.), *Rethinking the departure puzzle: New theory and research on college student retention* (pp. 127–156). Nashville, TN: Vanderbilt University Press.

Rendón, L. I., & Muñoz, S. M. (2011). Revisiting validation theory: Theoretical foundations, applications, and extensions. *Enrollment Management Journal, 2*, 12–33.

Sáenz, V. B., & Ponjuan, L. (2009). The vanishing Latino male in higher education. *Journal of Hispanic Higher Education, 8*, 54–89.

Schnell, C., & Doekott, C. (2002). First year seminars produce long-term impact. *Journal of College Student Retention, 4*, 377–391.

Schrader, P., & Brown, S. (2008). Evaluating the first year experience: Students' knowledge, attitudes, and behaviors. *Journal of Advanced Academics, 19*, 310–343.

Scott, C. J., & Rodriguez, O. (2012). *Development, discouragement, or diversion? New evidence on the effects of college remediation.* NBER Working Paper No. 18328. August, 2012.

Smedley, B. D., Myers, H. F., & Harrell, S. P. (1993). Minority-status stresses and the college adjustment of ethnic minority freshman. *Journal of Higher Education, 64*, 434–452.

Solorzano, D., & Villalpando O. (2005). Educational inequality and Latina/o undergraduate students in higher education. In C. A. Torres & T. R. Mitchell (Eds.), *Sociology of education: Emerging perspectives* (pp. 211–224). Albany, NY: State University of New York Press.

Swail, W., Cabrera, A., & Lee, C. (2004). *Latino youth and the pathway to college.* Pew Hispanic Center Study, Washington, DC. Retrieved from http://www.pewhispanic.org/files/reports/31.pdf

Tierney, W. G. (1999). Models of minority college-going and retention: Cultural integrity versus cultural suicide. *Journal of Negro Education, 68*, 80–91.

Tinto, V. (2006a). Reconstructing the first year of college. *Planning for Higher Education, 25*, 1–6.

Tinto, V. (2006b). Research and practice of student retention: What next? *Journal of College Student Retention: Research, Theory & Practice, 8*, 1–19.

Tinto, V. (1975). Dropout from higher education: A theoretical synthesis of recent literature. *A Review of Educational Research, 45*(1), 89–125.

Wolniak, G. C., & Engberg, M. E. (2010). Academic achievement in the first year of college: Evidence of the pervasive effects of the high school context. *Research in Higher Education, 51*, 451–467.

Yosso, T. J. (2006). *Critical race counter-stories along the Chicana/Chicano educational pipeline.* New York, NY: Routledge.

Yosso, T. J., Smith, W. A., Ceja, M., & Solorzano, D. G. (2009). Critical race theory, racial microaggressions, and campus racial climate for Latina/o undergraduates. *Harvard Educational Review, 79*, 659–691.

Zusman, A. (2005). Challenges facing higher education in the twenty-first century. In P. G. Altbach, R. O. Berdahl, & P. J. Gumports (Eds.), *American higher education in the 21ˢᵗ century: Social, political, and economic challenges* (pp. 115–160). Baltimore: Johns Hopkins University Press.

Recognizing Counter-Stories of First-Generation Latina/o Graduate Students

ADVANCING THE LATINA/O GRADUATE COLLEGE CHOICE PROCESS

Fernando Valle and Cristóbal Salinas Jr.

ABSTRACT

This study focuses on the advancement of first-generation Latina/o graduate students and argues for inclusion in graduate college choice models to improve access, retention, and completion along the Latina/o educational pipeline. This qualitative study positions counter-stories of first-generation graduate students at the heart of the graduate choice process and models to reframe the master narrative of graduate education. Reviewing the college choice process from undergraduate Latina/o students and Latina/o graduate along with Latina/o critical theories frame the actualities of the graduate college choice experience. The authors center their own involvement in the graduate college choice process and the critical role regional institutions serve to foster graduate school knowledge as forms of capital for Latina/o graduate students. Participants include first-generation graduate Latina/o students and address family, work, graduate school fears, finance and career concerns. Data analysis provides insights, lessons, and recommendations for regional institutions, including Hispanic-Serving Institutions. Elvia Ramirez (2013) argues Latina/os' path to graduate school is imperative and especially critical to investigate in light of the social and political import of graduate education.

> A new #DoctoraLatina moment: I received a text from a former student yesterday letting me know that her Masters in Social Work program has officially begun today. In her text she thanked me for pushing her to dream a bigger dream for herself and ultimately her community. This chart was shown to me when I was accepted into three doctoral programs and was told how special

I am because I had the audacity to even apply to these programs as a Latina student. At first I felt wrong in believing that there was something "special" to advancing further into my education. But I became aware of all the obstacles that were in my path and remembered that higher education was not built for people like me—but that people like me are now responsible to reshape higher education for those that follow. Today I remind all students I encounter that they are special. They don't believe me until I show them this chart (Latina/o Pipeline). I say the following: You are special. You are magic. Go get that degree and figure out a way to leave this world better than you found it. And I am happy and proud to say that my students are doing just that . . .

Blanca E. Vega, EdD, August 28, 2015

INTRODUCTION

Educational reform and (mis)leadership in the United States is an ongoing agenda (Brooks, 2012). In 2009, President Obama set forth the U.S. postsecondary education completion agenda: to have the highest proportion of college graduates in the world by 2020. Latina/o population demographics are rapidly increasing inside and outside the classroom; and it is evident that Latina/o students' success in postsecondary education will be significant to meet the agenda goals. To support this postsecondary education completion agenda we must critically analyze access, retention, and completion of first-generation Latina/o students' experiences in postsecondary education.

In this article, we advance the *platica* (conversation) about reframing and improving access, retention, and completion for Latina/o students in graduate education. We expand on the importance of creating opportunities for first-generation Latina/o students to earn a master's, doctoral, or professional degree. Inspired by critical scholarship, we incorporate counter-narratives as rich counter-stories to structure the article through the amalgamation of first-generation graduate students entering, navigating, and persisting in the formal setting that is graduate school. At the heart of this counter-storytelling is the lived experiences of first-generation Latina/os fielding the graduate choice processes and reframing a master narrative of graduate education. Transmitting experiences of first-generation Latina/o graduate students and their college choice processes through counter-narratives and critical lenses allows us to avoid deficit narratives that blame this growing demographic. Instead, we agree with scholars (Hurtado & Carter, 1997; Irizarry, 2009; Nora, 2003; Rendón, 1994) that omit the narrative of blame and build a newer narrative suggesting Latina/o first-generation college students have the potential to achieve parity with other groups in terms of educational attainment, given the appropriate support.

LATINA/OS ON THE MOVE

The 2010 U.S. Census (2010) reported that Latinas/os made up 16% of the U.S. population, representing 50.5 million Latinas/os. In 2013, the U.S. Census (2013) estimated that the Latina/o population increased to 54 million, making Latinas/os the largest racial and ethnic minority group and largest marginalized group in the United States. It is projected that by 2050 Latinas/os will comprise 28% of the U.S. population (U.S. Census, 2013), yet, the Latina/o population will continue to increase and gain numerical power, but still will continue to remain oppressed (De Luca & Escoto, 2012). We recognize that the terms *Hispanic* and *Latina/o* are complex, being used interchangeably in the general population and in academia. For the purposes of this study we use the term *Latinas/os*. We also acknowledge that the *Latina/o* term is "problematic in that reinforces an arbitrary binary, limiting the social construction of gender to only two genders" (Irizarry, 2011, p. 2830).

Gándara and Contreras (2009) assert that Latina/o students' experiences in education is one of the most urgent challenges for the educational system in the United States. Furthermore, the Latina/o population continues to be perceived as a threat in the United States's political, economic, cultural, and social spheres inside and outside academia (Chavez, 2013). Some literature indicates that postsecondary education "endorse[s] diversity to the extend that it serves white students" (Yosso & Lopez, 2010, p. 89). Latinas/os have often been marginalized and targeted in education and continue to be invisible in history. Latina/o students' challenges include financial aid support, racial identity development, lack of same-race/ethnicity of faculty and staff, family, community transition, and college choice access and selection (Gándara & Contreras, 2009; Ramirez, 2013; Salinas, 2015).

"Society acts unaware of contributions that Latinos [and Latinas] have made to society" (Salinas, 2013, p. 72), which makes school uninteresting for Latina/o students. However, Latinas/os have influenced various aspects of life in the United States, including education, the economy, politics, science, art, and leadership, among other areas. From Focus on Hispanics (2010), we highlight a few extraordinary events and Latinas/os who have made a notable impact in various areas in the United States:

- In 1903, more than 1,200 Mexican and Japanese farm workers established the first farm workers' union, the Japanese-Mexican Labor Association.

- In 1912, New Mexico's state constitution prohibited segregation for children of "Spanish descent."
- In 1928, New Mexico's Octavio Larrazolo became the first Latino Senator in the United States.
- In 1932, Benjamin Nathan Cordoza became the first Hispanic person named to the United States Supreme Court.
- In 1963, the first bilingual education program in public schools was offered in Coral Way Elementary, located in Miami, Florida.
- In 1968, Chicana/o high school students presented a list of demands to the Los Angeles Unified School District Board of Education, desiring a better education.
- In 1988, Dr. Lauro Cavazos became the first Latino to be Secretary of Education and to serve in a President's cabinet.
- In 2002, Latinas/os became the largest racial and ethnic group in the United States, reaching 37.1 million.
- In 2009, Sonia Sotomayor became the first Latina to serve on United States Supreme Court.

Despite the invisible accomplishments, history, challenges, oppression, and marginalization that Latinas/os faced in the United States, we are confident that Latinas/os will continue to make a significant impact in education, politics, economics, leadership, sports, art, and many other areas. While the United States school system has been challenged with school reform for the past four decades, *The Futures of School Reform* by Mehta, Schwartz, & Hess (2012) maps out a variety of bold visions that push the boundaries of our current thinking and different courses of action for change. We argue that our school systems' procedures and reform efforts by scholars and practitioners across the P-20 pipeline must incorporate the growing Latina/o demographic, for Latinas/os will slowly change the landscape of the United States' educational system.

Adelante con la Educación

As the Latina/o population continues to grow, it is assumed that more Latina/o students will enroll in higher education institutions. For example, from fall 2002 to fall 2012 the number of Latina/o students enrolled in public elementary and secondary schools increased from 8.6 million to 12.1 million (from 18% to 24%). In contrast, during the same period the number of white students enrolled in public elementary and secondary schools

decreased from 28.6 million to 25.6 million (from 59% to 51%). Compara-
bly, Black student enrollment in public elementary and secondary schools
has also decreased during the same period of time, from 8.3 million to 7.8
million (from 17% to 16%) (U.S. Census, 2010).

In 1990, undergraduate enrollment in two- and four-year institutions
was 12.0 million students. There was an increase of 46% from 1990 to fall
2013, to 17.5 million students enrolled in two- and four-year institutions.
It is projected that undergraduate enrollment will continue to increase, and
by 2024, 19.6 million undergraduate students will be enrolled in two- and
four-year institutions. Despite the increasing number of Latina/o students
in public elementary and secondary schools, and in two- and four-year
colleges and universities, Latina/o students continue to be disfranchised in
the U.S. educational system (U.S. Census, 2010, 2013).

Contreras and Gándara (2006) state that Latina/o students are "less likely than any Blacks, Whites, or Asians to graduate from high school, go on to
college, and earn a degree." (p. 92). Their statement is supported by the data
presented throughout this article. In comparison, the number of Latina/o
students who apply to doctoral programs is significantly smaller than that
of any other ethnic group. The number of doctoral degrees conferred to
U.S. residents (including M.D., D.D.S., and law degrees) increased roughly
for all race/ethnicity groups in the span of ten years, from 1999–2000 to
2009–2010 (See table 1).

Arciniega (2012) asserts that education of Latina/o students "is not just
a Latino higher education issue: rather it is a national imperative" (p. 156).
Furthermore, Arciniega "recognizes that Latino [and Latina] students are
the cultural wealth of this country, as are all students, which makes their
future a national issue. It is imperative that all institutions across the coun-

TABLE 1. Status and trends in the education of racial and ethnic groups

LEVEL OF DEGREE AND RACE/ETHNICITY	1999–2000	2009–2010	1999–2000 BY %	2009–2010 BY %
Doctoral Degree	106,494	140,505	100	100
White	82,984	104,426	77.9	74.3
Black	7,080	10,417	6.6	7.4
Hispanic	5,039	8,085	4.7	5.8
Asian/Pacific Islander	10,684	16,625	10	11.8
American Indian/Alaska Native	707	952	0.7	0.7

Source: Adapted from the National Center for Education Statistics, 2012

try focus their efforts and prioritize their resources to directly impact the Latino [and Latina] students" (2012, 153). Understanding access, retention, and completion of first-generation Latina/o students' experiences in postsecondary education is significant to the success of the United States and the world's future.

ADVANCING THE LATINA/O COLLEGE CHOICE FRAMEWORK

According to a survey conducted March 2011 by the Pew Center, college remains a near universal aspiration in this country, even in the face of steeply rising costs. Among parents of children ages 17 or younger, 94% say they expect their child (or children) to attend college. We introduce this expectation that families believe in and policy makers support as *The hope of education*; the idea that a student can complete a post-secondary education in the United States. Studies continue to demonstrate that increased levels of postsecondary education lead to higher salaries, longer working lives, more career mobility, and an increased quality of life (Hossler & Palmer, 2006; Pascarella & Terenzini, 2005). The competition for student enrollment in undergraduate and graduate programs continues to play a significant role in university programming, budgeting, and leadership. Higher education is increasingly concerned with rising costs, declining appropriations and endowments, and increasing competition for students, through a growing marketplace orientation (Bok, 2003; Lewin, 2008). Identifying and recruitment of current undergraduates, targeted mailings, and maintaining an up-to-date website helps universities with their strategies to maintain interest in their schools and programs.

The increased interest in graduate choice and enrollment raises new questions about the most effective practices for attracting and recruiting graduate students. To help address this need for information, Noel-Levitz and the National Association of Graduate Admissions Professionals (NAGAP) partnered this spring to survey the nation's graduate recruitment and admissions professionals to find out what they think are the most effective recruitment practices for master's degree students (Maihan, n.d.). As recruitment and admission professionals report their graduate student recruitment practices with millennial students coming into graduate programs, the evidence of actual college choice from the graduate student perspective remains uncharted. Extensive research has been conducted on the college choice process of undergraduate students (Hossler & Gallagher, 1987) but there is limited attention to the college choice process of graduate student populations, especially with the growing Latina/o populations in universities across the country.

This research aims to add to the body of knowledge in the Latina/o graduate college choice processes by examining first generation graduate student college choices and experiences through counter-narratives and critical frames. The Hossler and Gallagher (1987) model, including predispositions, search process, and choice, is seminal and has influenced the kinds of questions and programs universities develop to entice selection of their colleges. While conceptualized for undergraduate college choice, the model has been widely used in studies at both the graduate and undergraduate levels (Mertz, Eckman, & Strayhorn, 2012) and is considered the "prevailing model" by college choice researchers (Ceja, 2006, p. 88). Because where one attends college has significant implications for professional mobility, and social inequality, it is imperative that scholars examine graduate students' college choice (Ramirez, 2013).

To further understand the Latina/o college choice process, influences that impact their decisions must be investigated and acknowledged. Perez (2010) discusses Latina/o research, which indicates four factors standing above the rest: financial aid, family, social network, and location. These factors shape a student's choice set (the colleges students apply to), as well as their ability to sway a student's final choice (Perez, 2010). Studies have found that graduate students are influenced by a variety of factors in their graduate school application and matriculation decisions, including program reputation, location, financial aid, characteristics of the graduate program, quality of the faculty, and input from spouse/partner (Ramirez, 2013). This article seeks to inform higher education practitioners, college administrators, and graduate programs by gaining the perspective of Latina/o graduate college students with these aspects of college choice.

THE POWER OF THE COUNTER-NARRATIVES

We follow in the wake of a lineage of Latina/o scholar advocates who provide a discourse of equity by advancing critical frames for Latina/o agency across the P-20 educational pipeline. Perez and McDonough (2008) advanced scholarship on Latina/o undergraduate college choice using chain migration theory within a social capital framework. Their research found the 106 primarily first-generation college students in their study relied heavily on siblings, peers, relatives, and high school contacts for purposes of postsecondary planning and for creating a college consideration and application set. Dolores Delgado-Bernal (2010) utilized critical race theory (CRT) and

Latina/Latino critical theory (LatCrit) to demonstrate how critical raced-gendered epistemologies recognize students of color as holders and creators of knowledge. She further argues students of color are holders and creators of knowledge and often feel as if their histories, experiences, cultures, and languages are devalued, misinterpreted, or omitted within formal educational settings (p.105). Tara Yosso (2005) provides a critical race lens that allows us to see that Communities of Color nurture cultural wealth through at least six forms of capital such as aspirational, navigational, social, linguistic, familial, and resistant capital.

This study is built on counter-narrative scholarship to advance Latina/o graduate choice process. Counter-narratives provided the authors capacity to frame Latina/o graduate experiences in ways that both honor lived experiences and convey them with integrity. Counter-narratives allow the researcher and participants to study and name a reality inconsistent with what might be considered the norm or pervasive otherwise (Ladson-Billings, 1998; Solorzano & Yosso, 2002). Connelly and Clandinin (1990) note that by nature people lead storied lives and tell stories of those lives. Narrative researchers describe such lives, collect and tell stories of them, and write narrative experiences to further understand ourselves and students educationally (Connelly & Clandinin, 1990, p. 2–3.). The educational importance of this line of work is that it brings theoretical ideas about the nature of human life as lived to bear on educational experiences lived (Connelly & Clandinin, 1990).

Latina/o counter-narrative and counter stories are personal stories that challenge the dominant narrative with truths and lived experiences. Richard Delgado (1989) reminds us that oppressed groups have known instinctively that stories are an essential tool to their own survival and liberation. To conceptually structure the study we use Solorzano and Yosso's (2002) frame of Strauss and Corbin's theoretical sensitivity (1990) and Delgado Bernal's cultural intuition (1998) to create counter stories from (a) data gathered from the research process itself, (b) the existing literature on the topics, (c) our own professional experiences, and (d) our own personal experiences.

As an example, the authors used critical lenses of race, gender, and class and the experiences of Chicana and Chicano undergraduate and graduate students, postdoctoral fellows, and faculty to examine the concepts of self-doubt, survivor guilt, imposter syndrome, and invisibility (Solorzano & Yosso, 2002, p. 34). The "composite" characters in this article developed in counter-narratives and counter-storytelling are grounded in real-life experience and actual empirical data, and are contextualized in social situations that are also grounded in real life (Solorzano & Yosso, 2002, p. 36). Research scholars further assert counter-stories serve the following four functions: (a) They can build community among those at the margins of society by putting a human and familiar face to educational theory and practice, (b) they can challenge the perceived wisdom of those at society's center by providing a context to understand and transform established belief systems, (c) they can open new windows into the reality of those at the margins of society by showing possibilities beyond the ones they live and demonstrating that they are not alone in their position, and (d) they can teach others that by combining elements from both the story and the current reality, one can construct another world that is richer than either the story or the reality alone (Solorzano & Yosso, 2002).

LO LOGRAMOS! ADVANCING LATINA/O GRADUATE CHOICE PROCESS

We have a personal and professional interest in the topic as "there is no better point of entry into a critique or reflection than one's own experience" (Bannerji, 1992, 67). We embrace the scholarship of Flores Carmona (2011), and reflecting on the first-generation college student experience, we were privileged to attend universities where we learned to trust knowledge gained from lived experiences. We see our identities as Latinos, Mexican immigrants, migrant farmworkers, *fronterizos*, and bilingual students as assets. Scholars Burciaga and Navarro (2012) provide us with educational *testimonio* as critical pedagogy, an autoethnographic-style research tracing one's individual educational trajectory. Reading these assertions in critically framed literature provides an authentic space for the authors to share counter-stories of graduate choice through personal scholar narratives, embrace the wisdom and *apoyo de familia*, the impact of cultural wealth experiences, knowledge of finances, the power of social capital, and the location of the desired destination—graduate school. The first two counter-stories are ones of a braided effort, framing *testimonio,* counter-story reflection, and lived experience to the graduate process.

From "Waterboy" to Professor Fernando Valle

As a Mexican migrant family of six, we drove ten hours every summer, leaving San Juan in the Rio Grande Valley to work in the sorghum, cotton, and onion fields in towns across West Texas like Plainview, Lockney, Dumas, and Hereford. Our family was part of a caravan of *familias* from the U.S.-Mexico border, and, through *pláticas* and *testimonios* about their treatment, the workers painted a picture of the sobering reality of their labor, with twelve-hour work days for everyone. Referred to in West Texas migrant-worker-speak as *"el azadón, la pala y la cebolla,"* those experiences came with rattlesnakes in the fields, sun, dehydration, and children as young as ten working full days under foreman supervision. As the youngest, at six years old I became the helper and the "waterboy" for my family and many other *familias* working in the fields. We overcame many humbling and often demeaning experiences in the field and local towns, living and working in the worst of conditions—deplorable housing and man camps. Despite the hard labor, long hours, language obstacles, and oppression, my father was proud to have his *familia* by his side. In a true leader's voice he organized families in the fields, teaching, modeling, and encouraging working families with a rally cry, *"¡Ánimo al cuadro! ¡Ánimo al cuadro!"*

My *familia* encouraged and transmitted a strong work ethic in all aspects of life. Our parents' relentless work, as our first *maestros*, pushed us to work and graduate from high school. "No le tengas miedo al trabajo, don't be afraid of work," they would tell us, always encouraging us, patting us on the back on the way to school. My father's schooling ended in sixth grade, but the school of life and the knowledge of Mexican culture was our asset. Our parents' work ethic later replaced work in the fields, and they started a family roofing and construction business. They were the encouragement and source of inspiration for us to pursue education beyond high school—to take the risk and *"seguir adelante."*

The migrant narrative in public school was both a curse and a blessing. I was tracked in public school; in elementary school I was identified as a Gifted and Talented (GT) student, and in middle school the migrant labeled placed me in courses with no learning—only remediation. My parents knew I belonged in "regular" classes and advocated for my education. In high school, the migrant status opened doors for financial aid and college funding. Higher education was becoming a reality.

As a first-generation Latino student, like so many, I relied on friends and family, my sister especially, for advisement to navigate college. I worked 40 hours a week, lived at home, and attended the local college my first year. I still felt lost, insecure, unadvised and was reminded in college classes full of Latino students taught by white males to "look to your right and left, most of you will not make it to the end of the semester"—an intimidating verbal reminder of a statistic. It came true, many of my *amigos/as* stopped coming after the first semester. With no bus system and lacking other transportation, working full time to contribute to the household, marriage and other life events took many of my classmates on paths other than college. I was quickly following that path, and in my second year I rallied my friends to apply and move with me to San Antonio for school. Three of us applied, and after two backed out I was left with the decision to transfer to the University of Texas–San Antonio to "make it." I faced fears of failure and not belonging. Always with "¡*Animo!*," always "¡*Adelante!*" in my head, my *familia* ever-present in my heart, knowing prayers and candles were lit to protect and guide me. The experience changed my life, as I met and found other students like me, living off financial aid, sharing meals and rides, and using our cultural wealth to navigate the school system and bring our roots with us into higher education—speaking Spanish, singing *tejano* and *corridos*, dancing *cumbias* and *guapangos*, playing *lotería*, and eating menudo on Sundays. These cultural spaces provided a sense of belonging and the strength to persist through the insecurity and loneliness of college completion.

I graduated and returned home to teach middle-school science. The first three years, it was science fairs, science sponsor, helping to coach in the University Interscholastic League (UIL), sponsoring teams and field trips to competitions. The students in my classes were kids from my hometown, my streets and neighborhood. They provided lessons of life and shared their own experiences of understanding *cultura*, poverty, *ganas*, gang culture, and resilience. After the third year it was not enough; I was thirsty for more. I wanted more than the field of education had to offer. I overheard colleagues at work talking about "going back to school for their master's." I talked to them, inquired, and followed suit with an application to the master's in counseling education program. I was terrified of the GRE and felt I would not make the program; I wrote the letter of interest, completed the application, and turned in dismal GRE scores. The letter from The University of Texas–Pan American read "accepted." Again I learned from peers at work and friends what courses to start with, how to navigate the program, what financial aid opportunities existed, how to use the payment plans, and in general what to do. Folders full of old copies, handwritten notes, and course schedules were handed down in a gritty binder, which became my graduate road map and provided my graduate advising.

I did not have mentoring relationships with any professors during my undergraduate experience. I went through the motions, checked off the boxes, took tests, and graduated. In graduate school—especially in a counseling program—the professors engaged us, made us uncomfortable, talked to us, and most importantly, listened. Having *pláticas* with professors opened the collegial professional space, a space of privilege. The graduate program provided the first time a *profesor latino* shared his challenges and the story of the sacrifice, the work, and how nervous he was in his dissertation defense. It was the first time I made the cultural and academic connection. This was possible. I remember looking around, and I saw that all of the students in the class hung on his every word; we were all part of a powerful personal conversation, one decoding the PhD degree through life experiences like mine, ones with *familia*, culture, and the lived experience of the Mexican American border. I learned about myself as a student and professional and realized that I am by nature a *consejero*. I became a high school counselor and had both the valedictorian and students faced with being school dropouts all coming in and out of my office. I saw the realities and missed opportunities in our schools through an emotional and affective lens. My principal encouraged me to obtain a second master's, in educational leadership. The second time around I felt comfortable in graduate school but was challenged with school leadership, politics, and the nuances of leading versus managing a school. For an assistant principal, 50- to 60-hour weeks are the norm, and if you do not hustle to run the school, the school will run you.

During the next five years, I worked to build rapport and reputation as an administrator with the different principals coming in and out of our school. Talk of the doctoral program finally came to our regional college. Fears surfaced of taking the GRE again, producing writing samples, interviews, and navigating doctoral studies—the tensions of a lost first-generation and first-year student happened all over again. I applied, wrote, was interviewed, and again received the letter that read "accepted." True and stable, my *familia* encouraged and supported me when I dropped out after the first year of doctoral studies; I did not balance family, the work of a school administrator, and the depth of work required as a doctoral student. Humbled by the experience, it woke me up to seek help and succeed, to persist with a modeled work ethic, and to fight for the opportunity. In May of 2008, I defended my dissertation and completed my doctorate. I interviewed for and accepted a tenure-track position back in West Texas as a professor at Texas Tech University. In the fall of 2008, I left the Rio Grande Valley to become a professor of educational leadership. I never thought I was going to move back to a place that left us with bitter memories of mistreatment working as a migrant family in the fields of West Texas. I have come full-circle in my education, and this time I am not riding in the back of the truck with the *familia* leaving the fields. I am proud to be in a space of privilege, contributing and quenching my thirst, like the waterboy, for knowledge, working in higher education as a tenured professor, advocating for Latina/o graduate students to "*seguir adelante con ánimo.*"

From the ESL Classroom to Professor Cristobal Salinas Jr.

I migrated from Mexico to the United States at a young age. This experience was challenging; I had to develop new friendships, adapt to a different culture, and learn a new language. Furthermore, I was challenged to learn new social, political, and educational expectations that the educational system in the United States had set for me as a Latino student. First, I felt that having brown skin was "associated with ugliness and carries with it stigma of being significantly less human than White people" (Salinas, 2013, p. 72). Then, I learned that I was no longer allowed to identify as Mexican in governmental documents; rather, I only had the option to identify as Hispanic and sometimes as Latino. Last, in educational settings I was expected never to leave the English as a second language (ESL) classroom, and my Mexican-American accent meant ignorance and limited success in education. Throughout my experiences of being marginalized and oppressed because of my racial group and physical appearance in eighth grade, I understood that xenophobia was evident in the United States, especially in educational settings. I was reminded by my teachers, classmates, and politicians that I was their "panic;" yet, they are the ones who made me identify as *His-Panic*.

Mrs. Moyer, my first ESL teacher, helped me to overcome those challenges that I faced as I entered the educational system in the United States. Teachers like Mrs. Moyer—who invested, believed, and were not scared of me—as well as my parents providing me with the support system to become successful despite these challenges. Although my parents only possess a seventh-grade education, they have always given me sound direction and inspiration to further my studies. My parents inspired me to choose a career where I can make a difference. I have chosen education as my career, because in my culture being a teacher is more than wisdom; it is about respect, transforming lives, equality, and justice.

Growing up I did not know I was going to be in the field of education—I always dreamed of returning home to Mexico. During my senior year of high school, I attended the Nebraska Cultural Unity Conference for high school students at the University of Nebraska at Kearney (UNK). The conference experience exposed me to postsecondary education opportunities, scholarships, financial aid, student life, and other Latina/o students—from which I have learned about their experiences, and visualized myself in college in the United States. This visualization was scary and intimidating, because I knew that my parents could not afford to pay for my education; I had to take the ACT and was afraid that my low scores on a standardize test would determine my future; I questioned if I could be successful inside the classroom, because often a few teachers stated by their actions or words that Latina/o students should not attend a two- or four-year institution. Regardless of being scared and intimidated by this system and culture that I did not know, I got accepted to UNK.

My experiences of marginalization and oppression as an undergraduate student helped me understand that there was an education revolution going on in higher education. We needed more Latina/os as administrators, student affairs professionals, and faculty to advocate for other marginalized and targeted communities, with an emphasis on Latina/o students. More specifically, in my undergraduate college career I ran for student body president; during the election I received an anonymous threat that stated, "Take your name off the ballot before you get hurt. We do not want a fag and Mexican as student body president." As a result of this, I removed my name from the ballot. My mentors and friends were supportive through this process, but the university policy and college administrators did not complete an investigation of this hate crime. This moment made me reflect that my past experiences are no different to today's Latina/o students' experiences; Latina/o students are challenged by a system that has often rejected us.

Based on my experiences and recognizing that we need an educational revolution to change the landscape of higher education, I decided to apply for graduate programs that would empower and prepare me to be a critical thinker and leader of this revolution. I applied to graduate programs that my friends and mentors recommended. Through the process of choosing and applying to graduate programs, I did not receive advice or guidance from my parents, for they did not fully understand and know the educational system in the United States. Rather, I kept in consideration the location of the university and distance to my parents' home, funding, and financial aid (i.e., graduate assistantship positions), and master's programs that did not required the GRE, as I was afraid that the standardized test would threaten my enrollment in graduate school.

During my master's program in educational leadership and leadership studies at Iowa State University, I had the opportunity to present at various conferences. Presenting at conferences exposed me to other faculty who look and sound like me. I was inspired and motivated to continue doing research, writing, and presenting on my findings and thoughts. I believe that my experiences in conferences socialized me to academia. Therefore, I applied to doctoral programs that were nationally recognized in my field, with graduate research/teaching assistantship positions, and faculty that would support my research interests. My decision in selecting a doctoral program was based on my own personal experiences, and the advice of my mentors. Throughout my PhD career I faced forms of oppression similar to those that I had experienced previously, and also gained an understanding of my privilege as a doctoral student. This form of privilege comes with responsibility, to advocate through research and teaching for marginalized and oppressed communities. I was aware that earning my PhD was going to prepare me to pursue a career as a scholar and faculty member at a college or university, where I could then provide an opportunity to engage future educators in coursework and practical applications that will challenge their critical thinking skills through the lens of social justice. On April 1, 2015, I defended my dissertation and now I am an assistant professor at Florida Atlantic University.

LATINA/O FIRST GENERATION GRADUATE CHOICE: COUNTER-STORIES OF RESILIENCE

Wait, What, You Have Two Master's Degrees?

Sisters Mari and Letty's educational journey from high school to bachelor's degree to their graduate college choice and experience included moments of resilience, doubt, and much persistence. They are part of a family with four first-generation siblings; three with bachelor's degrees, two with master's degrees. and the youngest enrolled at a two-year institution. As the oldest, Mari lead the education pathway. She is a middle-school Spanish teacher with a bachelor's degree in Spanish and has two master's degrees: one in Spanish and the second one in applied linguistics. Letty has a master's degree in higher education and works at a local university as a science, technology, engineering, and mathematics (STEM) advisor. The third sister also has a bachelor's degree in multidisciplinary studies, and the youngest brother plans to transfer from the local community college to a larger four-year university, two hours from home, to finish his bachelor's degree. Mari quickly notes in the interview, "My little brother now has the master's degree as the education level he is shooting for. 'How can I not,' he says—'my sisters have master's degrees.'"

Mari recalls that she has been asked by teachers at work, "You? You have two master's degrees? How did your family do it? How did they produce four first-generation children with college degrees?" Letty and Mari both smiled during this part of the interview and Mari acknowledged, "My parents work really hard and are very supportive; how could we not?"

Letty reflects, "Thanks to them [my parents], we do not have to work as hard as they do physically in their jobs." Both Letty and Mari admit their *familia* was at the center of the conversation and college choice processes. Geographical proximity has been an important component of these choices: "For us as single Latinas it has been part of our education, and journey." Letty explains, "we first started at a local community college in town, then we moved to a college 30 minutes away, and then we moved further, two hours away for our masters."

Mari is the oldest and admits she has this "self-placed" pressure to advance and lead the way, "*por ser la mayor.*" After completing her bachelor's degree, she focused on finding a graduate program. She searched online and found a Spanish graduate degree, took the courage to apply and began the journey. She reflects that the first couple of semesters did not fulfil her. "I was taking Spanish Literature courses," she recounts, "*pero no me llenaba.*" Also, she did not want to lose her culture and language, "I was a Spanish major in undergrad; I did not want to lose my language." The courses, although part of the program, were unfulfilling and did not satisfy her intellectual spirit. The dissatisfaction she felt with the curriculum matched her experience with minimal advisement. Mari was very clear about this experience, "I was the one on top of my hours and courses. There was only one advisor. I basically presented the plan of courses and the faculty advisor would just sign." She explored curriculum options and took up a minor in applied linguistics. Not fulfilled with the master's degree in Spanish, she used her minor to pursue a second master's. Mari recalls, "I wanted guidance from my graduate program on career opportunities, on internships, my future jobs, and the real world." She did not receive assistance. "Now I feel like I did not need to get two master's degrees to be a Spanish middle-school teacher." She has completed the second master's degree. Reflecting on her own disengaged master's experience and with a new goal in front of her, "I am now thinking I want to be a *profesora*; I am interested in the PhD."

Letty listens to her sister intently and professes that she pursued graduate studies because her sister set the bar, "She was doing it, so I wanted to do it as well." Letty was a middle-school science teacher. "I went to a science magnet high school. I wanted to do environmental science for graduate studies, and I found out it was not for me." She explored the career center in college for professional direction and came across higher education studies. "I looked online at local colleges for higher education programs; I did not get responses from many, and decided on the college my sister was attending." Letty asserts, "I like my classes and I like my job as an advisor, but I know I want more. We have a brother coming up." Letty is currently enrolled in graduate courses for a second master's degree and has been proactive in applying for positions in STEM at the university to advance her knowledge and career. Letty concludes her reflection on their graduate school choices: "We have our parents' support to advance and keep going; what more could we ask for?" Letty has discussed considering PhD programs and is seeking Latina/o mentorship. Mari continues to cheer her sister on, admiring her ground-breaking journey and creating a path for her as well to pursue the PhD.

It's for Me and My Community

Marcos is in the process of graduating from college and shared his experience searching for MBA graduate programs across the state. "At first I was looking at websites, calling professors—some actually called me back—and I asked a lot of questions about their programs." As Marcos describes his brief excitement about choosing MBA programs and the financial stressors and realities that altered his outlook,

> I have to leave and move. I have to adjust. I know it's hard, and I really do not have a lot of money to do that. It's not fair to ask my family for more money. I already know the professors here, and they have been talking to us about their MBA. I have stability here; I have a job. For me relationships matter, and I have that here.

He described his passion for work in his community, of opening a medical clinic with his family in his hometown. "I am going to run the business and computer side of the clinic, my brother and sister will do the medical part." Helping his community, serving the poor, and advocacy work continued to create the backdrop for Marcos's experience in choosing a graduate school. Marcos has enrolled in the MBA program in his home institution and is excited about the possibilities of doing his internship in a medical facility.

How Will I Pay for Mija's College?

Rodrigo is a high school teacher and coach. He worked his way through college running his father's mechanic shop and attended school part time. "I know, I know, I am the poster boy for the ten-year plan" he jokes, "had to retake a lot of classes." Rodrigo admits that as a first-generation student and now as a professional, "It took me a long time to get my education, to get married, to buy my house—we had to save and sacrifice. I never thought about a master's degree." When his daughter was born the desire to provide, to model, and to pass on education was at the center of his aspirations. "My daughter is going to have a *quinceañera*, and she's going to college." Aspirations for increased income and the need to save for college fueled the effort to balance and save for an online master's degree program. As husband-and-wife educators, their partnership at home and work reflects the reality of their lives, financial commitments, saving, living on a budget, and the ongoing effort to invest in themselves and their family. "Coaching brings in the extra money. Really thought I was too old to go back to school. I looked at programs; you see the 20 and 30 thousand price tags." Struggling during college entrance requirements and the fear of the GRE are obstacles, "*Te da miedo* . . . Did not know if I would get in . . . I always think, I want *mija* to know her old man did it. Online classes were cheaper and worked for all of us." Rodrigo is in his final semester of his master's degree in educational leadership. He looks forward to using his graduate degree to advance his career.

I Realized I was one of Two Latina/os in the Program

Yolanda completed her undergraduate and graduate degrees in a predominantly white institution. Active in leading a campus organization, she focused her energies on the Latina/o centric groups. As a first-generation working professional, Yolanda recalls her college choice process: "I was working in the center for campus life in my twenties and was told if I did not have a master's I would not be promoted."

> When I was an undergrad, there were a few of us who were leading Hispanic organizations on campus; you can say we were the *crème de la crème* of the Hispanic leaders and the university recruited us as work-study to work on campus. My friend Marissa wanted to be a doctor, a PhD, Susanna wanted to be an elementary school teacher, and I wanted to pursue public relations. Marissa and Susanna were both recruited into the master's program in higher education. I felt they gave up their goals and dreams because our home college became a "safe" place to work. I left to be a recruiter for another college.

Yolanda reflects on her decision to pursue her master's: "My decision to get out of higher education work was the reason I wanted the master's degree. I saw others doing it and thought, I could be done in two years? Ok, yeah, then let's do this." For Yolanda, sharing her master's journey was an after-the-fact moment. She decided to leave her job as a recruiter and come back to her home institution, where she had capital with friends, professors and family.

"I had not told anyone that I was interested in a master's. I called my mom and told her, 'Well I had class tonight, Mom.' My mom was elated because I was back in town." Conversations with parents for Yolanda included payment plans and asserting to them, "I can pay for this."

Her experience in the program was one of survival, working and paying for graduate school. "I was given a sheet of paper and those were my classes. I may have talked to the advisor once or twice because I needed an independent study, but I just checked off my classes." Yolanda further recognizes her journey and choices. Many valuable lessons were learned from various faculty: "There was one Latina/o faculty, and he was the only one who listened. I leaned on him."

It was crystallized moment and realization for Yolanda, "I never thought I was the Hispanic recruit, but looking back at the program, I guess I was. There was me and Manuel, and . . . no that's it, it was just me and Manuel in the nonprofit master's program." Yolanda is currently a PhD student in media and communications studies and is in her last year of the program. She looks forward to conducting her research and returning to the professional world as *Doctora* Yolanda.

FINDINGS AND CONCLUSIONS OF THE LATINA/O GRADUATE CHOICE PROCESS

Efforts from high school to community college are well documented for Latina/o first generation students. Few studies examine the Latina/o graduate school college choice process. We continue the *plática* for first-generation Latina/o graduate students to extend and strengthen the Latina/o educational pipeline. The counter-stories share the essence of various participants and their lived experiences. They are part of a larger study and an amalgamation of counter-narratives that represent the spirit of first-generation Latina/o graduate students. The participants represent the 10% of the Latina/o U.S. population with master's degrees, and many aspire to be part of the 2% with a doctorate degree. First-generation graduate students utilize various forms of capital and community cultural wealth (Yosso, 2005) and utilize aspirational and resistant forms of capital to dismantle contemporary forms of deficit thinking (Valencia, 2010).

The bleak data pictures used to represent Latinas/os during the past four decades as dropouts, unemployed, poor, and uneducated must be changed. Latina/o graduate students are present in graduate programs across the country and universities, and colleges would be wise to capture and document experiences that enhance the recruitment and retention of first-generation Latina/o graduate students. The findings in this article from the counter-narratives resonate with Perez and Ramirez's work mentioned in this article. The importance of familial and financial support was a strong theme in every session. Both close and extended role models and mentors were formed the basis of persistence for first-generation Latinas/os becoming first-generation graduate students. Many navigated Web pages for program details and information. Although some received emails and messages from colleges and programs, many stayed at the home institution because of the lack of communication, comfort, and connection with institutions during the selection process. Yolanda stressed during her interview,

> In my master's and PhD program, I came in with first-generation problems and issues, unaware of the environment, culture of the program, and research requirements. My master's was a non-thesis program and I was a working professional. I experienced the attitude early in the PhD program that, since I had been through a master's program, there should be no first-generation-like issues. I experienced the attitude that first-generation issues don't exist beyond undergrads. When you are in an environment with no Latina/o faculty, few students like you; you are back where you started. With Latina/o undergrads you have organizations, programs, and supports. The few of us in a doctoral program, have to make and create our own supports.

Ramirez (2013) asserts that future research should be attentive to how social inequality impinges on Latinas/os' graduate school selection process. Ramirez further cites Solórzano and Yosso's work (2000) as the scholars suggest: to adequately understand the educational conditions of Latina/o students, scholarly research must incorporate a race, class, and gender analysis. The fact is that all the participants were encouraged by *familia*: partners, siblings, and colleagues and were encouraged to continue to their education despite feeling out- "classed" and out- "raced" for graduate school acceptance. Mari leans in to her sister during the interview and whispers, "You should do this" when the discussion of the PhD arises. Letty admits she wants to, but like many first-generation graduate student she has questions and some fears; yet her spirit is unwavering. These are missed conversations and discourse the participants sought. Advising Latina/o graduate students takes more than a list of courses. It is an opportunity for universities to retain and recruit Latina/o students and not wait two decades for demographic changes to lead them into Hispanic-Serving Institution territory.

Marianismo and *machismo/caballerismo* are quite prevalent in Latina/o theoretical literature and were also present in first-generation graduate conversations. Latina/o first-graduate students all referenced their roles, responsibilities, and their identities within and among their extended families with a rich desire to give back, ever present in their thinking and actions. The counter stories of lived graduate choices came to life. They acknowledge *familia* as a big part of their inspiration and support for sustainability. Latina/o first-generation graduate students worked to stay financially afloat, some as working professionals, others at odd jobs, and survived off student loans and financial aid. Experiences in and out of graduate studies sphere of influence that expanded as they pursued graduate school. Even without mentors to guide them during their choice of graduate studies many participants with minimal advisement advocated for themselves and others as they investigated programs. Using cultural wealth, they navigated (Yosso, 2005) and persisted through their graduate school choices and are now in graduate programs with the *ganas* to succeed.

REFERENCES

Arciniega, T. A. (2012). The crucial role of Hispanic-serving institutions in the education of Latina/o youth. *Journal of Latina/os and Education, 11*(3), 150–156.

Bok, D. (2003). *Universities in the marketplace: The commercialization of higher education*. Princeton, NJ: Princeton University Press.

Brooks, J. S. (2012). *Black school, white school: Racism and educational (mis)leadership*. New York, NY: Teachers College Press.

Burciaga, R., & Cruz Navarro, N. (2015). Educational testimonio: Critical pedagogy as mentorship. *New Directions for Higher Education, 2015*(171), 33-41.

Ceja, M. (2006). Understanding the role of parents and siblings as information sources in the college choice process of Chicana students. *Journal of College Student Development, 47*(1), 87–104.

Chávez, L. R. (2013). *The Latino threat: Constructing immigration, citizens, and the nation* (2nd Ed.). Stanford, CA: Stanford University Press.

Connelly, M. F., & Clandinin, J. D. (1990). Stories of experience and narrative inquiry. *Educational Researcher, 19*(5), 2–14.

Contreras, F. E., & Gándara, P. (2006). The Latina/o Ph.D. pipeline: A case of historical and contemporary under-representation. In J. Castellanos, A. M. Gloria, & M. Kamimura (Eds.), *The Latina/o pathways to the Ph.D.* (pp. 91–111). Sterling, VA: Stylus.

De Luca, S. M., & Escoto, E. R. (2012). The recruitment and support of Latino faculty for tenure and promotion. *Journal of Hispanic Higher Education, 11*, 29–40.

Delgado, R. (1989). Storytelling for oppositionists and others: A plea for narrative. *Michigan Law Review, 87*, 2411–2441.

Delgado-Bernal, D. (1998). Using a Chicana feminist epistemology in educational research. *Harvard Education Review, 68*(4), 555–582.

Delgado-Bernal, D. (2002). Critical race theory, Latino critical theory, and critical race-gendered epistemologies: Recognizing students of color as holders and creators of knowledge. *Qualitative Inquiry, 8*(1), 105–126.

Flores Carmona, J. (2014). Cutting out their tongues: Mujeres' testimonios and the Malintzin researcher. *Journal of Latino/Latin American Studies, 6*(2), 113-124.

Focus on Hispanics. (2010, December). Invisible no more: The Latino struggle for civil rights. Retrieved from http://www.nea.org/assets/docs/HE/Hispanicsfocus 10.pdf

Gándara, P., & Contreras. F. (2009). *The Latino educational crisis: The consequences of failed social policies.* Cambridge, MA: Harvard University Press.

Hossler, D., & Gallagher, K. S. (1987). Studying student college choice: A three-phase model and the implications for policymakers. *College and University, 62*(3), 207–221.

Hossler, D., & Palmer, M. (2008). Why understand research on college choice? In National Association of College Admissions Counselors (NACAC) (Ed.), *Fundamentals of college admission counseling: A textbook for graduate students and practicing counselors* (2nd ed., pp. 42–53). Arlington, VA: Kendall Hunt Publishing.

Hurtado, S., & Carter, D. F. (1997). Effects of college transition and perceptions of the campus racial climate on Latino college students' sense of belonging. *Sociology of Education, 70,* 324–435.

Irizarry, J. (2011). *En la lucha*: The struggles and triumphs of Latino/a pre-service teachers. *Teachers College Records, 113*(2), 2804–2835.

Irizarry, Jason. G. (2009). Cultural deficit model. Retrieved from http://www.educa tion.com/reference/article/cultural-deficit-model/

Ladson-Billings, G. (1998). Just what is critical race theory and what's it doing in a nice field like education? *International Journal of Qualitative Studies in Education, 11*(1), 7–24.

Lewin, T. (2008). Private colleges worry about a dip in enrollment. *The New York Times.* Retrieved from http://www.nytimes.com/2008/12/22/education/22college .html?ref=todayspaper&_r=0

Maihan, S. (n.d.). What's working in graduate student recruitment and marketing? [Blog]. Retrieved from http://blog.noellevitz.com/2012/08/06/working-graduate -student-recruitment-marketing/

Mehta, J., Schwartz, R. B., & Hess, F. M. (2012). *The Futures of School Reform.* HarvardEducation Press: Cambridge, MA.

Mertz, N., Eckman, E., & Strayhorn, T., (2012). Entering student affairs: A comparative study of graduate school choice. *College Student Affairs Journal, 30*(2), 1–14.

National Center for Education Statistics. (2012). The condition of education 2012 (NCES 2012-045), Indicator 47. Retrieved from https://nces.ed.gov/fastfacts /display.asp?id=72

Nora, A. (2003). Access to higher education for Hispanic students: Real or illusory? In J. Castellanos & L. Jones (Eds.), *The majority in the minority: Expanding representation of Latino/a faculty, administration and students in higher education* (pp. 47–67). Sterling, VA: Stylus Publishing

Pascarella, E. T., & Terenzini, RT. (2005). *How college affects students, Volume 2, A third decade of research.* San Francisco, CA: Jossey-Bass.

Pérez, J. D. (2010). *Beyond admissions: Latino college choice.* (Master's thesis). Stanford University.

Pérez, P., & McDonough, P. M. (2008). Understanding Latino and Latino college choice. *Journal of Hispanics in Higher Education, 7*(3), 249–265.

Pew Research Center. (2012). Most parents expect their children to attend college. Retrieved from http://www.pewresearch.org/daily-number/most-parents-expect-their-children-to-attend-college/

Pino, N. W., Martinez-Ramos, G. P., & Smith, W. L. (2012). Latina/os, the academic ethic, and the transition to college. *Journal of Latina/os and Education, 11*(1), 17–31.

Ramírez, E. (2013). Examining Latinas/as' graduate school choice process: An intersectionality perspective. *Journal of Hispanic Higher Education, 12*(1), 23–36.

Rendón, L. (1994). Validating culturally diverse students: Toward a new model of learning and student development. *Innovative Higher Education, 19*(1), 23–32.

Salinas, C. (2013). Social justice from a point of view of an 8-year-old boy. *Broad: A Feminist & Social Justice Magazine; Living in Color, 55*(1), 70–72. Loyola Chicago University; Chicago, IL.

Salinas, C. (2015). Understanding and meeting the needs of Latina/o students in higher education. In P. Sasso, & J. Devitis (Eds.), *Today's college students* (pp. 21–37). New York: Peter Lang.

Solórzano, D., & Yosso, R. (2000). Toward a critical race theory of Chicana and Chicano education. In C. Tejada et al. (Eds.), *Charting new terrains: Chicana(o)/Latina(o) education* (pp. 35–65). Cresskill, NJ: Hampton Press.

Solórzano, D. G., & Yosso, T. J. (2002). Critical race methodology: Counter-storytelling as an analytical framework for education research. *Qualitative Inquiry, 8*(1), 23–44.

Strauss, A., & Corbin, J. (1990). *Basics of qualitative research: Grounded theory procedures and techniques.* Newbury Park, CA: Sage.

U.S. Census Bureau. (2010). *Community facts—Find popular facts and frequently requested data about your community.* American Fact Finder. Retrieved from http://factfinder.census.gov/faces/tableservices/jsf/pages/productview.xhtml?src=CF

U.S. Census Bureau. (2013). *Changing nation; Percent Hispanic of the U.S. population: 1980-2050.* U.S. Department of Commerce. Retrieved from http://www.census.gov/content/dam/Census/newsroom/facts-for-features/2014/cb14-ff22_graphic.pdf

Valencia, R. R. (2010). *Dismantling contemporary deficit thinking: Educational thought and practice.* New York: Routledge.

Yosso, T. J. (2005). Whose culture has capital? A critical race theory discussion of community cultural wealth. *Race Ethnicity and Education, 8*(1), 69–91.

Yosso, T. J., & Lopez, C. B. (2010). Counterspaces in a hostile place a critical race theory analysis of campus culture centers. In L. Patton (Ed.), *Culture centers in higher education: Perspectives on identity, theory and practice* (pp. 83–101). Sterling, VA: Stylus Publishing.

Schooling Space

CREATING SPATIAL JUSTICE IN CAROLINA DEL NORTE

Juan F. Carrillo

In 2012, I visited family in Ciudad Juárez, Mexico for the Christmas holiday. During our stay in Mexico, I decided to organize a family trip to the mountains of northern New Mexico. I wanted all of us to create some memories in the snow. As things turned out, we would write a few songs, sing, play guitar, joke, and get a little elevation sickness in the process. Still though, I remember the drive from Juárez to Red River, NM. Aside from taking in the stunning beauty of the area's landscapes, before making it through the Albuquerque region, I recall my spouse saying something to the effect of, "this is it, this is home, this the heart of Aztlán."[1] She felt a connection. After feeling somewhat culturally and spiritually displaced in North Carolina, this trip and that comment made me reflect on the power of "home," and the power of place in nurturing feelings of inclusion and/or exclusion. When I returned to North Carolina a few days later, I once again got that strange, hollow feeling in my gut that gave me the sense of being "away from home" and "away from my heart's center." I wondered: how do we create "home" in the New Latin@ South? More specifically, how can the states' universities contribute to developing these types of spaces? Instead of feeling hopeless, this was all part of a reflexive process that encouraged me to reflect critically and begin to act.

At the current moment, whether it is the University of Missouri, Yale, or Princeton University, debates are surging around racialization of college spaces. Many students do not feel safe or recognized and respected in any holistic sense. *New York Times* columnist Charles Blow (2015) concedes that

---

1. Term used by Chican@s and others to refer to the ancient homeland of the Aztec-Mexica, which is associated with the U.S. Southwest.

universities are racialized spaces that are often alienating and there is a need for safe spaces for students of color. In the South, a heritage industry has largely omitted Latin@s. Latin@s are, in many ways, dehistoricized, and left out of the regions' set of symbols and self-talk related to "place." Nonetheless, from Georgia, to Kentucky, to North Carolina, Latin@s continue to call this region home. UNC Chapel Hill, as the nation's first public university, is an interesting case in terms of how these issues play out in the New Latin@ South. In fact, we know very little about how the UNC-CH has provided opportunities for memory, space, and belonging as it relates to Latin@ college students. These types of questions are underexplored in the region's colleges and universities.

In this article, I utilize a *spatial justice* (Soja, 2010) lens to explore the development of the Latin@ Education Research Hub (LERH) at the University of North Carolina Chapel Hill School (UNC-CH) of Education. Since my arrival in 2011, UNC-CH has to had face its historical "racial record" as part of ongoing student activism. Moreover, Latin@ students are beginning to engage their voices as well. Specifically, in this chapter, I will (1) focus on how relevant research on North Carolina Latino male college students influenced the development of this space, (2) address LERH's goals and vision, and (3) unpack the role of LERH in developing a spatial justice approach for addressing Latin@ education issues at UNC Chapel Hill. At the core of this focus is the fact that the new Latin@ South remains a "space in the making" with incomplete and fragmented narratives of how schooling and Latin@s will shape North Carolina's future. This chapter will makes links between these issues as well as explore the important and critical connections between power, geography, space, and Latin@ college students in the state.

The New Latin@ South

North Carolina has one of the fastest growing Latin@ populations in the United States. In fact, from 2000–2011, North Carolina had a 120 percent increase in its Latino population (*The Latino Population Booms in the South: Pew*, 2013). Research on Latin@ education in North Carolina has explored issues such as paternalism, xenophobic politics, deficit thinking, the politics of language and education, the role of race and social class, and the power of sports to cultivate community and empowerment (Cervantes-Soon, 2014; Cuadros, 2006; Villenas, 2001; Wortham, Murillo, Jr., Hamann, 2002). Yet no spatial justice lens exists within the research on North Carolina higher education with links to Latin@ students.

Suffice it to say, part of my frustration has been that the research and data that shows Latin@s moving into the Southeast are somehow framed or stuck in the PowerPoints of "numbers," "immigrants," and the "pobrecito" syndrome surrounding the question of how to help the Latin@ "other." This chapter intends to unpack and center the role that Latin@s can have in moving beyond this gaze within a university space and embark in a much more expansive set of narratives related to the Latin@ community and Latin@ college students.

Spatial Justice

> Collective memories in places are not just preserved and contested in the landscape, but through work, practice, and performance as well. (Hanna, 2008)

According to Soja (2013), "Everything that is social (justice included) is simultaneously and inherently spatial, just as everything spatial, at least with regard to the human world, is simultaneously and inherently socialized" (p. 5–6). In this view, geography plays a key role in how we organize power. For Soja, we need a spatial justice consciousness in ways that can lead to social justice and help guide strategic decisions. In the U.S. South, and specifically in its colleges and universities, there currently is a spatiality that has provided minimal access to Latin@ stories, history, and identities. The development of space is politically charged, and it can increase a sense of alienation and unequal distribution of resources and varying feelings of inclusion or exclusion. Soja draws from the work of many, including Foucault (1977; Foucault & Miskoweic, 1986), Harvey (1996), Lefebvre (1974/1991), and Said (1979) (among others) to shape his ideas around spatial justice. This work is grounded in the ways in which geography and space are linked to oppression while it also provides the impetus for imagining how space and social justice can be linked. Interestingly, the work of Soja and Lefebvre revolved around the rights to the urban city. In North Carolina, much of the space is rural or semi-rural. Moreover, as Villenas (2001) observes, the dynamics of new settlement patterns nurture struggles over rights and over who narrates what Latin@s need to achieve equity and access to resources. Space in North Carolina has long been negotiated among a Black-White binary, and Latin@s provide a new set of interests, relationships, and needs.

Marcuse (2009) also reminds us that spatial justice must be positioned in a historical context. Space is embedded in a dynamic and contextual context framed by historical conditions. In North Carolina, the Latin@ student body is framed as a "new group" and what they "deserve," or why, is still being negotiated. Moreover, I agree with Marcuse that ". . . much broader changes in relations of power and allocation of resources and opportunities must be addressed if the social injustices of which spatial injustices are a part are to be redressed" (p. 5).

In sum, a spatial justice approach will serve as the theoretical lens for this article. I am inspired by the potential to take geography and space seriously as a means by which to expand opportunities for Latin@ college students in the state, and, in a overall holistic sense, to nurture dynamic and empowering identities that push back against subtractive and assimilationist rhetoric.

METHOD

In this section, I briefly outline my methodological approach to this article. Specifically, this work draws from (1) my ongoing research on Latino male college students in North Carolina and (2) my reflections related to the development of LERH and the role of spatial justice at UNC-CH.

My qualitative research on Latino male college students in NC consists of life history interviews (Hatch & Wisniewski, 1995), a reflexive journal, and document analysis. To date, I have conducted more that 36 life history interviews. I have interviewed each participant at least three times (and a total of 12 participants at this point) for one to 1.5 hours. Drawing from Erlandson, Harris, Skipper, and Allen (1993), I used a reflexive journal so that I can reflect on the research process, with specific attention to research questions and evolving themes.

Participants

Participants for the work that I draw from and link to the development of LERH were selected based on the following criteria: Latino males, most of their K-12 schooling and higher education in North Carolina. The interviews were conducted while all of the participants were students at a top-tier university located in North Carolina.

ANALYSIS

In this section, I briefly discuss some of the primary themes that I derived from my research on Latino male college students in North Carolina, and I discuss the development and importance of LERH.

Latino Males in North Carolina Universities

Before LERH came to fruition, my initial experiences in North Carolina were significantly shaped by my research on North Carolina Latino male college students (Carrillo, 2016). This work was and continues to be a central part of how LERH is developed. Thus far, some of themes that have come from this work are (1) struggles over a sense of belonging in school, (2) an ongoing fight for developing a sense of "home" in North Carolina, (3) a desire to pursue social justice goals related to Latin@ students, (4) struggles over Latino identity development, a (5) lack of "Latin@ spaces" on and off-campus, a (6) need for the development of Latin@ historical knowledge with links to the region (NC), and a (7) the need for more Latin@ educators at all levels of the schooling pipeline. For the most part, the Latino male college students that I interviewed often felt alienated and marginalized in their university spaces.

Additionally, this work is situated within a larger context of Latin@ settling in nontraditional gateway regions like North Carolina. Many of the participants had spent some time in major cities that have large Latin@ populations, and they discussed the degree to which North Carolina has fewer Latin@-centric and inclusive spaces, compared to places like Los Angeles, New York City, and Houston. While some see hope in staying in North Carolina and fighting for social justice ends, others have pointed out that they miss the feelings of "home" and the respect and dignity that they associated with some aspects of traditional gateway regions, and for these reasons plan to move back to those areas.

These findings have contributed to developing LERH and centering the role of a spatial justice approach. In the next section, I explore these connections in more detail.

From Theory to Action: Spatial Justice and the Development of the UNC-Chapel Hill's Latin@ Education Research Hub (LERH)

> The challenges and pain we are seeing here and around the nation are real, and deserve the significant attention they continue to receive. It is our belief that we have an opportunity to highlight and reinvigorate our efforts to address the issues and gaps that keep anyone from feeling a complete sense of equality and belonging at Carolina.
>
> Carol L. Folt, Chancellor
> James W. Dean, Jr., Executive Vice-Chancellor and Provost
> Felicia A. Washington, Vice-Chancellor for Workforce Strategy, Equity and Engagement
> Winston Crisp, Vice-Chancellor for Student Affairs
> (University of North Carolina Chapel Hill, 2016)

According to Inwood and Yarbrough (2010), "Racialization of place is a process of constructing particular geographical landscapes that help define and reinforce racialized social hierarchies, thus facilitating domination and exploitation" (p. 299). In the South, iconography of space and place have led to centering of symbols and heritage stories that leaves many people, identities, and political orientations out of its spatial imagination. Latin@s are often left out of the narrative or denied the authoring of their mode of entry and positioning. As UNC Chapel Hill deals with the renaming of buildings to rid them of those associated KKK leanings and other racist roots, space and naming has become a part of highly contested debates among administrators, students, and faculty. Students have also protested and been in solidarity with University of Missouri students related to their struggles over racial equity concerns. As previously stated, drawing from Soja and my ongoing research on Latino males in North Carolina universities, I position LERH as one space where spatial justice serves as a place for social action, critical dialogue and research, and the ongoing imagining of geographic space to create narratives that bring Latin@ education away from paternalism, invisibility, and integrationist rhetoric that may harm larger political projects. My ongoing research in North Carolina makes it evident that many Latin@ students feel isolated and have a need for finding a sense of place and community and a desire to have space where their social justice work is supported. In places like California and Texas, there is a longer historical record of Latin@ activism and the development of Latin@-centric spaces at universities, such as El Centro Chicano at the University of Southern California and the Center for Mexican American Studies (CMAS) at the University of Texas at Austin. North Carolina is at a crucial crossroads, and this is a great time to move from talk to action and develop these types of spaces.

Below, I outline three ways by which spatial justice will be part of LERH and by doing so, attempt to provide a more inclusive space for Latin@ students. I also acknowledge that LERH is still in its infancy stages and may go through additional changes.

Creating a Sense of "Home"

> Locational discrimination, created through the biases imposed on certain populations because of their geographical location, is fundamental in the production of spatial injustice and the creation of lasting spatial structures of privilege and advantage. The three most familiar forces shaping locational and spatial discrimination are class, race, and gender, but their effects should not be reduced only to segregation. (Soja, 2009, p. 3)

As my research (2016) on North Carolina Latino male college students has suggested, many of these students crave for a place to call home at their university campus and in the larger community. UNC Chapel Hill has an opportunity to provide a space where Latin@s students and other committed stakeholders make decisions about how "home" can be created on campus. LERH is one small piece of this struggle. Currently, a UNC-CH Latin@ student organization meets at LERH and the UNC-CH School of Education (where LERH is located) has never had a space dedicated to Latin@ students and research. There is tremendous potential in nurturing spatial justice by providing opportunities for organic meetings where students, community members, and faculty can build their sense of home within LERH. The hope is not to make LERH a bureaucratic and token space, but a truly compassionate and open avenue for developing a holistic and inclusive set of stories and safe space in which to tell them and be supportive of one another.

Community-School Partnerships: Spatial Justice Projects

> In the broadest sense, spatial (in)justice refers to an intentional and focused emphasis on the spatial or geographical aspects of justice and injustice. As a starting point, this involves the fair and equitable distribution in space of socially valued resources and the opportunities to use them. (Soja, 2009, p. 2)

A key piece of spatial justice involves efforts to achieve various forms of social justice. Turning theory into social action is a central piece of LERH. Nurturing connections to community via university partnerships with the local community will also be a big part of LERH's vision. Within this context, students from K-12 schools and university faculty and students can also connect and share. At the current moment, LERH has been part of university-middle school partnership that addresses issues of power and identity among Latin@ students. Similarly, LERH has been collaborating with the University of North Carolina, Asheville on pertinent Latin@ education issues. A spatial justice approach will guide these partnerships. As such, thinking spatially about Latin@ students and the larger community will potentially push back against paternalistic rhetoric and assimilationist policies and schooling practices.

Critical Latin@ Education Research

> Thinking spatially about justice not only enriches our theoretical understanding, it can uncover significant new insights that extend our practical knowledge into more effective actions to achieve greater justice and democracy. Obversely, by not making the spatial explicit and assertive, these opportunities will not be so evident. (Soja, 2009, p. 1).

Thinking spatially about our research is an important tool for spatial justice. LERH is positioned to center critical work on Latin@s (in North

Carolina and nationally). My initial focus will be on UNC-CH faculty and students who are willing to contribute to this end. In North Carolina, much work remains to be done in ways that are additive, empowering, and geared toward advocacy and social change. Currently, work on Latino males as well as critical approaches to literacies and arts education have been discussed as important work that will likely be incorporated into LERH's initial phase. Additionally, we are currently developing a research policy arm in an effort to have a say related to state level policies that have an impact on Latin@ students and families.

In sum, these are just three of the areas that will be part of LERH. We are developing these areas as we speak. Nonetheless, a spatial justice framework will guide our work and continue to push us to flesh out our goals and links between theory and social action.

CONCLUSION

> Combining the terms spatial and justice opens up a range of new possibilities for social and political action, as well as for social theorization and empirical analysis, that would not be as clear if the two terms were not used together. (Soja, 2009, p. 4)

On November 19th, 2015, UNC Chapel Hill Chancellor Carol Folt hosted a community town hall meeting on the UNC-CH campus to address issues of inclusivity and race. This event is part of a larger search and struggle over how to create a campus that provides space(s) for multiple identities, experiences, and backgrounds. To date, I have heard very little about what the larger context of displacement and marginalization means for Latin@ students. Maybe it is part of a larger conversation that will come to the fore. Yet, as these discussions enter various levels of policy or rhetorical development, this article positions LERH as one avenue by which Latin@ identities, assets, and struggles can be part of a spatial justice framework that advocates for equity-centric goals.

So I ask: how do we make higher education accessible for Latin@ students and a place of social justice commitments and inclusiveness in the New Latin@ South? LERH is positioned to move beyond the discourses of demographic "challenges," or conversations around "integration" and noncritical use of the term "immigrant." Villenas (2001) has long pointed out that Latin@s in North Carolina small towns are often seen through a paternalistic lens. LERH seeks to provide an additive and empowering space for those that are interested making college a place where Latin@ students and other committed stakeholders can contribute to their sense of belonging.

There is much work ahead, but I highlight how a spatial approach is being used at a university located in the New Latin@ South. As Latin@s continue to move into the region, we need to come out of the "demographic shadows" and push back against various dimensions of paternalism. We have a great opportunity to build a spatially conscious vision where we get to name and create our goals, research, concerns, and contributions, all in an effort to build the university that we deserve.

REFERENCES

Blow, C. (2015, November 16). Race, College and Safe Space. *The New York Times*. Retrieved from https://www.nytimes.com/2015/11/16/opinion/race-college-and -safe-space.html?_r=0

Carrillo, J. F. (2016). Searching for "home" in Dixie: Identity and education in the new Latin@ south. *Educational Studies*, 52(1): 20-37.

Cervantes-Soon, C. G. (2014). A critical look at dual language immersion in the New Latin@ diaspora. *Bilingual Research Journal*, 37(1): 64–82.

Cuadros, P. (2006). *A home on the field: How one championship team inspires hope for the revival of small town America*. New York: Harper Collins.

Erlandson, D., Harris, E. L., Skipper, B. L., & Allen, D. S. (1993). *Doing naturalistic inquiry: A guide to methods*. Newbury Park, CA: Sage.

Foucault, M. (1977). *Discipline and punish: The birth of the prison*. New York: Vintage Books.

Foucault, M., & Miskowiec, J. (1986). Of other spaces. *Diacritics, 16*(1): 22–27.

Hanna, S. P. (2008). A slavery museum?: Race, memory, and landscape in Fredericksburg, Virginia. *Southeastern Geographer, 48*(3): 316–337.

Harvey, D. (1996). *Justice, Nature and the Geography of Difference*. Malden, MA: Blackwell Publishers.

Hatch, J. A., & Wisniewski, R. (1995) *Life history and narrative*. Abingdon, Oxon, UK: RoutledgeFalmer.

Inwood, J. F., & Yarbrough, R. A. (2010). Racialized places, racialized bodies: The impact of racialization on individual and place identities. *GeoJournal, 75*(3): 299–301.

Lefebvre, H. (1974/1991). *The production of space*. Oxford: Blackwell.

Marcuse, P. (2009). Spatial justice: Derivative but causal of social injustice. *Spatial Justice, 1*(4): 1–6.

Said, E. (1979). *Orientalism*. New York: Vintage.

Soja, E. W. (2010). *Seeking spatial justice*. Minneapolis: University of Minnesota Press.

Soja, E. (2009). The city and spatial justice. *Justice Spatiale, Spatial Justice, 1*, 31–39.

The Latino Population booms in the south: Pew. *The Huffington Post*. Retrieved from http://www.huffingtonpost.com/2013/09/03/latino-population-growth_n _3860441.html

University of North Carolina at Chapel Hill (2016), "Update from university leadership on race relations," Office of the Chancellor.

Villenas, S. Latina mothers and small-town racisms: Creating narratives of dignity and moral education in North Carolina. *Anthropology & Education Quarterly*, 32(1): 3–28.

Wortham, S., Murillo, Jr., E. G., & Hamann, E. T. (2002). *Education and policy in the new Latino diaspora*. Westport, CT: Greenwood Publishing Group

progress

Immigrant and Native Hispanic Students and Post-High School Pathways

Leticia Oseguera and Wil Del Pilar

For many immigrants and children of immigrants, the U.S. system of education provides a disparate pathway for upward mobility. While the participation of Hispanic students in higher education has increased from 3 percent to 12 percent since 1976,[1] what is not clear is whether these increases are experienced by native or by immigrant students and how the students move through the educational pipeline after high school. Research has shown contrasting achievement of immigrant populations, with Asian[2] and Black[3] immigrants experiencing an educational advantage and Hispanic[4] immigrants a disadvantage. In fact, the Hispanic immigrant population is the least educated population in the

---

1. Thomas A. Snyder and Susan D. Dillow, Digest of Education Statistics 2010 (Washington, DC: National Center for Education Statistics, Institute of Education Sciences, U.S. Department of Education, 2011), 282.

2. Min Zhou and Carl L. Bankston, *Growing Up American: How Vietnamese Children Adapt to Life in the United States* (New York: Russell Sage Foundation, 1998); Min Zhou and Susan S. Kim, "Community Forces, Social Capital, and Educational Achievement: The Case of Supplementary Education in the Chinese and Korean Immigrant Communities," *Harvard Educational Review* 76, no. 1 (2006): 1–29.

3. Pamela R. Bennett and Amy Lutz, "How African American Is the Net Black Advantage? Differences in College Attendance Among Immigrant Blacks, Native Blacks, and Whites," *Sociology of Education* 82, no. 1 (2009): 70–99; Douglas S. Massey, Margarita Mooney, Kimberly C. Torres, and Camille Z. Charles, "Black Immigrants and Black Natives Attending Selective Colleges and Universities in the United States," *American Journal of Education* 113, no. 2 (2007): 243–71.

4. Consuelo Arbona and Amaury Nora, "The Influence of Academic and Environmental Factors on Hispanic College Degree Attainment," *The Review of Higher Education* 30, no. 3 (2007): 247–69.

United States, with 52 percent of the population having less than a high school diploma or general-education diploma (GED). Interestingly, as time in country increases, the educational achievement of subsequent generations decreases.[5] There is some evidence of a Hispanic immigrant advantage, however, which shows that being a first- or second-generation immigrant increases the odds of enrolling in college compared to third-generation-plus (native) students.[6]

Many factors have been examined in relation to the educational decline among Hispanics as time in country increases—including socioeconomic status (SES), family structure, parental education, geography, and home language—but absent from these analyses is the function of schools as a socializing agent. Serving this population has acquired supreme importance for at least two reasons: the growth of the Hispanic population in the United States, and a labor market that increasingly requires some postsecondary schooling. In 2014 the Hispanic population in the United States reached 55 million,[7] accounting for 24 percent of students enrolled in K–12 public schools.[8]

As an increasing share of children and youth enrolled in schools are of Hispanic heritage, it is crucial that the educational pipeline provide a pathway to postsecondary education, not just for their welfare but for the benefit of U.S. economic and political institutions. A review of the literature reveals that little research unpacks how or whether an immigrant advantage influences postsecondary access, comparatively, among immigrant and native students from the same racial/ethnic group. To address this gap, this article considers the immigrant advantage phenomenon as it relates to Hispanic students' access to college and specifically examines the pathways that Hispanic students take from high school and into college, the military, or the labor force.

Much of the research concerning the educational aspirations and attainment of immigrants and their children is mixed and sometimes points in opposite or unexpected directions. In general, research shows that immi-

5. Richard Fry, *Hispanics, High School Dropouts and the GED* (Washington, DC: Pew Hispanic Center, 2010), http://pewhispanic.org/files/reports/122.pdf

6. Lucrecia Santibañez and Maria E. Zárate, "Bilinguals in the U.S. and College Enrollment," in *The Bilingual Advantage: Language, Literacy, and the Labor Market*, ed. Rebecca M. Callahan and Patricia C. Gándara (Bristol, UK: Multilingual Matters, 2014), 211–33.

7. Jens Manuel Krogstad and Mark H. Lopez, "Hispanic Population Reaches Record 55 Million, but Growth Has Cooled," *Pew Research Center*, June 25, 2015, http://www.pewresearch.org/fact-tank/2015/06/25/u-s-hispanic-population-growth-surge-cools/.

8. "Racial/Ethnic Enrollment in Public Schools," *National Center for Education Statistics*, October 15, 2015, http://nces.ed.gov/programs/coe/indicator_cge.asp.

grants perform well in school,[9] but upon closer inspection this trend does not hold for all immigrant groups. For instance, while almost all students (regardless of race/ethnicity or immigrant generation) aspire to attend college,[10] many Hispanic students wind up never entering higher education or dropping out before completing their degrees.[11] The path from aspiration to attainment seems disjointed for Hispanic students, and while participation for Hispanic eighteen- to twenty-four-year-olds has increased 240 percent since 1996, the role that their K–12 schooling experience and the immigrant generation has in their educational attainment is less clear.[12]

Whether Hispanic students continue on to postsecondary education and what type of institution they attend are matters that greatly influence the likelihood of completion and the type of degree or credential they earn.[13] Thus, this article is situated at the critical junction for Hispanic immigrants, children of Hispanic immigrants, and native-born Hispanic students alike: the end of their high school careers and the transition to higher education. We present where immigrant, children-of-immigrant, and native-born students begin their postsecondary education journey and what the related factors are for selecting those respective paths. This article concludes with recommendations for deeper investigation into high schools as socializing agents that shape different pathways for Hispanic students of different immigrant generation statuses.

Immigrants

The literature on immigrants consistently finds an educational advantage within this population.[14] The research shows that immigrants perform

9. Grace Kao and Marta Tienda, "Optimism and Achievement: The Educational Performance of Immigrant Youth" *Social Science Quarterly* 76, no. 1 (1995): 1–19; Alejandro Portes and Rubén G. Rumbaut, *Immigrant America: A Portrait,* 2nd ed. (Berkeley: University of California Press, 1996).

10. Grace Kao and Jennifer S. Thompson, "Racial and Ethnic Stratification in Educational Achievement and Attainment," *Annual Review of Sociology* 29 (2003): 417–42.

11. Michelle C. Liu, *Trends in Latino College Access and Success: Investing in Higher Education for Latinos* (Denver, CO: National Conference of State Legislatures, 2011); Jens Manuel Krogstad and Richard Fry, "More Hispanics, Blacks Enrolling in College, But Lag in Bachelor's Degrees," *Pew Research Center*, April 24, 2014, http://www.pewresearch.org/fact-tank/2014/04/24/more-hispanics-blacks-enrolling-in-college-but-lag-in-bachelors-degrees/.

12. Ibid.

13. Jens Manuel Krogstad, "5 Facts About Latinos and Education," *Pew Research Center*, May 26, 2015, http://www.pewresearch.org/fact-tank/2015/05/26/5-facts-about-latinos-and-education/.

14. Kao and Tienda, "Optimism and Achievement: The Educational Performance of Immigrant Youth."

equivalently to and even outperform natives.[15] The superior academic performance of immigrants has been attributed to immigrant optimism,[16] the role of immigrant parents, cultural superiority, and positive selectivity. The immigrant advantage not only improves performance in high school but also increases the likelihood of attending college.[17] However, the educational trajectories of immigrants tend to diverge along racial and ethnic lines,[18] with Black and Asian immigrants experiencing the greatest benefit from their immigrant status.[19]

The educational advantage of Asian immigrants is well documented in the literature.[20] Asian achievement has been attributed to several causes: immigrant parents,[21] positive selection,[22] tendency to come from higher-SES households,[23] and cultural arguments around the value of education.[24]

15. Grace Kao, "Racial Identity and Academic Performance: An Examination of Biracial Asian And African American Youth," *Journal of Asian American Studies* 2, no. 3 (1999): 223–49; Kao and Tienda, "Optimism and Achievement: The Educational Performance of Immigrant Youth"; Portes and Rumbaut, *Immigrant America: A Portrait, 2nd ed.*; Alejandro Portes and Rubén G. Rumbaut, *Immigrant America: A Portrait, 3rd ed.* (Berkeley: University of California Press, 2006); Kathryn H. Tillman, Guo Guang, and Kathleen M. Harris, "Grade Retention Among Immigrant Children," *Social Science Research* 35, no. 1 (2006): 129–56.

16. Carola Suárez-Orozco and Marcelo M. Suárez-Orozco. *Transformations: Immigration, Family Life, and Achievement Motivation Among Latino Adolescents* (Stanford, CA: Stanford University Press, 1995).

17. Ursula Keller and Kathryn H. Tillman, "Post-Secondary Educational Attainment of Immigrant and Native Youth," *Social Forces* 87, no. 1 (2008): 121–52.

18. Frank D. Bean and Gillian Stevens, *America's Newcomers and the Dynamics of Diversity* (New York: Russell Sage Foundation, 2003); Kao and Tienda, "Optimism and Achievement: The Educational Performance of Immigrant Youth"; Portes and Rumbaut, *Immigrant America: A Portrait, 3rd ed.*; Min Zhou, "Growing Up American: The Challenge Confronting Immigrant Children and Children of Immigrants," *Annual Review of Sociology* 23 (1997): 63–95.

19. Keller and Tillman, "Post-Secondary Educational Attainment of Immigrant and Native Youth."

20. Kao and Tienda, "Optimism and Achievement: The Educational Performance of Immigrant Youth"; Georges Vernez, Allan F. Abrahamse, and Denise D. Quigley, *How Immigrants Fare in U.S. Education* (Santa Monica, CA: Rand, 1996); Zhou and Bankston, *Growing Up American: How Vietnamese Children Adapt to Life in the United States.*

21. Kao and Tienda, "Optimism and Achievement: The Educational Performance of Immigrant Youth."

22. Cynthia Feliciano, "Educational Selectivity in U.S. Immigration: How Do Immigrants Compare to Those Left Behind?" *Demography* 42, no. 1 (2005): 131–52.

23. Alejandro Portes and Rubén G. Rumbaut, *Legacies: The Story of the Immigrant Second Generation* (Berkeley: University of California Press, 2001).

24. Zhou and Bankston, *Growing Up American: How Vietnamese Children Adapt to Life in the United States*; Zhou and Kim, "Community Forces, Social Capital, and Educational Achievement: The Case of Supplementary Education in the Chinese and Korean Immigrant Communities."

Despite these advantages, the evidence is not all positive for Asian students. Asian immigrants experience declines in college attendance as generations increase; beyond the third generation the educational achievement of Asian students diminishes and becomes similar to that of White students.[25-]

A similar body of evidence exists regarding the educational achievement of Black immigrants. Black immigrants are quantitatively different than African Americans.[26] Black immigrants are more likely to come from two-parent families,[27] attend private school, and come from higher-SES families ($43,275 compared to $33,790).[28] While Black immigrants have a significant advantage over all other immigrant populations, it is relatively short-lived, extending only to the first generation.[29] First-generation Black immigrants are significantly more likely than Whites to attend college,[30] particularly at the most elite and selective campuses. Divergent from the experience of Asian immigrants, the Black immigrant advantage benefits only the first generation; by the second generation the educational outcomes of the children of Black immigrants are no different from those of natives.

The literature on Hispanic youth illustrates the differential pathways this population navigates through high school and into postsecondary education. Despite being[31] among the least likely to graduate from high school

25. Kao and Tienda, "Optimism and Achievement: The Educational Performance of Immigrant Youth"; Keller and Tillman, "Post-Secondary Educational Attainment of Immigrant and Native Youth."

26. John R. Logan and Glenn Deane, "Black Diversity in Metropolitan America," *Lewis Mumford Center for Comparative Urban and Regional Research, University at Albany*, August 15, 2003, http://mumford.albany.edu/census/BlackWhite/BlackDiversityReport/black-diversity 01.htm.

27. Bennett and Lutz, "How African American Is the Net Black Advantage? Differences in College Attendance Among Immigrant Blacks, Native Blacks, and Whites."

28. Rubén G. Rumbaut and Alejandro Portes, *Ethnicities: Children of Immigrants in America* (Berkeley: University of California Press, 2001); Mary C. Waters, *Black Identities: West Indian Immigrant Dreams and American Realities* (New York: Russell Sage Foundation, 1999).

29. Kao and Tienda, "Optimism and Achievement: The Educational Performance of Immigrant Youth."

30. Keller and Tillman, "Post-Secondary Educational Attainment of Immigrant and Native Youth."

31. Arbona and Nora, "The Influence of Academic and Environmental Factors on Hispanic College Degree Attainment"; Katherine M. Conway, "Exploring Persistence of Immigrant and Native Students in an Urban Community College," *Review of Higher Education*, 32, no. 3 (2009): 321–52; Richard Fry, *Latinos in Higher Education: Many Enroll, Too Few Graduate* (Washington, DC: *Pew Hispanic Center*, 2005); Richard Fry, *Hispanic Youth Dropping out of U.S. Schools: Measuring the Challenge* (Washington, DC: Pew Hispanic Center, 2003); Edward Eric Telles and Vilma Ortiz, *Generations of Exclusion: Mexican Americans, Assimilation, and Race* (New York: Russell Sage Foundation, 2008).

or college,[32] Hispanic immigrants in both the first and second generation experience an educational advantage over the third generation.[33] Part of the advantage is attributed to having immigrant parents. The phenomenon, termed the immigrant paradox, credits family cohesion, support, work ethic, and stern discipline as factors of in the educational performance of immigrant youth.[34] Several recent studies also point to the impact of bilingualism on the educational performance of Hispanic youth. These studies report a link not only between being bilingual and educational success but also between the level of fluency and a decrease in the likelihood of dropping out of high school.[35] Additional research has found that "high use" Spanish bilingual students were more likely to go to college, and they were more likely to go to a four-year college.[36]

Because of the dramatic increases in the Hispanic population, due to higher birth and immigration rates, Richard Fry emphasizes the importance of distinguishing between the arrival ages of Hispanic immigrants.[37] Hispanic immigrants who arrive above the age of fifteen experience the highest risk of dropping out of high school (constituting 60 percent of Hispanic high school dropouts). Fry argues that these youth do not reflect on the performance of U.S. schools but rather are a reflection on Latin American schools and the reason for immigration (work or family unification, etc.).[38] Compelling evidence against this

32. Arbona and Nora, "The Influence of Academic and Environmental Factors on Hispanic College Degree Attainment"; Krogstad, "5 Facts About Latinos and Education."

33. Patricia Gandara, "Is There Really a Labor Market Advantage to Bilingualism in the U.S.?" *ETS Research Report Series* 2015, no. 1 (2015): 1–34; Lingxin Hao and Han Soo Woo, "Distinct Trajectories in the Transition to Adulthood: Are Children of Immigrants Advantaged?" *Child Development* 83, no.5 (2012): 1623–39; Rubén G. Rumbaut, "English Plus: Exploring the Socioeconomic Benefits of Bilingualism in Southern California," in *The Bilingual Advantage: Language, Literacy, and the Labor Market*, ed. Rebecca M. Callahan and Patricia C. Gándara (Bristol, UK: Multilingual Matters, 2014), 182–205; Santibañez and Zárate, "Bilinguals in the US and College Enrollment"; Telles and Ortiz, *Generations of Exclusion: Mexican Americans, Assimilation, and Race*.

34. Robert Crosnoe, *Preparing the Children of Immigrants for Early Academic Success* (Washington, DC: Migration Policy Institute, 2013); Hao and Woo, "Distinct Trajectories in the Transition to Adulthood: Are Children of Immigrants Advantaged?"; Grace Kao, "Parental Influences on the Educational Outcomes of Immigrant Youth," *International Migration Review* 38, no. 2 (2004): 427–49.

35. Rumbaut, "English Plus: Exploring the Socioeconomic Benefits of Bilingualism in Southern California."

36. Santibañez and Zárate, "Bilinguals in the US and College Enrollment."

37. Fry, *Hispanic Youth Dropping out of U.S. Schools: Measuring the Challenge.*

38. Ibid.

stance is provided by Jamie Lew,[39] who emphasizes the failure of U.S. schools in educating Korean American youth, focusing on the structural, social, and educational organizations that fail dropouts. U.S. schools, particularly urban schools in traditional sending areas, seem to provide students with an educational context that lacks rigor, resources, expectations, and institutional attachment.[40] School-level factors not only affect high school completion but also influence the postsecondary pathways that students take.[41]

The type of institution at which immigrant students begin their education can be a factor in whether they ever attain a bachelor's degree. Although community colleges can be a viable access point for students interested in transferring to a four-year university, evidence reviewed by Ernest Pascarella and Patrick Terenzini suggests that simply beginning the path to a bachelor's degree at a community college can reduce the likelihood of degree attainment by 15 to 20 percent.[42] This finding is quite troubling given that immigrants are 20 percent more likely than natives to begin their education at a community college.[43] Compared to other groups, Hispanics are most likely to attend a community college[44] but are least likely to graduate.[45] In fact, of the 2.2 million Hispanics enrolled in college in 2013, 46 percent were enrolled in community college—a higher proportion than any other racial/ethnic group.[46]

In spite of this trend, immigrant optimism may carry these students through community college. A study on immigrants at community colleges

39. Jamie Lew, "Korean American High School Dropouts: Overcoming Institutional Barriers," in *Asian Americans in Class: Charting the Achievement Gap Among Korean American Youth*, ed. Jamie Lew (New York: Teachers College Press, 2006), 45–60.

40. Hao and Woo, "Distinct Trajectories in the Transition to Adulthood: Are Children of Immigrants Advantaged?"

41. Patricia M. McDonough, *Choosing Colleges: How Social Class and Schools Structure Opportunity* (Albany: State University of New York Press, 1997).

42. Ernest T. Pascarella and Patrick T. Terenzini, *How College Affects Students: A Third Decade of Research, Vol. 2* (San Francisco: Jossey-Bass, 2005).

43. Maryann J. Gray, Georges Vernez, and Elizabeth Rolph, "Student Access and the 'New' Immigrants: Assessing Their Impact on Institutions," *Change* 28, no. 5 (1996): 41–47.

44. Amaury Nora, Laura I. Rendon, and Kristen G. Cuadraz, "Access, Choice, and Outcomes: A Profile of Hispanic Students in Higher Education," in *Education of Hispanics in the United States: Politics, Policies, and Outcomes, Vol. 16*, ed. Abbas Tashakkori and Salvador H. Ochoa (New York: AMS Press, 1999), 175–200; Vernez, Abrahamse, and Quigley, *How Immigrants Fare in U.S. Education.*

45. Conway, "Exploring Persistence of Immigrant and Native Students in an Urban Commuity College."

46. Krogstad, "5 Facts About Latinos and Education."

in New York found that immigrants earn more credits and are more likely to complete an associate's degree than are natives.[47] These findings were confirmed by an expanded study, which found that immigrants acclimate quickly to the collegiate environment, earning more credits and higher grade point averages than natives.[48] There also appears to be a small difference regarding place of birth. Foreign-born students who graduate from U.S. high schools are more likely to enroll at a four-year university than are native-born students. Foreign-born students who graduate from high school abroad are more likely to enroll at two-year colleges.[49]

An additional factor affecting the educational accomplishment of immigrants is generational status. The evidence is clear that first- and second-generation immigrants have an educational advantage over later generations.[50] First- and second-generation immigrants have higher levels of college attendance than immigrant students beyond the third generation. Despite structural barriers, they are able to achieve educational gains over their parents.[51] Immigrant optimism and social and cultural capital appear to provide first-generation students with shelter from structural deficiencies that may impede attainment.

Immigrants in the first generation appear to benefit the most from their status and, as previously discussed, the guidance of immigrant parents.[52] First-generation students have slightly higher grades, math scores, and aspirations than students in the third generation or beyond. There also

---

47. Thomas Bailey and Elliot B. Weininger, "Performance, Graduation, and Transfer of Immigrants and Natives in City University of New York Community Colleges," *Educational Evaluation and Policy Analysis* 24, no. 4 (2002): 359–77.

48. Conway, "Exploring Persistence of Immigrant and Native Students in an Urban Community College."

49. Bailey and Weininger, "Performance, Graduation, and Transfer of Immigrants and Natives in City University of New York Community Colleges."

50. Jennifer E. Glick and Michael. J. White, "The Academic Trajectories of Immigrant Youths: Analysis Within and Across Cohorts," *Demography* 40, no. 4 (2003): 759–83; Keller and Tillman, "Post-Secondary Educational Attainment of Immigrant and Native Youth"; Krista M. Perreira, Kathleen M. Harris, and Dohoon Lee, "Making It in America: High School Completion by Immigrant and Native Youth," *Demography* 43, no. 3 (2006): 511–36; Santibañez and Zárate, "Bilinguals in the US and College Enrollment."

51. Perreira, Harris, and Lee, "Making It in America: High School Completion by Immigrant and Native Youth."

52. Keller and Tillman, "Post-Secondary Educational Attainment of Immigrant and Native Youth"; Kao and Tienda, "Optimism and Achievement: The Educational Performance of Immigrant Youth"; Chunyan Song and Jennifer E. Glick, "College Attendance and Choice of College Majors Among Asian-American Students," *Social Science Quarterly* 85, no. 5 (2004): 1401–21; Vernez, Abrahamse, and Quigley, *How Immigrants Fare in U.S. Education.*

appears to be a small advantage for the second generation. Jennifer Glick and Michael White[53] found that the second generation was more likely to complete high school and was significantly more likely to have some college or beyond compared to those beyond the third generation.[54]

In comparison with earlier generations, the third generation is the least advantaged. Often called third-generation decline, this population is significantly different from the earlier groups.[55] Nancy Landale, Salvador Oropesa, and Daniel Llanes found that third-generation Mexicans were the most likely to drop out of high school.[56] This pattern holds true for other populations as well. Asian and Hispanic students were found to graduate at higher rates than their parents, but they lose ground in comparison to other groups.[57] What is missing in discussions of immigrant generation status is how the school context might shape the educational pathways of students. This work addresses this gap by examining post-high school pathways of students from different generation statuses.

FRAMEWORK

Similar to U.S. society, the educational outcomes of immigrants are stratified based on myriad factors, including the ways immigrants are received and assimilated or acculturated into society. Two dominant theories have guided the discourse on assimilation: classical assimilation theory[58] and segmented assimilation theory.[59] Classical assimilation (also known as

---

53. Glick and White, "The Academic Trajectories of Immigrant Youths: Analysis Within and Across Cohorts."

54. Ibid.; Keller and Tillman, "Post-Secondary Educational Attainment of Immigrant and Native Youth."

55. Portes and Rumbaut, *Legacies: The Story of the Immigrant Second Generation.*

56. Nancy S. Landale, R. Salvador Oropesa, and Daniel Llanes, "Schooling, Work, and Idleness Among Mexican and Non-Latino White Adolescents," *Social Science Research* 27, no. 4 (1998): 457–80.

57. Portes and Rumbaut, *Legacies: The Story of the Immigrant Second Generation.*

58. Richard Alba and Victor Nee, "Rethinking Assimilation Theory for a New Era of Immigration," *International Migration Review* 41, no. 4 (1997): 826–74; Richard Alba and Victor Nee, *Remaking the American Mainstream: Assimilation and Contemporary Immigration* (Cambridge, MA: Harvard University Press, 2003).

59. Alejandro Portes and Patricia Fernández-Kelley, "No Margin for Error: Educational and Occupational Achievement Among Disadvantaged Children of Immigrants," *The Annals of the American Academy of Political and Social Science* 620, no. 1 (2008): 12–36; Alejandro Portes and Min Zhou, "The New Second Generation: Segmented Assimilation and Its Variants," *The Annals of the American Academy of Political and Social Science* 530, no. 1 (1993): 74–96.

straight-line) theorists argue that immigrants follow a straight line until they reach a point of convergence over time, adopting the values, norms, behaviors, and characteristics of the majority culture. Segmented assimilation theorists argue that there are multiple pathways to assimilation, as stratified social structures lead to divergent assimilation outcomes. A variety of factors influences immigrants' segmented assimilation pathways, including national origin, SES, human capital, social capital, family structure, and context of reception.[60] These factors influence how and into what strata of society immigrants are likely to assimilate. Contrary to classical assimilation theory, immigrants can choose to acculturate selectively, maintaining the values and attitudes of their home country to inspire achievement for their children. Immigrants may also follow the straight-line path, purported by classical assimilation theorists, entering the middle class, while some immigrant groups may experience downward assimilation into an oppositional culture.[61]

Similarly, the U.S. system of higher education is stratified, with selective institutions at the top of the hierarchy and for-profit institutions at the bottom, with no college attendance conceivably being the lowest level of selectivity as students do not secure postsecondary training. What is unclear is how immigrant groups from distinct generations integrate into the U.S. higher education hierarchy. Thus, this work seeks to explore how assimilation factors (SES, human capital, social capital, family structure, and context of reception) influence the stratification of Hispanic immigrants, children of Hispanic immigrants, and native-born Hispanic students into different segments of education. Schools serve as a major socializing force for immigrants and therefore are one of the significant agents guiding the educational outcomes of this population. School effects will be conceptualized as the context of reception in the segmented assimilation theory model.

To effectively capture school effects on the educational pathways of immigrants, aspects of Jeannie Oakes' framework,[62] which outlines the seven critical conditions for college access, will be used as a proxy for the context of reception. This framework offers a broad organization of the

60. Portes and Fernández-Kelley, "No Margin for Error."

61. John U. Ogbu, *Minority Education and Caste: The American System in a Cross-Cultural Perspective* (San Diego, CA: Academic Press, 1978).

62. Jeannie Oakes, *Critical Conditions for Equity and Diversity in College Access: Informing Policy and Monitoring Results,* University of California All Campus Consortium on Research for Diversity, February 2003, https://ucaccord.gseis.ucla.edu/publications/critical-conditions-for-equity-and-diversity.

critical conditions that ideally need to be present to ensure movement into college after high school and will help us to determine the school effects on the educational outcomes of immigrants from distinct generations. These conditions include: (1) safe and adequate school facilities, (2) college-going school culture, (3) highly qualified teachers, (4) intensive academic and social supports, (5) rigorous academic curriculum, (6) opportunities to develop a multicultural college-going identity, and (7) family-neighborhood-school connections focused on college-going. Three of these conditions can be viewed primarily as related to individual-level academic and personal identity: rigorous academic curriculum, intensive academic and social supports, and multicultural college-going identity. Another three conditions reference within-classroom and within-school context: safe and adequate school facilities, college-going school culture, and highly qualified teachers. The final condition connects schools to families, communities, and neighborhood.

Context of reception focuses on government, society, and community policies and attitudes toward immigrant communities.[63] Since this analysis is focused on the effect of schools as socializing agents, our analysis focuses on school-level conditions (safe and adequate school facilities, college-going school culture, and highly qualified teachers). To better understand variation in educational outcomes, this work uses conceptual frameworks described above to examine the link between variations in the conditions for college access for immigrant populations by generational status.

METHODS

Data Source and Sample

The data are drawn from the Educational Longitudinal Study (ELS) 2002–2006 panel, collected for the National Center for Education Statistics (NCES) by the National Opinion Research Center. In 2002, the NCES surveyed 14,000 U.S. tenth-graders whose responses are weighted to represent the population of tenth-graders nationally. These same respondents were resurveyed in 2004 and again in 2006. Information was collected from the sampled students and their parents, teachers, and school administrators. Data are weighted using panel weights provided by ELS to reflect the responses of all U.S. students who were tenth-graders in 2002, twelfth-graders in 2004, and two years post-high school in 2006, assuming a traditional high

63. Portes and Zhou, "The New Second Generation: Segmented Assimilation and Its Variants."

school path. Consequently, these results can only be generalized to those students who were tenth-graders in 2002. Students for whom data are available for all three time points are included in this work.

Missing Data

To account for the common problem of missing data on surveys, we used multiple imputation to deal with missing values that were missing at random due to item nonresponse.[64] Multiple imputation uses information from the sample distributions of the variables themselves to replace missing values with randomly generated but contextually appropriate values. Our actual imputation procedure uses Imputation by Chained Equations (ICE) in the Stata software. ICE draws imputed values from a posterior distribution using OLS regression models to replace missing values for continuous variables and logit models to replace missing values for binary or ordinal variables.[65] Since the imputed data sets themselves have no missing values, sample size was preserved.

MEASURES

Generational Status

The main variable of interest in this study is generational status. The literature on immigrant generation has no consensus regarding the cutoff age of arrival to determine immigrant generation. This work defines immigrant students as any student who is foreign-born and children of immigrants as any student born in the United States to at least one foreign-born parent. In the literature on immigrants these groups are traditionally considered first, one-point-five, second, and two-point-five immigrant generation students.[66] Although the literature on immigrant generation highlights some differences among these populations,[67] because of data limitations the categories were merged to allow for statistical analysis. We plan to flag important factors such as age of arrival in multivariate analyses of these groups. Native

64. Donald B. Rubin, *Multiple Imputation for Nonresponse in Surveys* (New York: Wiley, 1987).

65. Patrick Royston, "Multiple Imputation of Missing Values," *The Stata Journal* 4, no. 3 (2004): 227–41.

66. Barry R. Chiswick and Noyna DebBurman, "Educational Attainment: Analysis by Immigrant Generation," *Economics of Education Review* 23, no. 4 (2004): 361–79.

67. Portes and Rumbaut, *Immigrant America: A Portrait, 2nd ed.*; Kao and Tienda, "Optimism and Achievement: The Educational Performance of Immigrant Youth."

students are defined as those who are born in the United States to two U.S.-born parents. These definitions yield an immigrant Hispanic sample size of 530, a children of Hispanic immigrant sample size of 496, and a native-born Hispanic sample of 713.

Control Variables

Many of the traditional control variables are included as part of the framework of this article (gender, race/ethnicity, home language background,[68] and family structure).

Segmented assimilation theory variables. The literature on college choice has shown that the type of institution that a student selects is largely mediated by income level, with higher-income students enrolling in more selective institutions.[69] To examine different educational pathways and the effect of income level, we use SES divided into quartiles as a variable.

Human capital. To capture human capital, parents' level of education is used. While immigrant parents may be unable to translate education from a foreign country into occupational prestige (used in ELS as a component of SES) in the United States, the value of education and the cultural capital that comes with higher education allows these parents to provide resources (e.g., help with homework, motivation, etc.) to their children. In addition, the academic achievement of the student will be used as a measure of human capital. Math has been found to be a strong predictor of later educational outcomes,[70] so a student's highest math enrollment will be used as a measure of a student's human capital.

---

68. We tested home language background in the analyses, but it was not significant in these samples so we ultimately excluded it from the analyses.

69. Anthony P. Carnevale and Stephen J. Rose, *Socioeconomic Status, Race/Ethnicity, and Selective College Admissions* (New York: Century Foundation, 2003), 101–56; Scott Swail, Alberto F. Cabrera, and Chul Lee, "Latino Youth and the Pathway to College," *Pew Research Center*, June 23, 2004, http://www.pewhispanic.org/2004/06/23/latino-youth-and-the-pathway-to-college/.

70. Clifford Adelman, *Answers in the Tool Box: Academic Intensity, Attendance Patterns, and Bachelor's Degree Attainment* (Washington, DC: U.S. Department of Education, Office of Education Research and Improvement, National Institute on Postsecondary Education, Libraries, and Lifelong Learning, 1999); Clifford Adelman, *Principal Indicators of Student Academic Histories in Postsecondary Education 1972–2000* (Washington, DC: US Department of Education, Office of Vocational and Adult Education, 2004); Leticia Oseguera, *Making the Case for Applying Oakes' Critical Conditions for College Access Framework to the Educational Longitudinal Survey (ELS) Data* (Los Angeles, CA: UC ACCORD, 2010).

Social capital. Our measure of social capital will include preconditions of social capital. Leticia Oseguera, Gilberto Conchas, and Eduardo Mosqueda highlight the fact that social capital becomes capital only after it is activated and leads to some measurable outcome.[71] As such, there are preconditions that must exist for social capital to be measured. In this work, we define social capital as the extent to which parents and children communicate about school and post-high school experiences. We call this school-related social capital, and it is a five-item factor.[72]

Context of reception. Lastly, context of reception (COR) is measured, using safe and adequate school facilities, college-going school culture, and highly qualified teachers. Safe and adequate facilities are schools free from overcrowding, violence, or other unsafe or unsanitary conditions. Dilapidated or unsafe schools directly (and negatively) influence student achievement and motivation for success.[73] We operationalize this condition using the aggregated students' opinion of poor school climate[74] and the counselors' opinion of the learning environment.[75] A college-going school culture is a school environment where teachers, administrators, parents, and students expect all students to have access to experiences that will enable high achievement. "These high expectations are coupled with specific interventions and information that emphasize to students that college preparation is a normal part of their childhood and youth."[76] We opera-

---

71. Leticia Oseguera, Gilberto Q. Conchas, and Eduardo Mosqueda, "Beyond Family and Ethnic Culture: Understanding the Preconditions for the Potential Realization of Social Capital," *Youth & Society* 43, no. 3 (2011): 1136–66.

72. Provide advice about plans for college (.70); provide advice about applying to college/school after high school (.69); provide advice about selecting college (.58); provide advice about jobs to apply after high school (.60); provide information about community/national/world events (.46). Alpha =.75.

73. Michelle Fine, *Framing Dropouts: Notes on the Politics of an Urban Public High School* (Albany: State University of New York Press, 1991); Jonathan Kozol, *Savage Inequalities: Children in America's Schools* (New York: HarperPerennial, 1992).

74. There are gangs in school (.66); racial/ethnic groups often fight (.61); student does not feel safe at school (.40). Alpha=.68.

75. How often physical conflicts a problem at school (.74); how often vandalism a problem at school (.65); how often robbery/theft a problem at school (.64); how often gang activity a problem at school (.61); how often class cutting a problem at school (.60); how often possession of weapons a problem at school (.55). Alpha=.77.

76. Jeannie Oakes, Julie Mendoza, and David Silver, "Informing and Monitoring California's Progress Toward Equitable College Access," in *Expanding Opportunity in Higher Education Leveraging Promise*, ed. Patricia Gandara (Albany: State University of New York Press, 2006), 30–31.

tionalize this condition using the percent of the student body that continues on to a four-year college. Highly qualified teachers include the requisite training and certification of teachers but also the ability of teachers to make "highly valued knowledge accessible to students of diverse backgrounds."[77] In this work, we also measure high-quality teaching from the student perspective of whether teachers at the school are interested in students,[78] but we aggregate this variable by school ID to create a school-level measure of whether students collectively believe teachers at the school are interested in the students.

Stratified School System (Outcome Variable)

Defining a stratified system of education can be done in a variety of ways. Our operational definition of selectivity is based on sector. We include a measure for students who do not enter postsecondary institutions. If we are truly attempting to measure a stratified educational system and the effects of school, we have to recognize that there are populations of students who fall along the lowest stratum.[79] We grouped institutions by sector, defining educational selectivity as (1) four-year college or university, (2) open-access community colleges, (3) broad-access proprietary/for-profit college, and (4) no college. Since the focus of this article is the examination of post-high school pathways, community colleges were used as the reference group, as they are open-access institutions and the predominant choice of Hispanic students.[80]

ANALYTIC METHOD

A series of descriptive and multivariate analyses are employed to examine immigrant generational status differences. To examine immigrants of distinct generation statuses into our definition of a stratified postsecondary educational system, we use multinomial logistic regressions. This approach allows us to simultaneously examine the relationship between immigrant generation and various postsecondary educational pathways, and compare

---

77. Ibid., 30.

78. Teachers are interested in students (.74); the teaching is good (.66); teachers praise student effort (.55); students get along well with teachers (.47); in class, often (do not) feel put down by teachers (.41). Alpha=.73.

79. Michael J. Piore, *Birds of Passage: Migrant Labor and Industrial Societies* (Cambridge, UK: Cambridge University Press, 1979).

80. Krogstad, "5 Facts About Latinos and Education."

the extent to which Alejandro Portes and Min Zhou's segmented assimilation framework explains immigration generation status differences across sectors.[81] In a similar analysis, Cynthia Feliciano and Mariam Ashtiani argue that using a multinomial analysis rather than an ordered analysis is more appropriate, introducing less measurement error.[82] Pat Goldsmith adds that multinomial logit models are appropriate because educational attainment is both a nominal and an ordinal variable.[83] The possible outcomes in this study include no college and into labor force, broad-access for-profit college enrollment (either two- or four-year level), open-access community college enrollment, and four-year college enrollment. Community college is the reference group as we want to compare an open-access system to all the other possible pathways, including not attending college at all and moving directly into the labor force or military. We produce three different multinomial models (one for each generation status). Table 1 provides an overview of the outcome by generation status, and Table 2 presents the means and standard deviations of the variables in the analyses by generation status.

FINDINGS

Results: Hispanic Immigrant Students

In this section, we highlight the segmented assimilation variables that are related to three possible outcomes: labor force participation, for-profit college attendance, or four-year college attendance relative to open-access community college enrollment among the Hispanic immigrant sample (see Table 3 for results). It is possible that students who are attending college are working, but we defined labor force as full-time labor force and no college attendance. Among immigrants in this first model, those students who moved directly into the labor force versus students who enrolled in a community college, SES, family structure, human and social capital variables operated as they are theorized. That is, lower-SES immigrant students were more likely to enter the labor force immediately after high school than to attend a community college, and immigrant students who completed slightly less advanced math than general math were more likely to move

81. Portes and Zhou, "The New Second Generation: Segmented Assimilation and Its Variants."

82. Cynthia Feliciano and Mariam Ashtiani, *Poverty and Postsecondary Educational Pathways* (Los Angeles: UC ACCORD, 2010).

83. Pat R. Goldsmith, "Schools or Neighborhoods or Both?: Race and Ethnic Segregation and Educational Attainment." Social Forces, 2009. doi:10.1353/sof.0.0193.

TABLE 1. Hispanic post-high school pathway by generation status

	IMMIGRANT	CHILDREN OF IMMIGRANTS	NATIVES
Labor Force/ Military	38.3	27.5	33.6
For-Profit College	6.3	6.5	8.3
Community College	33.7	38.8	34.0
Not-for-Profit Four-Year College	21.7	27.3	24.1

TABLE 2. Means and standard deviations for variables in model by generation status

VARIABLES	IMMIGRANT MEAN	STD. DEV.	CHILDREN OF IMMIGRANTS MEAN	STD. DEV.	NATIVES MEAN	STD. DEV.
STUDENT LEVEL VARIABLES						
Female	0.51	0.50	0.48	0.50	0.51	0.50
SES Quartile	1.74	1.00	1.69	0.98	2.17	1.02
Family Structure	0.57	0.50	0.63	0.48	0.50	0.50
HUMAN CAPITAL Advanced math course-taking pipeline	0.28	0.45	0.29	0.46	0.29	0.45
SOCIAL CAPITAL Parents discuss school activities and post-high school plans (10th grade)	2.03	0.55	2.08	0.58	2.17	0.52
HIGH SCHOOL LEVEL VARIABLES						
COR: SAFE & ADEQUATE FACILITIES Student opinion of poor school climate (10th grade)	2.25	0.44	2.26	0.42	2.17	0.48
COR: COLLEGE GOING CULTURE Graduates went to four-year college	3.93	1.07	3.98	1.12	3.96	1.17
COR: HIGH QUALITY TEACHING Student opinion that teachers are interested in students	2.80	0.30	2.75	0.28	2.72	0.37

TABLE 3. Multinomial logistic regression: Predicting Hispanic immigrant student pathways (Reference = Open Access Community College)

VARIABLES	LABOR FORCE/ MILITARY				FOR-PROFIT COLLEGE OR UNIVERSITY				FOUR-YEAR COLLEGE OR UNIVERSITY			
	B	STD. ERROR	SIG.	EXP (B)	B	STD. ERROR	SIG.	EXP (B)	B	STD. ERROR	SIG.	EXP (B)
STUDENT LEVEL VARIABLES												
Intercept	1.623	.109	.000		−.126	.178	.479		−1.863	.115	.000	
Female	−.413	.014	.000	.662	−.368	.025	.000	.692	.377	.017	.000	1.457
SES Quartile												
Quartile 1	1.883	.038	.000	6.572	.339	.056	.000	1.404	−.416	.027	.000	.659
Quartile 2	1.463	.040	.000	4.317	.726	.058	.000	2.066	−.154	.031	.000	.858
Quartile 3	1.254	.041	.000	3.505	.452	.061	.000	1.571	.223	.030	.000	1.250
Family Structure	−.218	.014	.000	.804	−.010	.025	.681	.999	−.009	.017	.588	.991
HUMAN CAPITAL												
Advanced math course-taking pipeline	−.753	.018	.000	.471	−.384	.031	.000	.681	1.127	.017	.000	3.088
SOCIAL CAPITAL												
Parents discuss school activities and post-high school plans (10th grade)	−.201	0.013	.000	.818	.098	.023	.000	1.103	.262	.015	.000	1.300
HIGH SCHOOL LEVEL VARIABLES												
COR: SAFE AND ADEQUATE FACILITIES												
Student opinion of poor school climate (10th grade)	.769	.019	.000	2.159	.210	.033	.000	1.233	−.326	.020	.000	.722
COR: COLLEGE GOING CULTURE												
Graduates went to four-year college	.345	.007	.000	1.412	−.153	.012	.000	.858	.200	.008	.000	1.221
COR: HIGH QUALITY TEACHING												
Student opinion that teachers are interested in students	−.575	.026	.000	.469	−.644	0.042	.000	.525	.094	.028	.001	1.099

directly into the labor force than to attend a community college. Immigrant students without a two-parent family unit and immigrant students who reported lower likelihood that their parents spoke with them about their post-high school plans were more likely to enter the labor force and not move on to the community college. Immigrant Hispanic men were more likely to enter the labor force than attend a community college than were their female counterparts.

Among the school context of reception variables, being in a high school with a larger proportion of students attending a four-year college actually results in a greater likelihood of immigrant students themselves entering the labor force versus attending a community college, as does being in a high school where the mean class report that there is a poor school climate. However, being in a school context where students report that teachers are interested in students is related to lower likelihood that a student will go into the labor force and instead will enter a community college. In general, among the immigrant sample poorer school contexts are related to moving directly into the labor force rather than attending a community college.

In the second model, examining the relationships of the tested variables to for-profit college enrollment versus open access community college enrollment, we see a slightly different picture with the immigrant students. First, family structure had no relationship to for-profit versus community college enrollment. In this model, when students spoke with their parents about post-high school plans, students ended up in a for-profit college and not a community college. Thus, the poor school climate did not determine for-profit versus community college enrollment as clearly as it did for labor force participation.

Finally, in the third model, examining four-year college enrollment versus community college enrollment, arguably the higher selectivity college pathway, we see some aspects of the segmented assimilation theory play out, but not others. That is, family structure did not distinguish between four-year college enrollees and community college enrollees. School context reinforced the segmented assimilation framework. Among immigrant students, the school context of reception appears to matter for predicting four-year college enrollment rather than choice of the open-access (less selective) community college. Being in high school environments in which a greater proportion of the student body goes to college, where students report teachers are interested in students, and where there are fewer reports of poor school climate is positively related to enrolling in a four-year college among immigrant students.

With respect to the school context variables, the immigrant students appear to go directly into the labor force and not to college when in school environments seemingly unconducive to success. In other words, ideas of immigrant optimism may not play out among immigrant students who are exposed to environments where there are poorer reports of school climate and less teacher interest in students and where the relationship between moving into the labor force and not attending community college plays out. Where there is a positive context of reception, immigrant students are predicted to enroll in a four-year college.

Results: Children of Hispanic Immigrants

Moving to the models for the children of immigrants, we again present the findings in the context of the theoretical framework and identify where differences among the post-high school outcomes arise (see Table 4 for results). For the pattern for the children of immigrants and the relationship with labor force participation over community college enrollment, we see expected effects with family structure, human capital, and social capital variables and what predicts labor force participation.

Briefly, poorer math performance and less discussion with parents about post-high school plans also predict labor market incorporation rather than community college attendance. SES effects appear to reinforce the literature on the upward mobility of certain immigrant students. That is, among children of immigrants, lower-SES children of immigrants were more likely than their higher-SES counterparts to enroll in a community college than to enter the labor force directly out of high school. Where we see additional divergent patterns is with the school context of reception. Among children of immigrants, being in a poor school climate increases the odds that a student will directly enter the labor force instead of attending a community college. Additionally, being in an environment where more students move on to four-year colleges and more teacher interest in students is reported slightly increases the odds of labor force participation over attending a community college. These findings suggest that among children of immigrants, the context of reception is related to whether children of immigrants go straight to work or instead enroll in college. Additionally, among the children of immigrants, the lowest SES levels relative to the highest SES level are less likely to enter the labor force and instead move on to community college.

Moving to the second model for children of immigrants and the variables that predict for-profit enrollment over community college enrollment, family composition matters. That is, coming from a two-parent family increased

TABLE 4. Multinomial logistic regression: Predicting Hispanic children of immigrant student pathways (Reference = Open Access Community College)

VARIABLES	LABOR FORCE/ MILITARY				FOR-PROFIT COLLEGE OR UNIVERSITY				FOUR-YEAR COLLEGE OR UNIVERSITY			
	B	STD. ERROR	SIG.	EXP (B)	B	STD. ERROR	SIG.	EXP (B)	B	STD. ERROR	SIG.	EXP (B)
STUDENT LEVEL VARIABLES												
Intercept	−.824	.124	.000		−5.035	.209	.000		−1.834	.120	.000	
Female	−1.646	.017	.000	.193	−1.037	.025	.000	.355	.024	.016	.137	1.024
SES Quartile												
Quartile 1	−.204	.039	.000	.815	−.171	.060	.004	.843	−.812	.029	.000	.444
Quartile 2	−.896	.042	.000	.408	−.254	.063	.000	.776	−1.033	.032	.000	.356
Quartile 3	−.268	.044	.000	.765	−.785	.073	.000	.456	−.425	.033	.000	.654
Family Structure	−.304	.016	.000	.738	1.493	.035	.000	4.450	.171	.017	.000	1.186
HUMAN CAPITAL												
Advanced math course-taking pipeline	−1.260	.024	.000	.284	-.180	.031	.000	.836	1.519	.016	.000	4.566
SOCIAL CAPITAL												
Parents discuss school activities and post-high school plans (10th grade)	−.397	.014	.000	.672	-.355	.022	.000	.701	.207	.014	.000	1.230
HIGH SCHOOL LEVEL VARIABLES												
COR: SAFE AND ADEQUATE FACILITIES												
Student opinion of poor school climate (10th grade)	.757	.021	.000	2.133	−.189	.035	.000	.828	−.381	.021	.000	.683
COR: COLLEGE GOING CULTURE												
Graduates went to four-year college	.163	.007	.000	1.177	−.060	.012	.000	.942	.137	.007	.000	1.147
COR: HIGH QUALITY TEACHING												
Student opinion that teachers are interested in students	.088	.030	.003	1.092	1.529	.051	.000	4.614	.471	.029	.000	1.601

the likelihood of enrolling in a for-profit over a community college for the sample of children of immigrants. Children of immigrants who report more post-high school plan discussion with parents are less likely to enroll in a for-profit over a community college. Reporting discussion with parents about post-high school plans was also identified in the immigrant sample and community college enrollment. Reports of school climate and teacher opinion worked inversely in the model, predicting for-profit college enrollment rather than labor force participation. Being in an environment where students report teacher interest actually increases the likelihood of attending a for-profit over a community college, but poorer school climate reports reduce odds of for-profit enrollment compared to community college enrollment. Being in a school environment where larger proportions of graduating students move on to four-year colleges reduces the odds of for-profit enrollment, and thus the children of Hispanic immigrants are more likely to enroll in the community college sector. Again the school context of reception matters for the children of immigrants and what post-high school path they pursue. Among the children of immigrants, lower-SES students were less likely to attend a for-profit than a community college.

In the model predicting four-year enrollment for the children of immigrants sample, family structure was significant, with children of immigrants enrolling in a four-year college if they resided in a two-parent family. Other patterns in human and social capital were in the expected direction with four-year enrollment except SES levels. Across all three SES levels, children of Hispanic immigrants were less likely to enroll in a four-year college over a community college than their highest-quartile peers. Among the context of reception variables, we see healthier school contexts predicting four-year college enrollment for the children of immigrants sample. Similar to the conclusion for immigrant students, school context of reception variables are related to pathways and can explain difference by sector of enrollment.

Results: Native-Born Hispanic Students

Returning to the model predicting labor force participation among the native Hispanic student sample, we describe variables that related to entry into labor force participation over community college enrollment (see Table 5 for results). Among native Hispanic students, lower-SES native students were more likely to move into the labor force than to attend community college. Among the native Hispanic sample, different patterns emerged in terms of labor force relationships. Being in an environment where students report a poorer climate reduces the odds of moving into

TABLE 5. Multinomial logistic regression: Predicting native Hispanic student pathways (Reference=Open Access Community College)

VARIABLES	LABOR FORCE/ MILITARY				FOR-PROFIT COLLEGE OR UNIVERSITY				FOUR-YEAR COLLEGE OR UNIVERSITY			
	B	STD. ERROR	SIG.	EXP (B)	B	STD. ERROR	SIG.	EXP (B)	B	STD. ERROR	SIG.	EXP (B)
STUDENT LEVEL VARIABLES												
Intercept	3.307	.071	.000		.399	.115	.001		1.072	.079	.000	
Female	−.308	.012	.000	.735	−.065	.019	.001	.937	.221	.014	.000	1.247
SES Quartile												
Quartile 1	.333	.023	.000	1.395	.305	.036	.004	1.357	−.542	.023	.000	.582
Quartile 2	.492	.023	.000	1.635	.058	.037	.117	1.060	.168	.022	.000	1.183
Quartile 3	.034	.024	.153	1.035	.419	.037	.000	1.521	−.315	.022	.000	.730
Family Structure	−.190	.012	.000	.827	.159	.019	.000	1.172	.249	.014	.000	1.283
HUMAN CAPITAL												
Advanced math course-taking pipeline	−.924	.017	.000	.397	.179	.022	.000	1.196	1.284	.015	.000	3.611
SOCIAL CAPITAL												
Parents discuss school activities and post-high school plans (10th grade)	−.051	.012	.000	.950	−.159	.018	.000	.853	.710	.014	.000	2.035
HIGH SCHOOL LEVEL VARIABLES												
COR: SAFE AND ADEQUATE FACILITIES												
Student opinion of poor school climate (10th grade)	−.405	.014	.000	.667	.729	.024	.000	2.074	−.926	.016	.000	.396
COR: COLLEGE GOING CULTURE												
Graduates went to four-year college	−.210	.006	.000	.811	−.393	.009	.000	.675	−.024	.006	.000	.976
COR: HIGH QUALITY TEACHING												
Student opinion that teachers are interested in students	−.511	.017	.000	.600	−.734	.027	.000	.480	−.571	.019	.000	.565

the labor force and in favor of going into a community college. However, so does being in an environment in which more graduating students attend four-year colleges, and stronger reports of teacher interest also reduce the odds of moving into the labor force and instead going on to college. In this model, the native Hispanic student outcomes differed from the Hispanic immigrant and children of Hispanic immigrants samples.

In the native Hispanic student model that predicts for-profit college enrollment, among native students, having an intact family structure and enrolling in advanced math courses predict for-profit enrollment over community college enrollment. This group was the only one in which advanced math completion predicted for-profit enrollment. Lower-SES native students were more likely than their highest-SES peers to attend a for-profit than a community college. Attending a school with poorer reports of school climate was a strong predictor of enrollment in a for-profit over a community college, while a high school environment of peers who are attending four-year colleges and stronger reports of teacher interest reduce the odds of moving into a for-profit college and instead go on to community college.

Finally, in the native-born Hispanic model predicting four-year enrollment versus community college enrollment, the relationships are what one might expect. Intact family, higher math course completion, reports of discussing post-high school plans with parents, and women Hispanic native-born students all are predictors of greater likelihood of enrolling in a four-year college over a community college. SES patterns also differ for this group. The first- and third-quartile native samples are less likely than their second- and fourth-quartile peers to attend a four-year college than a community college. Perplexing is that among the native sample, if students attend schools where greater proportions of students go on to four-year colleges and more teachers report interest in students, these circumstances are related to a lower likelihood of enrolling in a four-year college; native students enroll in community college. The positive school context of reception effect does not seem to extend to native-born Hispanic students. Poorer reports of school climate also reduce likelihood of four-year attendance over community college attendance.

SUMMARY DISCUSSION AND SEGMENTED
ASSIMILATION THEORY REVISITED

The summary of the three models identifies some general patterns but overall shows different relationships among the three population groups of interest in this study. School context mattered for the groups but operated differently among the groups and within the groups, sometimes in their prediction of different college types and labor force participation. Some salient differences emerge when we examine the role of SES for immigrants, children of immigrants and natives, SES generally predicts labor force for immigrants, community college enrollment among children of immigrants and is mixed for native students but their patterns more closely follow the immigrant students. Family structure mattered for the children of immigrants sample and native student sample but less so for the immigrant sample. School context of reception played out in different ways among the three groups in this study. For some, poorer school climate reports appeared to be overcome, although the likely college enrollment destination was a community college.

What this work begins to identify preliminarily is that once other variables are controlled, school context of reception plays a role in students' post-high school pathways. While we make note of family structure, SES, human capital, and social capital relationships, we also identify how school context relates to various post-high school pathways. Among the native Hispanic sample in particular, students do not appear to receive the positive effects of school climate, and that may be a glimpse into why there is a decline in attainment of this generation. When examining students of different immigrant generation statuses, high school context of reception does seem to matter, and this work begins to operationalize and identify some of those school contexts that help understand different outcomes beyond individual and family effects.

Latinas/os and U.S. Community Colleges

A GATEWAY TO OPPORTUNITY AND SUCCESS

Victor B. Sáenz and DeAna Swan

INTRODUCTION

For those who might not otherwise attend college, America's community colleges are a catalyst for opportunity, and they increasingly serve as the primary entry point to postsecondary education for many students. There are more than 1,100 community colleges in the United States, enrolling about seven million credit-seeking students. Another five million are enrolled in other curricular pathways (AACC 2015). Almost 1.5 million of these community college students are Latinas/os[1], a number that has almost doubled since 2000 (NCES 2015). Indeed, Latinas/os represent one of every five credit-seeking community college students (21.7 percent), and more than half (57 percent) of all Latina/o students enrolled in postsecondary education are enrolled within this sector (NCES 2015).

These trends underscore an important and long observed reality for the fast-growing U.S. Latina/o community, namely that the community college sector is a crucial gateway to postsecondary access and success (de los Santos Jr. and de los Santos 2003). However, gains in community college enrollment for U.S. Latinas/os have not translated into gains in overall educational attainment for this fast-growing group of students. Indeed, this

---

1. This article uses the words Latina/o and Hispanic interchangeably. While it would be preferable to further disaggregate these groups by national origin (e.g, Mexican origin, Puerto Rican, etc.), it is often difficult given the inherent limitations within the reporting data that are available for research use. Unless otherwise noted, all references to whites or African Americans refer to non-Hispanics.

gateway to opportunity is constricted by the persistent completion gaps for Latinas/os, gaps that remain a major concern for community college stakeholders and policymakers across the country. This concern takes on an increased urgency in light of the changing demographic reality for our nation, one that is increasingly Hispanic.

This article provides a summary of contemporary trends, challenges, and opportunities facing Latinas/os in the community college sector. We begin by establishing the national context of Latina/o student enrollment and completion, and then we offer a broad overview of key institutional differences within the sector. We recognize the vast diversity that exists among public and private community colleges, among urban and rural colleges, among technical colleges and Hispanic-serving institutions. This rich diversity of institutional contexts defines the community college sector and provides for a variety of experiences for Latina/o students.

Next, informed by the most current research on the topic[2] we discuss persistent challenges and opportunities for Latina/o community college students, including remedial and developmental education, dual enrollment, and the transfer function. Fourth, we review current research on success factors for Latinas/os in community colleges with a spotlight on proven student success models (e.g., Puente Program, Guided Pathways, Achieving the Dream, minority male consortia, etc.). Finally, we canvass emerging perspectives about the important role of community college faculty and leadership in facilitating Latina/o student success. We conclude our article by offering key considerations for a future research agenda focused on Latinas/os in community colleges.

NATIONAL CONTEXT:
ENROLLMENT AND COMPLETION TRENDS
FOR LATINAS/OS IN COMMUNITY COLLEGES

The U.S. community college sector is generally seen as a decisive pathway for upward social and economic mobility, especially for Latina/o students and other students of color whose numbers in higher education are steadily increasing. No matter what indicator we examine, the number and proportion of Latina/o students enrolling in and completing community colleges is

---

2. This topic calls for an inordinate amount of review of existing research and would easily warrant an entire book. However, for purposes of this article, we took great care in selecting primarily emerging and contemporary research on Latinas/os in community colleges. For this reason there are only a few references prior to the year 2000.

growing. Table 1 displays enrollment trends data for two-year[3] institutions from 1976 to 2013.

Almost half of all students of color and forty percent of under-resourced students are enrolled in community colleges (Sandovall-Lucero, Maes, and Klingsmith 2014). The number of Latina/o students enrolling in community colleges has been accelerating at a faster rate than any other group, numbering close to 1.5 million in the fall 2013 headcount (NCES 2015).

In fact, Latinas/os are more likely to enroll in community colleges than any other group. Figure 1 examines the proportion of students in higher education who enrolled in community colleges from 1976 to 2013. In fall 2013, 48.2 percent of Latinas/os in any type of higher education institution were enrolled in community colleges, compared to African American (37.4 percent), Asian (33.0 percent), and white (31.4 percent) students (NCES 2015). These rates have been declining steadily for most groups since 1976, but Latinas/os remain more likely than their peer groups enroll in this sector. Researchers find that even after controlling for socioeconomic status, academic preparation, degree intention, and other factors, Latina/o students are still more likely to begin their postsecondary education at community colleges for a host of reasons (e.g., affordability, flexible course scheduling, accessibility, etc.) (Kurlaender 2006).

TABLE 1. Enrollment in two-year institutions by race/ethnicity, Fall 1976 to Fall 2013

	1976	1980	1990	2000	2005	2010	2013
White	3,077.1	3,558.5	3,954.3	3,804.1	3,998.6	4,321.3	3,636.1
Black	429.3	472.5	524.3	734.9	901.1	1,198.9	1,073.1
Hispanic	210.2	255.1	424.2	843.9	981.5	1,393.0	1,491.2
Asian/Pacific Islander	79.2	124.3	215.2	401.9	434.4	463.1	415.7
Total	3,795.8	4,410.4	5,118.1	5,784.8	6,315.6	7,376.3	6,616.1

Note: Numbers are in thousands.
Source: "Digest of Education Statistics, 2014" (2015), Table 306.20.

---

3. We use the term "two-year institutions" as the descriptor instead of "community colleges" because our data source categorizes these institutions as such. We do not use these terms interchangeably unless we are directly citing a source (as is this case here). Otherwise we use the term community college to describe our institution of interest.

FIGURE 1. Proportion of students in higher education enrolled in two-year institutions, by racial/ethnic group, 1976 to 2013

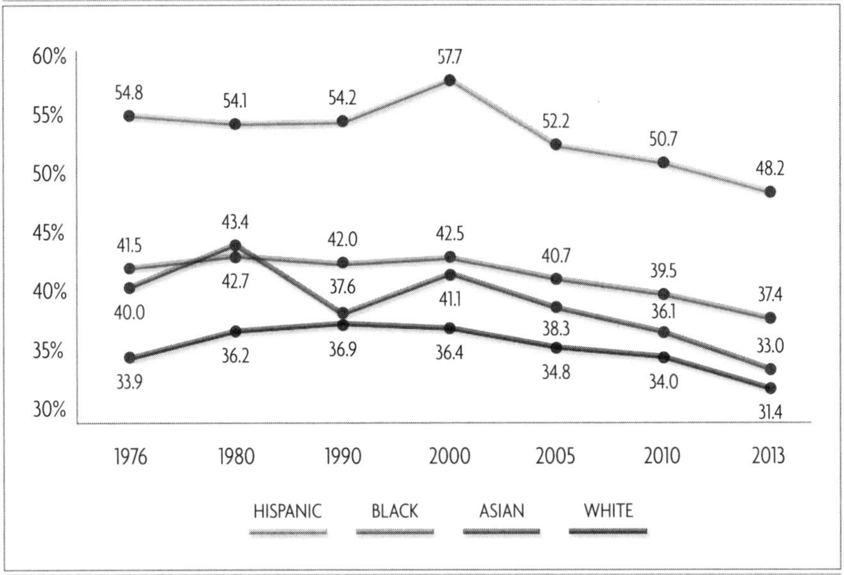

Source: "Digest of Education Statistics, 2014" (2015), Table 306.20.

When examining the proportion of all students enrolled in two-year institutions, the growth of Latina/o students within this sector is especially apparent. Figure 2 displays these figures across selected racial/ethnic groups. As a proportion of all students enrolled in two-year institutions, Latinas/os represented only 5.4 percent in 1976. By 2005 that proportion had almost tripled, and in fall 2013 it was 21.4 percent. This means that more than one of five students enrolled in two-year institutions in 2013 was Latina/o, a proportion poised to increase even further in light of demographic projections across the country. These enrollment trends are a clear illustration of the growing importance of the community college sector to the Latina/o community, but they tell only a part of the story.

Part-Time, Full-Time, and Mixed Enrollment Status

When they arrive at two-year institutions, Latina/o students are less likely than their peers to be enrolled full time and more likely to have mixed or part-time enrollment, suggesting a very inconsistent and potentially tenuous prospect for degree completion. In October 2011 only 78

FIGURE 2. Proportion of students across race/ethnicity that are enrolled in two-year institutions, 1976–2013

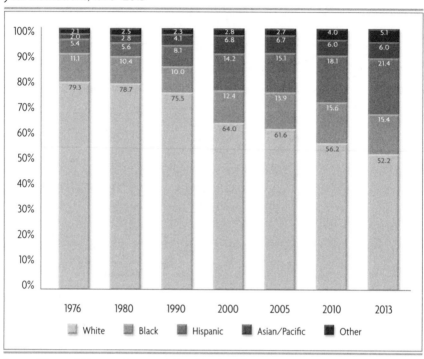

Source: "Digest of Education Statistics, 2014" (2015), Table 306.20.

percent of Hispanic 18- to 24-year-old college students were enrolled full time. By comparison, 85 percent of similar whites were enrolled full time (Fry and Taylor 2013). Indeed, less than half of Hispanics in two-year colleges pursue their education exclusively as full-time students over their entire academic career, and many have mixed or part-time enrollment (Fry 2004).

Mixed enrollment means students enroll full time for some terms and part time for other terms. In their national study of the 2009 cohort of entering college students, researchers with the National Student Clearinghouse noted that 53.9 percent of the cohort of students they tracked for six years were mixed enrollment students while another 6.9 percent were exclusively part-time and 39.1 percent were exclusively full-time (Shapiro et al. 2015). The six-year completion rate for students who started at two-year institutions was 38.2 percent. It was much higher for those who enrolled exclusively full-time (54.6 percent) and it was slightly lower for those with mixed enrollment (35.1 percent). However, 22.3 percent of mixed enrollment students are still enrolled in a postsecondary institution as of fall 2015, suggesting that those students can still persist and may ultimately complete their degree (Shapiro et al. 2015).

No cohort data for Latina/o students who started at two-year institutions is available through the National Student Clearinghouse data. The inconsistent enrollment status for Latinas/os enrolled at community colleges represents a key opportunity for further research and study, especially given the established empirical links to degree completion.

Latinas/os and Educational Attainment

Despite gains in college enrollment, Hispanics continue to lag behind all other racial and ethnic groups in the percentage who earn bachelor's or associate's degrees (Melguizo 2009). Indeed, Latinas/os have the lowest educational attainment rate of any racial/ethnic group—only 22 percent of Latino adults twenty-five and older have at least an associate's degree or higher compared to 46 percent of whites, 60 percent of Asians, and 31 percent of African-American adults (Santiago, Calderon Galdeano, and Taylor 2015). These gaps in educational attainment between Latina/o and white adults, consistently large across states, are particularly noticeable in states that have sizeable Latina/o populations (Liu 2011).

Nonetheless, Latinas/os have made notable progress in recent years. In fact, between 2004 and 2013, the number of Latinas/os earning an associate's degree or higher increased 71 percent, from 3.8 million to 6.5 million (Santiago, Calderon Galdeano, and Taylor 2015). In 2010 Latinos represented 15.7 percent of all associate's degrees earned, a proportion that has more than tripled since 1990 (NCES 2015). These are significant gains, and they portend a continuing upward trend in overall educational attainment, but the prevailing gaps for Latinas/os as compared to their peers must continue to be a focus of our student success and completion efforts.

INSTITUTIONAL AND REGIONAL DIFFERENCES ACROSS COMMUNITY COLLEGES

The hallmark of the American higher education system is the rich diversity of its institutions which number in the thousands. Nowhere is this diversity more evident than in the community college sector, where a rich collage of public and private institutions, technical colleges, Hispanic-serving institutions, and proprietary institutions provide countless pathways for students to choose from. Hispanic students' institutional choices differ considerably from those of their peers; only a small percentage of Hispanics enroll in private community colleges (5 percent, compared to 15 percent of whites), and they are more likely (41 percent) to be found in large urban colleges than their white peers (28 percent of whom enroll in large urban colleges) (Alfonso 2006). In fact, Latinas/os who do enroll in community colleges are concentrated in two states, Texas and California.

In 2012–13, 62 percent of all Latinas/os enrolled in American community colleges attended an institution in either California or Texas (Santiago, Calderon Galdeano, and Taylor 2015). Within each state, Latinas/os also increasingly represent a larger share of students. In fall 2013 Latinas/os represented 40 percent of students enrolled in the California Community College (CCC) system (Acevedo-Gil et al. 2015) and 32.7 percent of students in Texas (Hernandez, Slate, and Joyner 2015). What's more, about 80 percent begin their postsecondary career in the community college sector, underscoring the importance of this pathway for Latinas/os (Moore and Shulock 2010) As for associate's degree completion rates, for Latina/o community college students these do vary across the country; just over 50 percent of Latina/o students in two-year institutions in Florida earn a degree within three years: in New York, the graduation rate is 17 percent; in California the graduation rate is 37 percent; in Texas the graduation rate is 33 percent (Liu 2011).

Hispanic-Serving Institution Status

When considering how institutional diversity intersects with the experiences of Latina/o community college students, we focus more intently on an exploration of the fastest growing sector of community colleges, the Hispanic-Serving Institution. The U.S. Department of Education defines Hispanic-Serving Institutions (HSIs) as those eligible for federal programs specifically designed to assist colleges serving large numbers of first-generation, low-income Hispanic students. At least 25 percent of enrolled Hispanic students attend full-time, and at least half of all students must qualify for need-based financial aid (Brennan and Lumina Foundation for Education 2011).

For most Latina/o students the pathway to higher education is through an HSI and, most likely, a Hispanic-serving community college (Flores, Horn, and Crisp 2006). Some quick facts about HSIs: there are over 370 HSIs, and they enroll more than half of all Latina/o undergraduates; about half of HSIs (48 percent) are community colleges (178), and 4 percent

(15) are private not-for-profit two-year institutions (Santiago, Calderon Galdeano, and Taylor 2015). Also, nearly half of all HSIs are located in Texas and California, and most of these are community colleges (Perrakis and Hagedorn 2010).

Currently more than half of U.S. community colleges qualify as HSIs, yet not enough of these institutions engage their qualifying status for federal funding to directly contribute to Latina/o student success (Lorch 2014; Nora and Crisp 2009). Enrollment and demographic trends forecast more Hispanic-Serving Institutions in the near future, and also that Latina/o students will be disproportionately enrolled in them. Thus, this sector of community colleges represents a key success pathway for Latina/o students, one that must be increasingly scrutinized thoughtfully.

CHALLENGES AND OPPORTUNITIES FOR LATINA/O COMMUNITY COLLEGE STUDENTS

In recent years, community colleges have made significant strides in improving the academic achievement of students through the expansion of innovative policies and programs to enhance student success. In particular, formal collaboration between K-12 school districts, two-year institutions, and four year universities has increased at local and state levels. Whether through the adoption of dual enrollment practices, the forging of transfer agreements, or the overhaul of developmental education, systems change is rampant within and across all sectors of education, and community colleges are right in the center of this activity. This dynamic environment has brought unique challenges to our understanding of Latina/o community college student pathways, but it has also brought new opportunities.

Dual Enrollment

Dual enrollment allows eligible high school students to participate in college level courses and earn college credit while with the understanding that students benefits by greater access to a wider range of rigorous courses, savings in time and money on a college degree, efficiency of learning, and enhanced admission to college (Kleiner and Lewis 2005). These dual enrollment pathways can include traditional course-based offerings (e.g., advanced placement), academies for high-achieving students, the Early College High School model (courses & program of study), dropout recovery programs (leveraging dual-credit with most at-risk), career and technical education dual credit models (traditional vocational, etc.), and academic core programs (e.g., international baccalaureate).

In a strategic attempt to support the goals of two- and four-year institutions, dual enrollment processes must be as seamless and effective as possible for students (Flores, Horn, and Crisp 2006). The collaboration between school districts and institutions of higher education has shown significant promise, and these partnerships have helped to fuel the growth and demand for dual enrollment pathways across the country.

Developmental Education

Discussions addressing the topic of developmental or remedial education of community college students are pervasive in the educational literature. For Latina/o students specifically, more than half (58 percent) who attend a two-year college require at least one remediation course, compared to 68 percent of African Americans and 47 percent of White students (Santiago, Calderon Galdeano, and Taylor 2015). However, participation trends in remedial education is rarely disaggregated by race and ethnicity, making it difficult to better understand key differences across races and ethnicities.

In a study of all remedial and nonremedial students, Crisp and Nora (2010) found that students who delay college enrollment are more likely to need remedial education. However, for those students who were enrolled in remedial education, educational standing made a difference on their success, with first-year students being most influenced by their status as a remedial education student (Crisp and Nora 2010). Of course this makes sense, considering that students who persist to their third year of college are a fairly selective group who have found success navigating the campus. Students who did not accept the utility of remediation and developmental courses had a much lower likelihood of remaining enrolled in college (Nora and Crisp 2009).

While a large number of students participate in remediation courses, scholarship is inconsistent when it comes to the benefit of remedial education for Latina/o community college students. Solorozano, Acevedo-Gil, and Santos (2013) assert that many of the students who enroll in basic skills courses do not progress to college-level coursework, creating extra burdens and impeding timely progress toward a degree. However, Crisp and Nora (2010) found that students who required remediation in at least one area and were enrolled in a developmental course benefited from that experience through the end of their second year of college. Among first-time community college students, those placed into English and math remediation courses persisted at similar rates to those not enrolled in developmental courses. Furthermore, remediation increased nontraditional older students' likelihood of transferring or earning a credential (Crisp and Nora 2010).

Transfer

Not only are the majority of Latina/o students attending community colleges, but most enroll with an intention to transfer to a four-year university (Acevedo-Gil et al. 2015), although less than one quarter actually do (Crisp and Nora 2010). In contrast, white youth who begin at a community college are nearly twice as likely to finish a bachelor's degree than Hispanic youth (Fry 2004). Across all student demographics, enrolling in a two-year program instead of a four-year institution inhibits a student's likelihood of achieving a four-year degree (Fry 2004); nevertheless many Hispanic students follow this path. Furthermore, literature suggests correlations among social class and gender when it comes to transfer rates, with high SES and male students more likely to transfer (Kurlaender 2006).

Scholars have offered several factors that contribute to low student transfer to four-year institutions. The absence of a "transfer culture" has been found to discourage Latina/o students from attaining a four-year degree (Nora and Crisp 2009). Some additional findings include a lack of articulation agreements between two-year and four-year colleges, poor academic guidance and counseling, low expectations of community college faculty, misinformation about the transfer requirements and process, and increasing costs of four-year institutions (Nora and Crisp 2009) (Zarate and Burciaga 2010). In a study conducted at Esperanza college, Latina/o students also faced significant barriers to the transfer process. Many were forced to balance multiple roles and responsibilities outside of their studies while attending college; many also felt that they were academically and socially unprepared for college (Ornelas and Solorzano 2004). Yet, some scholars such as Melguizo (2009) attest that the negative effect of community colleges in terms of low baccalaureate degree attainment is actually much smaller than previous studies have suggested. However, policymakers at the state and federal levels have stressed the need to increase community college transfer as a mechanism to expand access to the baccalaureate (Dowd 2007).

Reverse Transfer

Another trend that has affected the success of Latina/o students and many other community college students is reverse transfer. Today's college students are as likely to move from a four-year university to a community college (e.g., reverse transfer) as they are to move from a community college to a four-year university (vertical transfer) (LeBard 1999). Reverse transfer allows a student to earn an associate's degree from an accredited two-year institution even if they have also attended a four-year institution (Brennan and Lumina Foundation for Education 2011). The key to these agreements is that they allow students to combine credits earned at two-year colleges with those earned at four-year institutions to earn their associate's degree (Bautsch 2013). An increasing number of states (e.g., Colorado, Missouri, Tennessee, and Texas) are allowing community colleges to take credit for awarding associate degrees through reverse transfer, which they often cannot do with typical transfer students. This has been a focus in recent state legislative sessions, and an additional ten or more states have reverse transfer agreements in place or are in the process of developing them (Bautsch 2013).

In one example of this policy, El Paso Community College (EPCC) partnered with the University of Texas El Paso (UTEP) to offer students who attend UTEP an opportunity to earn a credential even if they do not complete the required hours for a bachelor's degree (Brennan and Lumina Foundation for Education 2011). Through this partnership, more than 1,100 students received an associate's degree from EPCC while attending UTEP in 2010. Over 80 percent of students enrolled at each institution are Latina/o, so it stands to reason that reverse transfer is a having a positive effect on Latina/o student success within that region. Indeed, while a large number of Latina/o students—and the community colleges they are enrolled in—may be benefitting from dual enrollment and reverse transfer opportunities, data are not readily available to help identify exactly how many are participating in such programs at the state or national level. Further, with the growth of dual enrollment and reverse transfer programs, key stakeholders and educational leaders have raised important questions about how to keep pace with growing demand while maintaining the academic rigor of these offerings.

COMMUNITY COLLEGE STUDENT SUCCESS MODELS THAT TARGET LATINA/O STUDENTS

Latina/o community college students are a special target population of many different student success models and programs in recent years, some garnering more acclaim at the national level than others. Such efforts include the New Mathways Project (The Charles A. Dana Center 2015), Achieving the Dream (Achieving the Dream 2015), and common course numbering. Many are also home-grown or boutique initiatives that emerged through accreditation activities or in response to ongoing strategic planning and data gathering efforts.

Some of these models and programs at the national, state, or local level focus on first-generation or low-income students; others are anchored in curricular pathways or focus on specific areas of coursework such as math developmental education. These efforts are often intended to improve degree outcomes for community college students, and they are showing positive signs of success. The common denominator is often Latina/o students who fall into some or most of the target criteria. Given the growing number of programs across the country, we cannot possibly provide an exhaustive listing of these initiatives. Nonetheless, our summaries that follow provide a glimpse into some of the more prominent efforts that move the needle on Latina/o community college student success.

Puente

The Puente Program (Puente Program 2015) has received considerable praise over the last few decades, thanks to its documented success in high school retention and college preparation (Gandara 2002). The Latino-specific program was initiated in 1981 and currently serves fifty-five two-year colleges and thirty-six high schools in California (Martinez and Fernández 2004). It has recently launched an expansion in Texas led by a non-profit called Catch the Next; six Texas community colleges are participating in the Puente Program as of fall 2015, with more poised to join in the near future (Catch The Next 2015). Designed to assist students in successful transfer to a four-year institution, Puente provides culturally relevant counseling, mentoring, and accelerated writing courses that are rooted in a multi-cultural bilingual curriculum (Acevedo-Gil et al. 2015). Scholars have acknowledged the validating environment and success that the program offers (Acevedo-Gil et al. 2015; Cejda and Rhodes 2004; Cox, Joyner, and Slate 2011; Martinez and Fernández 2004; Gandara 2002) and have recommended expansion.

Completion by Design

Serving Texas and three other states, Completion by Design was a program briefly funded by the Bill and Melinda Gates Foundation to serve low-income students attending community colleges (Hernandez, Slate, and Joyner 2015). The program provided additional funding to support community colleges across Texas serving a large proportion of Latina/o students. Although the brief existence of the funding source did not allow for much assessment of the program, some research has reported statistically significant gains in enrollment and educational attainment for Latina/o students attending community colleges from 2000 to 2001. This preliminary evidence suggests an incentive to continue applying strategies advanced by Completion by Design (Hernandez, Slate, and Joyner 2015).

Guided Pathways

An increasing number of community colleges across the country are adopting a "guided pathways" approach that simplifies students' course-taking patterns with a stated goal in mind (Jenkins 2014). Some argue that community colleges are "designed for access not success" because of the overwhelming number of degree choices for students presented with little to no guidance, the uncertain career prospects, and the general incoherence of curriculum that leads too many students into dead end mazes and non-credit-earning courses. By focusing on a specific degree or credential pathway from the beginning, "guided pathways" pushes students to commit to a highly structured academic program with "degree maps" and predictable schedules as well as ongoing tracking and support from dedicated advisors and counselors. The intensity of "guided pathways" includes intrusive advising and early alert systems, hallmarks of a high-tactile approach that theoretically moves students toward their ultimate goals but without limiting their options. Many of the institutions that have adopted guided pathways serve high proportions of Latina/o students.

Achieving the Dream

In addition to colleges in California and Texas, institutions across the nation participate in initiatives designed to serve Latina/o students in community colleges. Achieving the Dream is a national initiative launched in 2004 to increase the academic success of community college students, with an emphasis on low-income students and students of color (Rutschow et al. 2011). El Paso Community College is one of many institutions that have attributed the program's efficacy to a boost in graduation rates and decline in remediation courses among their largely Latina/o student population (Brennan and Lumina Foundation for Education 2011).

Single Stop

Single Stop (Single Stop 2015) is a program designed to serve seventeen community colleges across the country to rethink the services they offer students (Santiago, Calderon Galdeano, and Taylor 2015). Eight of the colleges are Hispanic-Serving Institutions serving a student population that is greater than 25 percent Latina/o (Santiago, Calderon Galdeano, and Taylor 2015). The program aims to offer a site where students can receive help filing taxes, applying for government benefits, and attaining financial and legal counseling as a way to reduce the financial stress faced by Latina/o students—ultimately leading to their educational success (Santiago, Calderon Galdeano, and Taylor 2015). Research on its impact notes that the program helps Latina/o community college students identify resources that ease financial barriers and thus helps them to take full advantage of academic and social support services that institutions provide (Santiago and Stettner 2013).

Men of Color Consortia

Two emerging institutional consortia models focus on improving outcomes for male students of color enrolled at community colleges in Texas and California. The Texas Education Consortium for Male Students of Color (TECMSC 2015) cultivates a statewide network of public K-12 schools and higher education institutions, practitioners, policymakers, and other key stakeholders to positively influence educational outcomes for males of color from high school through post-secondary education. The Consortium counts over fourteen community colleges among its members and advances best practices for male students of color in the state of Texas. The Minority Male Community College Collaborative ("M2C3" 2015, 3) is based at San Diego State University with the goal of partnering with community colleges across the United States to enhance access, achievement, and success among minority male community college students. M2C3's research and practice agenda prioritizes men who have been traditionally underrepresented and underserved in postsecondary education.

THE ROLE OF COMMUNITY COLLEGE FACULTY AND LEADERSHIP

Among the most important jobs facing community college leaders is how to build a team that can serve the needs of an increasingly diversifying student population and create a more welcoming learning environment for all students. One response is to build a team of faculty and administrators that better reflects the racial, ethnic, and gender diversity among the community college student population (Lujan, Gallegos, and Harbour 2003). This legacy-shaping activity can go a long way in supporting Latina/o students, as faculty of color play an important role in affecting student success. To recruit more faculty and administrators of color, leadership must be fully committed to creating and sustaining a campus culture that embraces diversity and inclusivity (Brennan and Lumina Foundation for Education 2011; Nora and Crisp 2009).

Building the Team: Hiring Practices

Research on hiring practices in community colleges points to some key factors that correlate with a given college campus's hires of faculty and administrators (Lujan, Gallegos, and Harbour 2003). In their wide-ranging study, Lujan, Gallegos, and Harbor (2003) found the ethnicity of the vice president for academic affairs is a positive predictor for a greater number of Latina/o faculty as well as the amount of contact s/he has with minority students and faculty (Lujan, Gallegos, and Harbour 2003). They also concluded that the presence of minorities on community college boards of trustees is also a positive predictor, as is the recruitment of minorities from the private sector to teach part-time career-related courses (Lujan, Gallegos, and Harbour 2003).

Too often, however, the response from leadership is that qualified applicants are simply not plentiful or that resources are not available. CEOs of Hispanic-serving institutions reported funding cuts and inadequate budgets as a top concern of the institutional progress and effectiveness (de los Santos Jr. and de los Santos 2003). Also, the low representation of Latina/o faculty on some campuses was attributed to a challenge finding quality applicants, particularly for science, math, and engineering departments. Further, the learning complexities associated with students who are English language learners challenges human resources to find leadership at community colleges to respond proactively to changing student needs (de los Santos Jr. and de los Santos 2003).

Role of Faculty and Administrators in Community Colleges

Having a higher proportion of Hispanic faculty and administrators, as we find in two-year HSIs (Nunez, Sparks, and Hernandez 2011), can offer enhanced understanding of students' cultural backgrounds and increase the number of faculty and staff to serve as mentors. Some who have investigated the effects of diversity on a college campus conclude that Latina/o students who perceive their campuses as being ethnically diverse are much more likely to remain enrolled (Hurtado and Ponjuan 2005; Nora and Crisp 2009). Administrators and faculty are obliged to examine and address campus climate in their service to Latinas/os attending community colleges. Nora and Crisp (2009) recommend that campus administrators prioritize clear transfer policies aimed at improving the educational outcomes for Latina/o students, because of the large number of Latinas/os whose postsecondary education pathway initially includes community college. Others have highlighted the need to build coalitions among the college, families, businesses, and the local community to best serve the Latina/o student population at community colleges and four-year institutions (Nora and Crisp 2009).

Research suggests a disconnect between what senior administrators perceive student needs to be and what Latina/o students report (Ornelas and Solorzano 2004). Student perceptions of prejudice and discrimination on campus—inside as well as outside of the classroom—can negatively affect attainment of an undergraduate degree. If Hispanic students perceive an environment of intolerance and discrimination, it can have a negative effect on their academic performance, specifically in the classroom. (Nora and Crisp 2009).

Role of Presidents and Trustees

Community college presidents and trustees must explicitly support Latina/o student success and they must do so enthusiastically by engaging with families and communities. In addition, community college leaders must provide a means of rewarding faculty and administrators who are successful in developing student talent and in serving the needs of their fast-growing Latina/o student populations. In 2014 *Excelencia* in Education launched *Presidents for Latino Student Success*, a new national effort designed to directly engage institutional leaders in the conversation to improve Latina/o student success rates (*Excelencia* in Education 2015). More of these symbolic and earnest initiatives are needed to directly engage community college presidents and board of trustees in the imperative of increasing Latina/o student success.

CONCLUSION AND
FUTURE RESEARCH

This article re-examines the role of American community colleges as a gateway to success for Latina/o students, the fastest growing group of college enrollees. It does not—indeed, cannot—provide an exhaustive review of the myriad issues and challenges facing Latinas/os in community colleges. Among the key issues that we did not address were the effect of financial aid on Latinas/os within this sector, the experiences of undocumented students, or the growth of technology in reshaping the educational experience (other articles may cover these topics among others). However, within the larger context of this edited book, our article serves as a worthwhile complement by focusing on enrollment and degree attainment trends, key matriculation challenges, student success models, and the role of faculty and leadership. For some this may be an introduction to key issues for Latinas/os in community colleges; for others it may serve as a reinforcement of the complex challenges that we must continue to study through further research.

The various Latina/o student success models that we reviewed represent only a sampling of the many past and ongoing efforts aimed at enhancing community college success for a wide array of students. These efforts may also play an increasingly important role in facilitating student success for the growing enrollment of Latina/o students; however, it is clear that more intentional and scalable efforts are needed to better understand empirically how these models work and whether they are truly moving the needle. Not enough is yet known about the specific outcome of these efforts on Latina/o students or whether they even have a direct or indirect effect. In light of the demographic and enrollment reality for many community colleges across the country, more research is needed to get a better grasp of the specific benefits of these innovative pathway models on Latina/o community college student success.

The emerging evidence suggests that community colleges must continue to adapt and improve their efforts for Latina/o student success. The future of the community college sector will depend on how it adapts to the changing needs of society as well as to the emerging demographic reality led by the growth of the Latina/o population. Our nation's social and economic prosperity is increasingly linked to the overall educational success of Latinas/os in postsecondary education. Community colleges represent perhaps the most important pathway to achieving that success.

REFERENCES

AACC. 2015. "AACC FactSheet." Accessed November 3. http://www.aacc.nche.edu/AboutCC/Documents/FactSheet2015.pdf.

Acevedo-Gil, Nancy, Ryan E. Santos, Luliana Alonso, and Daniel G. Solorzano. 2015. "Latinas/os in Community College Developmental Education: Increasing Moments of Academic and Interpersonal Validation." *Journal of Hispanic Higher Education* 14 (2): 101–27. doi:10.1177/1538192715572893.

Achieving the Dream. 2015. "Increasing Support to Latino Students." Accessed December 21. http://www.achievingthedream.org/intervention/14221/increasing-support-to-latino-students.

Alfonso, Mariana. 2006. "Hispanic Educational Attainment in Sub-Baccalaureate Programs." *New Directions for Community Colleges*, 133 (January): 17–25.

Bautsch, Brenda. 2013. "Student-Transfer.pdf." Accessed January 16. http://www.ncsl.org/documents/educ/student-transfer.pdf.

Brennan, Patricia L., and Lumina Foundation for Education. 2011. "Un Nuevo Dia: As Latino Population Grows, so Must College Attainment. Lumina Foundation Focus[TM]." *Lumina Foundation for Education*.

Catch the Next. 2015. "About Our Program." Accessed December 21. http://catchthenext.org/our-program/.

Cejda, Brent D., and Jeff H. Rhodes. 2004. "Through the Pipeline: The Role of Faculty in Promoting Associate Degree Completion Among Hispanic Students." *Community College Journal of Research and Practice* 28 (3): 249–62. doi:10.1080/10668920490256435.

The Charles A. Dana Center. 2015. "New Mathways Project." Accessed December 21. http://www.utdanacenter.org/higher-education/new-mathways-project/.

Cox, Shelly, Sheila A. Joyner, and John Slate. 2011. "Differences in Hispanic Graduation Rates at Texas Community Colleges over Time." *Community College Enterprise* 17 (2): 62–76.

Crisp, Gloria, and Amaury Nora. 2010. "Hispanic Student Success: Factors Influencing the Persistence and Transfer Decisions of Latino Community College Students Enrolled in Developmental Education." *Research in Higher Education* 51 (2): 175–94.

de los Santos Jr., Alfredo G., and Gerardo E. de los Santos. 2003. "Hispanic-Serving Institutions in the 21st Century: Overview, Challenges, and Opportunities." *Journal of Hispanic Higher Education* 2 (4): 377–91. doi:10.1177/1538192703256734.

Dowd, Alicia. 2007. "Community Colleges as Gateways and Gatekeepers: Moving beyond the Access 'Saga' toward Outcome Equity." *Harvard Educational Review* 77 (4): 407–19. doi:10.17763/haer.77.4.1233g31741157227.

Excelencia in Education. 2015. "College and University Presidents Join New National Effort to Improve Success for Latino Students in Higher Education." Accessed December 22. http://www.edexcelencia.org/media/press-releases/college-and-university-presidents-join-new-national-effort.

Flores, Stella M., Catherine L. Horn, and Gloria Crisp. 2006. "Community Colleges, Public Policy, and Latino Student Opportunity." *New Directions for Community Colleges* 2006 (133): 71–80. doi:10.1002/cc.229.

Fry, Richard. 2004. "Latino Youth Finishing College: The Role of Selective Pathways." *Pew Hispanic Center* 23.

Fry, Richard, and Paul Taylor. 2013. "Hispanic High School Graduates Pass Whites in Rate of College Enrollment." *Pew Research Center's Hispanic Trends Project.* http://www.pewhispanic.org/2013/05/09/hispanic-high-school-graduates-pass-whites-in-rate-of-college-enrollment/.

Gandara, Patricia. 2002. "A Study of High School Puente: What We Have Learned about Preparing Latino Youth for Postsecondary Education." *Educational Policy* 16 (4): 474–95.

Hernandez, Jack, John R. Slate, and Sheila A. Joyner. 2015. "Hispanic Student Enrollment and Attainment in Texas Two-Year Colleges: A Multiyear, Statewide Analysis." *Community College Journal of Research and Practice* 39 (11): 969–85. doi:10.1080/10668926.2013.873005.

Hurtado, Sylvia, and Luis Ponjuan. 2005. "Latino Educational Outcomes and the Campus Climate." *Journal of Hispanic Higher Education* 4 (3): 235–51.

Jenkins, Davis. 2014. "Redesigning Community Colleges for Student Success: Overview of the Guided Pathways Approach." Community College Research Center, Teachers College, Columbia University. Accessed January 16. http://www.ct.edu/files/ssc/DavisJenkins_CCRC_Guided_Pathways_Overview_August_2014.pdf.

Kleiner, Brian, and Laurie Lewis. 2005. *Dual Enrollment of High School Students at Postsecondary Institutions: 2002-03. E.D. TAB. NCES 2005-008.* ED Pubs, P. Accessed January 16. http://eric.ed.gov/?id=ED484632.

Kurlaender, Michal. 2006. "Choosing Community College: Factors Affecting Latino College Choice." *New Directions for Community Colleges* 2006 (133): 7–16. doi:10.1002/cc.223.

LeBard, C. 1999. Reverse transfers in the community college. *ERIC Digest.* Retrieved from http://files.eric.ed.gov/fulltext/ED433871.pdf.

Liu, Michelle C. 2011. "Investing in Higher Education for Latinos. Trends in Latino College Access and Success." National Conference of State Legislatures.

Lorch, Theresa M. 2014. "Goal Development of Latina/o Students in a Developmental Learning Community at a Community College." *Community College Journal of Research and Practice* 38 (4): 323–36. doi:10.1080/15363759.2011.559883.

Lujan, Linda, Loretta Gallegos, and Clifford P. Harbour. 2003. "La Tercera Frontera: Building upon the Scholarship of the Latino Experience as Reported in the Community College Journal of Research and Practice." *Community College Journal of Research and Practice* 27 (9–10): 799–813. doi:10.1080/713838283.

M2C3. 2015. "M2C3." Accessed December 22. http://consortium.cceal.org/about-us/.

Martinez, Magadelena, and Edith Fernández. 2004. "Latinos at Community Colleges." *New Directions for Student Services* 2004 (105): 51–62. doi:10.1002/ss.116.

Melguizo, Tatiana. 2009. "Are Community Colleges an Alternative Path for Hispanic Students to Attain a Bachelor's Degree?" *Teachers College Record* 111 (1): 90–123.

Moore, C., and Nancy Shulock. 2010. *Divided We Fail: Improving Completion and Closing Racial Gaps in California's Community Colleges.* Sacramento, CA: Institute for Higher Education Leadership and Policy.

NCES. 2015. "Digest of Education Statistics." Accessed November 3. https://nces.ed.gov/programs/digest/d14/tables/dt14_306.20.asp?current=yes.

Nora, Amaury, and Gloria Crisp. 2009. "Hispanics and Higher Education: An Overview of Research, Theory, and Practice." In *Higher Education: Handbook of Theory and Research*, edited by John C. Smart, 317–53. The Netherlands, Springer.

Nunez, Anne-Marie, P. Johnelle Sparks, and Eliza A. Hernandez. 2011. "Latino Access to Community Colleges and Hispanic-Serving Institutions: A National Study." *Journal of Hispanic Higher Education* 10 (1): 18–40.

Ornelas, Armida, and Daniel G. Solorzano. 2004. "Transfer Conditions of Latina/o Community College Students: A Single Institution Case Study." *Community College Journal of Research and Practice* 28 (3): 233–48. doi:10.1080/10668920490256417.

Perrakis, Athena, and Linda Serra Hagedorn. 2010. "Latino/a Student Success in Community Colleges and Hispanic-Serving Institution Status." *Community College Journal of Research and Practice* 34 (10): 797–813. doi:10.1080/10668921003723110.

Puente Program. 2015. "A National Model for Student Success." Accessed December 21. http://puente.berkeley.edu/.

Rutschow, Zachry, Elizabeth Lashawn Richburg-Hayes, Thomas Brock, Genevieve E. Orr, Oscar Cerna, and Dan Cullinan. 2011. "Turning the Tide: Five Years of Achieving the Dream in Community Colleges." SSRN Scholarly Paper ID 2031257. Rochester, NY: Social Science Research Network. Accessed January 16. http://papers.ssrn.com/abstract=2031257.

Sandovall-Lucero, Elena, Johanna B. Maes, and Libby Klingsmith. 2014. "African American and Latina(o) Community College Students' Social Capital and Student Success." *College Student Journal* 48 (3): 522–33.

Santiago, Deborah A., Emily Calderon Galdeano, and Morgan Taylor. 2015. "Factbook. The Condition of Latinos in Education." *Excelencia* in Education. Accessed January 16. http://www.edexcelencia.org/research/2015-factbook

Santiago, Deborah A., and Andrew Stettner. 2013. "Supporting Latino Community College Students: An Investment in Our Economic Future." *Excelencia* in Education. Accessed January 16. http://www.edexcelencia.org/research/supporting-latino-community-college-students-investment-our-economic-future

Shapiro, Doug, Afet Dunbar, Phoebe Khasiala Wakhungu, Xin Yuan, Angel Nathan, and Youngsik Hwang. 2015. "Completing College: A National View of Student Attainment Rates—Fall 2009 Cohort." Accessed January 16. https://nscresearch-center.org/wp-content/uploads/SignatureReport10.pdf.

Single Stop. 2015. "Community Colleges." Accessed December 21. http://singlestopusa.org/program/community-colleges/.

Solórzano, D., Acevedo-Gil, N., & Santos, R. 2013. Latina/o community college students: Understanding the barriers of developmental education. *Policy Report, 10,* 1-8.

TECMSC. 2015. "Aligning Texas Educators for the Success of Boys and Men of Color." Accessed December 22. http://ddce.utexas.edu/txedconsortium/about-us/.

Zarate, Maria Estela, and Rebeca Burciaga. 2010. "Latinos and College Access: Trends and Future Directions." *Journal of College Admission,* 209 (January): 24–29.

Latino College Students

A TRAJECTORY IN THE RIGHT DIRECTION
AFTER YEARS OF DESPONDENCY

Amaury Nora and Vincent D. Carales

For some time now, college completion has been identified as one of the top ten policy issues of our time (American Association of State Colleges and Universities 2012). Throughout the years, the data referring to Latina/o college completion has been sobering (Spruill, Hirt, and Mo 2014; Perna 2000; Ryu 2009; Strayhorn 2006). For example, it has been reported that out of every 100 elementary school children, only ten will graduate from college and only four will earn a graduate degree (Padilla 1999). This dismal scenario has been exacerbated by the limited research that exists on the positive and negative aspects of the Latina/o student college experience. Data documenting achievement gaps between students of color and white students have presented a compelling portrait of the lack of success as Latina/o students progress from kindergarten through undergraduate and graduate education. Gender gaps have also been reported as startling. Women students graduate from high school on time (75 percent) at higher rates than male students (68 percent). Despite recent increases in high school graduation, college enrollment, and degree completion rates for Hispanics (Fry 2011), Saenz and Ponjuan (2009) note that Latino males continue to have lower educational outcomes compared to Latina females. Not long ago, the White House Initiative on Educational Excellence for Hispanics provided a webinar on "Improving Outcomes" addressing the educational outlook for men of color (April 23, 2014). The webinar focused on the President's "My Brother's Keeper" initiative and improving educational and life outcomes for young Hispanic males in the United States. A report issued by the American Enterprise Institute (2010) highlighted that at the average college or university, 51 percent of Hispanic students complete a bachelor's degree in six years compared to 59 percent of white students at those same institutions. Even after accounting for the type of students colleges admit, Hispanic students graduate at lower rates than their white peers at all levels of admissions selectivity.

Based on relevant research literature, several key research gaps have been identified over the years that could provide some clue as to the discrepancy (Crisp, Taggart, and Nora 2014). However, much of this still limited knowledge about the overall college student experience especially for Latina/o students is based on older studies and assertions. While factors that account for student outcomes have been isolated, studies may not be delving deep enough into their analyses since the problem of student retention and completion has yet to be solved. Moreover, as a result of these previous findings a deficit perception (or model) of Latina/o students currently exists. Indeed, what is totally lacking in the literature is whether beliefs and perceptions that were drawn from previous studies (atheoretical for the most part) are still prevalent for today's Latina/o student populations. Are behaviors, cultural norms, and beliefs about Hispanic students today the same as they were in past years? Have many well-intended interventions, institutional strategies and activities, or educational programmatic efforts focused on prior research findings to the exclusion of the possibility that many assertions that are made regarding Hispanic males and females may no longer apply to more recent Hispanic student populations?

Of key concern in the literature are the completion rates of Latina/o students who enroll in Hispanic-Serving Institutions. The intent of the current article was to focus on Latinas/os at one Hispanic-Serving Institution from a more in-depth quantitative enquiry. Though many large databases may contain information on the number of Latina/o students that persist or graduate, much more useful information based on institutional records regarding their academic performance, persistence over a six-year period, enrollment and performance in developmental courses, enrollment status (full-time vs. part-time), type of student (native vs. transfer), and financial circumstances (e.g., family income, family contribution, Pell grant eligibility, loans, grants, scholarships, unmet need) are not available at the individual student level (Crisp, Taggart, and Nora 2014). Rather, much of the information gathered on Latina/o students is representative of aggregated data. Cross-tabulations by ethnicity, gender, type of student, and enrollment status are difficult to achieve when the data is of an aggregated nature. Moreover, the predictive character of specific constructs captured in institutional records is often not possible to measure in a single case study unless the data is at the student level.

The current article focuses on three separate research studies conducted at a Hispanic-Serving Institution (HSI). The first investigation examined six major assertions regarding Hispanic students in general through a more in-depth quantitative framework. These five assertions centered on: (1) the representation of Latino males in higher education among different racial/ethnic groups; (2) the college attendance patterns among Latina/o students; (3) Latina/o students' family backgrounds as they relate to social capital; (4) involvement and academic performance of Latina/o students in developmental courses; (5) the academic, persistence, and graduation performance of Latinas/os compared to their white counterparts; and (6) Latina/o student representation in STEM degrees earned.

The second research enquiry employed a conceptual framework capturing the underlying perspectives of five theoretical models (Nora's [2003] Student Engagement Model; Rendon's [1994] Validation Model; Crisp's [2010] Mentoring Model; Solórzano's Microaggressions Perspectives [2000]; and Yosso's [2006] Cultural Wealth Model) and tested the impact of the framework on a student's sense of belonging, a factor known to have an important influence on Latina/o student persistence and graduation (Hurtado and Carter 1997; Crisp, Taggart, and Nora 2014). The third inquest utilized the same conceptual framework as the one identified in the second study but examined the impact of that framework on academic performance within four different student classifications.

ASSERTIONS REGARDING HISPANIC STUDENTS

Perceptions Regarding Latina/o Students in Higher Education

Research indicates that the educational pipeline for Latina/o students leaks at every juncture (Yosso and Solórzano 2006). Sixty-three percent of young Latina/o adults earn high school diplomas and only 33 percent of Latina/o high school graduates go on to enroll in college, compared to 39 percent of African American and 46 percent of white high school graduates (Brindis et al. 2002). The literature further suggests that those Latinas/os who do enroll in college are characteristically different than many other college students. Latina/o students have been found to be more likely to come from lower income backgrounds (Merisotis and McCarthy 2005; Núñez and Bowers 2011), to be among the first in their families to attend college (Crisp, Nora, and Taggart 2009; Pino, Martinez-Ramos, and Smith 2012; Saenz et al. 2007), and to come from under-resourced schools (Gándara and Contreras 2009).

Perhaps because they enter college with these characteristics, they also experience college differently than other students. Latinas/os are believed to be more likely enrolled part-time (Benitez 1998; Crisp, Nora, and Taggart 2009), to work long hours (Longerbeam, Sedlacek, and Alatorre 2004), to receive higher levels of financial aid (Benitez 1998; Crisp, Nora, and Taggart 2009), and to drop out of school for financial reasons (Longerbeam, Sedlacek, and Alatorre 2004). These experiences are significant, particularly in light of Arbona and Nora's (2007) findings of positive relationships between Latina/o student enrollment full-time and continuous and bachelor's degree attainment. In the end, only one in ten young Latina/o adults have a college degree (Brindis et al. 2002), making it so that only 8.1 percent of the nation's bachelor's degrees are conferred to Latinas/os (U.S. Department of Education 2011).

Hispanic-Serving Institutions

HSIs are defined as accredited, nonprofit institutions of higher education with at least 25 percent of their undergraduate full-time equivalent students identifying as Hispanic or Latina/o (Contreras, Malcom, and Bensimon 2008; Laden 2001). As of 2004, there were 242 HSIs, over half of which were community colleges within the U.S. (Benitez and DeAro, 2004). And, although these HSIs make up only 7 percent of all nonprofit two- and four-year institutions, they enroll 54 percent of all Hispanic college students (Benitez and DeAro 2004). However, since all but three HSIs have been designated as such simply by virtue of their enrollment figures, many of them do not include within their missions the specific and explicit intentions to serve the needs of Hispanic students and communities (Contreras et al. 2008). For this reason, Gasman (2008) suggests that HSIs cannot be assumed to provide supportive or intimidating environments for their Latina/o students.

Indeed, the literature is mixed as to whether or not HSIs contribute to better outcomes for Latina/o students than do other types of institutions. Cuellar (2014) finds that, though Latina/o students at HSIs may begin college with lower levels of academic self-concept than their peers who are enrolled at non-HSIs and emergent HSIs, this difference is leveled after four years in college. This suggests that there is something about the HSI environment, more so than other types of environments, that bolsters the development of academic self-concept among Latina/o students. Perhaps in a similar vein, Crisp, Nora, and Taggart (2009) find evidence that, whereas Hispanic students are largely underrepresented in STEM fields,

Hispanic ethnicity increases the odds of declaring a STEM major within an HSI setting.

One certain difference in the environment of HSIs versus other institution types is the proportion of Hispanic students. Related to this, Hagedorn et al. (2007) found that a critical mass of Hispanic students and a critical mass of Hispanic faculty both have independent, positive relationships with Hispanic students' overall success, including their cumulative GPAs and course success ratios. Yet, while data indicates that HSIs also confer degrees to larger proportions of Hispanic students at all levels than do other institutions (Laden 2004), there is also evidence that they still do not confer degrees to Hispanics at rates that are equitable to local racial and ethnic demographics (Contreras et al. 2008).

Social Capital and Latina/o Students

The concept of social capital recognizes social networks as resources that may provide individuals and/or communities with connections and means for obtaining other forms of capital (Bordieu 1986). Yosso (2006) describes social capital as one form of community cultural wealth among Latinas/os. According to her model, it includes networks of people and community resources that may be used to navigate through and gain access to various societal institutions, including education. The extant literature helps to illustrate how this plays out. For instance, Pérez and McDonough (2008) find that Hispanic students depend on their relationships with multiple people, including parents, siblings, other relatives, peers, teachers, school counselors, other school staff, acquaintances, as well as institutional informants and support networks, as they make their decisions of where to attend college. They continue to rely on their relationships with others as they make their transition into college as well. Pino, Martinez-Ramos, and Smith (2012) find that while Latina/o second generation college students are more likely to find their parents to be helpful during this transition, Latina/o first generation college students are more likely to consider freshman orientation as a helpful resource during their transition to college. Saunders and Serna (2004) further highlight that the social networks that Latina/o first generation college students both bring to college and create while in college are key to their persistence. They emphasize, however, that those who manage to create new social networks within the college setting are also able to gain a greater sense of comfort and confidence within it.

While many second generation Latina/o students look to parents for information regarding college attendance, Ceja (2004), in an earlier study, noted that the important role their parents played was much more focused on encouraging their children's educational aspirations and academic success. Unlike in many middle-class white families, the parents of these students did not always depend on their own educational success as they provided their children with school advice. Oftentimes, they encouraged their children to succeed in school as they reflected on their own economic, social, and occupational struggles.

THE RESEARCH SITE: A DESCRIPTIVE PROFILE

With 42 percent of students being Latina/o, the four-year institution is classified as a Hispanic-Serving Institution (HSI). The institution is also an emerging Tier I research institution focused on increasing four- and six-year graduation rates. The vast majority of students starting their academic careers in the six-year time period for the study were first-year students who enrolled in college right out of high school. A total of 4,487 freshman students enrolled represented 64 percent of the entire entering student population. The second largest group of students enrolling during the same time period were transfer students enrolled as freshmen (N=303; 11.7%), sophomores (N=1007; 39%), juniors (N=972; 37.7%), and seniors (N=295; 11.5%) totaling 2577. The largest student subgroup was Hispanic at 42 percent, followed by white students (40 percent). African American and Asian American students were equally represented at 8 percent and 7 percent, respectively. Hispanic and white students, collectively, represented 82 percent of the entire entering students in Fall 2006. The representation of Hispanic males and females within each ethnic group are similar with those of their white counterparts. Other than major differences between Hispanic and white students and African American and Asian American students, similarities noted within each ethnic group were consistent across all groups.

FINDINGS FROM THE TREND ANALYSIS

Social Capital

For purposes of the investigation, social capital was operationally defined as the highest level of education reached by the student's parents. The assumption was made that parents who attained a higher level of education would provide much more information to students, not only focused on the application and admissions processes in college, but on the nature of an educational experience on a campus. The largest difference in father's educational attainment (24.4 percent) was found between Hispanic and white students who reported fathers having some college, a bachelor's degree, or a graduate/professional degree. Hispanic male students who started college right out of high school reported that 48 percent of their fathers had at least some college while Hispanic female students also right out of high school reported that 45 percent of their fathers had the same level of educational attainment. Among Hispanic male transfer students, they reported 41.5 percent having reached those goals followed by Hispanic female transfer students at 32 percent.

The largest difference in mother's educational attainment was found between Hispanic and white students (roughly a 25 percent difference among mothers who reported some college, a bachelor's degree, and a graduate/professional degree). Nearly 50 percent of Hispanic male and female students starting college right out of high school, 42 percent of Hispanic female transfer students and 39 percent of Hispanic male transfer students reported that their parents started college or had earned some form of degree.

Students' Course

A total of 87.2 percent of all students were enrolled as full-time students with only 12.8 percent attending college on a part-time basis. The group with the largest percentage of students attending on a part-time basis consisted of male, transfer students. Among all Hispanic and white students, those enrolling full-time in college after graduating from high school represented 97.1 percent of the students. Among all transfer students, an average of 71.5 percent of the students were registered as having a full-time course load.

DEVELOPMENTAL STUDIES DURING
FIRST YEAR AT INSTITUTION

In fall of 2006, a total of 1488 students were enrolled in one or more developmental courses at the institution. Of those, 1077 successfully completed their remedial courses while 411 were not successful in completing their required developmental courses. During the spring 2007 academic semester, a total of 155 were found enrolled in one or more developmental course. At the end of the semester, 116 of the 155 successfully completed their required remediation leaving 39 that were not. When the data was broken down by ethnicity, the findings indicated that during the fall 2006 semester a total of 677 Hispanic students were enrolled in some type of developmental course. Of those, a total of 468 (69 percent) were successful in completing their courses. The remaining 209 Hispanic students (31 percent) did not successfully complete their remedial courses. In comparison, a total of 491 white students were enrolled in that fall 2006 semester of which 370 (75 percent) successfully completed their developmental courses leaving 121 (25 percent) who did not.

A Comparison of Student Outcomes

The next set of figures focuses specifically on measurable student outcomes including the student's academic performance, their persistence rates, graduation rates, and earned degrees.

Academic performance by year. An examination of the overall student academic performance at the end of the first semester revealed that the grade point average for all students was a GPA of 2.59. At the end of the four-year period, academic performance of all students stood at a GPA of 2.78. Extending the time period to six years revealed that the overall student academic performance was a GPA of 2.74, indicating that the academic performance for all students remained consistent from the time of entry to graduation or later.

Six-year graduation rate. The six-year graduation rates among all students that first enrolled in fall of 2006 was 39.84 percent. The total number of entering students (N = 7064) receiving degrees during the six-year period in the study was 2814.

Student persistence rates. To further arrive at a holistic profile, the data was disaggregated into four academic years. The first-to-second year persistence rate for all students was found to be 59 percent. The persistence rate at the end of the second year revealed that 43 percent of those entering in fall 2006 remained enrolled. At the end of the third year, the persistence rate dropped to 37 percent and, at the end of the students' fourth year at the institution, it dropped once more to 27 percent. Of all the Hispanic students that entered as freshmen in 2006, a total of 585 graduated at the end of the fourth year. Of all the white students that entered as freshmen in 2006, a total of 469 graduated at the end of the fourth year.

A similar breakdown of the data was made by ethnicity. Excluding all other racial/ethnic groups except Hispanic and white students, the persistence rates for Hispanics are higher than for the total student population and lower for white students.

TABLE 1. Comparison of persistence rates and overall academic performance between Hispanic and White freshmen students.

Hispanic Freshmen Students	Persistence Rate	Overall GPA at End of Academic Year
Fall 2006 to Fall 2007	63%	2.429
Fall 2006 to Fall 2010	31%	2.698
White Freshmen Students	Persistence Rate	Overall GPA at End of Academic Year
Fall 2006 to Fall 2007	55%	2.653
Fall 2006 to Fall 2010	24%	2.797

The data was further disaggregated by native versus transfer for Hispanic students. Of all the Hispanic transfer students that entered as freshmen in 2006, a total of 558 graduated at the end of the fourth year. Of all the Hispanic transfer students that entered as freshmen in 2006, a total of 27 graduated at the end of the fourth year.

TABLE 2. Comparison of persistence rates and overall academic performance between Hispanic native and transfer students.

Hispanic Freshmen Native Students	Persistence Rate	Overall GPA at End of Academic Year
Fall 2006 to Fall 2007	63%	2.429
Fall 2006 to Fall 2010	32%	2.748
Hispanic Freshmen Transfer Students	Persistence Rate	Overall GPA at End of Academic Year
Fall 2006 to Fall 2007	61%	2.247
Fall 2006 to Fall 2010	22%	2.772

Undergraduate STEM degrees awarded. While the majority of students from all ethnic groups declared a major in biology, roughly 21.9 percent earned a Bachelor's of Science at the end of a four-year period. The highest proportion of science degrees earned was reported for Hispanic males (4.9 percent) who enrolled in college right out of high school, followed by Hispanic males (4.2 percent) who transferred. Hispanic females recorded the third highest proportion of science degrees (3.6 percent). White students recorded the fourth highest proportion equally at 3.2 percent.

The groups with the lowest proportion of science degrees were: Hispanic female transfer students (2.6 percent), white female native students (2.0 percent), and white female transfer students (0.17 percent). Of the 604 science degrees that were earned in STEM fields, Hispanics earned 368 (61 percent) while white students earned 236 for 39 percent of the total number.

CURRENT ASSERTIONS AND COUNTERVAILING FINDINGS

The intent of the investigation was to provide an exploratory examination of specific student factors at a specific HSI four-year institution captured through student institutional records. The first part of the investigation focused primarily on a set of student characteristics that would provide a much more detailed picture of students over a six-year period. To date, widespread perceptions regarding Latina/o students are (1) that Latino males are disproportionately underrepresented in higher education among different racial/ethnic groups; (2) that the great majority of Latino students attend college on a part-time basis; (3) that a great majority of Latino students do not come from family backgrounds where social capital is available; (4) that Latino students enrolled in developmental courses fall into a "black hole of remediation" and do not continue their education; (5) that Latino academic performance is way below that of their white counterparts with regard to academic achievement, persistence, and graduation rates; and (6) that Latino students lag far behind white students in STEM degrees earned. Based on the findings from the current study, the following conclusions can be drawn, at least at one specific Hispanic-Serving Institution.

Social Capital (Prior Parental Educational Experiences)

While Hispanic students do record lower levels of social capital, as measured by the educational attainment of their mothers and fathers, nearly 50 percent of them come from families whose parents had acquired some level of college education or had earned degrees at the bachelor's, master's, or doctoral levels. Contrary to popular belief, knowledge of what it takes to attend college and the different processes involved in applying and enrolling in college is much more evident than what has been previously believed. It could be hypothesized that as more Hispanics began to attend or graduate from college, they subsequently encouraged their offspring to seek undergraduate degrees and are now providing the social capital necessary for Latina/o students to navigate through a higher educational system.

Postsecondary Participation
(Representation at an Aspiring Institution)

The second popular belief, that Latina/o students do enroll disproportionately compared to their white counterparts, was found to be untrue at the study institution. Forty percent of the student population at the HSI examined in the study consisted of white male and female students. However, Latino male and female students represented 42 percent of the total student enrollment, almost equal representation at an emerging Tier 1 institution where the expectation remains that white students will outnumber minority students. Even as the study institution is engaged in seeking Tier 1 status, the representation of Hispanic students remains high.

The Myth of the Vanishing Latina/o Student

Moreover, while the trend among Latina/o students has been one in which Latinas far outnumber Latino students, such was not the case at the current institution. There was only a two-point percentage difference between Hispanic females (22 percent) and Hispanic males (20 percent). This pattern was also found among two-year HSI institutions in the city in which the HSI institution is located. At one community college, whose emphasis was on STEM and health-related fields, Hispanic male students outnumbered Hispanic female students by nearly 10 percentage points. The same pattern was found among Hispanic males and females even when disaggregated by transfer versus native enrollment.

Attending College Full-Time

The perception that Latina/o students mainly attend college on a part-time basis (Benitez 1998; Crisp, Nora, and Taggart 2009) was also not found to hold up in the findings. An overwhelming majority of Latina/o and non-Latina/o students enrolled in college on a full-time basis. Once again, when the data were disaggregated by native vs. transfer students and gender, native male (97 percent) and female students (96 percent) enrolled for full-time attendance. Surprisingly, 75 percent of transfer students also enrolled on a full-time basis.

The Black Hole of Remedial Education

A fourth perception regarding Latina/o students and remediation is that they do not do well in developmental courses and that, once enrolled in a developmental course, they do not continue with courses that count toward a specific degree. As was evident in the findings, 69 percent of Hispanic students enrolled in at least one developmental course were successful in completing the course and moving on to nonremedial, degree-counting courses.

The Under-Academic Performance of Latina/o Students

Another unconfirmed popular belief is that attrition rates among Hispanic students are much higher than for white students at all Hispanic-Serving Institutions. The truth is that persistence rates are dismal for all students. The four-year persistence rate among all undergraduate students at the study institution was a mere 27 percent. The first-to-second year persistence rate was 59 percent. No matter what racial or ethnic background students possessed, their four-year persistence was disappointing. However, among those who persisted to graduation, there were slight differences by ethnicity. Hispanic students actually fared a little better in first-to-second year persistence rates (63 percent) over white students (55 percent). The same could be found in first-to-fourth year persistence (graduation), where Hispanics recorded a 31 percent persistence rate over a 22 percent attrition rate for white students. Furthermore, the persistence rates and accompanying academic performance over a four-year period were found to be the same among Hispanic males and females. And, the same was found when compared to white male and female academic performance and persistence. On one side of the issue, Hispanic attrition remains too high to accept but, on the other side of the issue, Hispanics are performing as well or even a little better than their white counterparts in higher education, at least at one Hispanic-Serving Institution.

Hispanics and STEM Majors

The last perception held about Latinas/os in higher education is that far fewer Hispanic students than white students earn degrees in STEM fields (Crisp, Nora, and Taggart 2009). The findings from the current study suggest otherwise. Furthermore, an embedded perception within this belief is that Hispanic male students are not only vanishing at an alarming rate but that they are nowhere represented in significant number in those fields (Saenz and Ponjuan 2009). At the end of the four-year period (2006–2010), Hispanic male native students earned a total of 117 undergraduate degrees in a STEM discipline, with an additional 99 degrees earned by Hispanic male transfer students. To put this achievement into perspective, of the 604 science degrees earned in STEM, Hispanics earned 368 (61 percent) of those degrees while white students earned 236 (39 percent). Surprisingly, the proportion of degrees earned by the two groups mirrors the proportion of Hispanics and whites in the general population.

SENSE OF BELONGING AND ACADEMIC PERFORMANCE: THE IMPACT OF COGNITIVE AND PSYCHOSOCIAL FACTORS ON HISPANIC COLLEGE STUDENT SUCCESS

In the present era of accountability, higher education is continually challenged to improve student outcomes with a significant amount of focus placed on degree completion. While there has been some improvement in persistence and graduation rates over the years, undergraduate degree attainment among certain racial/ethnic groups remain disproportionately lower (Swail 2014). Programmatic efforts or interventions that have made a difference in retention and degree attainment have relied on theoretically tested perspectives guiding the development of such efforts (Nora 2003; Crisp 2010; Nunez, Hurtado, and Galdeano 2015; Hossler, Dundar, and Shapiro 2013). Extant research has identified an array of noncognitive or psychosocial explanatory factors affecting student persistence and degree attainment, including such constructs as social and academic interactions between students and their institutions, classroom validation, student engagement, educational and institutional commitments, mentoring experiences, and the role of significant others influencing re-enrollment and degree attainment. Among these sets of factors, a significant explanatory contribution to student persistence and degree completion has been found for a student's fit with his or her institution or, a sense of belonging, so much so that it has taken on an added significance as a major student outcome. Johnson et al. (2007, 526) point out that "sense of belonging illustrates the interplay between the individual and the institution." They also note that this relationship exchange between the student and the institution varies among students from different racial and ethnic backgrounds. It was hypothesized that this unique interaction between student and environment directly influenced the student sense of connectedness to the campus, and it served as the guiding principle in our study. The purpose of the investigation was to examine the validity of a set of student background characteristics, financial circumstances, and psychosocial factors in influencing a student's sense of belonging.

A Review of Sense of Belonging in the Literature

A student's sense of belonging, conceptualized in a variety of ways, has been extensively included in studies on student persistence (Hausmann,

Schofield, and Woods 2007). Previous models of student persistence have incorporated varying notions and definitions of sense of belonging in addition to such constructs as integration, student involvement, institutional fit, and commitment (Tinto 1987, 1993; Astin 1984; Bean 1985; Cabrera et al. 1992; Cabrera, Nora, and Castaneda 1993; Nora and Cabrera 1996; Strauss and Volkwein 2004). In their critique of two seminal models of student persistence; the *student integration model* (Tinto 1987, 1993) and *student involvement theory* (Astin 1984), Hurtado and Carter (1997) concluded that it was necessary to incorporate a psychological dimension of student integration, which they conceptualized to be a student's sense of belonging. Subsequently, studies have focused on the importance of this variable separate from academic and social integration, into which it was previously subsumed.

Recent research has positively linked academic motivation, peer interaction, participation in learning communities, experiences with diversity, and campus racial climate to a student's sense of belonging at an institution (Freeman, Anderman, and Jensen 2007; Hurtado and Ponjuan 2005; Hoffman et al. 2003; Maestas, Vaquera, and Zehr 2007; Nunez 2009; Strayhorn 2008). Research has also shown confidence in an academic setting as associated with a sense of belonging (Marra et al. 2012; Freeman, Anderman, and Jensen 2007). Faculty-student relationships are one of the more critical connections between academic integration and sense of belonging. Students who view faculty interactions more positively have shown to feel a stronger sense of belonging on their campuses (Freeman, Anderman, and Jensen 2007), and as Kuh et al. (2006) note, positive faculty interactions are related to better grades and increased likelihood of program completion. When students perceive that faculty show a greater interest in their development they are more likely to have higher levels of sense of belonging (Maestas, Vaquera, and Zehr 2007; Hoffman et al. 2003). Hoffman et al. (2003) have also discovered a positive relationship between supportive faculty and peer interactions and students' sense of belonging. Because sense of belonging plays an important role in the persistence process, a much more structured approach is needed that hypothesizes the different sets of cognitive and noncognitive variables that ultimately influence this very significant construct. The notion driving the current study is that because a student's sense of belonging is significantly intertwined with factors known to affect student persistence and degree attainment and that are instrumental in predicting student persistence as well, it is important to identify those academic and social experiences, financial circumstances, and behavioral and attitudinal constructs that impact this important variable.

Hurtado and Carter's (1997) notion of an undergraduate's sense of belonging brought attention to the psychological dimension of student integration theory in terms of connection, identification, and affiliation with the campus community. Strayhorn (2008, 17) extended their conceptualization of that latent construct by defining it as "students' perceived social support on campus, a feeling or sensation of connectedness, the experience of mattering or feeling cared about, accepted, respected, valued by, and important to the group or others on campus." He further indicated that both environmental and institutional settings play a role in the process of developing a sense of belonging. It is more about the experiences and characteristics of the student and less about the institution. The conceptualization of a student's sense of belonging for this study was based on a combination of the two perspectives.

The selection of the different explanatory variables in the hypothesized model was based on several theoretical models on student persistence that have been developed over the years and encompass some form of connection or belonging at an institution. The intent of the research was to focus on several theoretical approaches to student success that incorporate various aspects of students' social, academic, and interpersonal experiences as well as their cultural assets. Our conceptual framework (hypothesized model) was guided by research on student engagement (Nora 2003), mentoring (Crisp 2010), validation (Rendon 1994), community cultural wealth (Yosso 2005), and student assets (Rendon, Nora, and Kanagala 2014). These five theoretical perspectives were used as a guide in the selection of independent variables for the study. Based on the notion that a student's sense of belonging at their campus is influenced by the college environment for students that come from diverse backgrounds (Johnson et al., 2007), the selection of variables was closely aligned to these theoretical perspectives because they collectively incorporate dimensions of a student's diverse and cultural college experience.

RESEARCH METHODOLOGY

A nonexperimental research design was used for the investigation. The design was cross-sectional in nature, using a combination of online student survey and institutional data to test the theoretically based quantitative model among students attending an institution located in the Southwestern region of the United States. The online survey was administered to all enrolled students in the Spring of 2014. A total of 5484 students responded to the survey, for a 25 percent response rate. Demographic and other information was collected from both the survey and institutional records. Several institutional characteristics were matched with the student survey data. Financial aid-related variables including receipt of Pell grant, cost of attendance, unmet need, and demographic data (i.e., gender, ethnicity, enrollment); variables included in the model were provided by matching the institutional database record with the survey respondent's student ID. Data on background, financial and psychosocial characteristics including information on mentoring, faculty interaction, validation, family connections, student involvement, diversity and racial experiences, and others was collected through the online survey. Specific constructs and scales, borrowed from the theoretical frameworks previously mentioned, were identified to provide measures of the variables in the hypothesized model. The majority of the information was collected using a five-point Likert-type scale with responses ranging from 1 (Strongly Agree) to 5 (Strongly Disagree). The survey items captured the conceptualization of the independent variables included in the hypothesized model.

Results: Sense of Belonging

An examination of the influence of an array of cognitive, financial, and psychosocial factors on a student's sense of belonging at his or her institution revealed five major themes derived from the quantitative data analysis. These five groundings included (1) the importance of finances and financial aid, (2) the positive influence of psychosocial experiences on campus, (3) the negative bearing of racially-motivated attitudes and beliefs, (4) the carryover of prior high school academic performance, and (5) the notion of change in a student's life.

The first theme focused on the financial conditions of students. Three constituents of the first theme involved two clear components of financial assistance, the amount of Pell grant that was received by the student and the amount of unmet need for educational expenses, and one intangible component, worrying about college-related expenses (Nora and Cabrera 1994). In past discussions (Rendon, Dowd, and Nora 2011), the argument has been made (and validly so) that the receipt of financial assistance in the form of Pell grants helps to offset college expenses and, subsequently, increase the chances of a student persisting to graduation. In the current study, the finding revealed that the more the amount of financial aid in the form a Pell grant increased, the less a student felt a sense of belonging at their institution. Conceivably this finding can be explained by the knowledge that Pell grants provide but a small degree of relief in meeting educational costs (Rendon, Dowd, and Nora 2011). Concomitantly, this effect was also seen in the finding that as the amount of unmet need increased for students, a student's sense of belonging fell. Finally, those students who reported having financial stress and worry associated with meeting the costs of a college education also experienced a decrease in feeling a sense of belonging on campus. Why a negative relationship between these financial factors and the perception that a student belongs at an institution? Perhaps not having enough financial resources to purchase books, to engage in extracurricular activities that require money, or maybe just thinking that others have the financial means while they don't may lead students to feel they don't fit in at that institution.

The second theme established the value of validating and mentoring students and engaging in a collaborative undertaking on sense of belonging. For Hispanic students, knowing that they were validated in the classroom as well as outside of class was significant in enhancing their development of a sense of belonging on campus. When students felt that their opinions and life experiences were heard and valued in class and that at least one professor had shown concern about their academic progress, students reported higher levels of belonging on campus. Entrenched within this construct were two notions: at least one professor had inspired them to learn and at least one professor had made them feel cared about as a human being. In the end, the more Hispanic students perceived that faculty and staff at their institution reached out to them and made them believe they could be successful college students, the more likelihood that their sense of belonging at that institution would increase.

A second aspect in the second theme was the student's involvement in an informal mentoring experience, on- or off-campus. Students who perceived that someone in their lives had asked and encouraged them to express their feelings regarding their academic and social experiences on campus were more likely to feel at home and develop a sense of belonging at their institution. Four subparts of the second theme included the perception that someone in their lives had been involved in developing a realistic view of their skills and academic strengths, that there was someone who helped them to develop coping strategies enabling them to reach their academic goals, that somebody had taken the time to discuss their academic problems with them, and that somebody had engaged them in a discussion that required them to reflect on the skills needed to achieve their future goals. As Hispanic students experienced more of these aspects, their sense of belonging on campus increased. Related to this second aspect was the perception that being involved in collaborative learning experiences, such as studying with a group of students outside of class and joining in a study session for exams or work assignments, greatly increased their feelings that they belonged on their campus. Similarly related was the relationship between engaging in social experiences with college friends off-campus and feeling a sense of belonging back on campus. Perhaps the extension of friendships outside of a campus environment reinforces that relationship or connection back on campus.

The third theme focused on race-related issues dealing with identity, open discussion of race, resiliency in the face of negative putdowns, and campus climates. Rendon, Nora, and Kanagala (2015) noted that minority students often experience a set of negative barriers as they enter college. Those barriers include negative perceptions held by others, discriminatory attitudes expressed on campus, and microaggressions (Solórzano, Ceja, and Yosso 2000). The findings for the third theme revealed that those barriers consisted of the perception that discriminatory gestures and behaviors were observed in the classroom as well as outside the classroom and the perception that a Hispanic-Serving Institution may marginalize non-Hispanic students and perpetuate negative views about them. The perception that discriminatory gestures and behaviors exist on campus negatively influenced the perception of Hispanic students that they belonged and were accepted at their institution. As expected, the perception that a Hispanic-Serving Institution marginalizes students and perpetuates a negative profile of Hispanic students increases the chances of students not feeling that they belong. In contrast, however, the findings also revealed that as students engaged more in discussions surrounding racial issues with others of different races/ethnicities, the more they felt a sense of belonging.

The fourth of the five themes consisted of a student's high school academic performance. Graduating with a higher rank from high school had a positive carryover into college. The higher the rank of the student, the more likely they were to develop a sense of belonging once enrolled in college. The finding re-establishes the importance of a good academic performance, not only for admission purposes but for feeling at home on a campus.

The last theme dealt with the awareness upon entering college that life, as known in high school, was about to change in college. That change led to an increase in anxiety caused by feeling overwhelmed and stressed. As anticipated, as the level of anxiety rose for all students, the less they felt as though they belonged on a college campus. Surprisingly, the cost of attendance, social experiences off-campus, the number of hours attempted and earned, involvement in extracurricular activities on-campus, and the use of technology for assignments were not found statistically significant in accounting for the variance in a student's sense of belonging.

Results: Academic Performance

Five major themes surfaced from the findings on academic achievement. The first theme related more to the academic performance or engagement of Hispanic students at the different classification levels. The findings revealed that as the number of hours enrolled by students increased, the grade point average of the students decreased. Taking on a higher load of courses negatively affected the student's academic performance. While an increase in student engagement as defined by the number of hours enrolled in each semester might be perceived as staying on course, there comes a point where too many hours will interfere with a student's ability to deal with the course requirements. Evidence of this finding is seen in the positive impact that the number of semester hours that were earned by students had on their grade point averages. As the number of earned hours increased for students, so did their academic performance. What that exact number of hours attempted that will yield the desired outcome is the next step in the research.

The second theme was not evident for students during their freshman year—the influence of a student's high school experiences. In this component, three variables were involved: (1) the high school rank of the student at the time of graduation from high school, (2) the size of the student population in high school, and (3) the involvement of the student in their high school's extracurricular activities. In all cases, regardless of the student's classification, coming from a high school with a large student population, graduating in the higher ranks of their graduating class, and being involved in the many extracurricular activities available to them at their high schools all had very positive effects on the student's subsequent academic performance in college. While class size and graduating rank were not found to be statistically significant for freshman students, the one variable that was involved was the engagement of students in activities outside the classroom while in high school.

The third theme revealed in the findings encompassed the notions of validating and mentoring students and the strong positive impact on their academic performance. The strange aspect of the findings is that the constructs were not equally represented at the different classification levels. For Hispanic freshman students, being validated on campus was an important variable affecting their performance in class. Having a sense that their opinions and life experiences were valued in class and that at least one staff or faculty member had shown concern about their academic progress were but two aspects of the theme that influenced their grade performance in college. Embedded within this theme was the notion that at least one faculty member had empowered them to learn while at the institution as well as the notion that faculty had reached out to make them feel cared about as human beings. The more those students came to believe that faculty and staff at their institution reached out to them and ultimately made them believe that they could be successful college students, the greater the increase in their academic performance during their first year in college. What was surprising was that past the first year, the factor no longer played such an important role in the performances of students.

The second related variable in the third component was the student's involvement in an informal mentoring experience, on- or off-campus. This variable was significant for sophomores and juniors only. Students who sensed that someone in their lives had asked and encouraged them to express their feelings regarding their academic and social experiences on campus were more likely to perform better academically. Four of the most influential aspects of the third theme were the beliefs that someone in their lives had been involved in developing a realistic view of their skills and academic strengths, that there was a special individual that helped them to develop coping strategies that would enable them to reach their academic goals, that someone had taken the time to discuss their academic problems with them, and that an individual had engaged them in a discussion that required them to reflect on the skills needed to achieve their future goals. As sophomore and junior Hispanic students experienced more of these aspects, their academic performance in class increased. Quite puzzling was the fact that neither mentoring nor validation was statistically significant in predicting grade performance during the senior year. Perhaps as students mature and reach their final year in college, their self-confidence and esteem are no longer fragile and so students no longer require them in their academic life.

The fourth theme related to the financial circumstances of students. The three components of this fourth theme involved two tangible components of financial assistance, the amount of Pell grant that was received by the student and the amount of unmet need for meeting college costs, and one intangible component, worrying about college-related expenses (Nora and Cabrera 1994). These three aspects of financial circumstances were not found to negatively influence students' academic performance during their first year in college. However, their impact was felt during the junior and senior years. While it was expected that receiving financial assistance in the form of a Pell grant would offset college expenses, the finding revealed that as the amount of financial aid in the form a Pell grant increased, the academic performance of the student suffered. Perhaps this finding can be explained by the fact that Pell grants provide only a small relief in meeting educational costs (Rendon, Dowd, and Nora 2011). Further evidence of this impact was seen in the finding that as the amount of unmet need increased for students, academic performance was negatively affected. As anticipated, those students who experienced higher levels of financial stress and worry associated with meeting college expenses also experienced a decline in their academic performance.

The fifth theme dealt with the realization during the first year in college that life, as the student once knew it in high school, was different than life in college. That realization led to the student feeling overwhelmed and stressed while in college. An unexpected finding, however, was that feeling overwhelmed and stressed had no impact during the first two years in college, while it was a significant factor during the junior and senior years. As the level of anxiety rose for juniors and seniors, their academic performance was negatively affected. One could speculate that, as Hispanic students come closer to reaching their academic goals, anxiety associated with the realization of how different the "real world" can be compared to college life distracts students from fully concentrating on their studies.

The sixth and final theme focused on a "*choque*" factor. Rendon, Nora, and Kanagala (2015) describe that *choque* factor as a set of barriers that students come up against as they enter college from a different world. Those factors include negative perceptions held by others, discriminatory attitudes expressed on campus, and microaggressions (Solórzano 2012) as a few examples. In the current investigation, those *choque* factors were represented by two main variables: the perception that discriminatory gestures and behaviors were observed in the classroom as well as outside the classroom and the perception that a Hispanic-Serving Institution may marginalize some students and perpetuate negative views about them. The influence of these two factors was found only for freshmen and sophomores. For freshman students, the belief that discriminatory gestures and behaviors exist on campus negatively affected their academic performance. Moreover, the stronger the perception that a Hispanic-Serving Institution marginalizes students and perpetuates a negative profile for some students, the more students' academic performance is negatively affected.

CONCLUDING REMARKS

What foremost conclusion can be drawn from the findings? As with every other single-institution study, the generalizability of the results derived from the analysis is institution-specific. Nonetheless, at this one Hispanic-Serving Institution, Hispanics are keeping up, or at times, outperforming other racial and ethnic groups, and there is little evidence that Latino male students are disappearing or lagging far behind all other student subgroups. One could conclude that Latina/o students can be successful in earning more than their fair share of STEM degrees and persisting at a higher level than their white counterparts. However, while some of the empirical evidence would indicate this to be the case, the truth is that the attrition rate among all groups of students at this specific Hispanic-Serving Institution remains a target for further improvement. If there is a lesson to be learned from the investigation, that lesson must focus on minority and nonminority students who successfully complete an undergraduate program of study. Among those, both Latina and Latino students have performed on equal footing. One could speculate that, provided an environment of opportunity, Hispanics can easily compete and succeed (Crisp, Nora, and Taggart 2009).

What can we learn from the findings that negate a deficit viewpoint regarding Latina/o students? Maybe an indication that all students are beginning to benefit from the many retention-aimed interventions and activities found at institutions of higher education, or, maybe that our efforts at improving the persistence of Latino students from the first year to the second year in college are finally having an impact. And, it may be that while we see improvement in that critical first year, the four-year persistence and graduation rates of Hispanics still need to be fully addressed and that our models may be misspecified as to what affects the withdrawal of students at a later stage in their college lives.

As for conclusions drawn from the findings on sense of belonging, two inferences can be deduced. The establishment of an environment that allows for open discussion of racial and ethnic issues in-class as well as away from the classroom and provides the opportunity to learn more about someone of a different race/ethnicity adds more credibility to the argument that a diverse student body is a worthwhile goal for universities and colleges (Saunders and Serna 2004). Moreover, when perceptions of discriminatory words, behaviors, or gestures directed at minority students are minimized on a campus, the positive effects of those efforts can be easily seen in the academic performance of Latina/o students and in their sense of belonging at an institution. Coupled with those good efforts is the fact that the validation of our students by faculty and staff and theoretically grounded mentoring experiences also impact the academic and social lives of students in ways that are very rewarding. Taken together, the findings begin to point to the possibility of a new era for Latina/o students in culturally sensitive, validating, and caring Hispanic-Serving Institutions.

REFERENCES

American Association of State Colleges and Universities. 2012. "Top 10 Higher Education State Policy Issues for 2012" by Hurley, Daniel, Lesley McBain, Thomas Harnisch, Emily Parker, and Alene Russell. *AASCU: A Higher Education Policy Brief.* Washington, DC.

American Enterprise Institute. 2010. *2010 Annual Report.* Washington, DC.

Arbona, Consuela, and Amaury Nora. 2007. "The Influence of Academic and Environmental Factors on Hispanic College Degree Attainment." *The Review of Higher Education* 30 (3): 247–70.

Astin, Alexander. 1984. "Student Involvement: A Developmental Theory for Higher Education." *Journal of College Student Personnel* 25 (4): 297–308.

Bean, John. 1985. "Interaction Effects Based on Class Level in an Explanatory Model of College Student Dropout Syndrome." *American Educational Research Journal* 22 (1): 35–64.

Benitez, Margarita. 1998. "Hispanic-Serving Institutions: Challenges and Opportunities." *New Directions for Higher Education* 102: 57–68.

Benitez, Margarita, and Jessie DeAro, J. 2004. "Realizing student success at Hispanic-Serving Institutions." *New Directions for Community Colleges* 127: 35–48.

Bordieu, Pierre. 1986. "The Forms of Capital." In *Handbook of Theory and Research on the Sociology of Education*, edited by John Richardson, 241–58. New York: Greenwood Press.

Brindis, C. D., A. K. Driscoll, M. A. Biggs, and L. T. Valderrama, 2002. *Fact sheet on Latino youth: Education.* San Francisco, CA: University of California, San Francisco, Center for Reproductive Health Research and Policy, Department of Obstetrics, Gynecology and Reproductive Health Sciences and the Institute for Health Policy Studies.

Cabrera, Alberto, Amaury Nora, and Maria Castaneda. 1993. "College Persistence: Structural Equations Modeling Test of an Integrated Model of Student Retention." *The Journal of Higher Education* 64 (2): 123–39.

Cabrera, Alberto, Maria Castaneda, Amaury Nora, and Dennis Hengstler. 1992. "The Convergence between Two Theories of College Persistence." *The Journal of Higher Education* 63 (2): 143–64.

Ceja, Manual. 2004. "Chicana College Aspirations and the Role of Parents: Developing Educational Resiliency." *Journal of Hispanic Higher Education* 3 (4): 338–62.

Contreras, Francis, Lindsey Malcom, and Estela Bensimon. 2008. "Hispanic-Serving Institutions: Closeted Identity and the Production of Equitable Outcomes for Latina/o Students." In *Understanding Minority-Serving Institutions*, edited by Marybeth Gasman, Ben Baez, & Caroline Turner, 71–90. Albany: State University of New York Press.

Crisp, Gloria. 2010. "The Impact of Mentoring on the Success of Community College Students." *The Review of Higher Education* 34 (1): 39–60

Crisp, Gloria, Amanda Taggart, and Amaury Nora. 2014. "Undergraduate Latina/o Students: A Systematic Review of Research Identifying Factors Contributing to Academic Success Outcomes." *Review of Educational Research* 85 (2): 249–74.

Crisp, Gloria, Amaury Nora, and Amanda Taggart. 2009. "Student Characteristics, Pre-college, College, and Environmental Factors as Predictors of Majoring In and Earning a STEM Degree: An Analysis of Students Attending a Hispanic Serving Institution." *American Educational Research Journal* 46 (4): 924–42.

Cuellar, Marcela. 2014. "The Impact of Hispanic-Serving Institutions (HSIs), Emerging HSIs, and Non-HSIs on Latina/o Academic Self-Concept." *The Review of Higher Education* 37 (3): 499–530.

Freeman, Tierra, Lynley Anderman, and Jane Jensen. 2007. "Sense of Belonging in College Freshmen at the Classroom and Campus Levels." *The Journal of Experimental Education* 75 (3): 203–20.

Fry, Richard. (2011). Hispanic college enrollment spikes, narrowing gaps with other groups. Washington, DC: Pew Hispanic Center. Retrieved from http://www .pewhispanic.org/2011/08/25/hispanic-college-enrollment-spikes-narrowing -gaps-with-other-groups/

Gándara, Patricia, and Francis Contreras. 2009. *The Latino Education Crisis: The Consequences of Failed Social Policies*. Cambridge, MA: Harvard University Press.

Gasman, Marybeth. 2008. "Minority-Serving Institutions: A Historical Backdrop." In *Understanding Minority-Serving Institutions*, edited by Marybeth Gasman, Ben Baez, and Caroline Turner, 18–27. Albany: State University of New York Press.

Hagedorn, L. S., Chi, W. Y., Cepeda, R. M., & McLain, M. (2007). An investigation of critical mass: The role of Latino representation in the success of urban community college students. *Research in Higher Education* 48(1), 73–91.

Hausmann, Leslie, Janet Schofield, and Rochelle Woods. 2007. "Sense of Belonging as a Predictor of Intentions to Persist among African American and White First-Year College Students." *Research in higher Education* 48 (7): 803–39.

Hoffman, Marybeth, Jayne Richmond, Jennifer Morrow, and Kandice Salome. 2003. "Investigating 'Sense of Belonging' in First-Year College Students." *Journal of College Student Retention* 4: 227–56.

Hossler, Donald, Afet Dundar, and Douglas Shapiro. 2013. "Longitudinal Pathways to College Persistence and Completion: Student, Institutional and Public Policy Perspectives. In *The State of College Access and Completion: Improving College*

Success for Students from Underrepresented Groups, edited by Laura Perna and A.P. Jones, 140–65. New York: Routledge.

Hurtado, Sylvia, and Deborah Carter. 1997. "Effects of College Transition and Perceptions of the Campus Racial Climate on Latino Students' Sense of Belonging." *Sociology of Education* 70: 324–45.

Hurtado, Sylvia, and Luis Ponjuan. 2005. "Latino Educational Outcomes and the Campus Climate. *Journal of Hispanic Higher Education* 4: 235–51.

Johnson, Dawn, Matthew Soldner, Jeannie Brown Leonard, and Patty Alvarez. (2007). Sense of belonging among first-year undergraduates from different racial/ethnic groups. *Journal of College Student Development* 48(5), 525–542.

Kuh, George, Jennifer Buckley, Brian Bridges, and John Hayek. 2006. "What Matters to Student Success: A Review of the Literature." Commissioned Report for the National Symposium on Post-Secondary Student Success. Washington, DC: National Postsecondary Education Cooperative. Retrieved from http://nces.ed.gov/npec/pdf/Kuh_Team_ExecSumm.pdf.

Laden, Berta Vigil. (2004). Hispanic-serving institutions: What are they? Where are they? *Community College Journal of Research and Practice* 28 (3), 181-198.

Longerbeam, Susan, William Sedlacek, and Helen Alatorre. 2004. "In Their Own Voices: Latino Student Retention." *NASPA Journal* 41 (3): 538–50.

Maestas, Ricardo, Gloria Vaquera, and Linda Zehr. 2007. "Factors Impacting Sense of Belonging at a Hispanic-Serving Institution." *Journal of Hispanic Higher Education* 6 (3): 237–56.

Marra, Rose, Kelly Rodgers, and Barbara Bogue. 2012. "Leaving Engineering: A Multiyear Single Institution Study." *Journal of Engineering Education* 101 (1): 6–27.

Merisotis, Jamie, and Kirstin McCarthy. 2005. "Retention and Student Success at Minority-Serving Institutions. *New Directions for Institutional Research* 125: 45–58.

Nora, Amaury. 2003. "Access to Higher Education for Hispanic Students: Real or Illusory?" In *The Majority in the Minority: Expanding Representation of Latina/o Faculty, Administration and Students in Higher Education,* edited by Janette Castellanos and L. Jones, 47–67. Sterling, VA: Stylus Publishing.

Nora, Amaury, and Alberto Cabrera. 1996. "The Role of Perceptions of Prejudice and Discrimination on the Adjustment of Minority Students to College." *The Journal of Higher Education* 67 (2): 119–48.

Nora, Amaury, Libby Barlow, and Gloria Crisp. 2005. "Student Persistence and Degree Attainment beyond the First Year in College: The Need for Research. In *College Student Retention: Formula for Student Success,* edited by Alan Siedman, 129–54. Westport, CT: Praeger Publishers.

Núñez, Anne Marie. 2009. "A Critical Paradox? Predictors of Latino Students' Sense of Belonging in College." *Journal of Diversity in Higher Education* 2 (1): 46–61.

Núñez, Anne Marie, and Alex Bowers. 2011. "Exploring What Leads High School Students to Enroll in Hispanic-Serving Institutions: A Multilevel Analysis." *American Educational Research Journal* 48 (6): 1286–1313.

Núñez, Anne Marie, Sylvia Hurtado, and E. Calderón Galdeano, E. (Eds.). 2015. *Hispanic-Serving Institutions: Advancing Research and Transformative Practice.* New York, NY: Routledge.

Padilla, Raymond. 1999. "College Student Retention: Focus on Success." *Journal of Student Retention, Theory, and Practice* 1 (2): 131–45.

Pérez, Patricia, and Patricia McDonough. 2008. Understanding Latina and Latino College Choice: A Social Capital and Chain Migration Analysis. *Journal of Hispanic Higher Education* 7 (3): 249–65.

Perna, Laura. 2000. "Differences in the Decision to Attend College among African Americans, Hispanics, and Whites." *The Journal of Higher Education* 71 (2): 117–41.

Pino, Nathan, Gloria Martinez-Ramos, and William Smith. 2012. "Latinos, the Academic Ethic, and the Transition to College. *Journal of Latinos and Education* 11: 17–31.

Rendon, Laura. 1994. "Validating Culturally Diverse Students: Toward a New Model of Learning and Student Development. *Innovative Higher Education* 19: 33–52.

Rendon, Laura, Alicia Dowd, and Amaury Nora. 2012. *Priced Out: A Close Look at Postsecondary Affordability for Latinos.* Washington, DC: The Higher Education Subcommittee of President Barack Obama's Advisory Commission on Educational Excellence for Hispanics.

Ryu, Mikyung. 2009. *Minorities in Higher Education: Twenty-Third Status Report.* Washington, DC: American Council on Education.

Saenz, Victor, & Luis Ponjuan. 2009. "The Vanishing Latino Male in Higher Education." *Journal of Hispanic Higher Education* 8 (1): 54–89.

Saenz, Victor, Sylvia Hurtado, Doug Barrera, DeSha Wolf, and Fanny Yeung. 2007. *First in My Family: A Profile of First-Generation College Students at Four-Year Institutions since 1971.* Los Angeles, CA: Higher Education Research Institute.

Saunders, Marisa, and Irene Serna. 2004. "Making College Happen: The College Experiences of First-Generation Latino Students." *Journal of Hispanic Higher Education* 3 (2): 146–63.

Solórzano, Daniel, Miguel Ceja, and Tara Yosso. 2000. "Critical Race Theory, Racial Microaggressions, and Campus Racial Climate: The Experiences of African American College Students." *Journal of Negro Education* 69 (12): 60–73.

Spruill, Nicklaus, Joan Hirt, and Yun Mo. 2014. "Predicting Persistence to Degree of Male College Students." *Journal of College Student Retention* 16 (1): 25–48.

Strauss, Linda, and J. Fredericks Volkwein. 2004. "Predictors of Student Commitment at Two-Year and Four-Year Institutions. *Journal of Higher Education* 75 (2): 203–27.

Strayhorn, Terrell. 2006. "Factors Influencing the Academic Achievement of First-Generation College Students," *NASPA Journal* 43 (4): 82–111.

———. 2008. "Sentido de Pertenencia: A Hierarchial Analysis Predicting Sense of Belonging among Latino College Students." *Journal of Hispanic Higher Education* 7 (4): 301–20.

Swail, Watson S. 2014. "A Different Viewpoint on Student Retention." *Higher Learning Research Communications* 4 (2): 18–25.

Tinto, Vincent. 1987. *Leaving College: Rethinking the Causes and Cures of Student Attrition.* Chicago: University of Chicago Press.

———. 1993. *Leaving College: Rethinking the Causes and Cures of Student Attrition* (2nd Ed.). Chicago: University of Chicago Press.

U.S. Department of Education, National Center for Education Statistics. 2011. *The Condition of Education 2011* (NCES 2011-033). Retrieved from https://nces.ed.gov/pubsearch/pubsinfo.asp?pubid=2011033.

Yosso, Tara. 2005. "Whose Culture has Capital? A Critical Race Theory Discussion of Community Cultural Wealth." *Race Ethnicity and Education* 8 (1): 69–91.

Yosso, Tara, and Daniel Solórzano. 2006. "Leaks in the Chicana and Chicano Educational Pipeline" [Latino Policy & Issues Brief No. 13]. Retrieved from the UCLA Chicano Studies Research Center website: http://www.chicano.ucla.edu/files/LPIB_13March2006.pdf .

Nineteen Years after Prop 209

ARE LATINO/A STUDENTS EQUITABLY REPRESENTED AT THE UNIVERSITY OF CALIFORNIA?

Maria Estela Zárate, Chenoa S. Woods, and Kelly M. Ward

INTRODUCTION

In 2013 the Supreme Court remanded the latest case challenging the consideration of race in admissions, *Fisher v. University of Texas at Austin* (2012), to the lower court. The US Court of Appeals, Fifth Circuit, then found for UT Austin and, again, Fisher appealed. Finally, in June 2016 the Supreme Court ruled in favor of UT Austin, upholding the university's affirmative action program and in the process setting federal precedent for similar programs. The University of California (UC), a public university system like the University of Texas, provides a suitable example of the long-term effects of wholesale banning of the consideration of race in college admissions decisions. Nineteen years ago, voters in California passed Proposition 209, decreeing that public colleges and universities are forbidden from considering applicants' race, gender, and ethnicity in admissions decisions. This ballot measure closed one route to college for many Latino/a students, who often do not have access to adequate college preparatory curriculum and information in the high schools they attend to compete on the basis of rigid admissions criteria like test scores and grade point averages (Bryan et al. 2011; Contreras 2005a; Kimura-Walsh et al. 2008; Tornatzky, Cutler, and Lee 2002; Zárate and Pachon 2006).

When Prop 209 went into effect in 1997, reports documented an immediate decline in the representation of Latinos/as at UC campuses (Lomibao, Barreto, and Pachon 2004; Card and Kruger 2004). However, since 2003, the long-term implications of Prop 209 have not been documented to ascertain if Latinos/as have gained ground in acquiring access to college. We aim to fill this gap in the literature by examining how Latinos/as have fared in gaining access to UC, given the parameters of race-blind admissions practices.

Demographic, fiscal, and institutional policy changes that occurred in the past decade are grounds for continued examination of the representation of Latinos/as at UCs. First, according to the California Department of Education (2015), the proportion of high school graduates who are Latino/a has increased by more than 15 percent since 1995. Second, fiscal crises in the past decade have led the state to slash allocated spending to UC, forcing administrators to pass the financial burden on to students in the form of increased tuition (Johnson 2012). Fiscal woes have driven some institutions to decrease enrollment and reduce spending on admissions outreach programs (Johnson 2012; Wood 2004). Finally, admissions policy changes have been implemented with the goal of expanding the pool of UC-eligible students (BOARS 2002; University of California Office of the President [UCOP] 2002). All of these developments could have potentially changed access to the UC system, which motivated us to reevaluate Latinos/as' access to UC.

The objective in this analysis is to document whether parity has increased or been achieved for Latinos/as' access to UC since the approval of Prop 209. While most of the discourse on the merits of racial diversity on college campuses has focused on admissions decisions, we argue that completing high school, fulfilling requirements for admissions, submitting an application, and enrolling are also critical aspects of the college-going process in which Latino/a students often fall short despite having high expectations for enrollment in college (Hurtado et al. 1997; Zárate and Gallimore 2005). Thus, we examine nineteen-year trends in the preparation, application, admissions, and enrollment of Latinos/as at the University of California:

- Have Latinos/as gained equitable representation at the University of California over the past nineteen years?
- Has the representation of Latinos/as in the different stages of the high school-to-UC pipeline changed in the past nineteen years?

BACKGROUND

The University of California

The California Master Plan of Higher Education (California Joint Committee to Develop a Master Plan for Education 2002), implemented in 1960 and renewed in 1987 and 2002, is the framework guiding enrollment and informing the roles of the state's public higher education institutions. The Master Plan positioned the UC system as the state's public elite research university and commits the UC system to admit the top one-eighth of California's high school graduates, guaranteeing them a place at a UC campus as long as they are eligible. Currently, there are nine UC campuses across the state serving approximately 181,500 undergraduate students. Over the past twenty years, access to the University of California has become increasingly competitive, especially at the flagship institutions: UCLA and UC Berkeley admitted approximately 17 percent of freshman applicants for Fall 2015 (UCOP 2015). However, selectivity varies widely among the nine campuses, and the less selective campuses accept close to 65 percent of applicants.

Race as a Factor in Admissions to University of California

Since the 1990s, national political shifts and public backlash against affirmative action policies have driven multipronged campaigns to abandon the use of race in UC admissions considerations (Murphy 1995; Orfield 1998). Challenges to the use of race in admissions decisions have taken place across electoral, legal, and governance fronts. On the legal front, the Supreme Court case *Regents of the University of California v. Bakke* (1978) protected the use of race in admissions decisions as long as racial group quotas were not used in the process. The constitutionality of considering race in admissions decisions was most recently contested in *Gratz v. Bollinger* (2003) and *Grutter v. Bollinger* (2003). These Supreme Court decisions further narrowed the use of race and ethnicity in university admissions policies. These combined decisions endorsed the use of race in admissions decisions but outlawed assigning rank or weight to a student's race or ethnicity.

In California, ballot initiatives and university governance policies dictate how race is considered in admissions decisions. In 1995, the UC Board of Regents passed SP-1, prohibiting UC from considering race or ethnicity in admissions decisions. Shortly thereafter in 1996, Proposition 209, also known as California's Civil Rights Initiative, was passed by voters and eliminated the use of race/ethnicity or sex in consideration for employment in the public sector or admissions in public schools and universities. These two propositions effectively banned the consideration of race in admissions decisions at California public higher education institutions and continue to guide admission practices.

Existing Research

Latino/a enrollment at UC campuses has been examined in previous studies scrutinizing the effects of Proposition 209 on underrepresented minority (URM)[1] admissions rates (Contreras 2005b; Hicklin 2007; Santos, Cabrera,

---

1. The University of California classifies African Americans, American Indians and Chicanos/Latinos/as as historically and continually underrepresented minorities (URM) in institutions of higher education. (UCOP 2003).

and Fosnacht 2010; Card and Kruger 2004; M. Long 2004; Lomibao, Barreto, and Pachon 2004). A consistent finding was that post-Proposition 209, the representation of Latinos/as and other URMs in applications, admissions, and enrollment decreased at most of the UC campuses. The enrollment of Latinos/as at the UCs decreased by approximately five to eight percentage points at flagship campuses in the first year following the implementation of Prop 209, and though enrollment has rebounded slowly at the least selective campuses, as of 2004 their representation among the UC-wide freshman class and more selective campuses had not met pre-209 levels (Grodsky and Kurlaender 2010; Horn and Flores 2003; Lomibao, Barreto, and Pachon 2004).

Yet another documented implication of Prop 209 was the decline in the proportion of URM applicants, including Latinos/as, to UCs (Grodsky and Kurlaendar 2010; Card and Kruger 2004; M. Long 2004; Horn and Flores 2003). Scholars have proposed that URMs' low application rates may be, in part, the result of students' perceiving their chance of gaining admissions to UCs as severely diminished as a result of Prop 209 (Grodsky and Kurlaendar 2010; Hicklin 2007; M. Long 2004). Students from high schools with large Latino/a populations are particularly unlikely to apply for UC admissions (Martin, Karabel, and Jaquez 2005). Martin, Karabel, and Jaquez offer the explanation that these students lack application information and warns that budget cuts impact outreach programs that reach students who most need information and guidance.

The low representation of Latinos/as among UC applicants and enrollees is particularly troubling given their increasing representation among the state's high school graduates. Since 1995, there have been even larger increases in the number of Latino/a students enrolled in the twelfth grade in California public schools while the proportion of non-Hispanic white students has decreased (California Department of Education 2015). In fact, Latinos/as compose the greatest share of all California graduates since 2008. Because the existing research has not examined application, admissions, or enrollment trends at UC since 2003 (Lomibao, Barreto, and Pachon 2004), it is not known if the concentration of URMs in various stages of the application process has changed to reflect broader population changes.

In addition to shifts in the demographic characteristics of high school graduates, significant economic blows to California's economy in the past ten years have resulted in budget cuts that impact access to UC. The state of California spends $1.6 billion less on higher education than it did ten years ago, and the proportion of the state's budget spent on higher education has diminished (Johnson 2012). In response to the budget cuts, UC has increased tuition and fees, decreased enrollment, and cut staff and faculty (Johnson 2012; UCOP 2011). Four years after the beginning of the recession, tuition and fees increased by more than 80 percent (Williams, Leachman, and Johnson 2011). In 2004, UCs withheld admitting 7,600 students in exchange for lower fee increases (Wood 2004). Moreover, budget cuts have also targeted reductions in staff and outreach programs geared toward recruiting and supporting Latino/a and African American students (Torres 2004). Collectively, these fiscal challenges have created more competition for admissions and increased financial barriers for first-generation students, many of whom are Latino/a (Contreras 2005a).

Another important change to the UC admissions landscape was the implementation of a comprehensive admissions review policy, Eligibility in Local Context (ELC), in the fall of 2001. With ELC, the top 4 percent of each high school's graduates were guaranteed admissions to a UC campus in 2001, though not necessarily a flagship campus, provided they met the eligibility criteria. Although other studies examined cohorts of applicants one to two years following the implementation of ELC (Horn and Flores 2003; Lomibao, Barreto, and Pachon 2004; Santos, Cabrera, and Fosnacht 2010; UCOP 2002), there has been no long-term examination of UC admissions trends since the initial implementation. Simulation analysis of the potential effect of ELC (Geiser 1999) indicated that there would likely not be a large impact on the admissions of URM students, including Latinos/as, because many of the students qualifying for admissions under ELC were already represented in the eligible pool defined by previous eligibility standards. Moreover, due to variability in how different campuses apply comprehensive review policies (Comeaux and Watford 2006), it was difficult to predict whether admissions trends would shift UC-wide in the years after the implementation of ELC.

We agree with other scholars that, to the extent that public institutions remain accountable to the state, enrollment at UCs should reflect the racial and ethnic composition of California's high school graduates (Bensimon, Hao, and Bustillos 2006; Haycock, Lynch, and Engle 2010; Milem 2003). Because Latino/a students have especially increased their representation among public high school graduates in California, we would expect a commensurate increase in their representation at UC. Demographic shifts, economic hardship faced by UC, and continued implementation of comprehensive admissions review strategies have the potential to differentially impact various stages of the UC college application and enrollment process.

Relying in part on Bensimon, Hao, and Bustillos's (2006) Academic Equity Scorecard framework, we developed four indices to capture the ways Latinos/as participate in four different stages of a trajectory leading to the University of California, from high school completion to enrollment

FIGURE 1. The educational pipeline beginning with high school completion and continuing through college enrollment.

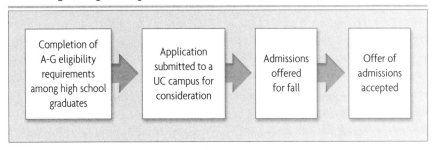

immediately following high school completion. We consider four critical stages of the college admissions process: eligibility, application, admissions, and enrollment (see fig. 1). Admittedly, there are different pathways to a baccalaureate-granting institution, and enrolling in a baccalaureate-granting institution immediately after high school is not the most frequent trajectory undertaken by Latino/a students (Fry 2004; Hurtado et al. 1997). Nonetheless, enrolling in college immediately after high school bypasses some of the pathways that often have higher attrition, such as transferring from a community college to a baccalaureate-granting institution (B. Long and Kurlaender 2009).

METHODS

Data

High school completion and A-G[2] eligibility requirement completion data from 1995 to 2013 were download from a dataset publicly available from the California Department of Education. This data is collected annually in October and reported in May. American Indian students and students who are of two or more races were omitted from the analytical sample due to their proportionally low representation. Asian, Pacific Islander, and Filipino students were collapsed into one Asian American category. This data only captures graduates of California public high schools. We are confident that the data used in this analysis account for the greater part of the eligible high school population for UC admission, since freshmen who graduated from California high schools make up the majority of applicants to UC (UCOP 2015).

---

2. A-G eligibility requirements consist of completing fifteen yearlong courses in the subjects of history, English, mathematics, science, a language other than English, visual/performing arts, and college-preparatory electives, with a grade of C or better in each course.

UC freshman application, admission, and enrollment data for California residents from Fall semester 1995 through 2013 were obtained from the University of California Office of the President (UCOP 2015). American Indian, "Other," and students of an unidentified race were omitted from the analyses because of their very small representation in this dataset. For the purposes of this paper, "UC" data refers to aggregate data for all UC campuses, except for the San Francisco and Merced campuses. San Francisco is omitted because it is dedicated specifically to the health sciences and therefore is not a traditional undergraduate university. Merced is omitted because data are available only for enrollment numbers from 2005 and later, after Proposition 209 was implemented. If a student applied or was admitted to several UC campuses in any year, they are counted as one applicant or admit in the data.

Analysis

Following others' use of equity indices to measure equity in various dimensions of higher education[3] (Bensimon, Hao, and Bustillos 2006; Perna et al. 2007), we created four equity indices, in which the numerator is the percentage of the target racial group in the available pool and the denominator is the concentration of the target racial group for each stage of the college-going process from 1995 to 2013. These equity indices measure a group's representation at each stage of the college-going process, based on their representation in the previous requisite stage. In this way, concerns about whether a student is eligible or a viable candidate for admissions are addressed, as the reference group is the eligible group (Bensimon, Hao, and Bustillos 2006). Equitable representation in this analysis is indicated by a 1:1 ratio between the proportion represented in the numerator and the proportion represented in the denominator. An index score of less than 1.0 indicates underrepresentation for the target racial group, and a score of greater than 1.0 indicates overrepresentation of the target racial group.

The equity indices we use in this analysis not only capture the stages in the college-admissions process that are least equitable, but also document whether conditions for URMs have improved over time (Bensimon, Hao, and Bustillos 2006). Moreover, the equity indices allow for comparisons across groups (Perna et al. 2007; Perna et al. 2011) and provide

---

3. Other researchers have used somewhat similar calculations to capture equitable representation, such as parity ratios (Contreras 2005b) or impact ratios (Santos, Cabrera, and Fosnacht 2010). Most use 1.0 as an indicator of equity (Bensimon, Hao, and Bustillos 2006; Contreras 2005b; Perna et al. 2007; Perna et al. 2011), others use 0.80 as a "significant" indicator (Santos, Cabrera, and Fosnacht 2010).

indicators of inequity rather than "gaps" in access and opportunity (Perna et al. 2007). In the following section we describe the four indices we apply in this analysis.

Equity Index A illustrates the representation of Latinos/as among A-G completers as a proportion of their representation among high school graduates. This index allows us to gauge whether the preparation of URMs for college is equitable in California public high schools.

$$\text{Equity Index A} = \frac{(\text{Latino A-G Completers} / \text{All A-G Completers})}{\text{Latino Graduates} / \text{All HS Graduates}}$$

Equity Index B depicts the proportions of the UC applicant pool that is Latino/a as a fraction of the proportion of their representation among students having completed A-G eligibility requirements.

$$\text{Equity Index B} = \frac{(\text{Latino Applicants} / \text{All Applicants})}{\text{Latino A-G Completers} / \text{All A-G Completers}}$$

Equity Index C depicts the proportion of Latino/a students among the admitted as a percentage of their representation in the applicant pool.

$$\text{Equity Index C} = \frac{(\text{Latino Admits} / \text{All Admits})}{\text{Latino Applicants} / \text{All Applicants}}$$

Equity Index D details the proportion of Latino/a entering UC each fall as a fraction of their representation among the admitted pool of students. This rate is commonly referred to as the yield rate. In this index, we examine for differences in yield rates between groups and across time.

$$\text{Equity Index D} = \frac{(\text{Latino Enrollees} / \text{All Enrollees})}{\text{Latino Adults} / \text{All Adults}}$$

RESULTS

Are URMs Completing High School Eligible for Admission to UC?

We find that A-G completion equity indices for Latino/a and African American students have remained consistently below equity for nineteen years (see fig. 2). While Latino/a students appear to have consistently, albeit slowly, gained ground in equitable representation among high school completers with A-G eligibility status, African American students have been persistently low. Asian American and non-Hispanic White high school graduates are consistently and increasingly overrepresented among high school graduates completing A-G eligibility requirements.

FIGURE 2. Index A: Proportion of students who complete the A-G requirements as a proportion of high school graduates.

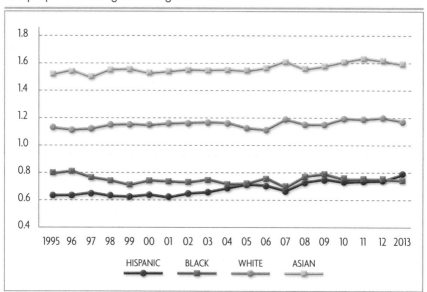

Are Eligible URMs Applying to UCs in Equitable Proportions?

In 1997, Latino/a students experienced a sharp decline in equitable representation among applicants to UCs, and they since have consistently fallen short of equity status in applications submitted (fig. 3). Like their non-Hispanic White peers, they are applying to UC campuses at rates well below what one would expect given their representation among students who have completed high school having fulfilled the A-G requirements. Interestingly, eligible African American high school graduates reached equity in applying to UCs beginning in 2007 and have sharply increased their representation among eligible applicants, so that most recently they are overrepresented among eligible applicants. Eligible Asian American high school graduates, on the other hand, are consistently overrepresented in submitting applications to UC campuses, albeit with declining representation in the past five years.

Are UCs Accepting URM Applicants in Equitable Proportions?

The most common illustration of how UC admission practices affect URMs maps representation among the admitted pool of students and in their admissions rates. However, this does not take into account the previous

FIGURE 3. Index B: Proportion of applicants as a proportion of students who have completed the A-G requirements.

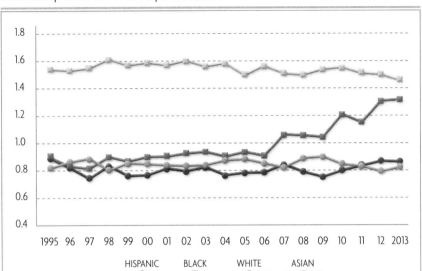

steps required to be eligible for admission. As seen above, students must first complete the A-G course requirements and apply to a UC campus. Thus, Equity Index C (fig. 4), which captures each group's admission rate in relation to its representation among applicants, is a more accurate representation of Latino/a students' equity in the admission process. Here, we observe that Latino/a and African American students' equity statuses fell in 1997 and have remained below equity. Latinos/as, after reaching equity in 1997, have fluctuated between 87 percent and 94 percent of equity status. Despite a brief upward trend between 2004 and 2007, African Americans' equity index has continued to decline between 2008 and 2013; as of 2013, African Americans remained below equity at 72 percent. Asian American students and non-Hispanic white applicants appear to be consistently at equity, with Asian Americans' sharp increase in equity beginning in 2011 and reaching 16 percent above equity.

Are Admitted URM Students Choosing to Enroll at a UC Campus in Proportions Equitable to Their Admission Rates?

In examining enrollment rates in relation to a group's representation in the admitted pool, Latino/a students have experienced a recent shift, with

FIGURE 4. Index C: Proportion of students who were admitted as a proportion of students who applied to the UC system.

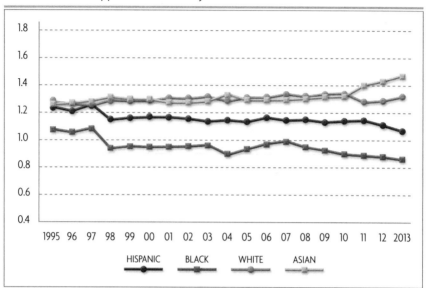

increases in equity beginning in 2010 and reaching equity in 2013 (see fig. 5). Non-Hispanic White students have enrolled at UC campuses at approximately 10 percent below equity, with a decline evident for the past ten years. Similarly, African American students experienced a drop in equity in 1997 to a low of 85 percent in 2006, yet they experienced wavering levels of equity in the following years, still under parity in 2013. In practical terms, non-Hispanic White and African American students, and Latino/a students before 2013, chose to enroll at a UC in lower proportions than their concentration among admitted representation. In contrast, Asian American students have consistently enrolled in higher proportions than their concentration among admitted students.

DISCUSSION

Using the "pipeline" analogy, we examined the stages where Latino/a students "leak" in the process between completing high school and enrolling at a UC campus. Specifically, we asked whether Latinos/as "trickled out" in meeting A-G eligibility requirements, applying for admissions, gaining admissions, and/or enrolling in a UC campus. Equity indices revealed the loss of potential Latino/a UC students at each stage of the process.

FIGURE 5. Index D: Proportion of students enrolled as a proportion of all students admitted.

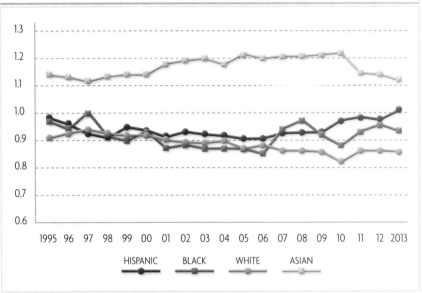

Although Latinos/as fell below equity across all indicators, fulfillment of A-G requirements (Index A) was the stage where Latino/a students exhibit the greatest discrepancy in equity levels compared to non-Hispanic White and Asian American students. While there has been an overall increase in equity for Latino/a students beginning in 2003, data from the past few years indicate increases to equity have leveled out, with Latino/a students remaining below equity. We speculate the trends are the result of a combination of lack of college advising in the early years, nonavailability of A-G curriculum, and tracking away from college preparation coursework (Contreras 2005b; Kimura-Walsh et al. 2008; Zárate and Pachon 2006). Although some school districts in California have implemented completion of A-G requirements as a graduation requirement (Helfand 2006; Jones 2012), the effects of these measures are either too small to be captured in statewide calculations, or the effects of these policies remain to be seen.

We make the assumption that California public high school graduates who have completed A-G requirements offer a reliable pool of potential Latino/a applicants to UCs. Our expectations of equitable representation of Latinos/as at UCs are grounded in the assumption that eligible students should be equitably represented throughout the admissions process. Unfortunately, not all Latino/a students who have completed A-G eligibility requirements apply for admissions to a UC campus (Index B). In this index, Latino/a students have been consistently below equity since 1997, with no visible improvement over time. In contrast, Asian American students appear to apply to UCs in a proportion that exceeds their representation among eligible students. This finding echoes Martin, Karabel, and Jaquez's (2005) finding that schools with high concentrations of Latino/a students had disproportionately fewer UC applicants. We are not certain as to what could hinder or sway eligible high school graduates from applying to a UC campus. One reason may be that some eligible students simply do not apply to UCs and apply exclusively to other colleges. Others have documented the tendency for URMs to enroll in less selective baccalaureate-granting institutions or community colleges (Grodsky and Kurlaender 2010). This leads us to speculate that perhaps UC-eligible Latino/a students apply to less selective institutions and self-select out of the UC admissions process because of (mis)perceptions of accessibility or fit with UCs.

Another reason eligible students may not be submitting applications to UCs could be that the additional admissions requirements, beyond completion of A-G requirements, present an insurmountable barrier. For example, perhaps eligible students learned too late about the test requirement in order to register and take the required tests. Several researchers have documented the gaps in college planning knowledge that pervade Latino/a and African American families (McDonough and Calderone 2006; Tornatzky, Cutler, and Lee 2002; Zárate and Pachon 2006), and because many of these students also lack access to adequate school-based college advising, they may not be completing all the application materials in time to apply to a UC.

The public discourse around admissions at a UC has centered on the legality of considering race in admissions decisions. Latino/a applicants have not reached equity levels in admissions since the mid-1990s (Index C). Although the discrepancy in equity between Latinos/as and Asian and non-Hispanic White students is not as wide as in other indices, the spread appears to be slowly increasing. It is clear that after the passage of Prop 209 in 1997, Latino/a students experienced an abrupt decline in their equitable representation among admitted students and have not gained ground in securing admissions to UCs.

Beginning in 2009, Latino/a students began to accept admission offers to UCs at an increasing rate (Index D). In 2013 the proportion of enrolled Latino/a students reached parity with the proportion of admitted Latino/a students. However, non-Hispanic White and African American students remain below equity while Asian students have been consistently overrepresented in enrollment as a proportion of their admission offers. It appears that recently, UC campuses have been more successful at attracting admitted

Latino students than in years past. These differences in enrollment decisions likely reflect different considerations of various factors. It is easy to focus on admissions practices when advocating for increased racial diversity on campus; however, this index illustrates the importance of considering students' perceptions and limitations when recruiting a diverse student body.

CONCLUSION

The implementation of Prop 209 initiated a change in the racial and ethnic composition of student bodies at UC campuses. During the past nineteen years, other factors affecting the fiscal and policy environments at UCs in addition to the state of California's changing demographics have undoubtedly affected application, admission, and enrollment decisions at UCs. All of these changes together undoubtedly affect Latino/a students differently than their peers. A closer look at the high school-to-college pipeline reveals multiple reasons for this underrepresentation.

There are many opportunities along the pipeline to address the inequitable representation of Latinos/as on UC campuses. The first step would be to determine why Latino/a high school students are not completing A-G eligibility requirements at rates similar to those of Asian and non-Hispanic white students. A more in-depth examination of application trends among Latinos/as would shed light on why Latinos/as have consistently remained below equity in applying to UCs. More needs to be learned about where these talented students are applying instead of UCs. Since immediately after Prop 209 was implemented, Latinos/as have consistently been below equity in getting admissions offers from UCs. What is it about these otherwise UC-eligible students that prevents them from being admitted? Equally concerning is the below-equity enrollment rates for African American, Latino/a and non-Hispanic white students at UCs. Further investigation on how students in California choose colleges and universities would shed light on this trend and may offer possible solutions to ensure that all populations are equally represented on UC campuses.

REFERENCES

Bensimon, E. M., L. Hao, and L. T. Bustillos. 2006. "Measuring the State of Equity in Public Higher Education." In *Expanding Opportunity in Higher Education: Leveraging Promise*, edited by P. Gandara and G. Orfield, 143–64. Albany, NY: SUNY Press.

Board of Admissions and Relations with Schools. 2002. *First-Year Implementation of Comprehensive Review in Freshman Admissions: A Progress Report*. Oakland: University of California.

Bryan, J., C. Moore-Thomas, N. L. Day-Vines, and C. Holcomb-McCoy. 2011. "School Counselors as Social Capital: The Effects of High School College Counseling on College Application Rates." *Journal of Counseling & Development* 89 (2): 190–99.

California Department of Education. 2015. "High School Enrollment Data." http://dq .cde.ca.gov/dataquest/EnrollEthState.asp?Level=State&TheYear=1995-96 &cChoice=EnrollEth1&p=2.

California Joint Committee to Develop a Master Plan for Education. 2002. *California Master Plan for Education.* http://www.ucop.edu/acadinit/mastplan /master_plan2002.pdf.

Card, D., and A. B. Krueger. 2004. "Would the Elimination of Affirmative Action Affect Highly Qualified Minority Applicants? Evidence from California and Texas." NBER Working Paper No. 10366, National Bureau of Economic Research, Cambridge, MA. http://www.nber.org/papers/w10366.pdf.

Comeaux, E., and T. Watford. 2006. *Admissions and Omissions: How "The Numbers" Are Used to Exclude Deserving Students: 2005–2006 CAPAA Findings.* Los Angeles: Ralph J. Bunche Center for African American Studies at UCLA. http://www .bunchecenter.ucla.edu/wp-content/uploads/2011/09/Bunche-Research-Report -June-2006.pdf.

Contreras, F. E. 2005a. "Access, Achievement, and Social Capital: Standardized Exams and the Latino/a College-Bound Population." *Journal of Hispanic Higher Education* 4 (3): 197–214. doi:10.1177/1538192705276546.

———. 2005b. "The Reconstruction of Merit Post-Proposition 209." *Educational Policy* 19 (2): 371–95. doi:10.1177/0895904804274055.

Fisher v. University of Texas at Austin. 2012. No. 11-345 (S. Ct. Oct. 12, 2012).

Fry, R. 2004. "Latino/a Youth Finishing College: The Role of Selective Pathways." Washington, DC: Pew Hispanic Center. ERIC database (ED485329).

Geiser, S. 1999. "Redefining UC's Eligibility Pool to Include a Percentage of Students from Each High School: Summary of Simulation Results." Oakland: University of California, Office of the President.

Gratz v. Bollinger. 2013. 539 U.S. 244.

Grodsky, E., and M. Kurlaender. 2010. "The Demography of Higher Education in the Wake of Affirmative Action." In *Equal Opportunity in Higher Education: The Past and Future of Proposition 209,* edited by E. Grodsky and M. Kurlaender, 33–59. Cambridge, MA: Harvard Education Press.

Grutter v. Bollinger. 2003. 539 U.S. 306.

Haycock, K., M. Lynch, and J. Engle. 2010. *Opportunity Adrift: Our Flagship Universities are Straying from Their Public Mission.* Washington, DC: The Education Trust. http://edtrust.org/wp-content/uploads/2013/10/Opportunity-Adrift_0.pdf.

Helfand, D. 2006. "A Formula for Failure in L.A. Schools." *Los Angeles Times,* January 30. http://www.latimes.com/news/local/la-me-dropout30jan30,0,1678653.story.

Hicklin, A. 2007. "The Effect of Race-Based Admissions in Public Universities: Debunking the Myths about Hopwood and Proposition 209." *Public Administration Review* 67 (2): 331–40.

Horn, C. L., and S. M. Flores. 2003. *Percent Plans in College Admissions: A Comparative Analysis of Three States' Experiences*. Cambridge, MA: The Civil Rights Project. http://civilrightsproject.ucla.edu/research/college-access/admissions/percent-plans -in-college-admissions-a-comparative-analysis-of-three-states2019-experiences /horn-percent-plans-2003.pdf.

Hurtado, S., K. K. Inkelas, C. Briggs, and B.-S. Rhee. 1997. "Difference in College Access and Choice Among Racial/Ethnic Groups: Identifying Continuing Barriers." *Research in Higher Education* 38 (1): 43–75. doi:10.1023/A:1024948728792.

Johnson, H. 2012. *Defunding Higher Education: What Are the Effects on College Enrollment*. San Francisco: Public Policy Institute of California.

Jones, B. 2012. "In Controversial Move, LAUSD's Deasy Wants to Raise High-School Graduation Requirements." *The Daily News Los Angeles*, May 5. http://www.dailynews .com/ci_20558014/controversial-move-lausds-deasy-wants-raise-high-school.

Kimura-Walsh, E., E. K. Yamamura, K. A. Griffin, and W. R. Allen. 2008. "Achieving the College Dream? Examining Disparities in Access to College Information Among High Achieving and Non-High Achieving Latina Students." *Journal of Hispanic Higher Education* 8 (3): 298–315. doi:10.1177/1538192708321648.

Lomibao, S. M., M. A. Barreto, and H. P. Pachon. 2004. *The Reality of Race Neutral Admissions for Minority Students at the University of California: Turning the Tide or Turning Them Away?* Los Angeles: Tomas Rivera Policy Institute.

Long, B. T., and M. Kurlaender. 2009. "Do Community Colleges Provide a Viable Pathway to a Baccalaureate Degree?" *Educational Evaluation and Policy Analysis* 31 (1): 30–53. doi:10.3102/0162373708327756.

Long, M. C. 2004. "College applications and the effect of affirmative action." *Journal of Econometrics*, 121 (1–2): 319–42. doi:10.1016/j.jeconom.2003.10.001.

Martin, I., J. Karabel, and S. Jaquez. 2005. "High School Segregation and Access to the University of California." *Educational Policy* 19 (2): 308-30. doi:10.1177 /0895904804274058.

McDonough, P. M., & S. Calderone. 2006. "The Meaning of Money about College Costs and Financial Aid." *American Behavioral Scientist* 49 (12): 1703–18. doi:10.1177 /0002764206289140.

Milem, J. 2003. "The Educational Benefits of Diversity: Evidence from Multiple Sectors." In *Compelling Interest*, edited by M. J. Chang, D. Witt, J. Jones, and K. Hakuta, 126–69. Stanford, CA: Stanford University Press.

Murphy, T. Y. 1995. "An Argument for Diversity Based Affirmative Action in Higher Education." *Annual Survey of American Law*. http://heinonline.org/HOL /Page?handle=hein.journals/annam1995&id=587&div=&collection=journals.

Orfield, G., and M. Miller, eds. 1998. *Chilling Admissions: The Affirmative Action Crisis and the Search for Alternatives*. Cambridge, MA: Harvard Education Publishing Group.

Perna, L. W., D. Gerald, E. Baum, and J. Milem, J. 2007. "The Status of Equity for Black Faculty and Administrators in Public Higher Education in the South." *Research in Higher Education* 48 (2): 193–228. doi:10.1007/sl.

Perna, L. W., J. Milem, D. Gerald, E. Baum, H. Rowan, N. Mar, and N. Hutchens. 2011. "The Status of Equity for Black Undergraduates in Public Higher Education in the South: Still Separate and Unequal." *Research in Higher Education* 47 (2): 197–228. doi:10.1007/sl.

Regents of University of California v. Bakke. 1978. 438 U.S. 265.

Santos, J. L., N. L. Cabrera, and K. J. Fosnacht. 2010. "Is 'Race-Neutral' Really Race-Neutral? Disparate Impact Towards Underrepresented Minorities in Post-209 UC System Admissions." *The Journal of Higher Education* 81 (6): 675–701.

Tornatzky, L. G., R. Cutler, and J. Lee. 2002. *College Knowledge: What Latino/a Parents Need to Know and Why They Don't Know It.* Claremont, CA: Tomas Rivera Policy Institute.

Torres, C. 2004. *Eliminating Outreach at the University of California: Program Contributions and the Consequences of Their Reductions.* Policy brief of the Tomas Rivera Policy Institute. ERIC database (ED502066).

University of California Office of the President (UCOP). 2002. *Eligibility in the Local Context: Program Evaluation Report.* Oakland: University of California.

———. 2003. *Undergraduate Access to the University of California After the Elimination of Race-Conscious Policies.* http://www.ucop.edu/sas/publish/aa_final2.pdf.

———. 2011. *The Facts: UC Budget Basics.* http://budget.universityofcalifornia.edu.

———. 2015. *UC Student/Workforce Data.* http://www.ucop.edu/institutional-research-academic-planning/data-reports/index.html.

Williams, E., M. Leachman, and N. Johnson. 2011. *State Budget Cuts in the New Fiscal Year Are Unnecessarily Harmful.* Washington, DC: Center on Budget and Policy Priorities. http://www.cbpp.org/files/7-26-11sfp.pdf.

Wood, D. B. 2004. "California Students Fall into State Budget Gap." *The Christian Science Monitor,* June 8. http://www.csmonitor.com/2004/0608/p02s01-usec.html.

Zárate, M. E., and R. Gallimore. 2005. "Gender Differences in Factors Leading to College Enrollment: A Longitudinal Analysis of Latina and Latino Students." *Harvard Educational Review* 75 (4): 383–489.

Zárate, M. E., and H. P. Pachon. 2006. *Gaining or Losing Ground? Equity in Offering Advanced Placement Courses in California High Schools 1997–2003.* Los Angeles: Tomas Rivera Policy Institute. ERIC database (ED502057).

"The Only Racism Left Is That against White People"

THE COMPLEX REALITIES OF THE CAMPUS RACIAL CLIMATE FOR LATINA/O STUDENTS

Nolan L. Cabrera

T he election of President Obama ushered in a paradoxical public response regarding the relevance of racism in contemporary society. First, many commentators argued that a black President meant that the US had entered a "post-racial era" (Bush and Feagin 2011). That is, for racial minorities, these commentators believed there were no longer systemic barriers in place that prevent upward mobility for racial minorities. Second, and in tension with the first development, white people on the aggregate believe that contemporary anti-white discrimination is more prevalent than anti-black discrimination (Norton and Sommers 2011). These two frameworks create a cohesive, dominant message that racism is no longer an issue unless it is targeting white people (Bush and Feagin 2011).

The racial dynamics of the larger society frequently play out on the college campus, and this creates a complicated dynamic for Latina/o[1] students. The college years are a formative time of racial/ethnic identity development, but a hostile campus climate can create a toxic environment in which growth may occur (Cabrera and Hurtado 2015). For example, the persistent message that racism is no longer an issue juxtaposed against the lived realities of being racially targeted can create what Gildersleeve, Croom, and Vasquez (2011) refer to as "Am I Going Crazy?" syndrome. This conceptual article interprets the campus racial climate (Hurtado et al. 2012) from the perspective of Latina/o students who are, to borrow

---

1. Throughout this article, I use the term "Latina/o" to refer to the pan-ethnic identity, which encapsulates students with Latin-American origins. It is more specific than the government-created "Hispanic," is broader than terms like "Chicana/o," and the use of the "a/o" avoids sexist language usage. I am not yet on board using the "x" ending, but am still deliberating.

from Lee (2005), "up against Whiteness." It then moves to interrogating white privilege in higher education as well as white responsibility for creating more racially inclusive campus environments. The article moves on to explore culturally sustaining pedagogies (Paris 2012) as a means of supporting Latina/o undergraduates as they continue to experience campus marginalization via the normalization of whiteness. It concludes with some considerations regarding how to frame race-conscious higher education practice in a postracial context that equates race-consciousness with "reverse racism" (Bush and Feagin 2011; McKinney 2003).

CAMPUS RACIAL CLIMATE AND WHITENESS

Racial climate describes the dynamic interplay of multiple components of a college campus that collectively serve to either support or inhibit student development. The different components consist of:

- an institutional legacy of inclusion/exclusion;
- compositional diversity;
- psychological dimension;
- behavioral dimension; and
- organizational dimension (Milem, Chang, and antonio 2005, 15–19).

An *institutional legacy of inclusion/exclusion* refers not only to history, but also to the ways in which institutions have responded to these legacies. A recent example of this is the University of Texas, Austin, removal of a statue of Confederacy President Jefferson Davis.[2] *Compositional diversity* refers to the proportion of students of color on campus, previously designated "structural diversity." The *behavioral dimension* encompasses the quantity and quality of cross-racial interactions on campus, while the *psychological dimension* involves perceptions of how inclusive or exclusive students believe the campus to be. The *organizational dimension* encompasses the ways in which diversity is (or is not) embedded in structures, policies, curricula, and decision-making processes of the institution.

The creation and application of campus racial climate initiatives and policies were intended as a means of creating more meaningful racial inclusion within institutions of higher education above and beyond simple numeric diversity (Hurtado et al. 1998; Milem, Chang, and antonio, 2005). When the focus shifts to racially privileged, white students, the waters

2. http://www.npr.org/sections/thetwo-way/2015/08/30/436072805/jefferson-davis-statue-comes-down-at-university-of-texas

become murkier because the very markers of racial inclusion can be seen as examples of racial exclusion (i.e., "reverse discrimination") (Cabrera 2014b; Cabrera, Watson, and Franklin 2016). For example, race-conscious recruitment and admissions policies are frequently framed as discriminatory against white people (Bonilla-Silva 2006; Cabrera 2014a). This belief is so strong and consistent, it was a primary rationale for attacks on affirmative action starting with *Regents v. Bakke* (1978), and running through *Hopwood* (1996), *Grutter* (2003), *Gratz* (2003), and the current Supreme Court case around Fisher. All of these cases are predicated upon one claim: if the plaintiffs were not white, they would have gained admission. While it is almost impossible for them to substantiate these claims, their cases highlight how increasing multiculturalism heightens perceptions of "reverse discrimination." Orozco (2011) takes this formulation one step further, and argues that white innocence exists only in the presence of minority aggression. Essentially, the empirical reality of white privilege is discursively flipped on its head first by establishing white innocence,[3] then by insulating this innocence by diverting attention to perceptions of "reverse discrimination."

This is common beyond issues of affirmative action. For example, Mexican American Studies in Tucson has recently been reframed as the "hate Whitey" curriculum (Cabrera, Milem, Jaquette, and Marx 2014; Cammarota and Romero 2014). Campus cultural centers are consistently asked to be more "open" and "inclusive," which implicitly means open to white students (Patton 2010). Even the presence of cultural centers can provoke leading and myopic questions such as, "Why don't we have a White Student Union?" (Cabrera, Watson, and Franklin 2016). Thus, markers of racial inclusivity are frequently framed as racially oppressing white students. Within this hotly contested area, the question arises: What is to be done?

Primary Responsibility: Whiteness and the Racially Privileged

Within institutions of higher education, there are frequent discussions of white privilege (e.g., McIntosh 1989), but rarely do these discussions move to the topic of the responsibility associated with unwarranted privileges. Instead of disrupting racial privilege, the focus tends to be on supporting

---

3. For example, a common refrain that establishes white innocence (on an individual level) is, "I am not *a* racist, so why should I have to pay for the sins of my ancestors?" (Bonilla-Silva 2006; Pierce 2012).

minoritized[4] groups, which can have unintended, negative consequences and implications. For example, when issues of educational marginalization arise for Latina/o students, a common interpretive focus lies on how to foster resiliency strategies among the targeted group (e.g., Arellano and Padilla 1996; Cabrera and Padilla 2004; O'Connor 2002). By resiliency, I mean that despite structured inequality, minoritized individuals experience educational success through a combination of individual drive and institutional support (O'Connor 2002). While I support the application of more "asset-based" analyses instead of "deficit-based" ones (Yosso 2005), there are two problems with focusing on resiliency. First, by placing minoritized individuals at the center of the analysis, it alleviates responsibility for the initial creation of inequality. That is, resiliency is only necessary to the extent that Latina/o students are marginalized, and the underlying question becomes: What were the structures, discourses, and social practices that created this marginalization in the first place?

Second, a relatively unexplored issue in education research is the concept of *John Henryism* (Bennett et al. 2004). John Henry was a railroad worker who challenged a machine to a rock-breaking race. Even though he won in an incredible feat of human will, he collapsed and died. His story has become a conceptual metaphor for the unintended negative consequences of resiliency. If students are embedded in toxic environments, they may be fostering resiliency at the cost of the physical, mental, and/or emotional health (Bennett et al. 2004). While the college environment and the campus racial climate may not be as toxic as the K-12 in many urban contexts (Duncan-Andrade 2009), there are a number of issues associated with it. For example, in the college environment students of color face microaggressions[5] from their peers on a regular basis, and constantly having to navigate this racially taxing interpersonal environment can lead to racial battle fatigue (Smith, Allen, and Danley 2007). Additionally, state-level anti-Latina/o policies such as Arizona's SB1070[6] can serve to further student racial stress and marginalization on a campus level (Mendez and Cabrera 2015).

---

4. By *minoritized*, I mean a racial minority group (i.e., non-white), but also one that is racially marginalized. Minoritized focuses on actions and systems that support the process of racial oppression. I prefer this term to "minority," as it focuses on a process of marginalization as opposed to simply a numerical description.

5. Microaggressions are "subtle, innocuous, preconscious, or unconscious degradations, and putdowns, often kinetic but capable of being verbal" (Yosso et al. 2009, 660).

6. SB1070 is also colloquially known as the "show me your papers" law. It required police officers during routine traffic stops to ask for proof of citizenship if they suspected the driver to be undocumented.

Thus, I center this analysis of Latina/o student campus marginalization on white responsibility for addressing racial conditions. There is a strong tendency in higher education scholarship and practice to use *diversity* as a code word for students of color. To the extent that there is a racial issue on campus, it is important to bring the voices of the marginalized to the forefront. That said, to limit the scope of the analysis to *only* people of color inadvertently misses the root cause of the problem. For example, every microaggression has a microaggressee and a microaggressor. We understand the experience of the former very well, but tend not hold the latter to account for their actions. Therefore, I am compelled by Applebaum's (2010, 53–90) conception that racial issues entail both white complicity and responsibility.

So, where is white complicity and responsibility within this formulation? First and foremost, it is the responsibility of white students, faculty, staff, and administrators to educate themselves about issues of race (Applebaum 2010; Cabrera 2012). While a number of important racial lessons can be gleaned by white people through cross-racial interactions, it is also emotionally and mentally taxing to make Latina/o students educate their white peers and can create problematic power dynamics when Latina/os are required to educate professors (Cabrera and Hurtado 2015; Leonardo and Porter 2010).

Whiteness is so engrained in the institutional structure of higher education (Gusa 2010; Harper and Hurtado 2007) that specific means of disrupting this normative structure are too many and too varied to list here. Instead, I will continue this discussion on a conceptual level, discussing core foci regarding the challenging of whiteness in higher education: a necessary prerequisite to fostering racial inclusion for Latina/o students. To this end, I focus on both the promise and limitations of white privilege pedagogy. White privilege refers to the unmeritocratic advantages that white people enjoy because they exist in a society where structured racism continues to create inequitable opportunity along the color line (Kendall 2006). Having white students, faculty, staff, and administrators begin to unpack the numerous ways that their advantages create disadvantages for students of color in general, and Latina/o students in particular, can help people understand how racial inequality is maintained in the absence of overt racial animus (i.e., "Racism without Racists," Bonilla-Silva 2006).

Engaging in white privilege pedagogy is not merely shifting perceptual realities and making white people aware of racism. It also requires a shift in many uninterrogated assumptions that many privileged people hold about interpersonal interactions. For example, demanding calm when discussing issues of racism is a manifestation of white privilege (O'Brien 2004). That is, the pain of racism is real, deep, profound, and dehumanizing. To say that people of color must "take the emotion out" when discussing racism only serves to cater to those unaffected by its adverse effects. Thus, white privilege pedagogy requires white people to frequently reconsider how they listen to people of color on the subject of racism. This also entails rejecting demands for social comfort as a prerequisite to engaging in racial dialogues (Cabrera, Watson, and Franklin, 2016; Leonardo and Porter 2010). When issues of racism are discussed, they can frequently make white people feel uncomfortable either because they are experiencing a new painful reality of which they were previously unaware (Cabrera, Watson, and Franklin 2016; Mills 1997) or because they feel targeted and blamed for issues of racism (Leonardo and Porter 2010; McKinney 2003). Whatever the rationale, the demand by racially privileged individuals for social comfort in cross-racial dialogues serves only to recreate white privilege because talking about racism is generally uncomfortable. To engage only when comfortable means that racially privileged individuals will engage only if they do not have to face these ugly, painful, and uncomfortable realities (i.e., they will talk about racism only if they do not have to actually engage racism).

Ultimately, white privilege pedagogy is meant to illuminate to racially privileged individuals the insidious nature of racism, while concurrently rejecting the counterproductive racial politics of "reverse racism" discourse (Kendall 2006; McKinney 2003). There are some scholars who critique the limitations of this approach. For example, Lensmire et al. (2013) highlighted the ways in which white privilege pedagogy in practice was limited because it functioned as a space for white people to confess their racial privileges, but with no connection to their social responsibility or social action. Leonardo (2004) has also criticized white privilege pedagogy for individualizing racism instead of directly linking the localized privileges of whiteness to the systemic reality of contemporary white supremacy. These are valid and important critiques that can be taken account of as future leaders develop and implement white privilege pedagogy, and it is therefore not necessary to throw the proverbial baby out with the racial bathwater.

Despite the limitations of white privilege pedagogy, there is an incredible amount of potential because a great deal of contemporary racism is both manifest and recreated in white space, behind closed doors (Cabrera 2014b; Picca and Feagin 2007). Within these white spaces, white people have unique access to what Picca and Feagin (2007, 91–143) refer to as "backstage performance," or racism that is performed for other white people in the absence of people of color. These behaviors and ideologies then creep into the larger campus environment, creating a foundation for the marginalization of students of color. To the extent that there are racial issues on college campuses, white people bear primary responsibility for addressing them as they are concurrently the ones privileged by the current system of racism (Bonilla-Silva 2006; Omi & Winant 1994). All too often, discussions of campus inclusion focus only on Latina/o student marginalization with no critical interrogation of white racial privilege. Attention can and should be paid to Latina/o students as well, but it takes a dramatically different form.

Secondary Responsibility: Supporting Latina/o Students Through Culturally Sustaining Pedagogies

The needs of Latina/o college students are so diverse that it would be foolhardy to attempt to list the specific ways they can be met. Instead, I offer some conceptual principles that can help guide campus practice. First, I begin with a tension. Yes, Latina/o students experience campus marginalization, but no, this does not mean they are "in need." I am guided by the multitude of scholars who reject deficit frameworks to understand the experiences of Latina/o students in particular (Yosso 2005) and students of color in general (Hurtado et al. 2012; Ladson-Billings 1995). By deficit framework, I mean framing the issue of minority underrepresentation as an issue of "cultural deficiencies" of minoritized communities with no consideration given the structural conditions that foster this inequality. Rather, the analysis focuses on the engrained assets of Latina/o students, and how to build upon them to best serve the needs of these minoritized students.

These additive approaches have been called "culturally relevant pedagogy" (Ladson-Billings 1995). By culturally relevant pedagogy, I mean pedagogies that "reposition the linguistic, literate, and cultural practices of working-class communities—specifically poor communities of color—as resources and assets to honor, explore and extend" (Paris and Alim 2014, 87). These pedagogical practices were engaged as a means of minoritized students developing repertoires in the dominant forms (i.e., white) of cultural expression, language, and knowledge. Paris (2012) has extended this concept in two critically important ways. First, he argues that instead of culturally relevant pedagogy, we need *culturally sustaining* pedagogy. That is, that the knowledge and cultural practices of minoritized students should be valued in and of itself, and pedagogical practices need to ensure that they maintain their cultural orientation while learning the dominant one. Second, Paris and Alim (2014) lovingly critiqued culturally relevant pedagogies for being insufficiently critical of the oppressive practices frequently embedded within the subcultures of youth of color. For example, hip-hop music can be a linguistically creative form of youthful expression and at the same time a manifestation of misogyny.

While these debates and theorizing about culturally sustaining pedagogies are largely rooted in K-12 education, a number of their areas are applicable to higher education scholarship. For example, a consistent theme in higher education scholarship is the presence of white space within predominantly white institutions of higher education (Harper and Hurtado 2007). By white space, I mean campus environments where whiteness is the cultural norm at the expense of the cultures of racial minorities. Gusa (2010) refers to this as the white institutional presence, and it creates an institutional pressure to give up one's native culture and assimilate into the dominant white paradigm. Instead, the institutional culture needs to change to not only engage but also to sustain Latina/o student native culture (broadly defined). This can occur in a number of ways, but consistent with the climate literature two key issues contextualize these approaches: 1) There is no magic silver bullet for creating campus inclusion, and 2) Local initiatives are only effective at changing institutional culture if they are coordinated (Hurtado et al. 1998; Milem, Chang, and antonio 2005).

Therefore, integrating culturally sustaining pedagogies (Paris 2012) and the campus racial climate (Milem, Chang, and antonio 2005) to support Latina/o students involves the following. First, it is necessary for PWIs (predominantly white institutions) to increase their enrollment of Latina/o students. It is very difficult to sustain one's native culture if there is no critical mass of same-race/ethnicity students on campus (Cabrera and Hurtado 2015; Garces and Jayakumar 2014; Gonzalez 2002). In addition, the institution needs to create space for increased quantity and quality of cross-racial interactions. A very promising approach involves intergroup dialogue, but it requires both a social justice focus and extremely skilled facilitators to be effective (Zuñiga et al. 2007). Additionally, institutions must be willing to address their historical legacies of inclusion and exclusion. This is frequently applied to issues of college access, but it can also mean within-institution segregation. For example, the traditional Greek system is both dominated by white students (also upper-middle-class ones), and also a site of racial-themed parties (Garcia et al. 2011; Syrett 2009). Disrupting this white space can be important in concurrently disrupting the pressures that Latina/o students frequently face at PWIs to either hide or give up their native culture.

From an organizational perspective, offering ethnic studies programs has been shown to be a very promising curricular intervention that can also support the goals of culturally sustaining pedagogies (Paris 2012; Sleeter 2011). Not only can ethnic studies promote increased educational achievement, but also sense of self and opportunities for self-exploration via seeing oneself in the curriculum (Hu-DeHart 1993; Sleeter 2011; Takaki 1993). Additionally, there needs to be space allocated for Latina/o students to further engage this cultural sustenance and self-exploration. This can take the form of Latina/o themed cultural centers, living and learning communities, or both (Patton 2010). Essentially, it becomes critically important within PWIs for space to exist where the cultural norm is not whiteness (Gusa 2010). Finally, Latina/o faculty can play a critically important role in supporting and sustaining Latina/o students (Anaya and Cole 2001; Santos and Reigadas 2002). However, diversifying the faculty does not happen by chance. Rather, it needs to be built into the organizational rewards and accountability structure of an institution (Milem, Chang, and antonio 2005).

Again, these initiatives, programs, and curricula are only required to the extent that Latina/o cultural identity is not valued within the larger institutional context. That said, they are all important for Latina/o students maintaining and further developing their cultural sense of self during the critically important undergraduate years—hence the importance of culturally sustaining pedagogy. Additionally, culturally sustaining pedagogy reframes the rationale behind these campus initiatives. A great deal of the diversity in higher education work is rooted in the "diversity rationale," which argues that fostering more inclusive campus environments improves educational outcomes for all students (Milem, Chang, antonio 2005). That is, diversity from a legal standpoint represents a compelling educational interest only to the extent that it benefits white students (James 2014). Instead, culturally sustaining pedagogy argues that offering culturally specific means of supporting minoritized students represents a justifiable end in and of itself (Paris and Alim 2014).

A key development that culturally sustaining pedagogy offers over more traditional culturally relevant approaches is that it offers an opportunity for a loving critique of Latina/o students. That is, it supports Latina/o students in their educational/cultural endeavors, but requires educators to critique their students when their students are engaging in oppressive behaviors (Paris 2012; Paris and Alim 2014). For example, in 2014 there was a Mexican-themed party at a University of Arizona sorority (Fernandez October 27, 2014). A number of Latina/o students were visibly upset by this blatant campus racism; however, several young Latino men decided to lodge their complaint against the sorority in misogynistic terms. The perspective of culturally sustaining pedagogy takes a two-fold focus on this issue. On the one hand, it supports the Latina/o students as they challenge campus racism. On the other, it requires a critique of the students' misogyny so that, to borrow from Freire (2000), that in their quest for liberation that the oppressed do not become the oppressor.

Thus, culturally sustaining pedagogy offers a great deal of promise, moving ahead when applied to Latina/o college students. It offers a method of engagement that supports marginalized students without tolerating the recreation of other forms of oppression. It is a race- and culturally conscious approach to higher education practice, which will concurrently make it controversial in postracial times where race-consciousness is framed as "reverse racism" (Bush and Feagin 2011). Thus, those engaging in this approach need to be prepared and willing to proactively frame the need for race-conscious social policies in the popular discourse.

The Final Step: Proactive Framing and Support of Latina/o Students in a Postracial Age

While an era of postracialism has put race-conscious and culturally specific college programming on the defensive, it is not a new phenomenon. Regardless, it creates a strong tension. On the one hand, race-neutral approaches to higher-education racial inequality tend to be ineffective. On the other, race- and culturally specific approaches frequently face attacks from those who see them as marginalizing white students. Thus, this work is not only about finding effective higher education strategies to support Latina/o students, but also about finding ways to proactively defend them. This requires effectively framing educational practice, and to explore how to do this I rely on the work of Lakoff (2008). Lakoff argues that a key reason political conservatives have, in recent memory, beaten liberals has to do with framing. He highlights three key components. First, the argument must have an explicitly articulated moral center. Second, the framers need to articulate what they are for as opposed to what they are against. Finally, the framing needs to be proactive instead of reactive.

The example of affirmative action is illustrative of framing. In the late 1990s and early 2000s, the liberal defense of affirmative action was "mend it, don't end it," while conservatives argued that consideration of race was racist, in particular, racist against white people (Crosby 2004). In this instance, the liberal frame holds no moral center, is reactive in its framing, and paints the issue in the negative ("don't end it"). Conversely, the conservative position has a strong moral center (i.e., racism is evil). It is proactive and positive in its framing (i.e., end racial discrimination now by eliminating affirmative action). This is only one example of dozens in modern political memory that highlights these differences in framing along political and ideological lines, and those offering culturally sustaining pedagogies to Latina/o college students need to be prepared to proactively defend these practices in the court of public opinion.

Lopez (2014) highlights why this work is critically important. He meticulously documents what he refers to as "dog whistle politics," whereby coded racism manipulated by savvy politicians appeals to the unconscious racism of white people in society and even makes them vote against their own economic interests. He explores issues such as Willie Horton, the rise of the Tea Party, undocumented immigration, and anti-Obama sentiment, finding a consistent theme. In a post-Civil Rights era, overt appeals to racism are largely ignored and demeaned, but underground racism is not only accepted but in many instances integral to political strategies. Lopez (2014, 178) elaborates on the strategy:

> Rather, dog whistle appeals remain inaudible to most, instead resonating with their unconscious racial anxieties and eliciting support only so long as they remain hidden. It seems that dog whistle politicians manipulate these background views and emotions, but succeed with most whites only so long as the racial appeals stay below conscious recognition.

There are two critically important components to this issue that Lopez articulates. First, and similar to Lakoff, conservative politicians have been extremely effective at garnering support by appealing to the unconscious racism of the voting populace. However, the underground nature of these appeals is also their weakness. Lopez further demonstrates that the more racist appeals are openly derided for being racist, the less effective racist appeals are because this moves the discussion out of an unconscious realm. Lopez (2014, 227) continues:

> Those who discuss racism are accused of being the real racists—again, as if pulling a fire alarm means one set the fire, or dialing 911 means one committed the crime. Refusing to be silenced, to defeat dog whistle racism and restore government to the side of the middle class will require as many of us as possible to go ahead and sound that alarm.

Thus, those creating and enacting Latina/o-specific programming are likely going to be accused of racism under the guise of colorblindness or post-racialism (Bush and Feagin 2011). However, the more these people are able to proactively label these coded appeals as racism, the less effect they will have. For example, the more proactively PWIs can be in defending the existence of Latina/o-specific cultural centers, the less effective appeals for a "White Student Center" will be. Additionally, the more proactive PWIs are at highlighting and critiquing the racism embedded in appeals for a "White Student Center," the less they will have to defend the existence of their Latina/o-specific cultural centers. The critical importance of this framing is that it allows practitioners to do the work. It can create a discursive shield against racist attacks, which means practitioners will ultimately be able to better serve Latina/o students in the process.

CONCLUSION

Massive battles are afoot within increasingly multicultural higher education, and demography is not destiny. That is, as the proportion of students of color increases, there is no guarantee that their needs will be met. To accomplish this, scholars, administrators, and practitioners need a multipronged strategy. They need to understand the unique educational needs of this population. They then have to creatively foster targeted ways of addressing these needs in a racially and culturally specific mechanism. They need to be willing to disrupt and challenge white racism within the ivory tower. Finally, they have to be willing to proactively defend these programs against myopic and racist attacks from people engaging in postracial discourse. Universal approaches have largely failed to effectively support Latina/o students, and targeted approaches are framed as either being divisive or even racist. Given these choices, many feel it is better to remain quiet and try to focus on the work at the expense of the public discourse. To this end, I offer the words of Audre Lorde in "A Litany for Survival" (1978, 31–32):

> and when we speak we are afraid
> our words will not be heard
> nor welcomed
> but when we are silent
> we are still afraid
>
> So it is better to speak
> remembering
> we were never meant to survive

Even though those supporting Latina/o students may be afraid to speak, the fear is still there during periods of silence. Thus, it is better to speak understanding that Latina/o-specific initiatives were never meant to survive postracialism. This is precisely why this additional facet of the work is so critically important.

REFERENCES

Anaya, Guadalupe, and Darnell G. Cole. 2001. "Latina/o Student Achievement: Exploring the Influence of Student-Faculty Interactions." *Journal of College Student Development* 42 (1): 3–14.

Applebaum, Barbara. 2010. *Being White, Being Good: White Complicity, White Moral Responsibility, and Social Justice Pedagogy.* Lanham, MD: Lexington Books.

Arellano, Adele R., and Amado M. Padilla. 1996. "Academic Invulnerability Among a Select Group of Latino University Students." *Hispanic Journal of Behavioral Sciences* 18: 485–507.

Bennett, Gary G., Marcellus M. Merritt, John J. Sollers III, Christopher L. Edwards, Keith E. Whitfield, Dwayne T. Brandon, and Reginald D. Tucker. 2004. "Stress, Coping, and Health Outcomes Among African-Americans: A Review of the John Henryism Hypothesis." *Psychology & Health* 19 (3): 369–83.

Bonilla-Silva, Eduardo. 2006. *Racism without Racists: Color-blind Racism and the Persistence of Racial Inequality in the United States.* 2nd ed. Lanham, MD: Rowman & Littlefield.

Bush, Melanie E. L., and Joe R. Feagin. 2011. *Everyday Forms of Whiteness: Understanding Race in a "Post-Racial" World.* 2nd ed. Lantham, MD: Rowman & Littlefield.

Cabrera, Nolan L. 2012. "Working through Whiteness: White Male College Students Challenging Racism." *The Review of Higher Education* 35 (3): 375–401.

———. 2014a. "But We're Not laughing: White Male College Students' Racial Joking and What This Says About 'Post-Racial' Discourse." *Journal of College Student Development* 55 (1): 1–15.

———. 2014b. "Exposing Whiteness in Higher Education: White Male College Students Minimizing Racism, Claiming Victimization, and Recreating White Supremacy." *Race Ethnicity and Education* 17 (1): 30–55.

Cabrera, Nolan L., and Sylvia Hurtado. 2015. "The Ivory Tower is Still White: Chicano/Latino College Students on Race, Ethnic Organizations, and Campus Racial Segregation." In *The Magic Key: The Educational Journey of Mexican Americans from K-12 to College and Beyond,* edited by R. E. Zambrana and S. Hurtado, 145–67. Austin, TX: University of Texas Press.

Cabrera, Nolan L., Jeffrey F. Milem, Ozan Jaquette, and Ronald W. Marx. 2014. "Missing the (Student Achievement) Forest for all the (Political) Trees: Empiricism and the Mexican American Studies Controversy in Tucson." *American Educational Research Journal* 51 (6): 1084–118.

Cabrera, Nolan L., and Amado M. Padilla. 2004. "Entering and Succeeding in the 'Culture of College': The Story of Two Mexican Heritage Students." *Hispanic Journal of Behavioral Sciences* 26 (2): 152–70.

Cabrera, Nolan L., Jesse Watson, and Jeremy Franklin. 2016. "Racial Arrested Development: A Critical Whiteness Analysis of the Campus Ecology." *Journal of College Student Development* 57(2): 119-134.

Cammarota, Julio, and Augustine F. Romero, eds. 2014. *Raza Studies: The Public Option for Educational Revolution.* Tucson, AZ: University of Arizona Press.

Crosby, Faye J. 2004. *Affirmative Action is Dead: Long Live Affirmative Action*. New Haven, CT: Yale University Press.

Duncan-Andrade, Jeffrey M. R. 2009. "Note to Educators: Hope Required When Growing Roses in Concrete." *Harvard Educational Review* 79 (2): 181–94.

Fernandez, Meghan. 2014, October 27. "Group Protests Sorority Over 'Culturally-Insensitive' Costumes." *Daily Wildcat*. Accessed November 15, 2015. http://www.wildcat.arizona.edu/article/2014/10/group-protests-sorority-over-culturally-insensitive-costumes.

Freire, Paulo. 2000. *Pedagogy of the Oppressed*, 30 Anniversary Ed. New York: Herder and Herder.

Garces, Liliana M., and Uma M. Jayakumar. 2014. "Dynamic Diversity: Toward a Contextual Understanding of Critical Mass." *Educational Researcher* 43 (3): 115–24.

Garcia, Gina A., Marc P. Johnston, Juan C. Garibay, Felisha A. Herrera, and Luis G. Giraldo. 2011. "When Parties Become Racialized: Deconstructing Racially Themed Parties." *Journal of Student Affairs Research and Practice* 48 (1): 5–21.

Gildersleeve, Ryan E., Natasha N. Croom, and Phillip L. Vasquez. 2011. "'Am I going crazy?': A Critical Race Analysis of African American and Latino Doctoral Student Experiences." *Equity and Excellence in Education* 44 (1): 93–114.

Gonzalez, Kenneth P. 2002. "Campus Culture and the Experience of Chicano Students in a Predominantly White University." *Urban Education* 37: 191–216.

Gratz v. Bollinger, 539 U.S. 244 (2003).

Grutter v. Bollinger, 539 U.S. 306 (2003).

Gusa, Diane L. 2010. "White Institutional Presence: The Impact of Whiteness on Campus Climate." *Harvard Educational Review* 80 (4): 464–89.

Harper, Shaun R., and Sylvia Hurtado. 2007. "Nine Themes in Campus Racial Climates and Implications for Institutional Transformation." In *Responding to the Realities of Race on Campus. New Directions for Student Services*, edited by S. R. Harper and L. D. Patton, 7–24. San Francisco, CA: Jossey-Bass.

Hopwood v. State of Texas, 78 F. 3rd 932, 5th Cir. (1996).

Hu-DeHart, Elaine. 1993. "The History, Development, and Future of Ethnic Studies." *Phi Delta Kappan* 75 (1): 50–54.

Hurtado, Sylvia, Jeffrey F. Milem, Alma R. Clayton-Pedersen, and Walter R. Allen. 1998. "Enhancing Campus Climates for Racial/Ethnic Diversity: Educational Policy and Practice." *Review of Higher Education* 21 (3): 279–302.

Hurtado, Sylvia, Cynthia L. Alvarez, Chelsea Guillermo-Wann, Marcela Cuellar, and Lucy Arellano. 2012. "A Model for Diverse Learning Environments: The Scholarship on Creating and Assessing Conditions for Student Success. In *Higher Education: Handbook of Theory and* Research, edited by J. C. Smart and M. B. Paulsen, 41–122.

James, Osamudia R. 2014. "White Like Me: The Negative Impact of the Diversity Rationale on White Identity Formation." *New York University Law Review* 89 (2): 425–512.

Kendall, Frances E. 2006. *Understanding White Privilege: Creating Pathways to Authentic Relationships Across Race.* New York, NY: Routledge.

Ladson-Billings, Gloria. 1995. "Toward a Theory of Culturally Relevant Pedagogy." *American Educational Research Journal* 32 (3): 465–91.

Lakoff, George. 2008. *The Political Mind: A Cognitive Scientist's Guide to Your Brain and its Politics.* New York, NY: Penguin Books.

Lee, Stacey J. 2005. *Up Against Whiteness: Racism, School, and Immigrant Youth.* New York, NY: Teachers College Press.

Lensmire, Timothy J., Shannon K. McManimon, Jessica D. Tierney, Mary E. Lee-Nichols, Zachary A. Casey, Audrey Lensmire, and Bryan M. Davis. 2013. "McIntosh as Synecdoche: How Teacher Education's Focus on White Privilege Undermines Antiracism." *Harvard Educational Review* 83 (3): 410–31.

Leonardo, Zeus. 2004. "The Color of Supremacy: Beyond the Discourse of 'White Privilege.' " *Educational Philosophy and Theory* 36 (2): 137–52.

Leonardo, Zeus, and Ronald K. Porter. 2010. "Pedagogy of Fear: Toward a Fanonian Theory of 'Safety' in Race Dialogues." *Race Ethnicity and Education* 13 (2): 139–57.

Lopez, Ian H. 2014. *Dog Whistle Politics: How Coded Racial Appeals Have Reinvented Racism & Wrecked the Middle Class.* New York, NY: Oxford University Press.

Lorde, Audre. 1978. A litany for survival. In *The Black Unicorn,* by A. Lorde, 31–32. New York: Norton.

McIntosh, Peggy. 1989. "White Privilege: Unpacking the Invisible Knapsack." *Peace and Freedom,* 10–12.

McKinney, Karyn D. 2003. "I Feel 'Whiteness' When I Hear People Blaming Whites: Whiteness as Cultural Victimization." *Race & Society* 6 (1): 39–55.

Mendez, Julian J., and Nolan L. Cabrera. 2015. "Targets but Not Victims: Latina/o Students and Arizona's Racial Politics." *Journal of Hispanic Higher Education* 14 (4): 377–91.

Milem, Jeffrey F., Mitchell J. Chang, and anthony l. antonio. 2005. *Making Diversity Work on Campus: A Research-Based Perspective.* Washington, DC: American Association of Colleges and Universities.

Mills, Charles W. 1997. *The Racial Contract.* Ithaca, NY: Cornell University Press.

Norton, Michael I., and Samuel R. Sommers. 2011. "Whites See Racism as a Zero-Sum Game That They Are Now Losing." *Perspectives in Psychological Science* 6 (3): 215–18.

O'Brien, Eileen. 2004. " 'I Could Hear You If You Would Just Calm Down': Challenging Eurocentric Classroom Norms Through Passionate Discussions of Racial Oppression." In *Identifying Race and Transforming Whiteness in the Classroom,* edited by V. Lea and J. Helfand, 68–86. New York, NY: Peter Lang.

O'Connor, Carla. 2002. "Black Women Beating the Odds from One Generation to the Next: How the Changing Dynamics of Constraint and Opportunity Affect the Process of Educational Resilience." *American Educational Research Journal* 39 (4): 855–903.

Omi, Michael, and Howard Winant. 1994. "Racial Formation in the 1960s to the 1990s." New York, NY: Routledge.

Orozco, Richard A. 2011. "'It is Certainly Strange . . .': Attacks on Ethnic Studies and Whiteness as Property." *Journal of Education Policy* 26 (6): 819–38.

Paris, Django. 2012. "Culturally Sustaining Pedagogy: A Needed Change in Stance, Terminology, and Practice." *Educational Researcher* 41 (3): 93–97.

Paris, Django, and H. Sammy Alim. 2014. "What are We Seeking to Sustain Through Culturally Sustaining Pedagogy? A Loving Critique Forward." *Harvard Educational Review,* 84 (1): 85–100.

Patton, Lori D., ed. 2010. *Culture Centers in Higher Education: Perspectives on Identity, Theory and Practice.* Sterling, VA: Stylus Publishing.

Picca, Leslie H., and Joe R. Feagin. 2007. *Two-Faced Racism: Whites in the Backstage and Frontstage.* New York: Routledge.

Pierce, Jennifer L. 2012. *Racing for Innocence: Whiteness, Gender, and the Backlash Against Affirmative Action.* Stanford, CA: Stanford University Press.

Regents of the University of California v. Bakke, 438 U.S. 265 (1978).

Santos, Silvia J., and Elean T. Reigadas. 2002. "Latinos in Higher Education: An Evaluation of a University Faculty Mentoring Program." *Journal of Hispanic Higher Education* 1(1): 40–50.

Sleeter, Christine E. 2011. *The Academic and Social Value of Ethnic Studies: A Research Review.* Washington, DC: National Educational Association.

Smith, William A., Walter R. Allen, and Lynette L. Danley. 2007. "'Assume the Position . . . You Fit the Description': Psychosocial Experiences and Racial Battle Fatigue Among African American Male College Students." *American Behavioral Scientist* 51: 551–78.

Syrett, Nicholas L. 2009. *The Company He Keeps: A History of White College Fraternities.* Chapel Hill, NC: The University of North Carolina Press.

Takaki, Ronald. 1993. *A Different Mirror: A History of Multicultural America.* Boston, MA: Back Bay Books. *Regents* of the *University* of *California v. Bakke,* 438 U.S. 265 (1978).

Yosso, Tara J. 2005. "Whose Cultural Has Capital? A Critical Race Theory Discussion of Community Cultural Wealth." *Race Ethnicity and Education* 8 (1): 69–91.

Zuniga, Ximena, Biren (Ratnesh) A. Nagda, Mark Chesler, and Adena Cytron-Walker. 2007. *Intergroup Dialogue in Higher Education: Meaningful Learning About Social Justice.* ASHE-ERIC Higher Education Report, 32(4): San Francisco, CA: Jossey Bass.

Acknowledgments

We acknowledge the advice and help from colleagues at Arizona State University's Hispanic Research Center (HRC), including Michael J. Sullivan, Karen S. Van Hooft, Melanie Magisos, and Ana María Regalado.

Michael, Executive Director for Science, Technology, Engineering, and Mathematics, has the uncanny ability to define problems clearly and succinctly, and based on that, to suggest the optimal solution. He also has a healthy and positive approach to problems: "Things will work out."

Karen, who has been with the HRC's Bilingual Press for four decades, first as Managing Editor and then Executive Editor, handled the extensive editorial queries and other communications with authors to produce the final manuscript as well as directing the books' physical production. Melanie, Executive Producer, Publishing and Product Development, also participated in the editorial and production processes.

We thank our coeditors, who include two old friends, Laura I. Rendón and Estela Mara Bensimón, and our colleagues at Educational Testing Service, Alberto Acereda and Richard J. Tannenbaum. They provided advice and counsel that helped the project move forward.

And finally, but not least, we thank Ana María Regalado, Director of Strategic Initiatives at the Hispanic Research Center, who provided organizational support for the project. This involved preparing the initial invitation letter to potential authors, receiving the manuscripts, keeping track of detailed information for more than 50 authors, receiving and filing the authors' biographical sketches, and more. As issues came up, Ana's response was positive and she always found a way to deal with the issue at hand. Without her help, this two-book project would not have happened.

About the Contributors

Estela Mara Bensimón is professor of higher education and director of the Center for Urban Education (CUE) at the University of Southern California Rossier School of Education. More information may be found on page 6 of the introduction to this volume.

Nolan L. Cabrera is an associate professor in the Center for the Study of Higher Education at the University of Arizona. He studies Whiteness, racism, and the controversy surrounding the Tucson Unified School District's Mexican American Studies Program. His work has been cited in a federal desegregation case and by the 9th Circuit Court of Appeals.

Emily Calderón Galdeano is a senior associate at *Excelencia* in Education and chief executive officer of Elevate Consulting Group. She has over fifteen years in the education policy arena at the national, state, and institutional levels. Her research agenda focuses on the intersecting trajectories of public policy and higher education, specifically as they relate to Latina/o student success.

Vincent D. Carales is an assistant professor in the Department of Educational Leadership and Policy Studies at the University of Houston. His research interests include examining the educational attainment of Latina/o community college students and the impact of state and institutional policy, college affordability, and financial aid reform.

Juan F. Carrillo is an assistant professor at the University of North Carolina, Chapel Hill School of Education. His primary research interests are in cultural studies in education, the identities of academically successful Latino male students, and Latin@ education in new gateway regions, with a specific emphasis on North Carolina.

Cheryl D. Ching is a postdoctoral scholar and research associate at the Center for Urban Education and the University of Southern California Rossier

School of Education. Her research focuses on how institutions of higher education—broadly understood to include colleges, intermediary organizations, and policy agencies—confront and wrestle with educational equity. Her dissertation on how "equity" is constructed and enacted at a community college received the 2017 Bobby Wright Dissertation of the Year Award from the Association for the Study of Higher Education.

Alfredo G. de los Santos Jr., the lead editor of this volume, is a research professor at the Hispanic Research Center of Arizona State University, emeritus vice-chancellor of the Maricopa Community College District, and founding president of El Paso Community College. More information may be found on pages 4 and 5 of the introduction to this volume.

Wil Del Pilar, PhD, serves as The Education Trust's vice president of higher education policy and practice. In this role, he spearheads Ed Trust's mission to highlight inequities and outline solutions in order to improve access, success, affordability, and completion in higher education for low-income students and students of color. Prior to joining Ed Trust, he served in Pennsylvania Governor Tom Wolf's administration as deputy secretary of postsecondary and higher education.

Eric R. Felix is a doctoral candidate in the urban education policy program at the University of Southern California. He is a research assistant working with Dr. Estela M. Bensimón at the Center for Urban Education. His research examines the role of higher education policy in addressing educational inequities for students of color, particularly within community colleges. Other research interests include college access and equity issues for Latinx students, community college finance, and improving the transfer process for racially minoritized students.

David R. García is an associate professor in the Mary Lou Fulton Teachers College at Arizona State University. He has extensive experience in state and national education policy, including serving as the Associate Superintendent of Public Instruction for the State of Arizona. His research is featured in numerous academic journals and books, and he has been recognized nationally for his public scholarship. García holds a BA from Arizona State University and a doctorate from the University of Chicago.

Tanya J. Gaxiola Serrano is a doctoral candidate at the University of California, Los Angeles, Graduate School of Education and Information Studies. Her research explores the experiences of Latinx community college students and institutional agents situated in contested localities including border regions. She also serves as the assistant director for the Center for Critical Race Studies at UCLA.

Gary Francisco Keller is Regents' Professor and director of the Hispanic Research Center at Arizona State University as well as publisher of the Bilingual Press. More information may be found on page 5 of the introduction to this volume.

Rubén O. Martínez is professor of sociology and director of the Julián Samora Research Institute at Michigan State University. He is book series editor of *Latinos in the United States* published by Michigan State University Press and coauthor of *Chicanos in Higher Education* and *Diversity Leadership in Higher Education* with Adalberto Aguirre, Jr.

Amaury Nora is professor of higher education, codirector of the Center for Research and Policy in Education, and associate dean for research in the College of Education and Human Development at the University of Texas at San Antonio. His research has focused on theoretical perspectives related to student persistence, the role of college on diverse student populations across different types of institutions, and the development of retention models that integrate economic theories and psychosocial perspectives within college persistence frameworks.

Leticia Oseguera is associate professor of education policy studies and senior research associate at the Center for the Study of Higher Education at the Pennsylvania State University. Her research focuses on program evaluation and assessment as well as college access and success for historically underserved and underrepresented student populations.

Belinda I. Reyes is director of the César E. Chávez Institute and associate professor in the Latina and Latino Studies Department at San Francisco State University. Reyes leads the Latino Educational Achievement Partnership to promote the advancement of Latino students in higher education. She holds a BS in economics from the University of Illinois Urbana-Champaign and a PhD in economics from the University of California, Berkeley.

Cristóbal Rodríguez is an associate professor in the Department of Educational Leadership and Policy Studies and director of graduate studies for the School of Education at Howard University in Washington, DC. For his works and contributions, in 2016 he received Faculty Honors from the

White House Initiative on Educational Excellence for Hispanics, an initiative within the US Department of Education.

Victor B. Sáenz is chair of the Department of Educational Leadership and Policy at the University of Texas at Austin. He is an associate professor in the Program in Higher Education Leadership, and he holds courtesy appointments with the Center for Mexican American Studies and the Department of Mexican American and Latina/o Studies. His research focuses on improving educational outcomes for underserved students in postsecondary education, with a special emphasis on young men of color.

Cristóbal Salinas Jr., PhD, is an assistant professor in the Educational Leadership and Research Methodology Department at Florida Atlantic University. He is the cofounder and managing editor of the *Journal Committed to Social Change on Race and Ethnicity*. His research promotes access and quality in higher education and explores the social, political, and economic context of educational opportunities for historically marginalized communities, with an emphasis on Latino/a communities.

Deborah A. Santiago is the cofounder, chief operating officer, and vice president for policy at *Excelencia* in Education. For more than twenty years, she has led research and policy efforts at local, national, and federal levels to improve educational opportunities and success for all students. She cofounded *Excelencia* to inform policy and practice, compel action, and collaborate with those committed and ready to act to increase student success.

José Luis Santos is a national expert on student success strategies and the founder and president of JLS Strategies Group, LLC, a consulting firm in the Washington, DC area that advocates for evidence-based strategies through data science and analytics, program evaluation, and policy development. He is the former vice president of higher education policy and practice at The Education Trust in Washington, DC and is a former professor at UCLA and Pepperdine University.

Umadevi Senguttuvan (PhD, Purdue University) is a senior researcher in the César E. Chávez Institute at San Francisco State University. She has a specialization in marriage and family therapy and is strongly committed to both research and clinical work. Her research interests are diverse and include youths' socioemotional development, family processes, culture, and social policies.

Daniel G. Solórzano is a professor of social science and comparative education at the University of California, Los Angeles. He has authored over 100 research articles, book chapters, and research reports on issues related to educational access and equity for underrepresented student populations in the United States. Professor Solórzano has received various awards including the UCLA Distinguished Teacher Award and the American Education Research Association (AERA) Social Justice in Education Award.

DeAna Swan is a doctoral student in the Program in Higher Education Leadership at the University of Texas at Austin. In her research she explores Latina/o college student access and success and is especially interested in the experience of Latina graduate student mothers. She received a BS from the University of Wisconsin-Madison and an MSEd from the University of Pennsylvania.

Adrián Trinidad is a doctoral student at the University of Southern California Rossier School of Education. Working with Dr. Estela Bensimón at the Center for Urban Education, his research explores transfer pathways for racially minoritized community college students, policy implementation, and organizational change in higher education.

Patrick L. Valdez is chief executive officer of the University of New Mexico Taos Branch Campus. He was previously dean of the undergraduate college and associate professor of education at the College of Mount Saint Vincent in New York City.

Fernando Valle is an associate professor of educational leadership at Texas Tech University. The competency-based work Dr. Valle leads through university and public school partnerships challenges deficit thinking and practices while centering culturally relevant practice. He continues to advance research on Latina/o educational leadership and the Latina/o education pipeline.

Kelly M. Ward is a doctoral student in the Department of Sociology at the University of California, Irvine. Her research explores the experiences of women of color in academia and how minority groups negotiate inclusion in majority spaces.

Timothy P. White is chancellor of the California State University (CSU) system, the largest four-year public university system in the United States. As the seventh chancellor to lead the CSU system, White is a champion of student success. He is a proponent of bringing individualized education to scale through the expansion of proven best practices. At the state and national level, White advocates for a comprehensive learning environment that links classroom learning to practice through research, creative activity, and community engagement. Born in Argentina, Dr. White received his PhD from the University of California, Berkeley.

Chenoa S. Woods (PhD, University of California, Irvine) is a research faculty member at the Center for Postsecondary Success at Florida State University. Her research focuses on the high school-to-college pipeline with an emphasis on out-of-classroom support programs and personnel. In her current position she analyzes developmental education policy in the state of Florida.

Maria Estela Zárate (PhD, University of California, Los Angeles) is professor of educational leadership at California State University, Fullerton, where she teaches future school leaders and principals. Her research program examines the educational and schooling trajectory of Latino and immigrant students.

Index

Download the index for this book at https://bilingualpress.clas.asu.edu /book/moving-forward-policies-planning-and-promoting-access-hispanic -college-students

"It is imperative that books like this one be read, studied, disseminated, and used as a blueprint for the promise of education for all the citizens of this country. The impressive educational gains and remaining obstacles for Latina/o students hold the key to prosperity, civic and social harmony, and ultimately, the success of this nation. A must read for all who see education as the great equalizer in our democracy."

Aída Hurtado, Luis Leal Endowed Chair
DEPARTMENT OF CHICANA AND CHICANO STUDIES
UNIVERSITY OF CALIFORNIA, SANTA BARBARA

"A select group of outstanding authors from across the country—from senior professors to emerging scholars, from policy experts and researchers to practitioners—has provided an insightful analysis of policy and practice and recommended new strategies and tools for improving both the assessment and achievement of Hispanic students. This volume is required reading for policy makers, administrators, and faculty, as well as those graduate students preparing to become leaders in higher education."

Loui Olivas, President
AMERICAN ASSOCIATION OF HISPANICS
IN HIGHER EDUCATION

"The editors of *Moving Forward* have assembled an impressive array of scholars who address important challenges and opportunities regarding the access of Latin@ students to higher education."

Jeffrey F. Milem, Dean and Professor
GEVIRTZ GRADUATE SCHOOL OF EDUCATION
UNIVERSITY OF CALIFORNIA, SANTA BARBARA

"This volume highlights how community colleges play an essential role in the educational pipeline, especially regarding the vital issues of access, affordability, and student preparation. It is incumbent on all universities— state and private—to partner with community colleges to help transfer students map their academic path and accelerate their time to degree."

Tomás D. Morales, President
CALIFORNIA STATE UNIVERSITY, SAN BERNARDINO

"*Moving Forward* is designed to motivate and engender creative strategies that will push for more change. . . . an inspiring and practical contribution to the cause of developing our greatest asset, our children and youth."

April Osborn, Executive Director
ARIZONA COMMISSION FOR
POSTSECONDARY EDUCATION

"This timely and thought provoking book sheds light on the importance of advocating for federal and state policies that benefit the increasing number of Hispanic students enrolling in our nation's colleges and universities. Both seasoned leaders in higher education and those new to academia can gain great insight from this book."

Eduardo Padrón, College President
MIAMI DADE COLLEGE

"This volume is on a critical topic at a critical moment. These authors are just the right group of scholars and policy analysts not only to assess the landscape but to offer informed opinions about what to do. The book is a breath of fresh air in a polluted environment."

William G. Tierney, University Professor
PULLIAS CENTER FOR HIGHER EDUCATION
UNIVERSITY OF SOUTHERN CALIFORNIA